Wittgensteinian Fideism?

Wittgensteinian Fideism?

Kai Nielsen and D. Z. Phillips

with critiques by
Béla Szabados, Nancy Bauer and Stephen Mulhall

scm press

British Library Cataloguing in Publication data

A catalogue record for this book is available from the British Library

ISBN 0-334-04005-1/9780-334-04005-7

First published in 2005 by SCM Press
9–17 St Albans Place, London N1 0NX

www.scm-canterburypress.co.uk

SCM Press is a division of
SCM-Canterbury Press Ltd

Typeset by Rowland Phototypesetting Ltd,
Bury St Edmunds, Suffolk
Printed and bound in Great Britain by
William Clowes, Beccles, Suffolk

Contents

Acknowledgements

The Claremont Annual Conference on the Philosophy of Religion is made possible by the generous financial support of Claremont Graduate University, Pomona College and Claremont McKenna College. I want to acknowledge the administrative support provided by Helen Baldwin, Secretary to the Department of Philosophy at University of Wales, Swansea and Jackie Huntzinger, Secretary to the School of Religion at Claremont Graduate University. I am also grateful to all the graduate students who helped to make the 2003 conference run smoothly. I am especially grateful to Robert Bolger, my research assistant at Claremont in 2003, for organizing the student helpers. Thanks are also due to Francis Gonzales, my 2002 research assistant, for typing first drafts of my papers and my 2004 research assistant, Mark Wright, for typing later versions of, and additions to, them.

Most of the chapters in the present book are new. The exceptions are as follows: Kai Nielsen's 'Wittgensteinian Fideism' was first published in *Philosophy* Vol. XLII No. 161 July 1967; 'Can Anything be Beyond Human Understanding?' was first published in *Philosophy and the Grammar of Religious Belief* ed. Timothy Tessin and Mario von der Ruhr, Basingstoke: Macmillan 1995; 'Wittgenstein and Wittgensteinians on Religion' was first published in *Naturalism and Religion*, Amherst, NY: Prometheus Press, 2001; D. Z. Phillips's 'Wittgenstein and Religion: Some Fashionable Criticisms' was first published in *Belief, Change and Forms of Life*, Basingstoke: Macmillan 1987. We are grateful for permission to reprint these papers here.

D. Z. Phillips
Claremont/Swansea

I would like to thank John Kerkhoven for his very conscientious reading of the proofs. He has saved me from many a slip, both stylistic and substantial.

Kai Nielsen
Concordia University, Montreal

Preface

In 1965, D. Z. Phillips published *The Concept of Prayer*, one of the first books, if not the first, which showed the influence of Wittgenstein's thought in the philosophy of religion. In 1967, Kai Nielsen published his famous article, 'Wittgensteinian Fideism' in the journal *Philosophy*. Their respective philosophical work has developed over the years, with Phillips becoming known as the leading proponent of Wittgensteinian philosophy of religion, and with Nielsen returning, again and again, to renew his investigation and critique of what he takes to be the fideistic implications of this mode of philosophizing. Yet, strangely enough, this is the first occasion on which Nielsen and Phillips have engaged each other in extended discussion. Their meeting occurred at the 2003 annual conference on philosophy of religion at Claremont Graduate University, California.

For Phillips, the term 'Wittgensteinian Fideism' has done more harm than good, since, for him, it misrepresents, and deflects us from, the main logical issues concerning language and reality in Wittgenstein's work. For Nielsen, on the other hand, Wittgensteinian Fideism constitutes the most powerful contemporary challenge to secular naturalism, one standing in urgent need of a fundamental critique of its basic assumptions. Wherever one stands in this dispute, there is much to learn from the exchanges in it, exchanges enhanced further by Béla Szabados's introduction to them, and the critiques of Nancy Bauer and Stephen Mulhall.

INTRODUCTION:

Wittgensteinian Fideism 1967–89
An Appreciation

BÉLA SZABADOS

The intention is one of retrieval, an attempt to uncover buried goods through rearticulation – and thereby to make these sources empower again, to bring the air back again into the half-collapsed lungs of the spirit. (Taylor, 1989, 520)

I   How to Approach the Question of Wittgensteinian Fideism?

1967 was a significant moment in twentieth-century philosophy of religion. Kai Nielsen identified and defined a fresh and creative current in the philosophy of religion that he called 'Wittgensteinian Fideism', and D. Z. Phillips edited a book of essays entitled *Religion and Understanding*, which made available under one cover some of the major contributions of philosophers who worked in a Wittgensteinian framework.

One way to approach the question 'What is Wittgensteinian Fideism?' is from the angle of a definition by genus and difference, especially since 'Wittgensteinian Fideism' is partly intended to classify some writers. We might say, the genus is 'fideism' and the difference is 'Wittgensteinian'. Another approach is to retrieve its history: ask who were the Wittgensteinian fideists, discern their characteristic motifs and motivations. We may also ask what use was made of this label in the philosophical lexicon in the second half of the twentieth century. What is more, to shed further light on Wittgensteinian Fideism, we may also return to its sources in Wittgenstein's neglected readings and ask whether it could have been understood differently.

I shall walk each of these paths, engage briefly each of these interconnected issues. But, is this not precisely the sort of approach that Wittgenstein cautions against when he remarks: 'People who are constantly asking "Why?" (or "What?") are like tourists, who stand in front of a building, reading Baedeker, and through reading about the history of the building's construction etc. are prevented from seeing it' (Wittgenstein 1980, 40). This may be read as a global repudiation of the history of philosophy, and then applied specifically to what we are doing here. This would be a mistake, since it is possible to study the history of a building and its construction, repairs to its structure and so on, with a view to better appreciating and making more appropriate use of it. I trust that in what follows there is no loss from sight of the foundations of possible homes that Wittgenstein laid, but rather a constant return to them by way of inspection, comparison and contrast.

In introducing the topic, I not only gesture to some salient points of interest on the landscape of Wittgensteinian Fideism, but also try to read its literature in the right spirit. Wittgenstein says somewhere that a philosopher who does not enter the discussion is like a boxer who does not step into the ring. There can be no doubt about Kai Nielsen and D. Z. Phillips having stepped into the ring. The analogy should not mislead us into thinking about knock-outs or ties. As the book title shows, what we are intent on is nourishing dialogue: a deepening understanding of ourselves and others through clarification.

II   Inventing 'Wittgensteinian Fideism'?

To begin with, here is a Wittgensteinian lens for appreciating Kai Nielsen's works in the philosophy of religion. 'The earlier culture will become a heap of rubble and finally a heap of ashes, but spirits will hover over the ashes' (Wittgenstein 1980, 3). In the last four decades Nielsen has written many valuable books in the philosophy of religion. He has hovered over the rubble and ashes of our earlier culture – attempting to rescue what is of value and burning the deadwood. From the beginning of his writings to his recent book *Naturalism and Religion*, Nielsen has thought that Wittgenstein and Wittgensteinians pose the strongest intellectual challenge to the project of a secular or post-religious culture yielding the fullest kind of human flourishing (Nielsen 2001, 14). The importance he attaches to Wittgensteinian treatments of religion is shown by his visiting and revisiting the subject over many decades, painting various portraits. These portraits differ in that both the subject of the portrait, Wittgenstein and Wittgensteinians, as well as the painter Nielsen have changed between sittings.

The first portrait can be viewed in the seminal essay of 1967, famously titled 'Wittgensteinian Fideism', the next chapter in the present work. It is a portrait painted in the absence and apparent unavailability of the subject – and all the more impressive for that. It defines, baptizes and evaluates a position in the philosophy of religion that is imaginatively reconstructed from the themes of Wittgenstein's later philosophy and from snippets of his disciples. At the time of this ground-breaking essay, Wittgenstein's *Lectures and Conversations on Aesthetics, Psychology and Religious Belief* were not in print, nor were they generally available in *samizdat* form. In fact, Nielsen's essay began with a strange admission:

'Wittgenstein did not write on the philosophy of religion. But certain strands of his later thought readily lend themselves to what I call Wittgensteinian Fideism ... as much as I admire Wittgenstein, it seems to me that the fideistic conclusions ... are often absurd' (see p. 21). Nielsen adds that there is no text that he can turn to for an extended statement of this position and that he is not sure whether Wittgenstein himself would have accepted the position, but Wittgenstein's work has been taken that way.

What then is the textual basis for Wittgensteinian Fideism? Nielsen explicitly speaks as if what we have here is a new theory in the philosophy of religion and he proceeds to map it by invoking some of the characteristic thought manoeuvres of Wittgenstein's work, *Philosophical Investigations*. One important theme in the later Wittgenstein is that there is a plurality of distinct forms of life with their associated language-games and rather different kinds of meaning and rationality. Another is that it is a mere prejudice of the dominant tradition in modern philosophy to suppose that a single standard or model must apply to them all. Connecting with this is the approach that to understand these different ways of living and speaking, we need to look and attend. 'What has to be accepted – the given, is – so one could say – are forms of life' (Wittgenstein 1958, 226). These in turn need no philosophical justification by giving them a foundation. The language-game 'is not based on grounds. It is not reasonable (or unreasonable). It is there – like our life' (Wittgenstein 1969, 73, par. 559). Good philosophy is descriptive of these language games. It does not provide theses, theories, justifications – it leaves everything as it is.

These features of Wittgenstein's thought are then applied. A Wittgensteinian fideist argues that religion is an ancient and ongoing form of life, with its own distinctive discourse, practices and criteria of meaning and rationality. Religious life and speech can only be understood and criticized from the inside, by someone who has a participant's understanding of this discourse. A philosopher's task is not to criticize or evaluate the religious language games and ways of life in terms of some alien norm, but to describe them where necessary, so as to break the perplexity concerning their operation. We can see then Nielsen at work as a classifier, as preparing the ground for placing some writers in the fideist as well as the Wittgensteinian camp. This seems to be genuinely informative and helpful, even though there may be controversy about what it is to be a Wittgensteinian and what is it to be a fideist.

Nielsen's essay shows another intention at work as well, namely, the business of criticism. Wittgensteinian Fideism is seen as a position in the philosophy of religion, with associated premises and arguments, a theory that challenges and competes with other theories. Hence, it is subject to evaluation. There are several compelling objections that Nielsen has voiced against the position of Wittgensteinian Fideism in his pioneering early work and later variations. First, Nielsen pointed out that to grant the fideist requirement to start from the inside does not necessarily imply agreement with religious beliefs. Second, Wittgensteinian Fideism compartmentalizes religion, and thus fails to notice that it, like other facets of our culture, is open to critique. Third, this critique can come from insiders who engage in its practices, from outsiders who do not, from insideroutsiders who did, but no longer do.

In later works on the subject, Nielsen drops some of these objections partly in response to corrections by Wittgensteinians, and partly because of a deepened understanding of Wittgenstein due to the many works relevant to religion that have become available: *On Certainty, Remarks on Frazer's* Golden Bough and *Culture and Value*. However, he continues to level and even sharpen the general charge, this time directly aiming at Wittgenstein himself, that Wittgenstein's philosophical outlook is ethically and politically irresponsible, since its attitude of quietism leads us to a pernicious disengagement from the world and robs us of the critical tools to assess our culture and change it for the better. To put it bluntly, a philosophy that leaves everything as it is hinders the struggle for social justice, peace and human flourishing. It is an obstacle to human solidarity. (It may strike some as ironic that one of the deepest critics of our culture, concerned with its reanimation, is charged with complacency and quietism.)

III   Who Were the Wittgensteinian Fideists?

Perhaps the time has come for a friendlier approach to the question of Wittgensteinian Fideism, namely, to meet some members of this philosophical family. The authors on Nielsen's original list are: Peter Winch, G. E. Hughes, Norman Malcolm, Peter Geach, Stanley Cavell, J. M. Cameron and Robert Coburn. The list is useful as a guide, because it identifies many of the significant players. However, it is both too narrow and too wide. Too narrow, since it omits some major contributors, such as Rush Rhees and D. Z. Phillips. This is understandable in the case of Rhees, since his book *Without Answers* was published only in 1969. The case of Phillips is somewhat different, since his incisive book *The Concept of Prayer* had already appeared in 1965. Thus in his later discussions Nielsen revises his list by including and attending to Rhees as well as privileging Phillips as a paradigmatic case.

The initial list also seems too wide in the sense that it includes philosophers, such as Stanley Cavell, whose significant contributions were not in the philosophy of religion, but in other, though perhaps related, areas. Notice, however, that Nielsen's placement of Cavell is right-headed, since Cavell is distinguished for his insightful interpretations and applications of Wittgenstein's methods to the philosophy of literature, and more broadly, of culture. And if Cavell is included, should room not be made also for Elizabeth Anscombe and O. K. Bouwsma?

Another concern about Nielsen's list might be that it lumps together writers with rather different views on a number of issues. Consider the sheer variety among them. While Rush Rhees and D. Z. Phillips are out of sympathy with Aristotle and St Thomas Aquinas, Elizabeth Anscombe and Peter Geach are in sympathy with them. Some are religiously committed, others are not. The committed come from a wide spectrum of Judaeo-Christianity, including Catholics and Protestants.

Now even though these differences are real, Nielsen's list is still helpful, and it is important to say why. Wittgenstein did not aim to put forth these or other doctrines in philosophy around which followers could congregate. He also accorded importance to tradition and culture, as well as to circumstances and needs, when issuing philosophical reminders to a particular purpose. The aim was to appreciate our forms of life by clarifying concepts and discourse, by devising different methods to tackle problems as they arose for us.

This is evident in his work, especially so in his lectures, notes and conversations with friends and students about religion. His remarks are expressive of an acceptance of, and respect for, the variety of expression in religious life. The imprint of William James is discernible here, as it is in Wittgenstein's rather pragmatic reaction to Drury's regret that he has not lived a religious life, possibly due to Wittgenstein's impact. Wittgenstein said: 'I believe it is right to try experiments in religion. To find out, by trying, what helps one and what doesn't . . . Now why don't you see if starting the day by going to Mass each morning doesn't help you to begin the day in a good frame of mind' (Rhees 1981, 179).

About his Catholic students, he said: 'I could not believe what they believe.' Notice, he did not say, what they believe is impossible or nonsense, or that they should not believe them. This recognition of difference as playing an important role in philosophical activity is coupled with Wittgenstein's disavowal of an ambition to found a school of thought. In light of this, it is natural to expect Nielsen's list to include writers with similarities and differences, rather than simply toeing an identical line.

IV Three Wittgensteinian Fideists: Rhees, Malcolm, Phillips

Who were the most influential among the writers mediating the Wittgensteinian legacy in the philosophy of religion? Who were Wittgenstein's builders? Rush Rhees is perhaps the most important figure in the first wave of Wittgensteinians, because it is this line of influence that bore most fruit and provided most nourishment through Peter Winch, Roy Holland and, most prominently, through the works of D. Z. Phillips. In the United States, Norman Malcolm and O. K. Bouwsma have been very influential through their teaching and publications. A few words then about Rhees, Malcolm and Phillips.

Early on in the 1950s and 1960s, Rush Rhees approached religious discourse in the light of Wittgenstein's legacy, building on it and applying it. His reflections are expressed in letters to friends, in discussions or at addresses to students' meetings. These contexts reveal philosophical activity as a real force in life, encountering actual tensions, clarifying them, thereby helping participants to come to grips with them. There is little mention of Wittgenstein in any of these interventions or discussions – it would have distracted from their focus by diverting attention from a practical concern to some exegetical issue. Rhees's book, *Without Answers*, is Wittgensteinian philosophy at its best. The importance of context, of particular cases and examples, of resisting certain metaphors that partly generate the problem in the first place, of inventing different analogies and hence different ways of looking at things, are salient features of Rhees's writings.

Here are a few passages that foreground some characteristic motifs. About the issue of reference: 'If you ask "Well, when we are talking about God, does our language not refer to anything?", then I should want to begin, as I have tried here, by emphasizing something of the special grammar of this language' (Rhees 1969, 132).

The theme of 'special grammar' is continued as Rhees turns to the question of the existence of God. Here he steers us away from the surface grammar of the sentence which suggests some grand metaphysical claim:

'God exists' is not a statement of fact. You might also say that it is not in the indicative mood. It is a confession – or expression – of faith. This is recognized in some way when people say that God's existence is 'necessary existence', as opposed to the 'contingency' of what exists as a matter of fact; and when they say that to doubt God's existence is a sin, as opposed to a mistake about the facts. (Rhees 1969, 131–2)

In 'Religion and Language', Rhees begins to explore the similarities and differences between religious discourse and the language of love. In particular, he suggests that 'The question of "what God is" could only be answered through "coming to know God" in worship and in religious life. "To know God is to worship him"' (Rhees 1969, 127). Later on he provides a striking analogy:

To say that we could come to know God without knowing that he was the Creator and Father of all things, without knowing his love and forgiveness, is like saying that I might come to know Winston Churchill without knowing that he had a face, hands, body, voice or any of the attributes of a human being. (Rhees 1969, 131)

About the traditional project of natural theology:

> The fault is in thinking of natural theology as the Foundation of the rest of religion, in some way. Here they bring in the whole confusion of metaphysics; whether Aristotelian or some other. Introducing a sense of 'fundamental' which is badly confused. Natural theology: 'Reason shows that there must be a God'. Some people cannot think of religion except in these terms; except in connexion with these ideas. And obviously there is nothing wrong with this. What is wrong is the attitude of: 'This is so, and we can prove it.' The expert talking to the ignorant upstarts . . . Those who hold to a rational theology seem to argue that a man might be brought to a belief in God, and also to a belief in immortality of the soul, by formal argument alone, even though he had never known anything like an attitude of 'trust in God'. Here I cannot follow them, and I wonder if I understand at all what they are saying.
>
> I feel like repeating what I have said more than once: I do not know any of the great religious teachers who have awakened men to religious belief in this way. When the author of Isaiah, or the author of the book of Job, or the authors of certain of the psalms were trying to keep the faith of the Jews alive during the exile – did they do anything of the sort? Do you find anything of the sort in the New Testament? (Rhees 1969, 111–12)

Notice then the following motifs. On the positive side, there is a 'philosophy at work' approach, a resolutely practical orientation. We are urged to look and see how religious concepts are actually used in religious life. Also, there is the philosopher as poet, who uses fresh similes and analogies to help us look at things differently, to break the spell of surface grammar on us. On the negative side, even though there is no general repudiation of theology as such, there is the rejection of natural theology understood as giving a foundation for religion by 'proof'. According to Rhees, we misconceive arguments for the existence of God as devices of reason whereby we can convince others that there is a God. As if these could have the desired effect without initiation or training in the religious way of life! These so-called proofs are really expressions of deepening wonder from within the religious life already. Even here, we see a probing as to what the use of such philosophical artifacts might be in the weave of religious life.

Now to Norman Malcolm. He wrote sparingly in the philosophy of religion, but what he wrote had great impact. His works are remarkably fresh, clear and direct. The anti-foundationalist motif is put right up front in the essay entitled 'The Groundlessness of Belief'. Malcolm argues against the traditional philosophical view that religious belief requires a rational foundation which would provide a justification for the religious way of life. The almost obsessive philosophical preoccupation with proofs for the existence of God is a piece of philosophical pathology:

> I do not comprehend this notion of belief in the existence of God which is thought to be distinct from belief in God. It seems to me to be an artificial construction of philosophy, another illustration of the craving for justification. Religion is a form of life; it is language embedded in action – what Wittgenstein calls a 'language-game.' Science is another. Neither stands in need of justification, the one no more than the other. (Malcolm 1977, 212)

In 'Anselm's Ontological Arguments' Malcolm makes important observations that show a continuation and further clarification of the motifs we encountered in Rhees. First, the concept of God has a place in the thinking and lives of human beings, hence it is presumptuous to think of it as self-contradictory. Second, there cannot be a deep understanding of the concept without an understanding of the phenomena of human life that give rise to it. Third, an account of belief in God must take the distinction between existence and eternity seriously. Fourth, Anselm's argument may have religious value in that it may help to remove philosophical scruples that stand in the way of faith. However, Malcolm goes on to say:

> At a deeper level, I suspect that the argument can be thoroughly understood only by someone who has a view of the human 'form of life' that gives rise to it from the inside not just from the outside and who has, therefore, at least some inclination to partake in that religious form of life. This inclination, in Kierkegaard's words, is 'from the emotions'. This inclination can hardly be an effect of Anselm's argument, but is rather presupposed in the fullest understanding of it. It would be unreasonable to require that the recognition of Anselm's demonstration as valid must produce conversion. (Malcolm 1960, in Phillips 1967, 61)

Malcolm's final contribution to the philosophy of religion is a book titled *Wittgenstein: A Religious Point of View?* in which he explores what Wittgenstein may have meant by the remark 'I am not a religious man but I cannot help but see every problem from a religious point of view' (Rhees 1981, 94). This was published posthumously with extensive commentary by Peter Winch.

And now a few snapshots of D. Z. Phillips who has been seen as the leading Wittgensteinian fideist by many secular philosophers. Nielsen, for example, writes that *The Concept of Prayer, Faith and Philosophical*

Enquiry and *Death and Immortality* amount to a detailed paradigmatic statement of Wittgensteinian Fideism. I read Phillips through the lens of Wittgenstein's remark: 'speak the old language . . . but speak it in a way that is appropriate to the new world, without on that account necessarily being in accordance with its taste' (Wittgenstein 1980, 60). Phillips has had a deep influence on the philosophy of religion as practised in the English-speaking world, partly through his many nourishing works, and partly because he took and handled the brunt of the criticism from those who disagreed with his orientation.

Wittgensteinian motifs, mediated by Rhees and Malcolm, as well as through the work of Peter Winch, are further elaborated, clarified and thus deepened by Phillips. I confine my discussion to his early works *The Concept of Prayer* and *Death and Immortality*. In these books, there is a double movement: Phillips describes and examines the roles that the practice of prayer and the belief in immortality play in religious life, and accompanies this by a critique of bad philosophy – by 'putting the slumlords of philosophy out of business' (Rhees 1981, 132). Philosophical theism views God as a metaphysical entity, construed as a Being among beings. It is bad philosophy, partly because of its epistemological foundationalism, partly because of its meaning-essentialism, partly because of its scientism – letting one method elbow all the others aside. Thinking of 'God exists' as a factual proposition, as making some kind of ontological claim about the furniture of the universe or its maker, generates the impression that 'coming to see that there is a God after all, is like discovering that an object which one thought did not exist, does in fact exist. If this were true, in coming to see that there is a God one would increase one's knowledge of facts, but not one's understanding' (Phillips 1965, 120).

Philosophical theism is a common assumption among Christianity's critics as well as its apologists, and by rejecting it, Phillips wants to rescue Christianity, in one fell swoop, from both. Consider how philosophical theism distorts the concept of prayer and the belief in immortality, thereby creating needless difficulties in people's lives. According to it, the standard picture of prayer is an instance of asking someone for something, or telling someone something, with the difference that this someone is a Super Being. This reduces prayer to a superstition, since the person praying would believe the prayer to be causally efficacious. Prayer becomes an ego-centred propitiation of God to intervene in the course of events so that it would fulfil one's desires. In the case of immortality, the standard philosophical picture involves a factual belief of personal survival in an after-life. This is 'hard to believe' as well as morally repugnant, since its evidently self-centred desire to exist for ever is out of alignment with the pursuit of unselfishness characteristic of genuine religiousness.

Looking at the employment of prayer in the context of religion, Phillips offers an account of prayer as a practice in which believers express and reflect on concerns that lie deep within them:

> When deep religious believers pray for something, they are not so much asking God to bring this about, as in a way telling Him of the strength of their desires. They realize that things may not go as they wish, but they are asking to be able to go on living whatever happens. In prayers of confession and prayers of petition, the believer is trying to find a meaning and a hope that will deliver him from the elements in his life which threaten to destroy it: in the first case, his guilt, and in the second case, his desires. (Phillips 1965, 120; see also Phillips 1967, 6)

Prayer then is intimately connected with and helps to effect an acceptance of the way things are. The key to prayer is: 'Thy will be done.'

Similarly, Phillips's account of immortality is expressive of a whole attitude towards the world: 'When we speak of immortality we really speak of what in human life is independent of chance and change, of morality, of eternal demands of us.' Genuine moral actions bear witness to 'something eternal in a man, . . . able to exist and grasped within every change' (Phillips 1970, 48). 'Eternity is not an extension of this present life, but this life seen under certain moral and religious modes of thought. This is precisely what seeing this life *sub specie aeternitatis* would amount to' (Phillips 1970, 49). A belief in eternal life is a rejection of self-centred temporal concerns and a pursuit of a self-effacing love of others.

Some critics, religious and secular, have read these passages as de-supernaturalizing Christianity. According to these critics, Phillips and other Wittgensteinian fideists, destroy or revise what they aim to preserve and protect from bad philosophy. What we have left after Phillips is a reduction to ethics, says Kai Nielsen. And Terence Penelhum says that, after reading Phillips, you can't go home again. For Christianity is a tradition of response, while Phillips's version is a 'response to the tradition' (Penelhum 1983, 166). Is it not possible, however, to read Phillips as a radical supernaturalist: as someone who resists all naturalistic/ontological treatments of God in the philosophical tradition? If we read Phillips this way, then we can still hear him speaking the old language, and making room for faith.

Are there differences among the Wittgensteinian fideists? Is Norman Malcolm's greater patience and sympathy with the architecture, context and expressiveness of the arguments concerning God indicative of such a difference? Again, at the end of 'The Groundlessness of Belief', Malcolm says: 'Belief in a God who creates, judges, and loves humanity is one form of religious belief. Belief in a mystical principle of causality according to which good produces good and evil produces evil is another form of religious belief' (Malcolm 1977, 216). Does this not suggest a contrast with Phillips who thinks that it is a form of superstition to bring matters of causality into this?

V   The Refusal of 'Wittgensteinian Fideism'

'Wittgensteinian Fideism' may then be seen as an informative and useful way of classifying a group of writers by bringing attention to their filiations. Yet Phillips has repeatedly repudiated the label. So we need to ask, why is it that the leading Wittgensteinan fideist cannot accept the label and recognize himself in the position? Roughly, his reasons are: Wittgensteinian Fideism is textually indefensible; it is not a position that he, or others on the list, ever held. Rather, it was set up as a straw man by critics hostile to religion. Furthermore, it misleads readers as to the real features and direction of Wittgenstein's philosophy.

In particular, Phillips goes on to cite passages from his own works, early and late, as textual evidence that show him to be arguing against the very theses he is said to be holding. Such passages may also be found in the other fideists; for example, Malcolm who says that there cannot be a deep understanding of the concept of God without an understanding of the phenomena of human life that give rise to it (in particular, he mentions the phenomenon of guilt). Thus, as early as 1964, three years before the birth of Wittgensteinian Fideism, Phillips says:

> I am anxious to avoid a position in which religious discourse seems to be a special language cut off from other forms of human discourse. Religion would not have the kind of importance it has were it not connected with the rest of life. Religious discourse has much in common with moral discourse. The naked are clothed and the starving are fed whether the motive is moral or religious. Religion, in the form of prayer, can often help to resolve moral difficulties. More important is the fact that we say that the later stages of a religion are deeper than the earlier stages; we say too that one person's faith is deeper than the faith of another person. These judgements can be made by non-believers, which suggests that religious concepts are not inaccessible to non-religious understanding. (Phillips 1967, 196)

In 1986, Phillips lays out the objections levelled against him in the literature, and responds to them point by point. Religious beliefs are autonomous and isolated from the rest of life; they can only be understood by religious believers and cannot be criticized from the outside; nor can they be affected by social or cultural events. Phillips convincingly cites himself to refute these charges:

Religion must take the world seriously . . . For example, some religious believers may try to explain away the reality of suffering, or try to say that all suffering has some point. When they say things like this, one may accuse them of not taking suffering seriously. Or if religious believers talk of death as if it were a sleep of long duration, one may accuse them of not taking death seriously enough. In these examples, what is said about suffering and death can be judged in terms of what we already know and believe about these matters. (Phillips 1986, 13–14)

Consider again: 'we have reason to distinguish between the case of the [religious] picture losing its hold for a given individual, with religious pictures losing their hold anyway not through the fault of any individual, but because of changes in the culture' (Phillips 1986, 89).[1]

Apart from this, there may also be a general reason for this refusal of Wittgensteinian Fideism, which has to do with its conception as a theory in the philosophy of religion, a theory that competes with, and is on the same level as, traditional philosophy of religion. If we take the 'Wittgensteinian' in 'Wittgensteinian Fideism' seriously, then the business of philosophy is not to advance theories or theses, but to put things right in front of us by describing the language game. No wonder then that Phillips is exasperated, since after all the work he has done to get philosophers to attend to and discuss the primary language of religion, Kai Nielsen's 'ingenious label' has stuck, and people are discussing the theory of Wittgensteinian Fideism! It is business as usual! Thus Phillips's humorous response to the question 'When did you decide to become a Wittgensteinian Fideist?' has a desperate edge to it: 'Shortly after the operation, as a matter of fact.'

VI   The Unfolding Character of the Dialogue

At this point, we might say, 'Do not ask for the meaning; ask for the use', and observe that 'Wittgensteinian fideist' has acquired a somewhat unsavoury flavor, if not an entirely negative use, in the philosophical lexicon. Indeed in the hands of some philosophers it has been used as a dismissive label. This cannot be plausibly said of Kai Nielsen's treatments of these writers. His works are characterized by exegesis and argument, and reveal that he is not altogether out of sympathy with their approach. Moreover, since some orthodox religious critics were also inclined to adopt Nielsen's reading of Wittgensteinians on religion, it is less than plausible to suggest that it was due to mere hostility to religion. So, how is it then that Phillips and other Wittgenstenian fideists have in fact been misread?

Phillips himself gives us a clue. He admitted that at one time he himself talked of religious beliefs as if they were autonomous language games and that he came to have misgivings about doing so. But then rather than looking for passages in his writings that may have misled others, there is only defensive reading. Indeed there are other passages in Rhees, Malcolm and even in Phillips that seem to have the import seized on by critics; for example, Rhees: 'To know God is to worship him' (Rhees 1969, 127) 'Special grammar' (Rhees 1969, 132); Malcolm: 'At a deeper level, I suspect that the argument can be thoroughly understood only by someone who has a view of the human "form of life" that gives rise to it from the inside not just from the outside and who has, therefore, at least some inclination to partake in that religious form of life' (Malcolm 1960, in Phillips 1967, 61). Perhaps then Wittgenstenians may have been partly responsible for having been misread. Clarity of expression is a difficult business. It is surely possible then to learn from how others read us – about them and about ourselves.

This opens up a promising Socratic dimension to the dialogue about Wittgensteinian Fideism. Neither fullness of meaning nor of use is present all at once. It is possible to see in both Nielsen's and Phillips's works a clarification and deepening, due to a growing self-examination, partly induced by their critics. Consider, for example, Nielsen, who partly in light of Phillips's concerns, becomes more cautious about, and eventually abandons, his use of the label 'Wittgensteinian Fideism'. By 1981, he refers to writers 'whom I have called – perhaps tendentiously – Wittgensteinian Fideists . . .' And in his recent book *Naturalism and Religion*, the single focus of his critique is what he calls Wittgenstein's 'quietism' (Nielsen 2001, 361–7 *passim*).

One welcome outcome of this dialogue is a crystallization of what was, and for some still is, worthwhile and nourishing in the family of writers called Wittgensteinian fideists. If we throw overboard the theory, what remains is a spirit of enquiry and a line of thinking that has revitalized the philosophy of religion. It directed attention to the patient description of religious forms of life and practices, to the characteristic uses of religious concepts and language. The phenomena were not lost from sight, or elbowed aside by some spurious or inappropriately applied method or theory.

One of the unnoticed merits of Kai Nielsen's essay 'Wittgensteinian Fideism' then is that it implicitly suggests a way of situating Wittgenstein historically as a member of a family of writers, and explicitly classifies a number of philosophers writing on religion as belonging to this family as well. Let us then return to Wittgenstein reading in the borderlands.

VII   Reading in the Borderlands

Georg von Wright tells us that Wittgenstein received deeper impressions from some writers in the borderland between philosophy, religion and poetry than from the philosophers, in the restricted sense of the word. We are also told that Wittgenstein could read only what he could whole-heartedly assimilate. Who are these writers? And what significance might they have for Wittgenstein's perspective on the philosophy of religion and on his philosophy as such? On the borderlands between philo-sophy and religion we find Wittgenstein reading St Augustine, Pascal, Kierkegaard, Dostoyevsky and Tolstoy. Von Wright remarks that 'The philosophical sections of St Augustine's *Confessions* show a striking resemblance to Wittgenstein's own way of doing philosophy. Between Wittgenstein and Pascal there is a trenchant parallelism which deserves closer study' (Von Wright 1982, 33) We might add that Wittgenstein made frequent allusions to Kierkegaard's insights. While details of indebt-edness are worthy of exploration, for present purposes the important thing is a way of thinking and a spirit of enquiry that these writers share.

What is this way of thinking or spirit of enquiry that Wittgenstein wholeheartedly assimilated and made his own? I suggest that this family of writers' line of thinking was fideistic in the sense that they believed in order to understand, that they endorsed the attitude '*Credo ut intelligam.*' This is an attitude to the activity of philosophizing that sees acceptance of rooted practices and ways of life as a given. Such an acceptance is not some peculiar and wilful act of belief, but an expression of reverence and a sense of wonder. This attitude takes what is given seriously. In contrast to traditional philosophy, which employs the method of sceptical doubt as a road to knowledge, fideist thinkers take an attitude of trust as fundamental to action, understanding and appreciation. They aim to do justice to what there is by overcoming forms of thought that distort and by providing perspicuous descriptions. It seems to me that Wittgenstein has a strong affinity to this family of writers and thinkers.

To say this is not to construe this family as having a common essence. That would be to see fideism narrowly as a doctrine or theory in the history of the philosophy of religion. A more promising way to under-stand a fideist perspective is through its central concern to leave room for faith by exposing the abuses and pretensions of reason involved in bad philosophy and the scientism of the age. Such an outlook has a venerable history, and that history is partly a history of resistance to and protection from ideological uses of reason involved in certain essentializ-ing and reductionist tendencies in Greek philosophy. The fear was that such ways of thinking would corrupt Christian faith and values. The key text here is St Paul's cautionary remark to the Colossians: 'Beware lest any man spoil you through philosophy and vain deceit, after the tradition of men, after the rudiments of the world, and not after Christ' (Col. 2.8 AV). Nothing here forces us to go along with Tertullian who reads this as a global rejection of reason or philosophy. There is a plausible alternative: Beware of bad philosophy, which obscures and undermines, rather than clarifies, a religious way of life, its moral and spiritual values.

A fideist approach and spirit of enquiry then protects the variety of our ways of life and their associated language games, including religious faiths and the distinctive values associated with them, from the incursions of bad philosophy. 'A bad philosopher is like a slumlord,' said Wittgenstein, 'it is my job to put him out of business' (Rhees 1981, 132). There is no rejection of reason here – just the exposure of the pathologies of reason.

To say then that Wittgenstein was out of sympathy with such fideist authors is contrary to what we know of his readings and sympathies, as well as of his comments concerning the thinkers he respected, kept on re-reading and recommended to others. Even more important than this filiation is that the attitude and substance of Wittgenstein's philosophical works show a fideist orientation. So it sheds light on our understanding of his work, and works done in his legacy, to say that they belong to this family of thinkers. Of course this does not mean the uncritical adoption of common doctrines or theories. Rather, it comes to this. Look at Wittgenstein and Wittgensteinians as belonging to a family of thinkers who share a certain lineage, who show striking resemblances, such as a spirit and attitude of enquiry, and who also show discernible differences. We might say, here is a fideist attitude, but with a Wittgensteinian twist. We need to recall in this connection that Wittgenstein did not hold that philosophy was a historical constant, but emphasized the contingency of philosophical activity, the importance of the culture in which it is carried out. Since the culture Wittgenstein operated in was radically different from that of Augustine, Pascal and even Kierkegaard, it is natural to expect marked differences between Wittgenstein and these other members of the fideist family.

VIII   Reading Each Other

To return to where I started: namely, the intention to uncover buried goods through re-articulation. How can we retrieve important moral sources from revisiting the history of Wittgensteinian Fideism? How may Kai Nielsen's and Dewi Phillips's struggles and dialogue empower us to bring the air back again into the half-collapsed lungs of the spirit? Here are some openings.

Consider their common rejections. Both aim to put an end to the philosophy of religion in the sense that they both reject the traditional philosophy of religion with its essentialism, foundationalism and scientism. We may see Nielsen as a left Wittgensteinian, who wants to put an end to the philosophy of religion as such, and Phillips as a right Wittgensteinian who wants to put an end to the traditional enterprise, but only to do philosophy of religion better.

Could these rejections be motivated by shared moral sources: the pursuit of clarity, transparency and doing justice? The blindspots of the 'isms' distort our understanding and thus hinder the works of justice.[2] Affirmations of further moral sources such as love, compassion and caring for others, are shown in the sustained attempts to rescue what is alive and of value in the religious tradition. To help us make green the valleys of the everyday, these moral sources need rescue from the prison house of distortions, dead languages, social complacency and withering institutions.

What are the differences that remain despite these affirmations? Could these be partly differences between temperaments? There are those who feel that if they kneel they could not get up. That their capacity for self-expression, self-reliance and judgement would be usurped. That their sense of responsibility for the state of the world would be diminished. Then there is the temperament that needs a light from above, for whom religion is the calm at the bottom of the raging sea, for whom that way of life and vocabulary makes possible greater self-expression and motivates good works. Is it possible to make generalizations here? Is it possible to say, 'Religion is inherently harmful?' without residual a priorism? Or do we need to speak for ourselves, after the tasks of clarification and reflection are done?

The dialogue between Kai Nielsen and D. Z. Phillips concerning Wittgensteinian Fideism invites us to engage in a dialogue with them about whether philosophy of religion is possible, about the impossibility and necessity of the philosophy of religion, and of religion itself. In this dialogue, we hear many different voices, the voices of the religious as well as of the secular, and we are given tools and nourishment to clarify or find a voice of our own.

This brings us back to Wittgenstein who explicitly says in the Big Typescript that the goal of his philosophy is justice, peace, as well as respect for particularity, to teach us differences. His concern in describing and examining different ways of using language is 'to see that every usage gets its due' and that we avoid over- or under-estimation by being on guard against a priori generalizations and narrow views. We may also remind ourselves that his way of philosophizing consists essentially of leaving the question of truth and asking about sense instead. Does the use of the religious picture nourish us? If it does, then we have bought the outfit of a tightrope walker, but neither Wittgenstein nor Phillips are impressed until they see what is done with it – do you use it to become more human? Nielsen keeps on telling us to forget about the outfit altogether – it masks our true humanity. Recall Wittgenstein's ethical *cri de coeur*: 'Let us be human' (Wittgenstein 1980). I trust that the questions of what that injunction means and of the many ways of struggling to be human, are also at the heart of our dialogue concerning Wittgensteinian Fideism.

Notes

1 Also consider Phillips 1970b, 76–8.
2 But do we not have blind spots of our own when we want to shut down efforts to revise and resume the traditional concerns expressed in the project of natural theology? Are there not foundationalists and foundationalists?

Bibliography

Malcolm, Norman (1960) 'Anselm's Ontological Arguments', *The Philosophical Review*; reprinted in Phillips 1967, 43–61.
—— (1977) 'The Groundlessness of Belief' in his *Thought and Knowledge*, Ithaca, NY: Cornell, 199–216.
—— (1994), *Wittgenstein: A Religious Point of View*, Ithaca, NY: Cornell.
Nielsen, Kai (1967), 'Wittgensteinian Fideism', *Philosophy*, 42, no. 161: 191–209.
—— (2001), *Naturalism and Religion*, Amherst, NY: Prometheus Books.
Penelhum, Terence (1983), *God and Skepticism: A Study in Skepticism and Fideism*, Dordrecht: Reidel.
Phillips, D. Z. (1964), 'Moral and Religious Conceptions of Duty', *Mind*; reprinted in Phillips 1967, 191–7.
—— (1965), *The Concept of Prayer*, London: Routledge and Kegan Paul.
—— (1967), *Religion and Understanding*, New York: Macmillan.
—— (1970a), *Death and Immortality*, London: Macmillan.
—— (1970b), *Faith and Philosophical Inquiry*, Routledge and Kegan Paul.
—— (1976), *Religion without Explanation*, Oxford: Blackwell.
—— (1986), *Belief, Change and Forms of Life*, London: Macmillan.
Rhees, Rush (1969), *Without Answers*. London: Routledge and Kegan Paul.
—— (1981), *Ludwig Wittgenstein: Personal Recollections*, Oxford: Basil Blackwell.
Taylor, Charles (1989), *Sources of the Self*. Cambridge, MA: Harvard University Press.
Von Wright, Georg Henrik (1982), 'A Biographical Sketch' in his *Wittgenstein*, Oxford: Basil Blackwell, pp. 15–34.
Wittgenstein, Ludwig (1958), *Philosophical Investigations*. Oxford: Basil Blackwell.
—— (1966), *Lectures and Conversations on Aesthetics, Psychology and Religious Belief*: Oxford: Blackwell.

—— (1969), *On Certainty*. Oxford: Basil Blackwell.

—— (1979), *Remarks on Frazer's* Golden Bough, ed. Rush Rhees, Retford: Brynmill.

—— (1980), *Culture and Value*. ed. G. H. Von Wright, Oxford: Basil Blackwell.

—— (1993), *Philosophical Occasions*. eds James Klagge and Alfred Nordmann, Indianapolis and Cambridge: Hackett Publishing Co.

PART ONE

Wittgensteinian Fideism? –
1967–89

1. Wittgensteinian Fideism

KAI NIELSEN

I

Wittgenstein did not write on the philosophy of religion.[1] But certain strands of his later thought readily lend themselves to what I call Wittgensteinian Fideism. There is no text that I can turn to for an extended statement of this position, but certain remarks made by Winch, Hughes, Malcolm, Geach, Cavell, Cameron and Coburn can either serve as partial statements of this position, or can be easily used in service of such a statement.[2] Some of their contentions will serve as targets for my argumentation, for as much as I admire Wittgenstein, it seems to me that the fideistic conclusions drawn by these philosophers from his thought are often absurd. This leads me back to an inspection of their arguments and the premises in these arguments.

These philosophers call attention to the linguistic regularities concerning 'God' that Ziff notes, but beyond anything Ziff claims they stress that religious concepts can only be understood if we have an insider's grasp of the form of life of which they are an integral part.[3] As Malcolm puts it, the very genesis of the concept of God grows out of a certain 'storm in the soul'. Only within a certain form of life could we have the idea of an 'unbearably heavy conscience' from which arises the Judaeo-Christian concept of God and of a 'forgiveness that is beyond all measure'. If, as Malcolm maintains, one does not have a grasp of that form of life from 'the inside not just from the outside' and, if as an insider, one does not have 'at least some inclination to *partake* in that religious form of life', the very concept of God will seem 'an arbitrary and absurd construction'. There cannot be a deep understanding of the concept of God without 'an understanding of the phenomena of human life that gave rise to it'.[4]

Certainly much of what Malcolm says here is unquestionably true. Anthropologists for years have stressed, and rightly, that one cannot gain a deep understanding of the distinctive features of a tribe's culture without a participant's understanding of the way of life of that culture. Concepts cannot be adequately understood apart from a grasp of their function in the stream of life. If a man has no experience of religion, has never learned God-talk where the 'engine isn't idling', he will not have a deep understanding of religion. But having such an understanding of religion is perfectly compatible with asserting, as did the Swedish philosopher Axel Hägerström, that the concept of God is 'nothing but a creation of our own confused thought' growing out of our need to escape 'from the anxiety and wearisomeness of life'.[5] And this comes from a philosopher who, as C. D. Broad's biographical remarks make evident, was once thoroughly immersed in the religious stream of life.

Malcolm's above contention is only one of the Wittgensteinian claims that I shall examine. The following cluster of dark sayings have, when they are accepted, a tendency to generate what I call Wittgensteinian Fideism:

1 The forms of language are the forms of life.
2 What is *given* are the forms of life.
3 Ordinary language is all right as it is.
4 A philosopher's task is not to evaluate or criticize language or the forms of life, but to describe them where necessary and to the extent necessary to break philosophical perplexity concerning their operation.
5 The different modes of discourse which are distinctive forms of life all have a logic of their own.
6 Forms of life taken as a whole are not amenable to criticism; each mode of discourse is in order as it is, for each has its own criteria and each sets its own norms of intelligibility, reality and rationality.
7 These general, dispute-engendering concepts, namely, intelligibility, reality and rationality are systematically ambiguous; their exact meaning can only be determined in the context of a determinate way of life.
8 There is no Archimedean point in terms of which a philosopher (or for that matter anyone else) can relevantly criticize whole modes of discourse or, what comes to the same thing, ways of life, for each mode of discourse has its own specific criteria of rationality/irrationality, intelligibility/unintelligibility and reality/unreality.[6]

A Wittgensteinian fideist who accepted such contentions could readily argue that religion is a unique and very ancient form of life with its own distinctive criteria. It can only be understood or criticized, and then only in a piecemeal way, from within this mode by someone who has a participant's understanding of this mode of discourse. To argue, as I do and as C. B. Martin has, that the very first-order discourse of this form of life is incoherent or irrational can be nothing but a confusion, for it is this very form of life, this very form of discourse itself, that sets its own criteria of coherence, intelligibility or rationality. Philosophy cannot relevantly criticize religion; it can only display for us the workings, the style of functioning, of religious discourse.

I agree with such Wittgensteinians that to understand religious discourse one must have a participant's understanding of it. However, this certainly does not entail that one is actually a participant, that one *accepts* or *believes* in the religion in question. But I do *not* agree that the first-order discourse of religion is in order as it is, and I do not agree that philosophy cannot relevantly criticize religions or forms of life. I shall examine these issues by examining some Wittgensteinian defences of the above approach to religion.

Let me remark at the outset that I am not sure to what extent Wittgenstein himself would have accepted a Wittgensteinian Fideism. But Wittgenstein's work has been taken in that way and it is thought in many quarters that such an approach will give us a deep grasp of religion and will expose the shallowness of scepticism. For this reason I shall carefully examine the view I call Wittgensteinian Fideism. But do not forget, what I indeed hope would be true, that Wittgenstein might well wish to say of Wittgensteinians what Freud said of Freudians. I shall start with G. E. Hughes who presents the most direct confrontation with my view.

II

In his discussion of G. B. Martin's *Religious Belief*, Hughes has defended in an incisive way the claim that, as a whole, rock-bottom, religious utterances or propositions are in order as they are.[7] He does not claim that they are *all* in order but only that generally speaking they are.

He starts by asking what are our criteria for conceptual confusion when we claim that en bloc first-order religious propositions are in conceptual disarray. He remarks, 'I should guess that it is possible to show any category of statements or expressions to be conceptually confused if one is allowed to insist that they must conform to the logic of some other category or categories of statements or expressions if they are to be said to make sense.'[8] Certainly, Max Black and a host of others have made it evident that if we try to treat inductive reasonings as if they were deductive ones, we would make nonsense of them. Similarly, if we try to construe moral statements as if they were empirical statements, and moral reasoning as if it were scientific reasoning, we would make nonsense out of morality. We have learned to treat these concepts and modes of reasoning as being *sui generis*; inductive reasonings and moral reasoning have, in the sense Ryle uses 'logic', a logic of their own. Our job as philosophers is to come to understand and display that logic, not to distort it by trying to reduce it to the logic of some other preferred type of discourse or to try to interpret it in terms of some ideal language like that found in *Principia Mathematica*. We should, Hughes argues, in doing the philosophy of religion adopt 'an alternative programme for meta-theology . . . that . . . consists in allowing the actual use of religious terms and statements to determine their logic, rather than trying to force an alien logic upon them'.[9] Hughes remarks that if we adopt this programme rather than the one Martin adopts (a programme similar to the one I have adopted) our philosophical arguments about religion can be seen in a quite different light. Arguments which show how religious statements generate contradictions when they are construed on the model of other types of statements 'can now be construed as showing some of the peculiarities of their own logic'.[10]

Hughes illustrates his argument with an example from Chapter 4 of Martin's *Religious Belief*. Martin argues there (pp. 40–1) that 'God' may be used in either of two ways: as a proper name referring to a particular being (a name such as 'Charles' or 'Sven') or as a descriptive term. Martin tries to show that using it in both ways at once leads to a contradiction. Hughes then remarks that Martin 'makes out a massive and powerful case for this contradictoriness *provided that the alternatives are as he states them*'.[11] That is to say, Martin's remarks are well taken about 'proper names and descriptive phrases *as applied to particular things*'.[12] But these acute remarks are all beside the point, Hughes contends, for God is not thought of as a 'particular thing' within orthodox Jewish and Christian thought. The 'patterns of what makes sense and what does not, in the case of names and descriptions of particular things, does not fit the pattern of usage of the word "God" on the lips of believers'.[13] It is about as sensible to speak of God as a particular being, as it is to speak of the number 18 or perfect moral virtue as a particular being. Moreover, it is worth remembering in this context that one piece of meta-theology which has won wide acceptance among the orthodox is that 'God' is not a substance-word (Aquinas in the formal mode).

On my approach and on Martin's approach 'the fact that the pattern of usage of a term such as "God" does not accord with that of other non-theological terms with which it is taken to be analogous, is made a basis for the charge that the use of the term is logically incoherent'.[14] But on Hughes' programme – a good programme for a Wittgensteinian fideist – the 'same non-accordance is regarded as showing that the terms are not as analogous as they have at first appeared, and the actual usage of religious terms within religious language is taken as normative for the logical type and the kind of meaning they have'.[15] Hughes goes on to remark that 'which of these programmes is preferable is perhaps the most important question for meta-theology (even, *mutatis mutandis*, for all meta-theorising)'.[16]

Hughes defends his crucial Wittgensteinian methodological preference on the grounds that religious language is a long-established fait accompli, and something which does a job which no other segment of language can do. It is because of this that he is tempted to think that religious statements are in order just as they are, that is, in their own kind of order and, as a whole, in a coherent order.[17] This is a significant claim the ramifications of which I will later consider in detail, but for now I will content myself with a brief sociological remark. We should counterpose against the fact that religious language is a fait accompli another fact, namely, that at all times and at all places, even among the most primitive tribes, there have been sceptics and scoffers, people who though perfectly familiar with the religious language game played in their culture would not play the religious language-game, not because they could not, but because, even though they were perfectly familiar with it, even though they had an insiders' understanding of it, they found it incoherent. But our first-order operations with what some *philosophers* call 'material object talk' and our actual operation with arithmetic are not in this state of controversy. (Meta-mathematics may be in a shambles, but not arithmetic or algebra.) But in this respect religion is very different. There are people who can play the language-game, even people who *want* very much to go on playing the language-game of religion, but they morally and intellectually speaking cannot continue this activity because their intellects, not their natural sympathies, make assent to Jewish or Christian doctrine impossible. Moreover their doubts are often much older than their acquaintance with theology or philosophy and they were only reinforced by their acquaintance with these disciplines. There are people – and among the educated a continually growing number of people – who find, or at least think they find, the religious language-game they have been taught as children either falderal or at best, in Santayana's celebrated phrase, 'moral poetry'. This seems to me to count heavily, though *surely* not decisively, against thinking that at rock-bottom such talk must have a coherent order.

Hughes' other consideration, that religious language does a job which no other segment of language can do, is more troubling. The truth of this very claim could be challenged, but this is not the tack I now want to take. Rather I want simply to point out that in a culture like ours, religious discourse is coming to fail to do its distinctive tasks because many people do not find it coherent. Perhaps they are profoundly deceived; perhaps it is after all a perfectly coherent mode of discourse, but, given their beliefs, to point out to them that such a language game is played is not enough. They perfectly well know how to use this discourse; they know that it is an ancient and venerated part of their culture; they know that it has a distinctive role in their culture. Knowing so well how to play the language-game, their very perplexity is over the apparent incoherence of just this familiar discourse. It is not that they are like

Moore, who was puzzled by what Bradley and other philosophers said about time but was not puzzled about time himself. (He could be puzzled about the correct analysis of 'time' without being puzzled about time.) But, characteristically at any rate, they are puzzled first and primarily about the very first-order God-talk itself and only secondarily about the theologian's or philosopher's chatter about this chatter. Moreover, if one looks over the range of practices that have counted as religions (if one looks at Confucianism and Theravada Buddhism for example) one finds functioning in cultures, and very ancient cultures at that, religions that in terms of our religions (not just in terms of our theologies) are atheistic or agnostic. Given this, it is perfectly possible that certain ersatz religions, for example, Spinoza's, Fromm's and perhaps even Comte's 'atheistical Catholicism', could, given certain cultural conditions, become religions. But given these facts and these possibilities, the fact – if it is a fact – that religious language does a job no other segment of language can do, does little to show that Christian or Islamic or Jewish first-order God-talk or God-talk at all is in a coherent order just as it is.

Hughes could reply that the part of religious talk that is in order just as it is, is what is really alive in religion; it is that which is essential to religion, constitutive of True Religion, that which is shared by all these religions and by ersatz religions as well. But if this reply is made we are likely to end up (1) with a very un-Wittgensteinian essentialist bogeyman, and (2) with treating religion or True Religion as little more than 'morality touched with emotion', that is, Santayana's 'moral poetry'. Given that the Christian Creed as well as the Christian code is crucial to Christianity, as understood by the orthodox, such a conclusion would be most unwelcome, and would, in effect, be a capitulation to the meta-theologian who claimed that Christian discourse, as it stands, is incoherent and not a vindication of the meta-theological claim that the bulk of Christian language is perfectly in place if only metaphysicians and theolologians would not tinker with it.

I do not want to claim that anything I have said so far settles anything. So far, I have only tried to show that there is something to be settled and that we cannot take this short Wittgensteinian way with the concepts of religion. The central considerations here are (1) is the first-order God-talk of Judaism, Christianity or Islam actually, for the most part, anyway, in order as it is, or is it in some way fundamentally incoherent, and (2) how could we decide this issue? These issues need a careful conceptual investigation.

III

These issues come up in an unsettling and probing way in the writings of Peter Winch. He does not directly attack the problem of the intelligibility of God-talk. Rather, Winch, in examining what it is to understand concepts radically different from our own, brings to the fore considerations which are central to an understanding and appraisal of Wittgensteinian Fideism.[18]

In trying to understand what it is to understand a primitive society, Winch examines the Azande conception of magic and subjects Evans-Pritchard's methodological remarks concerning it to a careful critical scrutiny. Evans-Pritchard indeed insists that in order to understand the Azande conceptions, we must understand them in terms of how they are taken by the Azande themselves and in terms of their own social structure, that is, forms of life. But he ceases to make common cause with Wittgenstein and Winch when he argues that nonetheless the Azande are plainly labouring under an illusion. There is no magic and there are no witches. We know that we, with our scientific culture, are right about these matters and the Azande are wrong. Our scientific account of these matters is in accord with objective reality while the Azande magical beliefs are not.

This certainly seems like a scarcely disputable bit of common sense, but Winch is not satisfied with such an answer. While trying to avoid what he calls a Protagorean relativism 'with all the paradoxes that involves', Winch still maintains that, though Evans-Pritchard is right in stressing that 'we should not lose sight of the fact that men's ideas and beliefs must be checkable by reference to something independent – some reality', he is 'wrong, and crucially wrong, in his attempt to characterise the scientific in terms of that which is in accord with objective reality'.[19] Evans-Pritchard is mistaken in thinking that, while the Azande have a different conception of reality from ours, our scientific conception agrees with what reality actually is like while theirs does not.[20]

Winch, moving from counter-assertion to argument, contends that 'the check of the independently real is not peculiar to science'.[21] It is a mistake to think, as Evans-Pritchard and Pareto do, that scientific discourse provides us with 'a paradigm against which to measure the intellectual respectability of other modes of discourse'.[22] At this point in his argumentation Winch uses an example from religious discourse to drive home his point. God, when he speaks to Job out of the whirlwind, takes Job to task for having lost sight of the reality of God. Winch remarks that we would badly misunderstand that passage if we thought that Job had made some kind of theoretical mistake, which he might have corrected by further observation and experiment. Yet, Winch argues, God's reality is independent of human whim or of what any man cares to think about it.

It is here that Winch makes a very revealing remark – a remark that could readily be used to put a Wittgensteinian Fideism into orbit. What God's reality amounts to, Winch says, 'can only be seen from the religious tradition in which the concept of God is used'.[23] Such a religious context is very unlike a scientific context in which we can speak of theoretical entities. Yet only within the religious use of language does 'the conception of God's reality have its place'.[24] As the concept of what is real or what is unreal vis-à-vis magic is only given within and only intelligible within the Azande form of life in which the Azande magical practices are embedded, so the concept of God's reality is only given within and only intelligible within the religious form of life in which such a conception of God is embedded. In both cases there is an ongoing form of life that guarantees intelligibility and reality to the concepts in question. God and Azande magic are not *simply* my ideas or Jewish or Azande ideas. Here we have baldly stated a major motif in Wittgensteinian Fideism.

'What is real?' or 'What is reality?', like 'What is there?', do not have a clear sense. When asked in a completely general way they are meaningless. We can only raise the problem of the reality of something within a form of life. There is no completely extra-linguistic or context-independent conception of reality in accordance with which we might judge forms of life.

> Reality is not what gives language sense. What is real and what is unreal shows itself in the sense that language has. Further, both the distinction between the real and the unreal and the concept of agreement with reality themselves belong to our language.[25]

Yet these distinctions, though surely not the words used to make them, would, Winch argues, have to be a part of any language. Without such distinctions we could not have a system of communication and thus we could not have a language. But how exactly the distinction between the real and the unreal is to be drawn is determined by the actual linguistic usage of some *particular* language. Evans-Pritchard and the man who would reject the whole mode of God-talk as unintelligible or incoherent are both unwittingly saying something that does not make sense, for their own conceptions of reality are *not* determined by the actual usage of 'reality' and they are mistakenly assuming that their very specialized use of 'reality' is something they can use as a yardstick with which to appraise any and every form of life. But they have given us no reasons for adopting this procedure or making this assumption.

If we have been brought up in a certain tradition and understand scientific discourse, we can, while working in that discourse, ask whether a certain scientific hypothesis agrees with reality. We can, given an under-standing of science, test this claim; but when Evans-Pritchard makes the putative statement that 'Criteria applied in scientific experimentation constitute a true link between our ideas and an independent reality', he has *not* asserted a scientific hypothesis or even made an empirical state-ment. His putative assertion is not open to confirmation or discon-firmation; and if 'true link' and 'independent reality' are explained by reference to the scientific universe of discourse, we would beg the ques-tion of whether scientific experimentation, rather than magic or religion, constitutes a true link between our ideas and an independent reality. There seems to be no established use of discourse by means of which the expressions 'true link' and 'independent reality' in Evans-Pritchard's assertion can be explained. At any rate – and to put Winch's contention in a minimal way – Evans-Pritchard does not give these expressions a use or show us that they have a use. Thus when we try to say that the idea of God makes no true link with an independent reality we are using 'true link' and 'independent reality' in a meaningless or at least a wholly indeterminate way.

This argument is reinforced by a further claim made by Winch in his *The Idea of a Social Science*. There Winch sets forth a central plank in any Wittgensteinian Fideism. Logic, as a formal theory of order, must, given that it is an interpreted logic (an interpreted calculus), systemati-cally display the forms of order found in the modes of social life. What can and cannot be said, what follows from what, is dictated by the norms of intelligibility embedded in the modes of social life. These finally determine the criteria of logical appraisal. Since this is so, 'one cannot apply criteria of logic to modes of social life as such'.[26] Science is one such mode and religion another; 'each has criteria of intelligibility peculiar to itself'. Within science or religion an action can be logical or illogical. It would, for example, be illogical for a scientist working in a certain area to refuse to take cognizance of the results of a properly conducted experiment; and it would also be illogical for a man who believed in God to try to pit his strength against God. But it makes no sense at all to assert that science or religion is logical or illogical, any more than it would make sense to speak of music as either well-coloured or ill-coloured or of stones as either married or divorced.

Winch's view here has rightly been taken to involve a claim to concep-tual self-sufficiency for all of the forms of life. It has also been thought that it involves a kind of compartmentalization of the modes of discourse or forms of life. Winch is indeed saying that we cannot criticize science or ethics by criteria appropriate to religion, and vice versa. Like Hughes, Winch is claiming that each mode of discourse must be understood in its own terms and that relevant criticism of that mode of discourse cannot be made from outside of that discourse, but can take place only from within it, when some specific difficulty actually arises in science or in religion.

There is much here that is very perceptive, but there is much that needs close scrutiny as well. Let me assume here what in reality is quite open to question, namely, that Winch is correct about the Azande. That is, let me assume that given the radically different conceptual structure embedded in their language, and given the role magic and witchcraft play in their lives, we can have no good grounds for saying, as Evans-Pritchard does, that our concept of reality is the correct one and theirs is not. But even making this very questionable assumption, it does not at all follow that in our tribe religion and science are related as Azande magic is related to our scientific beliefs. There is no 'religious language' or 'scientific language'. There is rather the international notation of mathematics and logic; and English, French, German and the like. In short, 'religious discourse' and 'scientific discourse' are part of the same overall conceptual structure. Moreover, in that conceptual structure there is a large amount of discourse, which is neither religious nor scientific, that is constantly being utilized by both the religious man and the scientist when they make religious or scientific claims. In short, they share a number of key categories. This situation differs from the Azande situation in a very significant sense, for in the former situation, we do not have in the same literal sense two *different* conceptual structures exemplifying two different ways of life. C. P. Snow to the contrary notwithstanding, we do not have two cultures here but only one.

Sometimes it is indeed tempting to think there really are two cultures. When I read a certain kind of religious literature – as in a recent reading of Simone Weil's *Waiting for God* – I have the *feeling* that I belong to another tribe: that what she can understand and take as certain I have no understanding of at all, beyond a Ziffian sense of her linguistic regularities. Leslie Fiedler tells us that Miss Weil 'speaks of the problems of belief in the vocabulary of the unbeliever', but that is not how I read her.[27] I find her unabashedly talking about religious matters in a way that I find nearly as incredible as some of the things the Azande say. She blithely accepts what I find unintelligible. Yet this initial impression is in a way misleading, for, as I read on, I discover that she is sensitive to *some* of the conceptual perplexities that perplex me. I find her saying,

> There is a God. There is no God. Where is the problem? I am quite sure that there is a God in the sense that I am sure my love is no illusion. I am quite sure there is no God, in the sense that I am sure there is nothing which resembles what I can conceive when I say that word . . .

When I ponder this, I realize that as much as we might differ, we are in the same universe of discourse. Miss Weil is not, after all, to me like the Azande with his witchcraft substance. We both learned 'the language' of Christian belief; only I think it is illusion-producing while she thinks that certain crucial segments of it are our stammering way of talking about ultimate reality. A very deep gulf separates us; we are not even like Settembrini and Naphta. But all the same, there remains a sense in which we do understand each other and in which we share a massive background of beliefs and assumptions. Given that, it is not so apparent that we do *not* have common grounds for arguing about which concepts of reality are correct or mistaken here.

Winch, as we have seen, argues against Pareto's and Evans-Pritchard's claim that scientific concepts alone can characterize objective reality. He is correct in his claim that their claim is an incoherent one. 'Scientific concepts alone make a true link with objective reality' is neither analytic nor empirical. No use has been given to 'true link' or 'objective reality'. When a plain man looks at a harvest moon and says that it is orange, or says that the sun rises in the east and sets in the west, or that his vineyard posts are solid, he is not making scientific statements, but he is not making *subjective* statements either. His statements can be perfectly objective; they can be about how things are, and they can be objectively testable (publically verifiable) without being scientific or without conflicting with science. But when it is claimed – as presumably people who seriously utter certain religious propositions claim – that the *facts* asserted by these religious propositions are such and such, their claims must be open to some possible confirmation or disconfirmation: their claims must be publically testable. As Austin puts it, they are making some assertion or trying to make some assertion about how things-are-in-the-world. But a claim like 'God created the heavens and the earth', when 'God' is used non-anthropomorphically, is not testable. That is to say, it is a claim that purports to assert a fact, yet it is devoid of truth-value. People who use such religious talk – partake of such a form of life – cannot determine how, even in principle, they would establish or disestablish such religious claims, but they still believe that they are factual assertions: that is to say that they have truth-values. It is a fact that there is a God; it is a fact that he created the world; it is a fact that he protects me and the like. Yet, how could we say what it would be like for God to create the world, if it is impossible in principle to say what would have to transpire for it to be false that God created the world? Or to put this verificationist point in a weaker and more adequate way, if we cannot even say what *in principle* would count as *evidence* against the putative statement that God created the world, then 'God created the world' is devoid of factual content.

This verificationist argument can, perhaps, be successfully rebutted,

32

KAI NIELSEN

but it is far less vulnerable than the claim that only scientific ideas correspond with reality. That is to say, given the concept of objective reality that plain men, including plain religious men, utilize in everyday life, a statement asserts a fact, actually has factual content, only if it is confirmable or disconfirmable in principle. To count as a factual statement, it must assert a certain determinate reality (a pleonasm); that is, its descriptive content includes one set of empirically determinable conditions and excludes others.[28] People who argue for this would, or at least should, claim that these last remarks are what Wittgenstein called grammatical remarks, that is, they hold in virtue of the linguistic conventions governing the crucial terms in question. But key religious utterances, though they purport to be factual statements, do not succeed in making what actually counts as a genuine factual statement. That is, as Strawson puts it, they are not actually part of that type of discourse we call a fact-stating type of discourse. Thus they lack the kind of coherence they must have to make genuinely factual claims.

I shall not here, though I have elsewhere, assess such a controversial claim.[29] Here I want only to note that even if it turns out to be mistaken, it is a far more powerful counter-thrust against Winchian claims to the conceptual self-sufficiency and the coherence of God-talk, than is the simplistic claim that only scientific ideas are in accord with objective reality. Such a verificationist claim – a claim utilized by Ayer and Flew – stands here as an unmet challenge to Wittgensteinian Fideism.

IV

Someone who wanted to use Winch to defend a Wittgensteinian Fideism might reply that a key religious claim like 'God created the heavens and the earth' does indeed have something to do with understanding the world. We could not have a deep understanding of our world if we did not understand *that*, but it must be realized that the understanding in question is not the narrowly factual or empirical one I have just been talking about. Supernatural facts are a *sui generis* kind of fact. They are not, as Austin would put it, 'a special kind of something in the world'; and they cannot be modelled on the garden variety concept of a fact. My argument, my critic might say, only shows that such religious statements are not factual in the way commonsensical, scientific and empirical statements are factual. It does not show religious statements are incoherent or pseudo-factual. Moreover, it in effect confirms the Wittgensteinian claim that religious discourse is one kind of discourse with its own distinctive logic while science and common sense are forms of life that constitute other quite distinct modes of discourse with their own unique criteria.

My reply is that the phrase 'logic of discourse' is a dangerous metaphor and that these discourses are not in actual life nearly so compartmentalized as the above argument would have it. The man perplexed about God is not like the man perplexed by Azande beliefs in witchcraft substance. He is not an outsider who does not know the form of life but an insider who does. So God spoke to Job out of the whirlwind. So how did he do it? Nobody, or at least nobody who matters, believes any more in a sky God up there, who might have done it in a very loud voice. But what did happen? How are we to understand 'God spoke to Job'? Maybe it was all Job's tortured imagination? Yet how do we even understand what it is that he was supposed to have imagined? And how are we to understand 'I am who am'? A man may be puzzled about the *nature* of time, but when his alarm clock rings at 5.30 a.m. and a little later the weather comes on over the radio at 6.00 and his clock shows 6.00 too, he does not, unless he is excessively neurotic, doubt what time it is. He is painfully aware what time it is. But perfectly sane men in a tribe where God-talk is an established practice, part of an ancient and venerated form of life, can and do come to wonder, to whom or to what they are praying, or what is being talked about when it is said that 'God spoke to Job'. God is a person, but we can't identify him; God acts in the world but has no body. Words here are put together in a strange way. What could it possibly mean to speak of 'action' or 'a person' here? These terms cut across activities; they are at home in religious and non-religious contexts. It is also true that some logical rules (the laws of contradiction, excluded middle and the like) most certainly seem to cut across forms of life. The forms of life are not as compartmentalized as Winch seems to imply, and as a Wittgensteinian Fideism requires. Insiders can and do come to doubt the very coherence of this religious mode of life and its first-order talk.

They indeed do, it will be replied, but in doing that they are philosophically confused. Careful attention to the concept of reality, and to the systematic ambiguity of norms of intelligibility, will show why. It is just here, it will be claimed, that Wittgenstein's insights are most enlightening. This takes us to what I regard as the heart of the matter, and here we need to consider some very fundamental arguments of Winch's.

Winch makes one central point which seems to me unassailable: to understand religious conceptions we need a religious tradition; without a participant's understanding of that form of life, there can be no understanding of religion. To understand it we must learn the rules of conceptual propriety distinctive of that form of life. Without a knowledge by *wont* of the norms of conceptual propriety associated with God-talk, we can have no grasp of the concept of God, and thus, without such knowledge by *wont*, there can be no quest for God or even a rejection of God. If 'we are to speak of difficulties and incoherencies appearing and being detected in the way certain practices have hitherto been carried on in a society, surely this can only be understood in connection with problems arising in the carrying on of the activity'.[30]

Surely we must start here. There could not even be a *problem* about God if we could not. But to start at this point is one thing, to end there is another. The need to start from 'inside' need not preclude the recognition of clefts, inconsistencies and elements of incoherence in the very practice (form of life). Once magic and belief in fairies were ongoing practices in our stream of life. By now, by people working from the inside, the entire practice, the entire 'form of life', has come to be rejected as incoherent.

We have seen, however, that Winch, after the fashion of a Wittgenstein fideist, argues that we cannot intelligibly assert the incoherence, illogicality, irrationality or unintelligibility of a form of life itself. The forms of life, he argues, have a conceptual self-sufficiency; operating with them, we can say that something does or does not make sense, is logical or illogical, for example, that was an illogical chess move. But we cannot say of the whole activity itself that it is illogical, irrational, unintelligible or incoherent, for example, chess is illogical.

The tide of metaphysics is running high here. Our everyday discourse, which is so important for a Wittgensteinian, will not support such a Winchian claim. 'An ongoing but irrational form of life' most certainly does *not appear* to be a contradiction. 'Foot-binding was for a long time an established institution but it was really cruel and irrational' may be false but it is not nonsense. 'Primogeniture had a definite rationale' and 'Magical practices are essential for the Azande' are not grammatical remarks, but this means that their denials are significant and this means that we can make judgements about the rationality of forms of life. Similarly, we can say, without *conceptual* impropriety, that gambling is illogical. We might even say that French is illogical because of its haphazard use of gender, or that the irregularities of English grammar make it illogical. All of these statements may be false, they may even be absurdly false, but they certainly do not appear to be self-contradictory or senseless. It is not at all evident that language has gone on a holiday here. But to establish his thesis Winch must show that, appearances notwithstanding, they are all either senseless or metaphorical.

It can be replied: how do you deal with (1) Winch's specific argument that 'the criteria of logic ... arise out of, and are only intelligible in the context of, ways of living or modes of social life as such'[31] and (2) his further contention that 'formal requirements tell us nothing about what in particular is to count as consistency, just as the rules of the propositional calculus limit, but do not themselves determine what are to be proper values of p, q, etc.'[32] I cannot consistently assert p and not-p, but what range of values the variable p takes is not uniquely determined by purely formal considerations. If I know that to say x is a bachelor entails *x* is not married, I know, by purely formal considerations, that I cannot assert *x* is a married bachelor. But what counts as 'a bachelor' or 'a married man' can only be determined by reference to the actual usage embedded in the form of life of which they are a part.

Unless we are prepared to accept the compartmentalization thesis, dear to Wittgensteinian fideists, the acceptance of the above claim about logic need not commit one to the paradoxical thesis that modes of social life cannot be appraised as logical or illogical, rational or irrational. Religion, morality and science may indeed each have 'criteria of intelligibility peculiar to itself'. This means that the criteria of application for 'God', 'Divine Person', 'perfect good' and the like is set by the first-order religious discourse itself. However, it also remains true (1) that discourse concerning God goes on in Swedish, German, English, French and the like, and (2) that there is no separate religious language. Given these two facts and given the overall universe of discourse of which religious discourse is a part, it may still be found that religious discourse, like discourse about fairies, is incoherent, for example, 'God is three and one', 'God is a person that one *encounters* in prayer but God is utterly *transcendent*'. Seemingly contradictory statements may indeed turn out not to be contradictory. When fully stated and understood, in terms of their distinctive contextual use, what *appears* to be contradictory or paradoxical may be seen to be straightforward and non-contradictory. Religious discourse is not something isolated, sufficient unto itself; 'sacred discourse' shares categories with, utilizes the concepts of, and contains the syntactical structure of, 'profane discourse'. Where there is what at least appears to be a contradiction, or where words are put together in a way fluent speakers *cannot* understand, a case must be made out for the contention that the contradiction is *only apparent*. What appears to be unintelligible, must be shown to have a use in the discourse or it must be given a use. That is to say, the words must be given an employment or shown to have an employment so that fluent speakers can grasp what is being said.

Many key religious statements at least appear to be contradictory or incoherent. That a *case* needs to be made out and perhaps even can be made out to show that they are not really contradictory or incoherent, shows that such a question can be raised about religious discourse. Given this fact and given the centrality of some of these religious statements, it becomes apparent that Winch's argument does not succeed in establishing that it is impossible to appraise whole ways of life as rational or irrational, intelligible or unintelligible. Furthermore, that we can ask questions about 'God is three and one' and 'A *transcendent* God is *encountered* in prayer' that involve appealing to criteria from the discourse as a whole and not just from religious talk, indicates that Winch's argument does not show that we can compartmentalize religious talk. In short, the Winchian arguments that we have examined do not show that we cannot raise questions about the rationality of a form of life or that religious discourse is so *sui generis* that its criteria of intelligibility are contained within itself.

We are not yet at the bottom of the barrel. The question 'What is real?' has no determinate sense. What is real and what is unreal is a very context-dependent notion. What in a specific context counts as 'real' or 'reality', as in 'a real trout', 'a real champion', 'an unreal distinction', 'the realities of the economic situation', 'a sense of reality', 'the reality of death' or 'the reality of God', can only be determined with reference to the particular matter we are talking about. We have no antecedent understanding of reality such that we could determine whether language agreed with reality, whether a specific language agreed with reality or whether a given form of discourse agreed with reality. With the exception of the *very last bit*, I agree with Winch about such matters, but alas it is this very last bit that is essential for a Wittgensteinian Fideism.

However, with this last Wittgensteinian claim, there are very real difficulties similar to ones we have already discussed. 'Reality' may be systematically ambiguous, but what constitutes evidence, or tests for the truth or reliability of specific claims, is not completely idiosyncratic to the context or activity we are talking about. Activities are not that insulated. As I have already remarked, once there was an ongoing form of life in which fairies and witches were taken to be real entities, but gradually, as we reflected on the criteria we actually use for determining whether various entities, including persons, are or are not part of the spatio-temporal world of experience, we came to give up believing in fairies and witches. That a language-game was played, that a form of life existed, did not preclude our asking about the coherence of the concepts involved and about the reality of what they conceptualized.

Without a participant's understanding of God-talk, we could not raise the question of the reality of God, but with it, this is perfectly possible and perfectly intelligible.

Indeed we sometimes judge the reality of one thing in terms of something utterly inappropriate, for example, moral distinctions are unreal because moral utterances do not make factual assertions. Here we do commit a howler. But, as my above examples show, this need not always be the case. 'Johnson ought to be impeached' can be seen, by an examination of the relevant forms of life, not to describe a certain happening. It is not a bit of fact-stating discourse asserting some actual occurrence, but rather it tells us to make something occur. 'Witches are out on Hallowe'en' is a putative factual statement. It supposedly does assert that a certain identifiable state-of-affairs obtains. It supposedly is like saying 'The Klan is out on Hallowe'en'. But the factual intelligibility of the former is not evident, for it is not clear what counts as a witch. To say that 'witch' refers to a unique kind of reality only intelligible within a distinctive form of life is an incredible piece of evasion. To reason in such a manner is to show that one is committed to a certain metaphysical theory, come what may. But, if one wants to be realistic and non-evasive, one will surely say that it gradually became apparent, vis-à-vis forms of life in which talk of witches was embedded, that in light of the meanings of 'fact' and 'evidence' in the overall discourse of which witch-talk was a part, that witch-talk was incoherent. Though there was a form of life in which the existence of witches was asserted, such a way of life is and was irrational. And even if for some baroque reason I am mistaken in saying that it is or was irrational to believe in witches, the fact that such a question can be intelligently raised about one form of life plainly demonstrates that Winch's a priori arguments against such an appraisal of a form of life as a whole will not wash.

Perhaps God-talk is not as incoherent and irrational as witch-talk; perhaps there is an intelligible concept of the reality of God, and perhaps there is a God, but the fact that there is a form of life in which God-talk is embedded does not preclude our asking these questions or our giving, quite intelligibly, though perhaps mistakenly, the same negative answer we gave to witch-talk.

Notes

1 This now turns out to be inaccurate. Since this was first written, the following book has been announced: Ludwig Wittgenstein, *Lectures and Conversations on Aesthetics, Psychology and Religious Belief.*

2 The scattered but central sources here are as follows: Peter Winch, *The Idea of a Social Science* (London: 1958); 'Understanding a Primitive Society', *American Philosophical Quarterly*, vol. I (October, 1964), pp. 307–25; G. E. Hughes, 'Martin's Religious Belief', *Australasian Journal of Philosophy*, vol. 40 (August, 1962), pp. 211–19; Norman Malcolm, 'Anselm's Ontological Arguments', *The Philosophical Review* (1960); 'Is it a Religious Belief That "God Exists"?'; *Faith and the Philosophers*, John Hick (ed.) (New York: 1964); Peter Geach, 'Nominalism', *Sophia*, vol. III No. 2 (1964); Stanley Cavell, 'Existentialism and Analytic Philosophy', *Daedalus*, vol. 93 (Summer, 1964); J. M. Cameron, *The Night Battle* (Baltimore: 1962); 'What Is a Christian?' *The New York Review of Books*, vol. VI (May 26 1966); Robert Coburn, 'A Neglected Use of Theological Language', *Mind*, vol. LXXII (July, 1963).

3 Paul Ziff, 'About God' in *Religious Experience and Truth*, Sidney Hook (ed.) (New York: 1961).

4 Norman Malcolm, 'Anselm's Ontological Arguments', *The Philosophical Review* (1960).

5 Axel Hägerström, *Philosophy and Religion* (London: 1964), p. 216.

6 I do not neccessarily lay all these *aperçu* at Wittgenstein's door, but all of them can clearly be found in one or another of his disciples.

7 G. F. Hughes, 'Martin's *Religious Belief*', *Australasian Journal of Philosophy*, vol. 40 (August, 1962), pp. 211–19.

8 Ibid., p. 214.

9 Ibid.

10 Ibid.

11 Ibid., pp. 214–15.

12 Ibid., p. 215.

13 Ibid.

14 Ibid.

15 Ibid.

16 Ibid.

17 Ibid., pp. 215–16.

18 The central essay here is his 'Understanding a Primitive Society', *American Philosophical Quarterly*, vol. I (October, 1964), pp. 307–25. But see also Peter Winch, *The Idea of a Social Science* (London: 1958).

19 Peter Winch, 'Understanding a Primitive Society', *American Philosophical Quarterly*, vol. I (October, 1964), p. 308.

20 Ibid.

21 Ibid.

22 Ibid.

23 Ibid., p. 309.

24 Ibid.

25 Ibid.

26 Peter Winch, *The Idea of a Social Science*, p. 100.

27 Leslie Fiedler, 'Introduction' to Simone Weil's *Waiting For God* (New York: 1951), pp. 3–4.

28 That 'determinate reality' is a pleonasm has been argued in a powerful way by Axel Hägerström in his *Philosophy and Religion* (London: 1964). It is surely to be hoped that the rest of Hägerström's writings in Swedish will soon be made available to non-Swedish readers. [See also paperback edition of Kai Nielsen, *Atheism and Philosophy*, Amherst, NY: Prometheus Press (2005).]

29 Kai Nielsen, 'On Speaking of God', *Theoria*, vol. XXVIII (1962, Part 2); 'Religion and Commitment', *Problems of Religious Knowledge and Language*; W. T. Blackstone and R. H. Ayers (eds.), forthcoming; 'Eschatological Verification', *Canadian Journal of Theology*, vol. IX (1963); 'God and Verification Again', *Canadian Journal of Theology*, vol. XI (1965); 'On Fixing the Reference Range of "God"', *Religious Studies* (October, 1966).

30 Peter Winch, 'Understanding a Primitive Society', *American Philosophical Quarterly*, vol. I (October, 1964), p. 319.

31 Peter Winch, *The Idea of a Social Science*, pp. 100–1.

32 Peter Winch, 'Understanding a Primitive Society', *American Philosophical Quarterly*, vol. I (October, 1964), p. 319.

2. Wittgenstein and Religion: Some Fashionable Criticisms

D. Z. PHILLIPS

It may be that Wittgenstein's influence on the philosophy of religion has aroused more hostility than any other aspect of his work. The years since World War Two have been described as 'a sorry time for the philosophy of religion in English-speaking countries', and this, it is said, has been due not least to the disastrous influence of Wittgenstein.[1] During the period referred to, the influence of Wittgenstein has been far-reaching in almost every branch of philosophy: philosophical logic, philosophy of mathematics, theory of knowledge, philosophy of mind, ethics, aesthetics, philosophy of the social sciences and so on. Adverse comments on his influence on the philosophy of religion, however, are not confined to those who think that Wittgenstein's philosophical influence in general has been a disaster. On the contrary, they are made, as in the instance quoted, by sympathetic commentators. Unfortunately, it cannot be denied that a philosophy by innuendo has grown up by which it is hinted, rather than argued, that what Wittgenstein is said to have said about religion and ritual is not closely related to the rest of his work. It has been suggested also that those influenced by him in the philosophy of religion have imposed alien features on Wittgenstein's work, and made use of certain of his terms, such as 'language-games', in ways of which he would not have approved.

It is hard to see how these charges can be sustained. If we look at some other areas of philosophy, we shall find a continuity between many of Wittgenstein's emphases there and those we find in his comments on religion and ritual. For example, logic, for Wittgenstein, is not an a priori realm which is, in some sense or other, prior to all experience. Distinctions between sense and nonsense have their life in activities and ways of living we share with one another. We see their force, not by reference to external, static standards, but by appreciating the different bearings things have on one another. In epistemology, Wittgenstein attacks the search for foundations. Our task, in face of scepticism, is not to show *how* we know, or to ask *whether* we know. Rather we are asked to reflect on the tendencies of thought which lead us to ask such questions. When these routes to our questions are revealed, we cease to be in the grip of scepticism. In the philosophy of mind, Wittgenstein argues that we do not need theories to provide us with foundations for human behaviour. When such theories are abandoned – various forms of mind-body dualism, various forms of behaviourism, various forms of physicalism – they can be shown to harbour conceptual confusions. But what is offered in replacement? Not an alternative theory, but release from those knots in the understanding which had led us to general theorizing in the first place. In ethics and aesthetics, the idea that philosophy should provide foundations or justifications for moral or aesthetic excellence is an example of the 'chatter' Wittgenstein said he wanted to put an end to in these contexts. Attempts at ignoring the heterogeneity of the moral and the aesthetic only lead to the construction of spurious unities. It has been observed that the variety in these contexts is important, not in order that we might fix our gaze on the unadulterated form, but to keep us from looking for it.[2] The search for essences in the philosophy of the social sciences, the desire to determine the essence of the difference between what is rational and what is irrational, has led to condescending misunderstandings of certain activities in our own culture and, more particularly, to condescending misunderstandings of activities in the culture of other peoples. By ignoring the concepts which characterized these activities, alien descriptions were imposed upon them.

We find, then, in all these areas of philosophy, a refusal to make philosophy the provider of foundations and justifications. Yet it is this very refusal which is resisted when philosophers turn to the philosophy of religion (and, interestingly, political philosophy). But here, too, the same emphases can be found in Wittgenstein's work. He refuses to look for proofs for the existence of God. He refuses to look for philosophical foundations and justifications for religious belief. Here, too, the task of philosophy is descriptive. Elsewhere, Kenny recognizes that this conception of philosophy is at work in Wittgenstein's discussions of religious belief:

> In saying that in philosophy there are no deductions Wittgenstein set himself against the type of philosophy which offers proofs, e.g. of the existence of God or immortality of the soul . . . Throughout his life he remained sceptical and hostile to philosophy of that kind. 'We must do away with all explanation,' he wrote, 'and description alone must take its place.' The point of the description is the solution of philosophical problems: they are solved not by the amassing of new empirical knowledge, 'but by the rearrangement of what we already know. (*P.I.* I, 109)[3]

Given this elucidation, it is curious that Kenny should suggest in 'In Defence of God' that philosophers influenced by Wittgenstein in the philosophy of religion are imposing *alien* features on his work. If we want a contrast to Wittgenstein's conception of philosophy in the philosophy of religion, we need not look further than Kenny's own work:

> Some theologians regard religion as a way of life which can only be understood by participation and therefore cannot be justified to an outsider on neutral rational grounds. Such people must consider any attempt at a philosophical proof of God's existence to be wrong-headed, and must find it inconceivable that such matters as whether everything in motion has a mover could have relevance to religion . . . To me it seems that if belief in the existence of God cannot be rationally justified, there can be no good grounds for adopting any of the traditional monotheistic religions.[4]

Clearly, on Kenny's own admission, Wittgenstein must be included among those who think that the desire for proofs of the existence of God is wrong-headed. Kenny also attributes to those influenced by Wittgenstein the view that only religious believers can understand religious belief. As we shall see, they do not hold such a view, but Kenny thinks, wrongly, that the only alternative to this view is the belief in the possibility of providing a neutral rational justification of religion. *Neither* thesis need be held. My aim, at the moment, however, is not to argue this point, but to clear the air regarding philosophical facts concerning Wittgenstein's influence on the philosophy of religion.

It has been argued, however, that whatever of Wittgenstein himself, those influenced by him in the philosophy of religion have gone much further than any of the emphases in Wittgenstein's work mentioned so far would warrant. They have, it is said, developed theses of their own. Any claim that these theses owe anything to Wittgenstein is an aberration on the part of those influenced by him.

Those influenced by Wittgenstein who have attempted to throw light on the nature of religious beliefs have been accused of wanting to shield religious belief against criticism. This alleged anti-intellectualism and conservatism has been given the name 'fideism', a term which, unfortunately, seems here to stay.[5] If the accounts of these critics were taken as a reliable guide to the nature of Wittgenstein's influence on the philosophy of religion, one would be led to conclude that philosophers so influenced embraced at least five theses concerning the nature of religious belief. Complaints about these theses have now been heard for almost 20 years.[6] Yet, staggering though it may seem, few have bothered to ask whether philosophers influenced by Wittgenstein have, in fact, ever propounded the five theses so confidently attributed to them. As a matter of fact, none of these theses, let alone all of them, have been held by the philosophers criticized most often in these terms. A philosophical prejudice, aided by a certain jargon, has simply generated a life of its own. It becomes necessary, therefore, to produce evidence of the misplaced character of these persistent criticisms. Since all these criticisms have been made most frequently of my work,[7] the textual evidence produced will be from that source.[8] I shall consider the five theses involved.

The first thesis attributed to philosophers influenced by Wittgenstein in the philosophy of religion is as follows: *Religious beliefs are logically cut off from all other aspects of human life.*

This is by far the most damaging claim made against philosophers of religion influenced by Wittgenstein. John Hick claims:

> The unacceptable feature of the position is that by treating religious language as autonomous – as a language-game with its own rules or a speech activity having meaning only within its own borders – it deprives religious statements of 'ontological' or 'metaphysical' significance ... The logical implications of religious statements do not extend across the borders of the *Sprachspiel* into assertions concerning the character of the universe beyond that fragment of it which is the religious speech of human beings. Religious language has become a kind of 'protected discourse', and forfeits its immemorial claim to bear witness to the most momentous of all truths.[9]

The route by which this alleged thesis is supposed to be arrived at, has been discussed most fully by Walford Gealy.[10] Gealy thinks that I have misconstrued the implications of one of the central developments in Wittgenstein's later philosophy. He expounds the development he has in mind as follows:

> Throughout the *Tractatus* Wittgenstein speaks of the general form of the proposition – the form which makes it possible for language to 'picture' reality. But in the *Investigations* the unity which language has is said to be informal and open-ended, and this unity is compared with that unity and relation which are all contained in the general term 'games'. And he emphasises that there is no one definite element which is common to all these activities.[11]

What Wittgenstein says here about language has two aspects, one of which, according to Gealy, I virtually ignore. The two aspects he has in mind are found in the following well-known passages in the *Investigations*. Here is the first:

> Consider for example the proceedings that we call 'games'. I mean board-games, card-games, ball-games, Olympic games, and so on. What is common to them all? – Don't say: 'There *must* be something

common, or they would not be called "games"' – but *look and see* whether there is anything common to all. – For if you look at them you will not see something that is common to *all*, but similarities, relationships, and a whole series of them at that. To repeat: don't think, but look! – Look for example at board-games with their multifarious relationships. Now pass to card-games; here you find many correspondences with the first group, but many common features drop out, and others appear. When we pass next to ball-games, much that is common is retained, but much is lost. – Are they all 'amusing'? Compare chess with noughts and crosses. Or is there always winning and losing, or competition between players? Think of patience. In ball-games there is winning and losing; but when a child throws his ball at the wall and catches it again, this feature has disappeared. Look at the parts played by skill and luck; and at the difference between skill in chess and skill in tennis. Think now of games like ring-a-ring-a-roses; here is the element of amusement, but how many other characteristic features have disappeared! And we can go through the many, many other groups of games in the same way; we can see how similarities crop up and disappear.

And the result of this examination is: we see a complicated network of similarities overlapping and criss-crossing: sometimes overall similarities, sometimes similarities of detail.[12]

Gealy also wants to call attention to the crucial preceding section where Wittgenstein writes:

Here we come up against the great question that lies behind all these considerations. – For someone might object against me: 'You take the easy way out! You talk about all sorts of language-games, but have nowhere said what the essence of a language-game, and hence of language, is: what is common to all these activities, and what makes them into language or parts of language. So you let yourself off the very part of the investigation that once gave you yourself most headache, the part about the *general form of propositions* and of language.'

And this is true. Instead of producing something common to all that we call language, I am saying that these phenomena have no one thing in common which makes us use the same word for all, – but that they are *related* to one another in many different ways. And it is because of this relationship, or these relationships, that we call them all 'language'.[13]

The two aspects of language which Gealy emphasizes in these passages are as follows: first, the distinctiveness of language-games. There is no one common element which accounts for them being language-games.

Thus we can make conceptual distinctions while comparing language-games. Second, the relationships between language-games: we could not have a language containing only one language-game. To belong to a language, a language-game must stand in some relation to some other language-game. This is necessary, for example, if we are to identify the language-game in question. Identity depends on contrasts and differences. On the other hand, it would be a confusion to ask how many language-games a language must contain, since that would be to assume that there are necessary and sufficent conditions for what is to count as language. This would contradict the view of the *Investigations* that the kind of unity language has is informal and open-ended.

Gealy's contention is that I stress the first aspect of language to which Wittgenstein calls our attention, but ignore the second aspect. In stressing the conceptual distinctiveness of religious beliefs, I forget, so Gealy claims, that this distinctiveness depends on the relation between religious beliefs and that which surrounds them in human life. On this view, I make religious belief an esoteric game. Different ways of speaking, different modes of language, are made absolutely autonomous. It is obvious that in these remarks Gealy is echoing the voices of many critics.

It may be thought that I myself recognize the justice of such charges. After all, in 1970, in my paper, 'Religious Beliefs and Language-Games' I made the following admission: 'I write this . . . as one who has talked of religious beliefs as distinctive language-games, but also as one who has come to feel misgivings in some respects about doing so.'[14] Later, however, I rejected this admission as premature. How, then, did I come to make it? I gave the following reason: 'I suspect that we have heard so-called fideistic . . . views attributed to us so often that we have almost come to believe in their accuracy ourselves without checking it!'[15] This is testimony enough to the hold which philosophical fashion can exert on philosophical enquiry. As a result of my suspicions, however, I underwent 'the self-inflicted penance of re-reading what I had said on these topics. I found no evidence of my having said that faith could not be challenged or overthrown by non-religious factors.'[16] Yet I cannot expect the critic to take my word for this, so what follows is a reminder of some of the ways in which I actually *oppose* the five theses which those influenced by Wittgenstein in the philosophy of religion are supposed to hold.

As early as my first book, *The Concept of Prayer*, I was anxious to stress that 'Religious concepts . . . are not *technical* concepts; they are not cut off from the common experiences of human life: joy and sorrow, hope and despair. Because this is so, an attempt can be made to clarify their meaning. The idea of prayer as talking to God presents us with this task.'[17] After all, the purpose of the whole book is to explore the connections which *do* exist between prayer and the events of human life. The fact of such connections is not contingently related to the meaning of prayer. How could God be thanked if there were nothing to thank God *for*? How could confessions be made to God if there were *nothing* to confess? How could petitions be made to God in the absence of purposes and desires? So far from denying the connections between prayer and these features of human life, I argued that if such connections are severed, the religious significance of the 'prayer' becomes problematic. I opposed writers like H. E. Fosdick, who rely on the fact that people often 'cry to God' in adversity, to prove that there is 'a spark of divinity' in all men. Whether the spark is indeed a spark of divinity depends on the part the cry plays in the life of the person concerned. Fosdick claimed that 'sometimes a crisis of danger lets loose this impulse, "I hadn't prayed in ten years", the writer heard a rail-road man exclaim when his train had just escaped a wreck; "but I prayed then".'[18] What do these prayers amount to? I replied:

> One would have to know more about each case before one could answer that question, but it is sufficient for my argument to show that unless prayers play a certain role in a person's life after the crisis is over, they are not characteristic of the *religious* role of prayer in the life of the believer. These prayers are far nearer superstition: kissing a rabbit's foot or touching wood.[19]

Compare the following examples. Bonhoeffer tells of an incident during a heavy bombing raid on a concentration camp where he was a prisoner:

> As we were all lying on the floor yesterday, someone muttered 'O God, O God' – he is normally a frivolous sort of chap – but I couldn't bring myself to offer him any Christian encouragement or comfort. All I did was to glance at my watch and say: 'It won't last any more than ten minutes now'.[20]

Bonhoeffer did not think the man's cry was a religious cry, or that he would have understood a religious response to it. Certainly he did not think that the cry was proof that the man had 'a spark of divinity' in him. The man was obviously breaking down, and Bonhoeffer comforted him as decently as he could by telling him that the raid would soon be over. Instead of crying, 'O God, O God' the prisoner could have said 'Mamma mia' as Hemingway's dying soldier did:

> One leg was gone and the other was held by tendons and part of the trouser and the stump twitched and jerked as though it were not connected. He bit his arm and moaned, 'Oh, mamma mia, mamma mia,' then, 'Dio ti salvi, Maria. Dio ti salvi, Maria. Oh Jesus shoot me

Christ shoot me, Mamma mia, mamma mia, oh purest lovely Mary shoot me. Stop it. Stop it. Stop it. Oh Jesus lovely Mary stop it. Oh Oh Oh,' then choking, 'Mamma mamma mia'.[21]

The cry which may take the form of a cry for God is in fact a cry for human help, or even a sheer exclamation. Whether this is so is seen, if it can be seen, from the context of the cry.

The appeal to contextual connections in determining whether responses are religious responses is no isolated emphasis confined to *The Concept of Prayer*. The same insistence is found over and over again throughout my work. I reiterate how anxious I am to show

> that religion is not some kind of technical discourse or esoteric pursuit cut off from the ordinary problems, and perplexities, hopes and joys, which most of us experience at some time or other. If it were, it would not have the importance it does have for so many people.

Taking eternal love, or the love of God, as my example, I was anxious to show in detail 'what significance it has in human experience, the kind of circumstances which occasion it, and the kind of human predicament it answers'.[22] In fact, I accused some of my critics of *their* readiness to divorce religious beliefs from their natural setting. It seemed to me then, as it does now, 'that the religious concepts discussed by Professors Hick, Hepburn and Ramsey' had 'been abstracted from the human phenomena that lie behind them, and so' had 'lost or changed their meaning'.[23]

The second thesis attributed to philosophers influenced by Wittgenstein in the philosophy of religion is as follows: *Religious beliefs can only be understood by religious believers.* Consider the following conversation between Ninian Smart and Bryan Magee:

> *Smart*: . . . That is the use of certain ideas and hints in Wittgenstein to evolve a philosophy of religion which implies that you have to believe in order to understand, so that religion is either true or meaningless. I am thinking in particular of the work of D. Z. Phillips in his *The Concept of Prayer* and some of his other writings . . . But I am person-ally not altogether favourable to this approach, because it would put me out of a job, or at least out of half a job, since it would make the study of religions other than one's own, presumably – (pause)
> *Magee*: – a waste of time?
> *Smart*: A waste of time.[24]

It is clear, however, that I argue against the thesis that religious belief can only be understood by religious believers. For example:

I am not arguing for a sharp separation between religious discourse and moral discourse. I cannot accept the account offered by some theologians which makes religion appear to be a technical language, cut off, alien and foreign to the language spoken by everyone else in the community. The picture is false and misleading. It cannot account even for religious phenomena, such as the traffic between unbelief and belief ... Religious doctrines, worship, ritual, etc. would not have the importance they do were they not connected with practices other than those which are specifically religious. When a man prays to God for forgiveness, for example, his prayer would be worthless did it not arise from problems in his relationships with other people. These problems can be appreciated by the religious and the non-religious alike. Because of such connections between religious and non-religious activity, *it is possible to convey the meaning of religious language to someone unfamiliar with it*, even if all one achieves is to stop him talking nonsense.[25]

But more than this may be attained. I have tried to show in my work

that there is a vast variety of different states and attitudes within the category of religious believers, since not all believers are worshippers. A person holding any of these may see the kind of thing atheism is and still reject it. Similarly, a man may see the kind of thing religious belief is and still call himself an atheist because he does not live by such beliefs ... The philosopher who wants to show what kind of belief religious belief is, or what kind of attitude atheism is, may have any of these attitudes or beliefs and still fulfil his task. Indeed, he may not want to describe himself in any of these ways,[26]

to call himself an atheist or a believer. True, religious believers call obedience to God a form of understanding. It would follow that anyone who did not practise such obedience in his life, lacked *that* understanding. But a philosopher can understand what I have just said about religious understanding and give an account of how obedience to God differs from other kinds of obedience, without being a believer himself, that is, in this context, without being obedient to God.

The thesis that only religious believers understand religious belief is closely connected in the minds of critics with the third and fourth theses of the five attributed to philosophers influenced by Wittgenstein in the philosophy of religion, namely, third: *Whatever is called religious language determines what is and what is not meaningful in religion.*

Kai Nielsen says:

To be such a conceptual relativist is to argue that what is to count as knowledge, evidence, truth, a fact, an observation, making sense and the like is uniquely determined by the linguistic framework used. But since our very conception of intelligibility, validity, knowledge and the like are a function of the linguistic system we use, it is impossible for us to attain a central Archimedean point in virtue of which we could evaluate the comparative adequacy of our own and other linguistic frameworks.[27]

And fourth: *Religious beliefs cannot be criticized.*

F. C. Copleston says, 'The idea of autonomous language-games, each of which can be understood only from within, by those who actually play the game in question, and which is therefore immune to all external criticism, seems to me open to objection.'[28]

It is not difficult to show that these two theses, like the two already considered, are theses I have argued *against*. It would be hard to deny that

> Religious believers make mistakes like anyone else. What they say, *if* it comes under the appropriate criteria of meaningfulness, must answer to these criteria. Hick is right . . . in saying that certain conceptions of God are confused, e.g. 'Yuri Gagarin's concept of God as an object that he would have observed, had it existed, during his first space flight'. It can be shown to be confused in two ways: first, by reference to what one can reasonably expect to observe in space, and secondly, by what is meant by the reality of God.[29]

Nonsense remains nonsense even if we associate God's name with it. So far from wanting to deny the possibility of subjecting anything called religious to criticism, I opposed philosophical moves which ran the danger of justifying nonsense. T. H. McPherson claimed:

> Religion belongs to the sphere of the unsayable, so it is not to be wondered at that in theology there is much nonsense (i.e. many absurdities); this is the natural result of trying to put into words – and to discuss – various kinds of inexpressible 'experiences' and of trying to say things about God.[30]

In response to such a view it has always seemed to me that J. A. Passmore's observation is devastatingly right: 'One difficulty with this line of reasoning, considered as a defence of religion, is that it "saves" religion only at the cost of leaving the door open to any sort of transcendental metaphysics – and indeed to superstition and nonsense of the most arrant sort.'[31] If criticism of this kind is to be avoided

> religion must take the world seriously. I have argued that religious reactions to various situations cannot be assessed according to some

external criterion of adequacy. On the other hand, the connections between religious beliefs and such situations must not be fantastic ... whether the connections are fantastic is decided by criteria which are not in dispute. For example, some religious believers may try to explain away the reality of suffering, or try to say that all suffering has some point. When they speak like this, one may accuse them of not taking suffering seriously.[32] Or if religious believers talk of death as if it were a sleep of long duration, one may accuse them of not taking death seriously.[33] In these examples, what is said about suffering and death can be judged in terms of what we already know and believe about these matters. The religious responses are fantastic because they ignore or distort what we already know. What is said falls under standards of judgement with which we are already acquainted. When what is said by religious believers does violate the facts or distort our apprehension of situations, no appeal to the fact that what is said is said in the name of religion can justify or excuse the violation or distortion.[34]

Rationalistic philosophers of religion want to go much further than these admissions would allow. They are not content with the recognition that connections between religious beliefs and other aspects of human life may reveal confusions in religion. They want to say further, that the religious beliefs which are not confused, can be justified, inferred, or given a foundation by reference to these other aspects of human life. Indeed, it is claimed that these possibilities constitute the rationality of the beliefs. This suggestion I have resisted. Consider the following example:

People react to the birth of children in various ways. Some say that the birth of a child is always a cause for rejoicing. Others may say that whether one rejoices at the birth of a child should be determined by the physical and mental health of the child, or by whether the family into which it is born can look after it properly. Others may say that one should always give thanks to God when a child is born. Others may condemn the folly of those responsible for bringing a child into a world such as this. All these reactions are reactions to the birth of a child, and could not mean what they do apart from the fact of the birth. But it does not follow that the various reactions can be inferred from the birth, or that they are conclusions for which the birth of the baby is the ground. All one can say is that people do respond in this way. Many who respond in one way will find the other responses shallow, trivial, fantastic, meaningless, or even evil. But the force of the responses cannot be justified; it can merely be shown.[35]

It is a conclusion such as this, however, which has led to the fifth thesis attributed to those philosophers influenced by Wittgenstein in the philosophy of religion, namely, *Religious beliefs cannot be affected by personal, social or cultural events.*

F. C. Copleston, speaking of the argument characterized by the four theses already considered, says, 'If it is carried to a point at which any fruitful dialogue between religious belief and critical philosophy is excluded, theology retreats into a kind of ghetto, cut off from the cultural life of which philosophy is one expression.'[36] Kenny quotes these remarks with approval.[37]

If we cannot give any rational justification for religious beliefs, does it not follow that religious beliefs have been made safe, incapable of being affected by personal, social or cultural events? No such conclusion does follow, and it is certainly not one that I have ever embraced. It cannot be denied that religious pictures which are free from conceptual confusion may nevertheless be eroded by values and developments of other kinds. Such erosion does not imply that the religious beliefs were mistakes or irrationalities of any kind. Far from denying the effects of cultural change on religious pictures I have drawn attention to them. I said we have reason

> to distinguish between the case of the picture losing its hold for a given individual, with religious pictures losing their hold anyway, not through the fault of any particular individual, but because of changes in the culture.[38] Certain religious pictures decline, and yet you can't ask 'But whose fault is it that they are declining?' You can't trace the decline to the biographical details of the life of any single individual ... a picture may die in a culture because believing it is not an isolated activity. To call the belief a language-game can be misleading if it does suggest an isolated activity. Other cultural changes can affect people's worship. For example, in *Brave New World* there is a decline in the notion of moral responsibility. In such a society one can see, without too much difficulty, how the notion of God as a Judge might also be in decline.[39]

I have simply given textual indications of the ways in which I have argued *against* the very theses attributed to myself and others who have been influenced by Wittgenstein in the philosophy of religion. The attribution of these theses has persisted despite the availability of *all* the counter-evidence. Putting aside the fact that philosophical fashion and jargon will not be deterred by mere facts, why do these theses persist?

Nothing said so far shows why Wittgenstein's own terminology should have led to the misunderstandings we have discussed. Why should

Wittgenstein's talk of language-games, for example, lead to so many misgivings among philosophers?

Notes

1 Anthony Kenny, 'In Defence of God', *The Times Literary Supplement*, 7 February 1975, p. 145. The title is the supplement's, not Kenny's.

2 Rush Rhees, 'Some Developments in Wittgenstein's View of Ethics' in *Discussions of Wittgenstein* (London: Routledge and Kegan Paul, 1970).

3 Anthony Kenny, *Wittgenstein* (Harmondsworth: Allen Lane, Penguin Press, 1973) pp. 229–30.

4 Anthony Kenny, *The Five Ways* (London: Routledge and Kegan Paul, 1969) p. 4.

5 See Kai Nielsen, 'Wittgensteinian Fideism', *Philosophy*, vol. 42 (1967), reprinted as Chapter 1 here.

6 For further references, see Bibliography, section C, *Belief, Change and Forms of Life* (Basingstoke: Macmillan, 1986).

7 I am described as a 'leading fideist' by Robert Herbert in *Paradox and Identity in Theology* (Ithaca and London: Cornell University Press, 1979) p. 13, and as the arch-Wittgensteinian fideist by Kai Nielsen in *An Introduction to the Philosophy of Religion* (London: Macmillan, 1982) p. 56. According to Nielsen, *The Concept of Prayer, Faith and Philosophical Enquiry* and *Death and Immortality* give 'a detailed paradigmatic statement of Wittgensteinian Fideism' (*An Introduction to the Philosophy of Religion*, p. 200).

8 I am confident that similar evidence could be found in the writings of O. K. Bouwsma, M. O'C. Drury, R. F. Holland, Norman Malcolm, Rush Rhees, Peter Winch and others. See Bibliography, section B, note 6 above.

9 John Hick, 'Sceptics and Believers', in John Hick (ed.), *Faith and the Philosophers* (London: Macmillan, 1964) pp. 239–40.

10 Walford Gealy, 'Ffaith a Ffydd' (Fact and Faith), *Efrydiau Athronyddol* (1977). It ought to be said that since writing the article Gealy has accepted the force of my textual refutations. He no longer thinks that I have ever held the thesis that religious belief is cut off from other aspects of human life, but he continues to disagree about the *character* of the connections between religious belief and other aspects of human life.

11 Ibid., p. 19.

12 Ludwig Wittgenstein, *Philosophical Investigations*, trans. G. E. M. Anscombe (Oxford: Basil Blackwell, 1953) I, 66.

13 Ibid., I, 65.

14 D. Z. Phillips, *Faith and Philosophical Enquiry* (London: Routledge and Kegan Paul, 1970) p. 78.

15 'Postscript' in Stuart C. Brown (ed.), *Reason and Religion* (Ithaca and London: Cornell University Press, 1977) p. 139.

16 Ibid., p. 138.

17 D. Z. Phillips, *The Concept of Prayer* (London: Routledge and Kegan Paul, 1965) p. 40 (issued as a paperback, Oxford: Basil Blackwell: New York: Seabury Press, 1981).

18 H. E. Fosdick, *The Meaning of Prayer* (London: SCM Press, 1915) p. 12.

19 Phillips, *The Concept of Prayer*, p. 116.

20 Dietrich Bonhoeffer, *Letters and Papers from Prison* (London: Fontana Books, 1959) p. 67.

21 Ernest Hemingway, *A Farewell to Arms* (Harmondsworth: Penguin Books, 1960) ch. 9, p. 47.

22 'Faith, Scepticism and Religious Understanding' (1967) reprinted in Phillips, *Faith and Philosophical Enquiry*, p. 21.

23 'Religion and Epistemology: Some Contemporary Confusions' (1966) reprinted in Phillips, *Faith and Philosophical Enquiry*, p. 143.

24 Bryan Magee (ed.), *Modern British Philosophy* (London: Paladin, 1973) p. 214.

25 'God and Ought' (1966) reprinted in Phillips, *Faith and Philosophical Enquiry*, p. 230. Italics added.

26 D. Z. Phillips, *Religion Without Explanation* (Oxford: Basil Blackwell, 1976) ch. 11, 'Religion, Understanding and Philosophical Method', p. 189.

27 Kai Nielsen, *Contemporary Critiques of Religion* (London: Macmillan, 1971) p. 96.

28 F. C. Copleston, *Religion and Philosophy* (London: Gill and Macmillan, 1974) p. viii.

29 'Religious Belief and Philosophical Enquiry' reprinted in Phillips, *Faith and Philosophical Enquiry*, p. 72.

30 T. H. McPherson, 'Religion as the Inexpressible' in A. G. N. Flew and A. MacIntyre (eds), *New Essays in Philosophical Theology* (London: SCM Press, 1955) p. 142.

31 J. A. Passmore, 'Christianity and Positivism', *Australasian Journal of Philosophy* (1957) p. 128.

32 I make such accusations at length in chapter 4 of *Belief, Change and Forms of Life*.

33 See D. Z. Phillips, *Death and Immortality* (London: Macmillan, 1970).

34 'Religious Beliefs and Language-Games' (1970) reprinted in Phillips, *Faith and Philosophical Enquiry*, pp. 92–9.

35 Ibid., p. 108.

36 Copleston, *Religion and Philosophy*, p. viii.

37 Kenny, 'In Defence of God'.

38 This theme is explored further in chapter 5 of *Belief, Change and Forms of Life*.

39 'Belief and Loss of Belief' (with J. R. Jones) reprinted in Phillips, *Faith and Philosophical Enquiry*, pp. 116–20.

3. D. Z. Phillips on the Foolishness
of Wittgensteinian Fideism

KAI NIELSEN

I

D. Z. Phillips thinks I and others create an unscholarly straw-man with our conception of Wittgensteinian Fideism. In his view it distorts what Wittgensteinians such as Norman Malcolm, Peter Winch, Phillips and indeed Wittgenstein himself say concerning religion. It is, Phillips claims, textually irresponsible, a false view of how religious discourse works and shows a very shallow understanding of religion. If it can be beaten down – exposed for the utter error it is – it should be excised from the serious discussion of religion.

I think the shoe is on the other foot. Phillips erects a straw-man of what Wittgensteinian Fideism is and then seeks to refute it. He does not even see what it is and what kind of challenge it poses from *within* a Wittgensteinian conception of philosophy.

Phillips, in Chapter 2, states and discusses five theses supposedly (according to him) definitive of Wittgensteinian Fideism and attempts to show that they do not apply to his views and that in any event they are absurd theses. That concentration on himself might seem self-centred, but it is actually fair enough for he has been taken to be a paradigm case of a Wittgensteinian Fideist. He is concerned to show that he, who supposedly is a Wittgensteinian Fideist, if there ever was one, does not hold any of the views expressed in his five theses. This, he adds, is true as well of other Wittgensteinian philosophers. He restates these theses and his criticism of them in both *Wittgenstein and Religion* (1993) and *Religion and the Hermeneutics of Contemplation* (2001), adding that 'no philosopher I know of has held the theses attributed to Wittgensteinian Fideism' (Phillips 2001, 15).

The five theses allegedly definitive of Wittgensteinian Fideism are:

1 'Religious beliefs are logically cut off from all other aspects of human life' (see Chapter 2, p. 42 and Phillips 2001, 26).

2 'Religious beliefs can only be understood by religious believers'
   (Chapter 2, p. 46 and Phillips 2001, 27).
3 'Whatever is called religious language determines what is and what
   is not meaningful in religion' (see Chapter 2, p. 47 and Phillips
   2001, 28).
4 'Religious beliefs cannot be criticized' (see Chapter 2, p. 48 and
   Phillips 2001, 29).
5 'Religious beliefs cannot be affected by personal, social or cultural
   events' (see Chapter 2, p. 50 and Phillips 2001, 29).[1]

Theses 2 and 4 are – as Phillips rightly avers – absurd theses and absurdly
false. But they are not even a part of Wittgensteinian Fideism, let alone
definitive of it. However, I do say that 1, 3 and 4, *properly disambiguated
and interpreted*, are a genuine part of Wittgensteinian Fideism. Moreover,
I think they are important elements in what I take to be the challenge of
Wittgensteinian Fideism. *As Phillips reads them*, I agree they are false,
even absurdly false. But he gives them a reading that distorts their role in
my account and shows an impoverished understanding of Wittgenstein,
Winch and Malcolm. A sensitivity to the texts would not have allowed
him to interpret 1, 3 and 4 as he does.

He takes 1 to be the claim that religious concepts are *technical* concepts
cut off from the common experiences of human life: joy and sorrow,
hope and despair (Phillips 1986, 8). This is something that was never
part of Wittgensteinian Fideism to deny, to disguise or even to downplay.
While God's love of his creation is quite different from a mother's love
of her child and God's creating the world is quite different from the
potter's creation of a vase and God's providential guidance is quite unlike
that of the guidance parents give to their children, yet there would be no
understanding (if indeed there is such understanding) of God's love, his
creation of humankind or his providential guidance without understanding the parallel 'mundane' practices. And so it is with God's speaking to
us. But there are things we can say or ask about the mundane uses of
these terms that we cannot say or ask, if we understand religious discourse, about the uses of the parallel terms in religious discourse. When
a potter makes a jug we can intelligibly, and sometimes with good reason,
ask what it was made of. We cannot do that for God's creating the world.
When we say God spoke to Moses or God spoke to Clinton of his sins
or to Bush of his arrogance, we cannot intelligibly ask what language he
used or whether he spoke loudly or softly or had a distinctive accent.
And when we say the eye of God is upon us and a child asks what colour
are God's eyes we correct him and say we cannot ask such questions
about God. There is no intelligible question about what colour God's
eyes are. To think otherwise just shows a misunderstanding of the *kind*
of reality God has. But this *initially* must sound very strange to the child.

He, if he is to have any religious understanding, has to get socialized, strangeness to the contrary notwithstanding, into the language-games distinctive of religion. For us, that is for most of the readers of this book, that is to be socialized into one or another of the Judaeo-Christian-Islamic strands. Someone who asks these questions shows that he does not understand such religious discourse.

Wittgensteinian philosophers who are what has been called Wittgensteinian fideists do not claim religious concepts are so Balkanized that they do not make contact with non-religious concepts. And both articulators of and critics of Wittgensteinian Fideism would assert with Phillips that religious practices would 'not have the importance they do were they not connected with practices other than those which are specifically religious' (see Chapter 2, p. 47). Consider someone who prays to God for forgiveness. '[H]is prayer would be worthless did it not arise from problems in his relationships with other people' (see Chapter 2, p. 47). Rather than say with 1 that religious beliefs are logically cut off from all other aspects of human life, Phillips – our alleged paradigm of Wittgensteinian Fideism – is

anxious ... to show that religion is not some kind of technical discourse or esoteric pursuit cut off from the ordinary problems, and perplexities, hopes and joys, which most of us experience at some time or other. If it were, it would not have the importance it does have for so many people. (see Chapter 2, p. 46)

This is exactly right. Religion would have no significance if this were not so. But philosophers such as myself, urging that such Wittgensteinian philosophers (O. K. Bouwsma and Norman Malcolm, for example) are also Wittgensteinian fideists, are as concerned as Phillips to claim that *in that way* religion has significance and makes those connections.

If Wittgensteinian fideists are to be taken to be asserting 1 at all, what they should be taken to be asserting is that religious discourse is a distinctive form of discourse with criteria of significance and truth that are distinctive of it. It is these criteria that principally govern what it makes sense to say when we speak religiously – what, if anything, can justify a religious belief and what it is to speak of a religious utterance as being true or false. These criteria are at work when it is acknowledged that we can intelligibly speak of the eyes of God being on us but not of the colour of his eyes. The claim – and this is how 1 is relevantly understood (if we are to talk of 1 at all) – is that religious concepts, while not being cut off from other concepts of everyday life, are distinctive, having criteria of significance, truth and reasonability that are principally determined by the distinctive form of life or mode of discourse that is religious. This in turn is shown in the distinctive uses of religious language in religious contexts, for example, God creates but creates out of nothing, God speaks but it makes no sense to ask what language or languages he speaks, he sees but it makes no sense to ask what colour eyes he has. These are just elementary things that we come to understand if we are to understand God-talk at all. There is, as it was once fashionable to say, a distinctive 'logic of God-talk'. In this way religious concepts are autonomous or, as I say in my 'Wittgensteinian Fideism', *sui generis* (Nielsen 1982, 67–72). They cannot be reduced to moral concepts, scientific ones, ordinary empirical concepts or to some technical or even metaphysical concepts. *In this way* religious discourse is a kind of protected discourse; it is *sui generis*.

Toward the end of his *Religion and the Hermeneutics of Contemplation*, Phillips in effect and unwittingly shows that this is what is at issue concerning Wittgensteinian Fideism. He starts with a frequently quoted passage from Peter Winch and then comments on it. I quote both the passage from Winch and Phillips's commentary in full. Winch writes:

> Criteria of logic are not a direct gift of God, but arise out of, and are only intelligible in the context of, ways of living or modes of social life. It follows that one cannot apply criteria of logic to modes of social life as such. For instance, science is one such mode and religion is another, and each has criteria of intelligibility peculiar to itself. So within science or religion actions can be logical or illogical . . . But we cannot sensibly say that either the practice of science itself or that of religion is either illogical or logical; both are non-logical. (Winch 1995, 100–01)

Then Phillips adds:

> By emphasizing the rules internal to each context, the impression is created of self-contained institutions which have little to do with each other. Passages such as these gave rise to the concerns about fideism discussed in section 6 of Chapter 1. Even at the time, Winch qualified his remarks immediately: '(This is, of course, an over-simplification, in that it does not allow for the overlapping character of different modes of social life. But I do not think this affects the substance of what I want to say, though it would make its precise expression in detail more complicated.)' But in his preface, Winch finds this qualification far too weak: 'Different aspects of social life do not merely "overlap": they are frequently internally related in such a way that one cannot even be intelligibly conceived as existing in isolation from others'. (Phillips 2001, 305)

However, the point concerning Wittgensteinian Fideism isn't to deny that religious discourse has features taken from different modes of social life. It is not to deny that there is an overlap here between different forms of discourse and that sometimes there are parts of these different modes of discourse that are 'internally related in such a way that one cannot even be intelligibly conceived as existing in isolation from others', for example, for God to have mercy on us it must be that we have done something untoward, suffered something untoward or the like.[2] If we could not get caught in such situations there would be no intelligibility in speaking of God's mercy. There would be nothing for him to exercise his mercy on. If things like this were not so religious discourse would not even be intelligible. But this is a necessary condition. It is nothing like a sufficient condition. And such qualifications, as Winch says himself, do not affect the substance of what he wants to say (Winch 1995, 100).

The core of that and the sense of 1 and a core thesis of Wittgensteinian Fideism is that criteria or significance or intelligibility are tied (logically tied) to distinctive ways of living or modes of social life. What it makes sense to say, what is reasonable to believe is principally determined by these ways of living, these modes of discourse, these forms of life. They leave no logical space, Winch has it, and Phillips follows him here, for speaking of criteria of intelligibility for *the modes of social life as such*. 'Science is one such mode and religion is another and each has criteria of intelligibility peculiar to itself' (Winch 1995, 100). Moreover, there is no super-language-game or super-form of life from which or with which we can view all other language-games or forms of life; there is no super-practice that allows us or gives us any kind of perch to survey and assess all other practices (Brandon 1994 and Rorty 1997). Thus there can be no standing outside of these modes of life (outside of these clusters of practices) where from the 'point of view of nowhere' or from 'the point of view of the universe' we can assess the intelligibility, reasonableness, rationality, acceptability or truth of these practices and modes of life. We can have no such sky-hooks. This is a – perhaps *the* – core claim concerning Wittgensteinian Fideism and it is a claim of not only Winch but of Wittgenstein, Malcolm and Phillips (Nielsen 1982, 43–139; Nielsen 1973, 23–40; Nielsen 1989, 102–33; and Nielsen 1991, 91–122). I have not created a straw-man here.

The reading I gave to what Phillips calls the first thesis of Wittgensteinian Fideism is also the reading I give to what he calls thesis 3. And, as we have seen above, they are plainly components of Wittgenstein's and Winch's way of viewing things (Nielsen 1982 and Nielsen 2001). As Phillips himself says, 'religious reactions to various situations cannot be assessed according to some external criterion of adequacy' (see Chapter 2, pp. 48–9).

What we have left is thesis 4. That is the claim that 'religious beliefs cannot be criticized'. Phillips responds that he – and repeatedly – criticizes religious beliefs. But the way he does – the sort of beliefs he criticizes – immediately gives the game away. Phillips says, rightly enough, that 'Religious believers make mistakes like anyone else. What they say, *if* it comes under the appropriate criteria of meaningfulness, must answer to these criteria' (see Chapter 2, p. 48). Suppose a Christian – to use Phillips's own example – is an astronaut and he goes on a space flight. He is, however, a very Neanderthal Christian for he has a conception of God 'as an object that he would have observed, had it existed, during his first space flight' (see Chapter 2, p. 48). He looks carefully during his flight and does not observe this God and as a result he ceases to be a Christian. This is a gross error in religious understanding and reasoning that anyone, whether religious or not, with a reasonable understanding of the form of life that Christianity is will immediately recognize to be an error. There is room aplenty within a religion for such criticism. Moreover, Phillips acknowledges that there are subtler forms of religious mistakes. The theistic proofs of the existence of God – even one as sophisticated as Anselm's – are such mistakes as is a belief in immortality where immortality is identified with endless duration. Religion, Phillips has it, must take the world seriously. But – and here he relies, as we have seen, implicitly on the reading I have given of 1 – 'religious reactions to various situations cannot be assessed according to some external criterion of adequacy' (see Chapter 2, pp. 48–9). Where there are some grounds for criticizing religion *Phillips's style* is where mistakes are made *within* the religious mode of reasoning as when it is claimed that there are good grounds for believing there is no God because no one has ever observed God or when it is asserted that God is a being among beings. People who make such claims simply do not understand developed Jewish, Christian and Islamic religious discourse. They do not understand the religious language-games characteristic of what Judaism, Christianity and Islam have become. They haven't got the hang of what religion is. They can call themselves Christians or religious as much as they want, and sincerely so regard themselves, but that does nothing to show they are either, anymore than a person can reasonably claim to be an experimental scientist if she claims she has, while doing experimental science, no reason at all to pay attention in the area in which she is working to the results of a well conducted experiment.

Phillips answers, 'what is said about suffering and death can be judged in terms of what we [presumably believers and non-believers alike] already . . . believe about these matters' (see Chapter 2, p. 49). Religious beliefs or theological doctrine cannot gainsay that. Suppose one's spouse is wracked with pain while dying of cancer and a Christian Scientist friend says that one's spouse is not really in pain and is not suffering. Pain and suffering, one is told, are unreal, illusory. But if someone says that, religion or no religion, that person, to understate it, has made a mistake. That *putative* religious response is in error for it conflicts with what we already securely know about suffering. But we do not need to, and should not, from a Christian point of view, reason in the way the Christian Scientist does. As Phillips well says, 'When what is said by religious believers does violate the facts or distort our apprehension of situations, no appeal to the fact that what is said is said in the name of religion can justify or excuse the violation or distortion' (See Chapter 2, p. 49).

None of this is to the point concerning Wittgensteinian Fideism. These mistakes are mistakes that come from a failure correctly to understand the mode of discourse or form of life that religion is. But where the form of life is adequately understood, Wittgensteinians have it, no relevant or well-taken criticism of the reality of God or religion is possible. It makes no sense on a Wittgensteinian understanding of things to say that God, where 'God' is properly construed, is a myth or that talk of God is meaningless or that religion is illusory. When 4 is asserted, i.e. that 'religious beliefs cannot be criticized', that is what is meant by people raising the challenge of Wittgensteinian Fideism and it is clear that Phillips, Malcolm and Winch accept that and proceed accordingly.

Phillips asserts:

> Rationalistic philosophers of religion ... are not content with the recognition that connections between religious beliefs and other aspects of human life may reveal confusions in religion. They want to say further, that religious beliefs which are not confused, can be justified, inferred, or given a foundation by reference to these other aspects of human life. Indeed, it is claimed that the possibilities constitute the rationality of the beliefs. This suggestion I have resisted. (see Chapter 2, p. 49)

This is good Wittgensteinianism and I think it is well-taken. But this is what I have been saying all along and, as well, attributing it to what I call Wittgensteinian fideists. However, there is another side of this as well which I take to be equally Wittgensteinian and it is something that 4, properly understood, gives to understand, namely that religious beliefs which are in accordance with that form of life cannot, in any fundamental way, be confused, cannot be mistaken and neither require nor can they have any justification. There are no philosophical foundations that ground them, but they are none the worse for all of that if they do not violate the logic of religious discourse. Such beliefs are in place as they are. They cannot be relevantly criticized or shown to be mistaken or be properly deemed to be illusory or mythical. They are in order as they are and, once confusions are dispelled concerning them, they need no philosophical defence. Indeed the rationalistic proclivity either to try to justify them or criticize them reveal both philosophical and religious errors of the most basic kind. Both Richard Swinburne and J. L. Mackie are out to lunch. This is both good Wittgensteinianism and yields a proper reading of 4. It is something that Phillips embraces and where deployed in defence of some religious faith (say, Christianity) is Wittgensteinian Fideism. It is a 'defence', as fideistic defences are, which argues that genuine religious beliefs neither can have *nor need* a defence – and most particularly a philosophical defence.

I want now to summarize and then add a coda. Phillips claims that the very notion of Wittgensteinian Fideism is at best absurdly false. It misrepresents the conceptions, beliefs and modes of reasoning of the philosophers taken by me and some others to be Wittgensteinian Fideism; the five theses Phillips takes to be core theses of Wittgensteinian Fideism, he has it, are held by none of the philosophers taken to be Wittgensteinian fideists and, apart from these textual matters, these theses are themselves false. In fine, the very notion of Wittgensteinian Fideism is an unscholarly mess best forgotten. This creation of straw-men and then predictably knocking them down, Phillips has it, deflects attention away from the important and distinctive work done by philosophers who write about religion under the influence of Wittgenstein. It is here where my account, Phillips has it, if taken seriously, can do genuine harm.

As the author of the very notion of Wittgensteinian Fideism, it is not unsurprising that I would resist.[3] My resistance can be summarized as follows. Phillips's theses 2 and 5 are not claims I have called Wittgensteinian Fideism and 1, 3 and 4 are not either *in the way Phillips reads them*. However, I give here unstrained readings of 1, 3 and 4 which I take to be core claims of Wittgensteinian Fideism and argue that they are attractive, though in ways puzzling, theses which are genuinely Wittgensteinian and are not up for easy dismissal. Phillips might resist by saying my readings of 1, 3 and 4, whatever I think, are actually strained and that his way of taking them is simpler. I agree they are simpler, but I do not agree that my readings are not plausibly Wittgensteinian or reasonable candidates for being true. Moreover, they capture better than Phillips's alternatives what is philosophically interesting and of significance for religion. They are, that is, both accurately Wittgensteinian and challenging philosophical considerations standing in need of careful scrutiny. However, if Phillips insists on taking 1, 3 and 4 *in his way* then I would counter that all five theses, *so understood*, are not theses that could reasonably be attributed to my conception of Wittgensteinian Fideism or are theses with which those people, such as myself, arguing against what I have called Wittgensteinian Fideism, are concerned with or should be concerned with. Phillips through and through creates figures of straw and then knocks them down. He does not help us to engage with the issues.

Now for the coda. I *think* Phillips thinks that I use 'Wittgensteinian Fideism' as a term of ridicule or abuse and that the conception Wittgensteinian Fideism is used by me as an ideological club with which to beat religion and those poor misguided philosophers who happen to be religious. But that is neither my intent nor is it how I use the term in my discussion of religion and of Wittgensteinian philosophers. If I were to become religious and if I were to seek some philosophical articulation of my faith I would be a fideist. Moreover, my reaction to rationalism in religion or in the philosophy of religion is much like Phillips's and like Kierkegaard's to Hegel. To try to give a metaphysical backing for religion seems to me a terrible error; it is bad philosophy and it blocks the way to an understanding of the importance of religion. The tradition of Tertullian, Pascal, Hamann and Kierkegaard, in coming to grips with religion, has a way of seeing and depicting the significance of religion that is lacking in Augustine, Aquinas, Paley and Hegel. And Richard Swinburne, Alvin Plantinga, George Mavrodes, Hugo Meynell and William Alston seem to me to turn the philosophical and intellectual clock back and make us engage in a lot of metaphysical disputes which Wittgenstein, if not Hume and Kant before Wittgenstein, should have taught us to set aside as houses of cards. And as much as I admire both Pascal and Kierkegaard, their use of philosophy in fideism's *articulation* is not, for philosophers, educated as we have been educated and standing where we now stand, as effective as that of the best Wittgensteinians and quasi-Wittgensteinians writing about religion. Among the Wittgensteinians writing about religion O. K. Bouwsma, Malcolm and Phillips are Christians, *perhaps* best characterized as fideist Christians, who philosophically discuss religions in a Wittgensteinian manner. Cavell, Rhees and Winch, who, I believe, are not believers, also philosophize about religion and other matters as well in a broadly Wittgensteinian way. And Wittgenstein himself, as intensely concerned as he was with religion, was not a believer. Yet Wittgenstein and those broadly speaking Wittgensteinian philosophers, some believers and some not, in my view present the strongest case for faith on offer. They clearly express – if 'making a case' sounds too crass – what is involved in being religious (a way of being and doing) with its integrally associated mode of discourse. And their articulation is more perspicuous than any other philosophical one that we have yet to come across. They show, while trying to avoid what Axel Hägerström well called metaphysical religiosity (Hägerström 1964, 175–223), how it is for we moderns and post-moderns (if you will) that religion can be a live option. As is perhaps put most clearly in my 'Wittgensteinian Fideism II' (Nielsen 1982, 101–39), I try to state Wittgensteinian Fideism in the strongest way I can muster, showing it clearly to be a live option for a reflective person who has some feel for religion and then I argue, if not with fear and trembling, at least with considerable philosophical hesitancy, though still with conviction, that, among our live options (things that we can be tempted reflectively to endorse) there is a form of secularism (not just any secularism) all the way down, that is a non-reductionist, non-scientistic and a holistic social naturalism that is still more attractive (Nielsen 1996 and Nielsen 2001). This I argue, though in a thoroughly fallibilistic spirit, is the better road to take in our context even for someone with those religious sensibilities where they have a good literary, philosophical and scientific education. Of what for us are the live options, secularism is, I both argue and narratively try to convey, everything considered, both philosophically and humanly speaking, the most compelling option. It is the road we should take in the yellow wood. *Perhaps* nothing is compelling here, but when we try to be as non-evasively reasonable as possible, taking everything that answers to our interests and meets our needs into consideration, we will, I argue, reflectively endorse such a secularism rather than what I have called Wittgensteinian Fideism or any other religious orientation. But to say that is not at all to say, or to give to understand, that Wittgensteinian Fideism is, either as a matter of philosophy or of life orientation, a silly or shallow view or even an ideological one or a way of seeing things that no knowledgeable, reflective and non-evasive human being, living here and now, could reasonably embrace.

I claim, my criticisms of Wittgensteinian Fideism to the contrary notwithstanding, and without taking them back, that what I have called Wittgensteinian Fideism remains a live option that should be brought up, not against what John Wisdom called the 'bar of reason' – there is no such thing – but up against our most careful – and to repeat W. D. Falk's favorite term again – non-evasive reflective assessment. I argue that against this bar Wittgensteinian Fideism will fail. But that this is so is certainly not obvious. And I never, even for a moment, any time in the past, thought that it was.

Notes

1 One distressing thing is that in discussing Wittgensteinian Fideism, something I wisely or unwisely am the creator of, Phillips makes no attempt at all to come to grips with my 'Wittgensteinian Fideism'. He gives his five theses that he takes to be the claims of people articulating and critiquing Wittgensteinian Fideism: claims that I examine in *this* text. But he entirely ignores the Wittgensteinian claims I state near the beginning of 'Wittgensteinian Fideism' and my claim that when accepted they have 'a tendency to generate what I call Wittgensteinian Fideism' (Nielsen 1982, 66–7). They seem to me (a) uncontroversially genuinely Wittgensteinian remarks, (b) not the same as Phillips's five theses and (c) they

have a tendency to generate Wittgensteinian Fideism. Perhaps some or all of these remarks are mistaken and they do none of these three things. But Phillips does not even consider them. He simply ignores them. The same is true of my remarks concerning Malcolm, including the citation of remarks of Malcolm's which seem clearly both perceptive and Wittgensteinianly fideistic in the sense I have specified and the same thing obtains for what I say about G. E. Hughes's articulation, in his acute criticisms of C. B. Martin's *Religious Belief* (Nielsen 1982, 65–72). They clearly set out what I call Wittgensteinian Fideism. Perhaps Wittgensteinian Fideism is the poor thing Phillips takes it to be, but if Phillips is to make even a start in showing this he must face such passages. It is both depressing and exasperating to try to converse with someone who stays at such a distance from what one actually says and then claims that what one is defending is absurdly false. If this is hermeneutics we are better off without it. I should also note that in the essays collected together in Phillips's *Faith and Philosophical Inquiry* we have vintage Wittgensteinian Fideism. I cite these essays for they conform perfectly to my characterization of Wittgensteinian Fideism and they powerfully articulate what I call the challenge of Wittgensteinian Fideism. See Phillips 1970.

2 This, however, cannot be exactly right. For there could be (as far as logical possibilities are concerned) an English-speaking tribe that had no understanding at all of God and God-talk that still intelligibly spoke of 'mercy' and the like. But it cannot go the other way around. Judaeo-Christian-Islamic talk of God would be unintelligible without an understanding of mercy and the like. And this is the point, I take it, that Phillips was intent, and correctly so, on making.

3 Though it is to be hoped, and indeed sometimes this obtains, that some of us sometimes change our minds even over fundamental matters. It is usually not a compliment to a philosopher to say that he has lived so long on his graduate school baby fat that he is saying the same sort of thing at the end of his career that he said in his doctoral dissertation.

Bibliography

Brandon, Robert (1994), *Making It Explicit: Reasoning, Representing and Discursive Commitment*. Cambridge, MA: Harvard University Press.

Hägerström, Axel (1964), *Philosophy and Religion*. Translated by Robert T. Sandin. London: George Allen & Unwin.

Nielsen, Kai (1973), *Scepticism*. London: Macmillan Press.

—— (1982), *An Introduction to the Philosophy of Religion*. London: Macmillan Press.

—— (1989), *God, Scepticism, and Modernity*. Ottawa, ON: University of Ottawa Press.

—— (1991), *After the Demise of the Tradition*. Boulder, CO: Westview Press.

—— (1996), *Naturalism Without Foundations*. Amherst, NY: Prometheus Books.

—— (2001), *Naturalism and Religion*. Amherst, NY: Prometheus Books.

Phillips, D. Z. (1970), *Faith and Philosophical Inquiry*. London: Routledge and Kegan Paul.

—— (1986), *Belief, Change and Forms of Life*. Atlantic Highlands, NJ: Humanities Press.

—— (1993), *Wittgenstein and Religion*. Basingstoke: Macmillan.

—— (2001), *Religion and the Hermeneutics of Contemplation*. Cambridge: Cambridge University Press.

Rorty, Richard (1997), 'What Do You Do When They Call You a "Relativist"?' *Philosophical and Phenomenological Research*. Volume LVII, no. 1, 173–7.

Winch, Peter (1995), *The Idea of a Social Science*. Second Edition. London: Routledge.

4. The Way We Were

D. Z. PHILLIPS

Kai Nielsen published what appears here as Chapter 1, 'Wittgensteinian Fideism', in 1967. I published what appears here as Chapter 2, 'Wittgenstein and Religion: Some Fashionable Criticisms', in 1986, 19 years later. Nielsen says of my paper in Chapter 3, 'D. Z. Phillips on the Foolishness of Wittgensteinian Fideism': 'It is both depressing and exasperating to try to converse with someone who stays at such a distance from what one actually says and then claims that what one is defending is absurdly false. If this is hermeneutics we are better off without it' (p. 63n1).

All my exchanges with Nielsen, except the one to which he refers, are direct responses to him. Perhaps this led him to think that my 1986 paper was about him also. It was not. It was about the phenomenon called 'Wittgensteinian Fideism'. I doubt whether Nielsen could deny its existence. Having let it go unchecked for nearly 20 years, I decided that something ought to be said about it. As for Nielsen's efforts to converse with me, it ought to be noted that I am not mentioned in Nielsen's original paper, nor is there any reason why I should be. More to the point is his admission that, until fairly recently, he had not read any of my work since 1970.

In Chapter 2, 'Wittgenstein and Religion: Some Fashionable Criticisms', for every criticism associated with the charge of Wittgensteinian Fideism, I name the philosopher who advanced it. I discuss Kenny, Copleston, Gealy, Smart, Hick and, of course, Nielsen himself. I claimed that many of the criticisms advanced are absurd. Nielsen says that he finds them absurd too. Can we, then, make this much progress, in agreeing that some of the criticisms associated with the phenomenon of Wittgensteinian Fideism are absurd? Can we also agree that attributing such themes to Wittgenstein or Wittgensteinian philosophers of religion is unscholarly?

What of Nielsen's own views? Unless we admit to how we were in 1967, we won't make progress in 2003. In 2003, Nielsen wants to say that Wittgensteinian Fideism, 'as a matter of philosophy or of life-orientation', is not something 'that no knowledgeable, reflective and non-evasive human being, living here and now, could reasonably embrace' (Chapter 3, p. 62). It is not *obvious* to Nielsen that it would fail the test of reflective reason, and he adds, 'And I never, even for a moment, any time in the past, thought that it was' (Chapter 3, p. 62). Nielsen seems to have forgotten quite a few 1967 moments. Here are some of them:

'. . . as much as I admire Wittgenstein, it seems to me that the fideistic conclusions drawn by these philosophers from his work are often absurd' (Chapter 1, p. 21); he claims to have shown, with respect to religion, 'that the very first-order discourse of this form of life is incoherent or irrational' (Chapter 1, p. 22); when Evans-Pritchard says that we are right and that the Azande are wrong about their magic, because while science corresponds to objective reality, magic does not, Nielsen responds, 'This certainly seems like a scarcely disput-able bit of common sense' (Chapter 1, p. 27); speaking of Simone Weil, he says, 'She blithely accepts what I find unintelligible' (Chapter 1, p. 30).

What happens if we try to marry Nielsen's 2003 claims with these 1967 remarks? The result would be something like this: 'I never even for a moment, at any time in the past, thought that an absurd, incoherent, irrational, unintelligible view, which flies in the face of common sense, is not open as a matter of philosophy, or life-orientation, to a knowledge-able, non-evasive, reflective human being today.' How can one combine 2003 with 1967 in any intelligible way?

In Chapter 5, 'Nielsen's Sceptical Strategies' I shall try to show that Nielsen is ambivalent, not only about 'Wittgensteinian Fideism', but about Wittgenstein's philosophical method. This ambivalence increases in his later chapters. In Chapter 2, I quoted a view of his which plays a major role in his subsequent discussions:

To be a conceptual relativist is to argue that what is to count as knowledge, evidence, truth, a fact, an observation, making sense and the like is uniquely determined by the linguistic framework used. But since our very conception of intelligibility, validity, knowledge and the like are a function of the linguistic system we use, it is impossible for us to attain a central Archimedean point in virtue of which we could evaluate the comparative adequacy of our own and their linguis-tic frameworks. (See pp. 47–8)

A great deal more will be said about comments such as these in the course of our exchange, but certain points need to be made at this early stage. In attributing such a view to me, Nielsen describes me as a 'conformist fideist'. I am alleged to think it 'reasonable to follow the habits of ordinary life without accepting metaphysical claims about a reality behind appearances' (Nielsen 1989, 2). But neither Wittgenstein nor I would speak of our practices as 'appearances'. To do so would be to perpetuate the very distinction between 'appearance' and metaphysical reality being combated. Further, neither Wittgenstein nor I are contrasting the claim that there *is* a metaphysical reality behind appearances, with the claim that there is no such reality. We are not discovering anything – that there is nothing behind the veil of appearances – but calling into question the intelligibility of this whole way of talking. These objections to Nielsen's way of construing the talk of 'appearance' and 'reality' is what I mean by the unscholarly use of these terms in the imputation of Wittgensteinian Fideism.

Similar conclusions can be drawn in relation to Nielsen's use of 'practice' and 'form of life' in relation to Wittgensteinianism. In his original paper, Nielsen repeatedly combines the view that it is reasonable to follow the habits of ordinary life, with the claim that it may be wrong to do so, and often has been wrong to do so, for the obvious reason that the habits of ordinary life may be, and often have been, incoherent. Nielsen argues that the de facto existence and persistence of such habits is not enough to guarantee their intelligibility. He claims that it is essential to 'Wittgensteinian Fideism' to deny the possibility of asking whether forms of life agree with reality.

The lapse in scholarship here comes from confusing what James Conant has called a *sociological* use of 'practice' with the *grammatical* use of the term (Conant 2005, 204). The sociological use simply refers to whatever happens, habits of ordinary life, including religious habits. These may be shot through with countless confusions. But the grammatical use of 'practice' refers to a conceptually distinct form of discourse. Therefore, it is no part of Wittgensteinianism to say that ordinary habits cannot be criticized. It is not even true that conceptually distinct forms of discourse cannot be criticized. What cannot be said of *them*, but can be said of ordinary habits, is that they are *confused*. But criticism does not always take the form of an accusation of confusion.

I think, in fact, that Nielsen's use of 'form of life' deviates from Wittgenstein's. There is no reason, of course, why it should not, but I do not think that Nielsen is aware of this fact. I insisted that I had never denied that religion is cut off from other aspects of human life. I said this in reaction to Nielsen's 'compartmentalization thesis' which he says is dear to Wittgensteinian fideists. But Nielsen claims that I failed to appreciate what his view of the thesis is. So let us try again to see what it amounts to.

In his original paper, the compartmentalization thesis depends on a curious argument concerning analogies. For example, it is said that we could not speak of God's eye unless there were ordinary eyes. The trouble, it seems, is that we cannot then go on to ask of God's eye many of the things we can ask of the other eyes. To which one might reply, 'Of course not, otherwise the relation would not be analogical.' Nielsen argues that it is precisely the differences that lead to the compartmentalization claim, namely, that the meaning of religious concepts are *sui generis*.

I say that I find this argument odd. If x has an analogy to y, features a and b may be similar, but features c and d may be different. If this difference is sufficient to merit the charge of fideism, it would follow that *all* analogies would have to be called fideistic.

There are deeper tensions in Nielsen's thought. On the one hand, Nielsen acknowledges that there is no general, overall substantive content that can be given to the distinction between 'the real' and 'the unreal'. On the other hand, he wants to speak of 'the overall structure of language by reference to which religious belief fails a reflective test'. I have yet to get clear about what Nielsen means by 'the overall structure' which does not reintroduce the overreaching conception of 'reason' and 'rationality' which he wants to reject.

When I spoke of connections between religious belief and other aspects of human life, I did not have in mind anything like the appeal to analogy, or to ordering habits of behaviour which Nielsen criticizes. I had in mind bearings that cannot be determined in any theoretical way, such as the connections between misdeeds and prayer for forgiveness, or between harvests and harvest festivals. Given these connections, it is odd to say that they are connections between linguistic frameworks or systems. We can speak of using systems, or frameworks, perhaps, if we are thinking of the use of categories in science, where one category may be used, rather than another, because of its greater fruitfulness. In that sense, one does not *use* language at all in the case of prayers of forgiveness or harvest festivals. One's life with the concepts involved is constitutive of the activity one is engaged in. The connections involved are neither formal nor inductive. They are connections *in our lives*; connections which make them the lives they are.

This is connected with Wittgenstein's claim that to imagine a language is to imagine a form of life. It is in the form of life that we come to appreciate the meaning of 'reason', 'mistake', 'confusion', 'value', 'the forbidden' and so on. I never suggested that such situations are static. After all the title of the book from which my paper is taken is *Belief, Change and Forms of Life*.

Different aspects of discourse though conceptually distinct, bear on each other, as do different aspects of our lives. If such distinctiveness is what Nielsen means by '*sui generis*', then, once again, *all* aspects of discourse become fideistic. But Wittgensteinian Fideism was supposed to be a critique of something peculiar to religious belief.

I had been influenced by Rhees's 'Wittgenstein's Builders' in my early work, but I did not appreciate it fully until I edited his *Wittgenstein and the Possibility of Discourse*, published in 1999. I must not read this fuller appreciation into what I wrote between 1967 and 1989. But I am inviting Nielsen to refrain from doing the same with respect to his own writing. This would involve, in my opinion, the recognition that he did make extravagant claims in 1967, which should be retracted. In short, he needs to face the following question: Can philosophy show that religious belief in general is incoherent, irrational or unintelligible? Does Nielsen still want to say that never in the past, not even for a moment, did he think it could?

Bibliography

Conant, James (2005), Voice B in 'Voices in Discussion' in *Religion and Wittgenstein's Legacy*, eds D. Z. Phillips and Mario von der Ruhr. Basingstoke: Palgrave.

Copleston, F. C. (1984), *Religion and Philosophy*. London: Gill and Macmillan.

Gealy, Walford (1977), 'Ffaith a Ffydd', *Efrydiau Athronyddol*.

Hick, John (1974), 'Sceptics and Believers' in *Faith and the Philosophers*, ed. John Hick. London: Macmillan.

Kenny, L. (1975), 'In Defense of God', *The Times Literary Supplement* 7, February 1975.

Nielsen, Kai (1967), 'Wittgensteinian Fideism', *Philosophy* XLII: 161, July 1967.

—— (1989), *God, Scepticism and Modernity*. Ottawa: Ottawa University Press.

Phillips, D. Z. (1986), 'Wittgenstein and Religion: Some Fashionable Criticisms', *Belief, Change, and Forms of Life*. Basingstoke: Macmillan reprinted as Chapter 2 here.

Rhees, Rush (1970), 'Wittgenstein's Builders', *Proceedings of the Aristotelian Society, 1959–60*. Reprinted in *Discussions of Wittgenstein*. London: Routledge and Kegan Paul.

Smart, Ninian (1973), 'Discussion' in *Modern British Philosophy*, ed. Bryan Magee. London: Paladin.

PART TWO

Reflecting on 'Wittgensteinian Fideism'

5. Nielsen's Sceptical Strategies

D. Z. PHILLIPS

I Background

The textual evidence from my work in Chapter 2 showed two things: first, that I do not hold the theses attributed to me in the name of Wittgensteinian Fideism; second, that the views I have expressed are the *exact opposite* of those attributed to me. It may seem surprising that until the present dialogue there has been no explicit reaction to this textual evidence. In 1979, Nielsen and I participated in a conference at the University of Notre Dame on the alleged autonomy of religious belief. Nielsen read a paper called 'Religion and Groundless Believing', and mine was called, 'Belief, Change and Forms of Life'.[1] In my paper, I argued that externalism, the view that religious belief is answerable to alien criteria of meaningfulness, and internalism, the view that religion has solely internal criteria of meaning, are both fallacies which feed off each other's deficiencies. My paper, however, also had an appendix that included some of the textual evidence which I developed later in my book, *Belief, Change, and Forms of Life*. That is the evidence I reproduce in Chapter 2 of the present work.

Perhaps the lack of a response from Nielsen is not so surprising, since his own relation to the term 'Wittgensteinian Fideism', from the outset of its use, is far from straightforward. The first claim he makes seems clear enough: 'certain strands of [Wittgenstein's] later thought readily lend themselves to what I call Wittgensteinian Fideism' (Chapter 1, p. 21; Nielsen 1967, 191).[2] But no sooner is this claim made than Nielsen confides, 'There is no text that I can turn to for an extended statement of this position' (Chapter 1, p. 21; Nielsen 1967, 191). In that case, what has happened to the strands in Wittgenstein's thought that 'readily lend themselves' to this view? Do they exist? Does Nielsen think so? I ask, since a little later he says that he is 'not sure to what extent Wittgenstein himself would have accepted a Wittgensteinian Fideism' (Chapter 1, p. 23; Nielsen 1967, 193). From this one might be led to conclude that Wittgensteinian Fideism is to be located, not in Wittgenstein himself, but in the work of certain Wittgensteinians who have read him in this way. That is what Nielsen leads us to think when he urges us, 'But do not forget, what I indeed hope would be true, that Wittgenstein might well wish to say of Wittgensteinians what Freud said of Freudians' (Chapter 1, p. 23; Nielsen 1967, 194). Nielsen rounds up a group he regards as the usual suspects – 'Winch, Hughes, Malcolm, Geach, Cavell, Cameron and Coburn' (Chapter 1, p. 21; Nielsen 1967, 191). They make for a mixed bunch, some of whom would be surprised to find themselves included. Nevertheless, at least we know where to look for the texts of Wittgensteinian Fideism – or so it seemed. But by 1979, we find Nielsen referring to his suspects as follows: 'Some, whom I have called – perhaps tendentiously – Wittgensteinian Fideists' (Nielsen 1979, 115). It is unclear whether Nielsen is expressing a doubt relating to the group as a whole, or only to some unspecified members of it. What we need, obviously, is a citation of a text or texts held, by Nielsen, to be unambiguous examples of Wittgensteinian Fideism. As early as 1973 it appeared that a text had come to the rescue, since I am described 'as a paradigm case of a Wittgensteinian Fideist' (Nielsen 1973a, 94). But, alas, five years later, we find Nielsen referring to 'Phillips, and those other philosophers whom I have (perhaps tendentiously) called Wittgensteinian fideists' (Nielsen 1979, 109). In the course of the present dialogue, my philosophical status, with respect to fideism, may well change again.

Given his ambivalence about Wittgensteinian Fideism from 1967 to 1989, the period of my concern in the present chapter, one may wonder why Nielsen bothered to associate Wittgenstein's name with fideism at all. He offers as an early justification the fact that 'Wittgenstein's work has been take in this way' (Chapter 1, p. 23; Nielsen 1967, 193). But *by whom*? The textual difficulty for Nielsen, between 1967 and 1989, is that he himself expresses doubts over whether Wittgenstein, or the Wittgensteinians he names, including myself, should be taken or read in this way. Certainly, no one I know of, who could be called a Wittgensteinian philosopher of religion, would be happy with being called a Wittgensteinian fideist. So who has read Wittgenstein, and certain philosophers influenced by him, in this way? Slowly, but surely, in a philosophical audience by now conditioned to think otherwise, the answer may begin to dawn: it is Nielsen himself, and the other philosophers I quote in Chapter 2, who read Wittgenstein in this fideistic way. So when Nielsen promises to 'carefully examine the view I call Wittgensteinian Fideism' (Chapter 1, p. 23; Nielsen 1967, 194), because Wittgenstein has been take in this way, he is promising to give careful attention to something he and others have created!

Readers may feel impatient with me for taking up this background. Why not go to the core of my philosophical disagreement with Nielsen, instead of squabbling over a label, and trying to decide who said what, where and when. I sympathize with this reaction, but it misses why this background is important. No doubt questions of scholarship are involved concerning exegesis of Wittgenstein's work, and its relation to the philosophy of religion, but that relation is only important if one believes, as I do, that it casts a liberating light on both belief and atheism. *Both* are rescued from philosophical distortion. I suspect that Nielsen would agree with me that Wittgenstein's work had little effect on mainstream philosophy of religion, whose problems remain firmly anchored in late seventeenth- and eighteenth-century epistemology, or in versions of post-Kantian metaphysics. I suspect that Nielsen would also agree that this lack of influence is a philosophical loss. That being so, it is important for us both to explore why. For that reason, the background to our present dialogue becomes part of this investigation.

It has been argued, recently, that Wittgenstein's place in contemporary philosophy of religion is a tragic one due to a fideistic reading of his work (see Clack 2001). Most of Wittgenstein's own remarks on religion were unavailable before 1966, but by then the fideistic reading had already taken hold. The ambiguity we have found in Nielsen is repeated in these remarks. The impression they are meant to give is that certain Wittgensteinians are responsible for this reading, whereas the fact of the matter is that it is other philosophers, including the author of the remarks, who read them in this way. Once this is realized, the philosophical tragedy, with which Wittgenstein is said to be associated, is radically relocated. The tragedy is not that Wittgenstein or certain Wittgensteinians are fideists, but that others have read them in this way. The greater tragedy is that the label 'Wittgensteinian Fideism' has gathered an autonomous use around itself, and is used as a label by which philosophers can refer 'knowingly' to works they have not studied seriously, or even read. Nielsen cannot be blamed for this traffic in a label, but he can hardly deny that it has happened. By exploring Wittgenstein's relation to the philosophy of religion, we not only raise questions concerning the conceptual character of belief and atheism to which I have already alluded. We also have to face fundamental questions about the nature of philosophical enquiry.

II Fideism

Following Penelhum's lead, Nielsen places Wittgensteinian philosophy of religion in the context of fideistic reactions to the Enlightenment. For Nielsen, the Enlightenment showed that the very conception of natural theology is misconceived. The counter-Enlightenment, he argues, 'accepted the Enlightenment's critique of natural theology and took a fideistic turn' (Nielsen 1989, 1). That turn itself took two forms, conformist fideism and evangelical fideism. According to the latter, 'scepticism has established that it is not unreasonable to believe in a reality behind appearances in ordinary life even though that belief is groundless' (Nielsen 1989, 2).

Such a view can be found in certain forms of Reformed epistemology. According to conformist fideism, of which my work is said to be an example, 'scepticism establishes that it is reasonable to follow the habits of ordinary life without accepting metaphysical claims about a reality behind appearances' (Nielsen 1989, 2). Nielsen sees his work as a continuation of the Enlightenment project of showing religion to be inherently incoherent, and he rejects both fideistic reactions to this endeavour.

Wittgenstein cannot be understood in this fideistic context. First, Wittgenstein would not say that scepticism establishes anything. On the contrary, for Wittgenstein, it does not succeed in making an intelligible claim. Second, this is why Wittgenstein does not *refute* scepticism. Such a refutation would consist of a counter-thesis, which shows either that there is or that there is not a reality behind appearances, and which grants, thereby, the intelligibility of these theses. Third, for Wittgenstein, through appreciating the unintelligibility of scepticism, we come to an appreciation of the reality of the ordinary. We do not *find out* anything about what is, or is not, behind appearances. Rather, we come to appreciate the place we are already at by giving it the right kind of conceptual attention. Fourth, the place we are at, the language-games and form of life we participate in, are not mere appearances. They are unpredictable, neither reasonable nor unreasonable, but there, like our lives.

It is important to say that, even between 1967 and 1989, this response, on my part, would not have surprised Nielsen. This is because his ambivalence towards Wittgensteinian Fideism is matched by his ambivalence towards Wittgenstein's philosophical method. Early on, Nielsen says, 'for as much as I admire Wittgenstein, it seems to me that the fideistic conclusions drawn ... from his thought are often absurd' (Chapter 1, p. 21; Nielsen 1967, 191). This is because Wittgenstein's contemplative view of philosophy thwarts what, at this stage, is Nielsen's essentialist thesis about the incoherence of religion: 'Philosophy cannot be for or against religion – it cannot reveal, as I try to do, the "groundlessness of religion", it can, when it knows its place, only elucidate it. It will forever remain impossible to show that the believer's religious discourse and therefore his religious form of life and faith is *intrinsically* incoherent or unintelligible' (Nielsen 1982b, 134). But neither Wittgenstein nor Wittgensteinians share Nielsen's essentialist enterprise. They do not counter his thesis that religious belief is inherently incoherent, with a thesis that religious belief in inherently coherent. Everything depends on what the religious belief turns out to be. Nothing is prejudged; one must speak as one finds. But this conceptual 'finding', according to Wittgenstein, demands a kind of attention to religion which, for various reasons, we are reluctant to give to it. It would be too strong to say that such a charge does not worry Nielsen, but not too strong to say that it does not worry him enough.

He says,

I feel here my philosophical commitments are pulling in several directions, often I am tempted to argue in just this Wittgensteinian way –
it sometimes seems to me so very right – and yet when translated into
the concrete . . . and when applied to talk of God, it seems to me to
have absurd consequences . . . Yet surely we cannot stand apart from
our forms of life with some criterion of conceptual propriety which is
not rooted in . . . form of life. Hence my ambivalence. But ambivalent
or not, if I cannot surmount these criticisms, my basic theses have
been undermined (Nielsen 1982b, 134)

Nielsen does not think his basic theses have been undermined, and
hence concludes that there is an inadequacy in Wittgenstein's philosophical method. To see how he comes to this conclusion, we will eventually
have to pay attention to what I call his sceptical strategies.

III Beliefs and Incommensurability

Tracing Nielsen's relation to my work is a complex matter. In this section, I simply want to show that, as early as 1973, there were certain
philosophical affinities between us, which could have been, but were not,
built on.

In 1973, Nielsen defended me against a claim that Wittgensteinian
Fideism contains an internal contradiction. The claim was made by Stuart
C. Brown who argued that there are two contradictory theses in my work
(Brown 1972). The first, the incommensurability thesis, states 'that there
is no common standard of reference by which the issues between belief
and unbelief could be rationally adjudicated' (Nielsen 1973a, 94). The
second, the truth thesis, simply states 'that there are criteria of truth and
falsity in religion' (Nielsen 1973a, 94). Brown argues that I try to combine
these theses. I cannot do so because the truth thesis, he claims, commits
me to holding that 'If there are criteria which determine certain beliefs
are true, then those beliefs, together with any to which someone who
holds them is thereby committed, are commensurable with any conflicting
beliefs' (Nielsen 1973a, 95). Nielsen shows, not only that the truth thesis
does not commit me to this view, but also that I have shown why in
early works such as *Death and Immortality* and *Faith and Philosophical
Enquiry*.

Brown and Nielsen agree that I do not seek an easy way out by
embracing a relativism in which 'true' simply means 'true for some particular group'. Nevertheless, Nielsen argues, although

Phillips does *not* give a relativistic reading of 'true', he does give a
distinctive reading for religious beliefs of 'true' and 'belief' . . . What
Phillips does (and here he also follows Wittgenstein) is to deny, given

the employment of 'true' in them, that the normal relations holding between matter-of-fact propositions hold for those distinctive situations where we cross types between religious propositions and purely matter-of-fact propositions. (Nielsen 1973a, 96)

Someone may believe that there is a God in heaven. Does that person have to hold that the truth of his belief is commensurable with the truth of the belief that astronauts have not seen God? Nielsen replies, 'Contrary to this, it is Phillips' contention – and it seems to me an entirely reasonable contention – that it shows an utter misunderstanding of what Christianity is all about to think that [the beliefs about the astronaut and God] could be possible utterances in that mode of discourse' (Nielsen 1973a, 96). The beliefs conflict with religious belief without being commensurable with it. An appeal to what the astronauts have not seen, shows that the person who makes it is not a believer, but, Nielsen argues,

> not in the way [a person] would who asserted 'There is no God; there is no heaven, the world is full of pointless, purposeless evil.' He says that these beliefs also qualify as infidel beliefs, but they are infidel beliefs which do not necessarily show a lack of understanding of religious beliefs, though they do categorically reject core Christian beliefs. [The belief concerning God and the astronauts, by contrast], show a lack of understanding of religious belief. They are conflicting beliefs but they are clearly not commensurable beliefs. They are beliefs, Phillips argues, which belong to a different language-game. The truth of 'God is in heaven' and the truth of any claim about what astronauts might see or fail to see is not settled in the same way. (Nielsen 1973a, 96–7)

If Brown were to react by saying that, in that case, there is no conflict, he would be accused of having a stipulative definition of 'conflict'.

If I hold that the beliefs of religion and atheism are not commensurable, must I hold that religious belief can only be true in some figurative way? Nielsen shows that I do not. I argue that religious beliefs 'could only be figuratively true, if we could at least in principle indicate something of what it would be like for (them) to be literally true' (Nielsen 1973a, 98). We do not have an original context of literal truth, which religious belief can be said to distort, or from which it can be said to deviate. 'But then we can hardly talk about its being figuratively true either' (Nielsen 1973a, 98).

If religious beliefs are not figurative, are not empirical hypotheses, and are not straightforward matter-of-fact propositions, how are they to be characterized? Nielsen attempts to give the following answer on my behalf:

To dispute about the truth here is very unlike arguing about whether
a prediction will come true or arguing over whether what a factual
statement alleges to obtain really does obtain, e.g. 'There are storks
in Iceland'. Rather it is to argue over an ethical matter, to wit, over
the worth of generosity. A man who says that he has come to see the
truth in the maxim that it is better to give than to receive is giving us
to understand that he will strive after generosity, and try to orient and
regulate his life in accordance with that maxim. A similar thing obtains
for anyone who assents to 'Christ is the truth, the life and the way'
or 'God is truth.' He is not taking a world-historical stance but is
announcing and affirming how he will strive to live. 'Truth', as 'belief',
has a very different use here than it has in scientific and factual
domains. (Nielsen 1973a, 100)

Without endorsing these remarks as a wholly satisfactory account of
my views at this time, it is still possible to note three conclusions reached
which could have been built on in a dialogue between Nielsen and myself:

1 The conflict between belief and unbelief need not be one between
  commensurable beliefs within a common system of reference. 'There
  is a God – There is no God' is unlike 'There are deer in the forest –
  There are no deer in the forest.' This is important for Nielsen's
  atheistic point of view, since he does not hold that religious beliefs
  are *false*, as a mistaken, contradictory belief would be, but holds,
  rather, that religious beliefs are unintelligible.
2 Religious beliefs are not true in some figurative sense of 'true'.
3 It is important that Nielsen notices that I say that religious beliefs
  are *similar* to moral beliefs. They are not equated, since there are
  important differences. Nevertheless, if one has to choose, religious
  beliefs are nearer to moral beliefs than they are to empirical hypotheses. Thus, the conflict between belief and unbelief is more like
  a conflict between different moral perspectives, than like conflict
  between competing factual propositions.

There is reason to think that, in 1973, Nielsen too thought these conclusions to be important. Referring to his account of my view, he says,
'There is something here which is important and has, I am convinced, "a
ring of truth about it"' (Nielsen 1973a, 100). But, in a way I find repeated
in Nielsen's argumentation, he draws back from the brink of conceptual
recognition and acknowledgement. He goes on to say, 'yet, I am also
convinced, it should be looked on with a very jaundiced eye' (Nielsen
1973a, 100). We shall see that, in subsequent discussions, it is 'the
jaundiced eye' that prevails.

IV Positivism and Verificationism

As we have seen, it seems, at times, as though Nielsen recognizes that it is a misunderstanding of religious beliefs to treat them as commensurable with non-religious beliefs; as beliefs to be weighed against others in a common system of assessment. Yet, early and late in his thought, we find him insisting that religious beliefs should meet criteria of meaning and truth that he has said do not apply to them. For example, he argues,

> It is a fact that there is a God; it is a fact that he created the world; it is a fact that he protects me and the like. Yet, how could we say what it would be like for God to create the world, if it is impossible in principle to say what would have to transpire for it to be false that God created the world? Or to put this point in a weaker and more adequate way, if we cannot even say what *in principle* would count as *evidence* against the putative statement that God created the world, then 'God created the world' is devoid of factual content. (Chapter 1, p. 31; Nielsen 1967, 203)

Here, Nielsen is treating the belief in God's creation as an empirical hypothesis, and says that it constitutes a challenge unmet by Wittgensteinian Fideism. But, as we have seen, he also holds that such a challenge misunderstands the nature of religious beliefs.

Nielsen is not arguing that only science gives us an acquaintance with reality. But he takes it to be a mark of any belief that it must be commensurable with the belief that denies it. He thinks that this marks grammatically, in Wittgensteinian fashion, what it takes for a belief to have 'objective reality' (see Chapter 1, p. 32; Nielsen 1967, 203). But we have seen already that Nielsen recognizes that a denial of a religious belief need *not* be commensurable with that belief. So where is the challenge religious belief has to meet in terms of such commensurability? Has Nielsen forgotten that he does 'not wish to attack Wittgenstein's claim that there is no logical form that underlies all language and is its rational foundation' (Nielsen 1982b, 110)? He calls Wittgenstein's claim 'a profoundly correct philosophical insight' (Nielsen 1982b, 110). Why does Nielsen go against his better judgment, then, in looking for a common form for all kinds of assent and denial?

The above issues are obviously relevant for disputes concerning the reality of God. We find a familiar oscillation in Nielsen's reactions to them. At times, Nielsen seems to hold that God cannot be discussed as an object among objects, a particular existent among existents. He seems to appreciate George Hughes's observation that 'God is not thought of as a "particular thing" within orthodox Jewish and Christian thought ... Moreover, it is worth remembering in this context that one piece of

NIELSEN'S SCEPTICAL STRATEGIES

meta-theology which has wide acceptance among the orthodox is that "God" is not a substance-word (Aquinas in the formal mode)' (Chapter 1, p. 24; Nielsen 1967, 195). Hughes is protesting against Nielsen's imposition on 'God' of an alien logic of proper names or definite descriptions. Nielsen, while half-accepting that the logic does not apply, draws back from investigating what logic does apply. Instead, he simply states that he can see no alternative. Thus, he says, 'God is plainly not some locatable reality "out there". Phillips makes this evident enough. But then *what* are we talking about when we speak of God?' (Nielsen 1973b, 32). Nielsen would do well to remember Wittgenstein's penetrating remark, 'The way you use "God" does not show you mean – but, rather, what you mean' (Wittgenstein 1984, 50e). We misread Wittgenstein, entirely, if we think Wittgenstein is substituting *what* we mean for *whom* we mean. He is denying that talking of God is like referring to a human being, or to an object. Nevertheless, if we pay attention to religious discourse we will find out what-we-mean by 'God'. Once again, Nielsen appreciates Wittgenstein's strictures against our craving for generality about the meanings of our words. But when it comes to religion, he reverts to fairly positivistic criteria of meaning.

Nielsen is well aware that I want him to appreciate that in discussing the reality of God we are discussing *a kind of reality*. He knows that I think this 'is comparable to the question of what *kind* of reality physical objects have. There is no *finding out* . . . whether God is real or not, as there is a finding out of whether unicorns are real . . . The real question in both cases is the question about the *kind* of reality physical objects and God have' (Nielsen 1979, 103). In making this claim, Nielsen thinks I commit 'the fallacy of the complex question. We assume, that is, that God *has* a reality and that God could be real when it is these very things that we want to query' (Nielsen 1979, 103).

Nielsen is wrong in the above conclusion. Scepticism has questioned the reality of physical objects and the reality of God. I was pointing out that when this happens, what is being questioned is the very possibility of intelligibility concerning such notions. That is why, for example, we cannot investigate the reality of physical objects in the way we investigate whether a particular physical object exists. Similarly, an investigation into the reality of God is an investigation into the possibility of sense in this context, a question that is logically prior to the truth or falsity of specific claims about God. The sceptical investigation is a logical investigation. Nielsen does not always recognize this, and turns it into an epistemological issue. He asks, 'Why can we not sensibly ask if what is *claimed* to be divine reality is *indeed* a reality at all? What is wrong with asking if that claimed reality is indeed something which actually exists?' (Nielsen 1979, 103). This is Nielsen reverting to the positivistic and verificationist strain in his thought. Until we investigate what we *mean* by God's reality, we are in no position to ask whether God exists. Nielsen's positivism does not do justice to his main position, which is not to deny that a God who might exist, in fact, does not, but to deny the intelligibility of discourse about God. In short, Nielsen is a sceptic in the sense I have elucidated.

No Wittgensteinian prejudges the intelligibility of a religious belief. One must wait on the belief to see what it amounts to. Wittgenstein and Wittgensteinians have recognized that one might unearth fundamental confusions as a result; confusions which, moreover, have caused a great deal of harm. Thus, they have no quarrel with Nielsen when he concludes that one may recognize the way religious people talk and still conclude that they do not do so 'intelligibly, coherently, reasonably, justifiably or truly' (Nielsen 1979, 104; cf. Chapter 1, p. 36; Nielsen 1967, 192–3; Nielsen 1973b, 26–7). Their quarrel with Nielsen is that, at this stage, this is *all* he sees in religion. He does not do conceptual justice to its other aspects. He cannot admit this. He is not prepared for his scepticism to be reduced to a personal confession on his part, such as, 'Religion doesn't mean anything to me' or 'I don't see the point of it.' At this stage, he still wants to claim that religion is inherently incoherent.

A tension in Nielsen's expression of his scepticism illustrates, inadvertently, a philosophical perspective I want Nielsen to embrace. On the one hand, as we have seen, he rightly wants to keep open the possibility that religious discourse may turn out to be unintelligible and incoherent. On the other hand, he compares the sceptic to 'some of Dostoevsky's sceptical characters, [who] very much see the point in such talk and yet remain quite incapable of belief' (Nielsen 1979, 105). But Nielsen's position does not allow him to say both: that religious talk is unintelligible and incoherent *and* that it has a point.

For Wittgenstein and Wittgensteinians, on the other hand, what Dostoevsky's characters portray is compatible with what may occur in contemplative philosophy. A philosopher may see the point of a religious belief without being able to appropriate it, make it his own, or live by it. Kierkegaard always insisted, as Wittgenstein does, that there is an infinite distance between conceptual clarity and faith. After all, in philosophy, we clarify the meanings of far more perspectives than we could possibly appropriate, if only because many of them are in conflict with each other. In relation to religious belief, these are distinctions that Nielsen cannot bring himself to allow. It would involve abandoning the positivism of a humanist tradition that prides itself on having seen through religion. It is no accident that the Enlightenment project Nielsen takes himself to be continuing, saw its criticism of religion as a means of liberating people from darkness, and bringing them into the light. That is why, I suspect, there was so much anger, in certain quarters, among some heirs to the Enlightenment, when Wittgenstein said that James Frazer, in *The Golden*

Bough, was more savage than the savages he discussed; that his explanation of primitive rituals was cruder than anything to be found in the
rituals themselves. Having said that, however, it is important to note that
Wittgenstein discusses *both* the confusion and depth in rituals in his
'Remarks on Frazer's *Golden Bough*' (Wittgenstein 1993). Nielsen's
positivism, at this stage, only shows him the *possibility* of confusion; a
possibility he turns into necessity.

V   Language and Wittgenstein's Philosophical Method

The issues we have been discussing lead Nielsen to voice some concerns
about Wittgenstein's philosophical method. There is an ambiguity in his
discussions of this method, comparable to the ambiguity we found in his
discussions of fideism. We will find him oscillating in his philosophical
attitude to it.

At first, Nielsen seems to share, with Wittgenstein, the desire to be
open to the conceptual and grammatical variety to be found in our
discourse. He takes to heart (or seems to) Hughes's caution 'that it is
possible to show any category of statements or expressions to be conceptually confused if one is allowed to insist that they must conform
to the logic of some other category or categories of statements or expressions if they are to be said to make sense' (Hughes 1962, 214). Nielsen
responds:

> Certainly, Max Black and a host of others have made it evident that
> if we try to treat inductive reasonings as if they were deductive ones,
> we would make nonsense of them. Similarly, if we try to construe
> moral statements as if they were empirical statements, and moral
> reasoning as if it were scientific reasoning, we would make nonsense
> out of morality. We have learned to treat these concepts and modes
> of reasoning as being *sui generis* ... Our job as philosophers is
> to come to understand and display that logic, not to distort it by
> trying to reduce it to the logic of some preferred type of discourse
> or to try to interpret it in terms of some ideal language like that
> found in *Principia Mathematica*. (Chapter 1, pp. 23–4; Nielsen 1967,
> 194)

Hughes wants to apply this lesson to religious discourse. It, too, should
not be distorted by trying to reduce it to the logic of some preferred type
of discourse. But Nielsen draws back from applying to religion the lesson
he seemed to approve of. In order to do so, he has to start talking in a
rather different way about language.

Nielsen's emphasis changes when he discusses religion. Suddenly, we
find him saying, ' "religious discourse" and "scientific discourse" are part

of the same overall conceptual structure . . . they share a number of key categories' (Chapter 1, p. 30; Nielsen 1967, 201). More confidently, he states, 'given the overall universe of discourse of which religious discourse is a part, it may still be found that religious discourse, like discourse about fairies, is incoherent' (Chapter 1, p. 35; Nielsen 1967, 207). Again, we are told, ' "Reality" may be systematically ambiguous, but what constitutes evidence, or tests for the truth or reliability of specific claims, is not completely idiosyncratic to the context or activity we are talking about' (Chapter 1, p. 36; Nielsen 1967, 208).

It seems, on this second view of Nielsen's, that religious discourse falls foul of rationality because it infringes the overall structure of the universe of discourse of which it is a part. It does so apparently by failing standards of evidence that transcend the diverse contexts in which evidence may be called for. But at no time, as far as I know, does Nielsen describe the overall structure of the universe of discourse, or the standards of evidence that are supposed to transcend all contexts. This is not surprising, since a little earlier he has been praising those philosophers who have exposed the confusions in such notions. But Nielsen needs the very notions he sometimes recognizes to be confused, to act as the standards religious discourse must meet. No wonder it can't meet them!

Let us continue, for a moment, to illustrate the philosophical oscillations in his argument. How can someone who speaks of 'the overall structure of discourse', also say, 'We have no antecedent understanding of reality such that we could determine whether language agreed with reality, whether a specific language agreed with reality or whether a given form of discourse agreed with reality. With the exception of the *very last bit*, I agree . . . about such matters, but alas it is this very last bit that is essential for a Wittgensteinian Fideism' (Chapter 1, p. 36; Nielsen 1967, 208)? But, even here, when he is endeavouring to express the extent of his agreement with Wittgenstein, he misunderstands what he is saying. Nielsen speaks of our inability to determine whether language agrees with reality. In Wittgenstein's thought, it makes no sense to speak of language either agreeing or disagreeing with reality, and so there is nothing for us to fail in determining. What agrees or fails to agree with reality is *what we say*. If we say that there is a chair in a room, when there is not, what we say fails to agree with reality. If we say a gesture is genuine when it is not, what we say fails to agree with reality. If we say we are worshipping God when we are worshipping an idol, what we say does not accord with reality. But the language in which true and false statements are made is not itself a description of anything. It is one of the deep pathologies of philosophy to think that the grammar of a discourse is itself a belief or description. Of course, philosophers raise questions about *the reality of discourse*, but these are questions concerning the *intelligibility* of what is said, true or false. Nielsen, of course, wants to deny the intelligibility of religious discourse. The appeal to an 'overall structure of discourse' will not allow him to do so.

There is something important to be rescued, however, from the confused appeal to the overall structure of language. We can rescue it by seeing why Nielsen thinks it important to appeal to such a structure. He does so, in reaction to a view of language he attributes to Wittgensteinians, in which language is said to be compartmentalized into domains which are logically distinct, and which have nothing to do with each other. This is why he keeps saying that 'the logic of discourse' is a dangerous metaphor, 'and that these discourses are not in actual life nearly so compartmentalized' (Chapter 1, p. 33; Nielsen 1967, 204). This conclusion is important for deep-going logical reasons that Nielsen does not appreciate. I want to show why.

First, Nielsen would have to recognize that Wittgensteinians have not held the view about the compartmentalization of language he attributes to them. Where my own work is concerned, this should be obvious from the texts quoted in Chapter 2. As I said there, 'As early as my first book, *The Concept of Prayer* [1965], I was anxious to stress that "Religious concepts . . . are not *technical* concepts; they are not cut off from the common experiences of human life . . . Because this is so, an attempt can be made to clarify their meaning"' (p. 44). Nielsen suggests that I once held the compartmentalization view, but came to renounce it (Nielsen 1979, 106). But he does not note the fact that I said later (quoted in Chapter 2), in rejecting this concession as premature, 'I suspect that we have heard so-called fideistic . . . views attributed to us so often that we have almost come to believe in their accuracy ourselves without checking it!' (p. 44).

This having been said, what is certainly true is that neither in my 1970 paper, 'Religious Beliefs and Language Games', nor in *Belief, Change and Forms of Life*, did I appreciate the depth of the logical points Rush Rhees was making in his paper 'Wittgenstein's Builders' (Rhees 1959–60). The compression of thought in that paper is formidable, and it took my editing of Rhees's *Wittgenstein and the Possibility of Discourse* to appreciate its far-reaching implications. These are implications for the notion of the logic of discourse. Unfortunately, Nielsen turns in exactly the wrong direction to appreciate them.

Nielsen says that 'when we reflect on . . . the various linguistic activities that we actually engage in – we will find that some are "ground floor" – an irreducible element of what there is. The other forms of discourse are in various ways parasitic on it and if in trying to assert the existence of something we make assumptions which run counter to it, we say something which is incoherent' (Nielsen 1982b, 135). Nielsen admits 'these remarks are vague, simply asserted rather than argued for and they remain programmatic' (Nielsen 1982b, 135). That is no accident. He faces a formidable Wittgensteinian challenge to produce his 'ground floor' – 'the irreducible element of what there is' – on which *all* other forms of discourse are parasitic. Failures to do just that began with the Presocratics, when they attempted to give a substantive answer to the question, 'What is the nature of all things?' As far as I know, Nielsen's claim remains programmatic, as does his other appeal to 'the overall structure of discourse'.

What is the important lesson to be found in the view that discourse is *not* made up of logically distinct domains that have nothing to do with each other? It is to be found in a notion that, for Nielsen, is a 'dark saying', namely, the notion of 'a form of life'. He asks, 'How distinctive and conceptually self-sufficient must something be in order to count as a form of life?' (Nielsen 1982b, 119) This question mires the logical role of the notion in Wittgensteinian thought.

Rhees says over and over again in *Wittgenstein and the Possibility of Discourse* that language makes sense if living makes sense. This is why he criticizes Wittgenstein's suggestion, in Part One of the *Investigations*, that the order 'Slab!', given by one builder to another on a building site, could be the whole language of a tribe. Rhees's objection is not to the limited vocabulary. He is denying that anything would be being said. It seems more like an automatic response to a signal. But, in fact, such an order would be given in the course of lived lives. That's what makes the giving and receiving of the order what they are. The order comes in the course of a day's work, work which itself has a place in people's lives; work to which people bring much that is not that work, and work which can be discussed, or reacted to, when it is over; work which stands in various relations to other aspects of life, a life which is part of a wider culture with its humour, art, music, social movements and so on. This is why Wittgenstein says that to imagine a language is to imagine a form of life. That is precisely what is hard to imagine within the parameters Wittgenstein gives to his builders.

Nielsen says, 'I do not, of course, object to "forms of life" being open-textured and I do not think language is calculus-like or should be treated as if it were' (Nielsen 1982b, 131). One of Rhees's objections to the analogy between language and games is that, whereas all games do not make up one big game, all language-games occur in *the same* language. Moreover, Rhees argues that Wittgenstein, in Part One of the *Investigations*, wanting to avoid the calculus-like unity of language argued for in his *Tractatus*, went to the other extreme of holding that each language-game is 'complete'. In short, he let the analogy with games run away with him. Rhees suggests that if one wants a centre of variation from which to discuss language, one would do far better to start from the notion of a conversation, than from the notion of a game. This would be connected with his insistence that language makes sense if living makes sense.

Nielsen thinks that ' "form of life" is a term of Wittgensteinian art and [that] it is too minimally articulated to bear the great weight Wittgenstein, Winch, Malcolm, Cavell and Phillips put on it' (Nielsen 1982b, 131). It is not my purpose here to defend every purpose to which the term has been put, but it is important to realize, as Nielsen does not, that the main weight the term has is one in logic – in the reasons Rhees brings out for the importance of saying that to imagine a language is to imagine a form of life.

The reasons why Nielsen has objections to the compartmentalization of language into forms of life are rather different. By not accepting that view, which he describes as 'dear to Wittgensteinian Fideists', he thinks we need not be committed to 'the paradoxical thesis that modes of social life cannot be appraised as logical or illogical, rational or irrational' (Chapter 1, p. 35; Nielsen 1967, 207). Further, he argues, 'it surely is question-begging to assert that this scepticism must simply be the result of conceptual blunders' (Nielsen 1973b, 27–8). On the other hand, Nielsen sees a tension between his claim that forms of life must be assessed rationally, and his recognition that 'our canons of criticism are set for us by the forms of life in question' (Nielsen 1982b, 112).

The tension in Nielsen's thought can be resolved if we pay attention to another Wittgensteinian term which he finds problematic, for reasons similar to his worries about 'forms of life'. That term is *practice*. We see this if we appreciate the importance of distinguishing, as we have seen James Conant does, between Wittgenstein's use of 'practice', and what might be called its 'sociological' use (Conant 2005, 204). In Wittgenstein's use, 'practice' refers to a conceptually and grammatically distinctive way of thinking or acting. In this use, it clearly would make no sense to speak of a confused practice. The sociological use of 'practice', however, simply refers to whatever goes on, or is done. If Wittgenstein's use is confused with the sociological use, one is led to the absurd thesis, attributed by Nielsen and others to Wittgensteinians, that no practice, no form of life, nothing that we do, can ever be confused![3] No wonder Nielsen thinks such a thesis is paradoxical. It is only through confusing the two uses of 'practice' that Nielsen thinks he is opposing Wittgenstein and Wittgensteinians when he says of their appeal to 'practice', 'But to start at this point is one thing, to end there is another' (Chapter 1, p. 34; Nielsen 1967, 205). It is the same confusion that leads him to suspect that Wittgenstein's philosophy harbours quietism in its claim that philosophy leaves everything where it is. But 'what there is', for Wittgenstein, will include reforms and criticisms, including reforms and criticisms of religion. It will also include resistance to reforms and criticisms. More importantly, for Nielsen, it includes the exposure of confusion. Does Nielsen think that Wittgenstein's philosophy advocates leaving confusion where it is? Of course not. Wittgenstein is insisting that what we need to

meet our philosophical puzzlement *already lies before us*. We are not
awaiting new information. Nothing is hidden. It is in *that* sense only that
philosophy leaves everything where it is.

VI Nielsen's Road to Scepticism

Nielsen thinks that I want to close the road to scepticism about religion.
Whether I want to do so depends on what scepticism amounts to. I
certainly want to oppose Nielsen's essentialist scepticism, by which I
mean his claim to have grasped 'the essence' of religion, and to have
exposed its inherent incoherence. In support of this scepticism, however,
he appeals to examples which he thinks, wrongly, I fail to recognize.
Examining these will reveal the nature of his own road to scepticism.

First, Nielsen points to the fact that people have come to regard the
beliefs they once held to be confused (see Chapter 1, p. 22; Nielsen 1967,
192). Why should I resist this claim? Perhaps their beliefs *were* confused.
The textual evidence in Chapter 2 shows that throughout my work I
have not denied this possibility.

Second, a believer may become a sceptic in the sense of no longer being
able to see the point of beliefs which do have a point. The person may
have been influenced by confused, but prestigious, philosophical accounts
of the beliefs. Having accepted these accounts, he can't stomach them in
the end, and his beliefs fall with the philosophy. Nielsen acknowledges
that I recognize this *personal* scepticism, but it does not satisfy his essentialist scepticism.

Third, a believer may become a sceptic about certain religious beliefs,
by listening to other religious attitudes that deride it. This would have
been the case if Job's Comforters, or his wife, had triumphed in the
advice they gave him. He would not have been able to say, 'The Lord
gave, the Lord hath taken away, blessed be the name of the Lord.' Nielsen
does not discuss this kind of case and, of course, it is far removed from
the essentialist scepticism he hankers after.

Fourth, however, we come to a sceptic close to Nielsen's heart, namely,
Nietzsche. Protesting, rightly, against philosophers who see depth in
belief, but none in atheism, Nielsen says,

> May I say that I find this talk of religious beliefs being deep as some-
> what *parti pris*. People are talking as though all religious beliefs are
> deep and secular perspectives are somehow not deep by comparison.
> But the distinction between depth and superficiality can be found on
> both sides of the fence. Voltaire is a superficial unbeliever and Paley
> is a superficial believer. On the other hand, Pascal and Kierkegaard
> are deep believers, while Hume and Nietzsche are deep unbelievers.
> Depth is not to be appropriated for religion alone.[4]

The question is whether Nielsen's views, up to 1989, can accommodate the kind of depth to be found in Nietzsche's atheism.

Nielsen wants an example of an atheism which sees the point in religious belief by seeing it to be essentially confused, not simply confused in a particular case. Nietzsche does not provide him with such an example. Nietzsche did not oppose Christianity because he thought it unintelligible, pointless. On the contrary, as has been said, he paid Christianity the compliment of seeing its point, but he hated it (see Holmer 1978, 194). A person would be an atheist with respect to religious belief, in this case, because its values would have been eroded, or despised from the outset, from the perspective of values of a very different kind.

This case should remind us of section III of the present chapter on 'Belief and Incommensurability', and the promise, in 1973, of an insight shared by myself and Nielsen, on which we could have built. We seemed to have appreciated that a clash between belief and unbelief is more akin to a clash between rival moral perspectives, than to a clash between rival factual hypotheses. In the end, Nielsen recommended that we look at the suggestion with a very jaundiced eye, and, as I said, it is the jaundiced eye that prevailed. We can see how when he says, later, of the 1973 insight, that 'religious claims are being modeled too nearly even for Phillips' taste on moral ones. Religion, so construed, is too close for comfort to morality touched with emotion and the distinctive putative truth-claims of religion have been lost' (Nielsen 1973b, 37). Nietzsche does not share this easy dismissal of the suggestion. On the contrary, he not only sees the threat in Christian spirituality, but sees also that what is at stake is obscured by the battle of truth-claims of the kind Nielsen, and so many other contemporary philosophers of religion, are concerned with. As Conant (1995, 317) has shown, there is a striking parallel between Wittgenstein and Nietzsche in this respect. Wittgenstein says:

> Christianity is not a doctrine, not, I mean, a theory about what has happened and will happen to the human soul, but a description of something that actually takes place in human life ... I believe that one of the things Christianity says is that sound doctrines are all useless. They have to change your *life* (or the *direction* of your life). (Wittgenstein 1984, 28, 53)

Nietzsche says:

> It is false to the point of absurdity to see in a 'belief', perchance the belief in a redemption through Christ, the distinguishing characteristic of the Christian: only Christian *practice*, a life such as he who died on the cross *lived*, is Christian ... *Not* a belief but a doing, above all a *not*-doing of many things, a different *being* ... States of consciousness,

beliefs of any kind, holding something to be true for example . . . are a matter of complete indifference . . . To reduce being a Christian, Christianness, to a holding something to be true, to a mere phenomenality of consciousness, means to negate Christianness. (Nietzsche 1990, 163)

In his views up to 1989, Nielsen does not take Conant's parallel to heart. Sometimes, he descends to examples that Nietzsche, and he (on better days), regard as absurd. Speculating on what it might mean to say that God spoke to Job out of the whirlwind, Nielsen asks, 'So how did he do it? Nobody, or at least nobody who matters, believes any more in a sky God up there, who might have done it in a very loud voice' (Chapter 1, p. 33; Nielsen 1967, 204). This is not Nielsen at his best. In the third section of the present chapter, I concurred with the scorn Nielsen poured on the suggestion that an appeal to the fact that astronauts had not seen God would be an argument against the belief that God is in heaven. In the grammatical space Nielsen has in mind, would an appeal to not having heard him fare any better? Is is not appropriate to adapt his own words, in Chapter 3, against any such suggestion? If so, he would support my contention, 'an entirely reasonable contention – that it shows an utter misunderstanding of what [Job's belief] is all about to think that [beliefs about sounds of God that astronauts did not hear] could be possible utterances in that mode of discourse' (Nielsen 1973a, 96).

Fifth, consider another atheist, Albert Camus, for whom, I suspect, Nielsen has a high regard. I want to compare their reaction to Simone Weil as an illustration of Nielsen's scepticism.

In Chapter 1, Nielsen told us that when he reads Simone Weil's *Waiting for God*, 'I have the *feeling* that I belong to another tribe . . . She blithely accepts what I find unintelligible' (Chapter 1, p. 30; Nielsen 1967, 202). But when she writes, 'There is a God. There is no God. Where is the problem? I am quite sure that there is a God in the sense that I am sure my love is no illusion. I am quite sure there is no God, in the sense that I am sure there is nothing which resembles what I can conceive when I say that word' (Chapter 1, p. 30; Nielsen 1967, 202), Nielsen thinks he sees enough common background 'for arguing about which concepts of reality are correct or mistaken here' (Chapter 1, p. 31; Nielsen 1967, 202). It is doubtful, however, whether he has appreciated the grammatical points she is making about God's identity, points which have been explored by Rush Rhees (1997).

Rhees shows that *nothing* of the ways in which we would determine whether two people are talking about the same person, the same planet, the same church, *actually* enter into the way we would determine whether two people are talking about the same God. The matter is settled by the presence or absence of a spiritual affinity between them. Rhees points

NIELSEN'S SCEPTICAL STRATEGIES 91

out that I could know that Winston Churchill existed without knowing that he was Prime Minister, but I could not know God without knowing that he is the creator of heaven and earth, the sources of grace and love. To think otherwise would be like thinking that I could know Winston Churchill without knowing that he had hands, feet, face etc. The grammatical point is that terms like 'love' and 'grace' stand to 'God', as hands, feet and face stand to 'human being'. The reality of God *is* the reality of love in this context. In claiming that this 'reality' is subsequent to a logically prior belief in God's existence (see Nielsen 1982a, 93–4), Nielsen, as we have seen, has Nietzsche as well as Wittgenstein ranged against him. What of Camus?

Nielsen has responded to Simone Weil-like analyses of 'God' and 'love'. He writes,

> This love, we are told, is the 'Spirit of God' and to possess it is to know God ... To love in this way is to believe in God. It is true that one could not believe in God without loving or at least having some affective attitude towards God. Knowledge of God – if indeed there is such – cannot be a purely theoretical knowledge ... But to equate belief, understanding and loving here is to confuse a necessary condition for religious beliefs with a sufficient one, and it is to convert atheists like myself ... into believers by stipulative re-definition. I do indeed believe in eternal love, characterised as Phillips characterises it – though I do not like to talk in this way – but I do not believe in God ... Here we have what in effect, if not in intention, is a form of apologetic advocacy of a radically reconstructed Christianity masquerading as a neutral analysis of Christian discourse. (Nielsen 1973b, 31–2)

But if the grammatical points are correct, what we have is not advocacy, but Wittgensteinian conceptual description. Camus is by no means as sure as Nielsen in his reaction to this analysis. His acquaintance with the thought of Simone Weil caused him to ponder deeply. On the one hand, he could not doubt that she was deeply religious. On the other hand, he could not deny that everything he had attacked in religion, she attacked with equal, if not greater, rigour. He had to admit that the depth in her religion was *not* what he attacked. He was still struggling with this issue at his untimely death.

Camus' uncertainty about Simone Weil is captured in his brilliant novel, *The Plague*. Faced by the horror of the plague, a priest preaches a second sermon, very different from his first, in which he sought to attribute the plague to the sins of the people. The second sermon, in fact, is Camus' grappling with Simone Weil's thought. Another priest in the novel, listening to the sermon, is uncertain about its content. When the preacher dies, they wonder whether he died of the plague – that is, do the horrors of the plague make nonsense of the second sermon as they did of the first? At the foot of the bed, the medical card reads, 'Doubtful case.'[5]

Camus did not deny a certain affinity between himself and Simone Weil, despite his atheism and her belief. It would not worry me, philosophically, or otherwise, if that turned out to be the case between Nielsen and myself. In fact, we are often agreed about what we oppose, an agreement that would be impossible without some positive affinity. Certain forms of atheism and belief may be closer to each other, than certain other forms of atheism and belief are to each other within those broad categories. After all, Simone Weil thought that a purifying atheism was a prerequisite for love of God, but she would never say that her aim was to reconstruct Christianity for apologetic purposes.

Camus saw that what he attacked was not what Simone Weil believed. He did not respond by saying that religious belief must be what he attacked. He found her views a 'doubtful case', but was eager to explore them. Too often in his views, up to 1989, Nielsen is not prepared even to say 'doubtful case'. His essentialist scepticism leads him to the claim that he has shown that religious belief is inherently incoherent. In the ensuing dialogue, I want to relax the hold that claim has on his thinking.

VII   The Pictures That Say Themselves

In the final section of the chapter, I want to introduce a topic that will serve as a link to the discussions in Part III. Nielsen is philosophically sceptical about Wittgenstein's use of the term 'picture' in connection with religious belief, and especially sceptical of the claim that these pictures say themselves. He says, 'This is a very odd use of "picture" in which we are to adhere to a picture and yet can have no independent access to what is pictured . . . there must be some notion of representation in virtue of which there must be something which the picture is a picture of' (Nielsen 1973b, 36). Nielsen's difficulties about Wittgenstein's use of 'picture' are akin to his difficulties with 'form of life' and 'practice'. They come from ignoring the logical role of the notion.

Long after his criticisms of the so-called picture theory of meaning in the *Tractatus*, the analogy between pictures and language continued to have an importance in Wittgenstein's work (see Rhees 2004). In Part I of the *Investigations*, in different contexts, Wittgenstein opposes a magical view of signs, the view that a sign gets its meaning 'all at once', from the mark on paper, or from the sound of the word. In criticizing this view, Wittgenstein emphasizes a logical view of signs, the view that a sign gets its sense from its place in the language, from the function it performs. This distinction is important in combating a magical view of religion, for example, the view that one's sins can be washed away like dirt – dirty one minute, clean the next; or the view that salvation can be possessed 'all at once' – what Kierkegaard called the desire 'to take eternity by storm' (Kierkegaard 1956).

Yet, important though the emphasis on a logical view of signs is, Wittgenstein gives a corrective to this use of language in the last part of Part I of the *Investigations*. He makes a distinction between representational pictures, such as the crowning of Napoleon and genre pictures, such as Cézanne's *The Card Players*. He insists that *both* pictures have an analogy with language. Speaking of the latter, Wittgenstein says, 'I should like to say "What the picture tells me is itself" ' (I: 523). What he is talking about, here, is clearly not confined to religion. This is made clear in the following important paragraphs:

> There might also be a language in whose use the 'soul' of the words played no part. In which, for example, we had no objection to replacing one word by another arbitrary one of our own invention. (I: 530)

> We speak of understanding a sentence in the sense in which it can be replaced by another which says the same, but also in the sense in which it cannot be replaced by another. (Any more than one musical theme can be replaced by another.)
>
> In the one case the thought in the sentence is something common to different sentences; in the other, something that is expressed only by these words in those positions (Understanding a poem.) (I: 531)

> Then has 'understanding' two different meanings here? – I would rather say that these kinds of use of 'understanding' make up its meaning, make up my *concept* of understanding.
>
> For I *want* to apply the word 'understanding' to all this. (I: 532)

If we take this lesson to heart, 'understanding a sentence' is shown to be something different from what often passes for 'the propositional element' in language. Wittgenstein writes:

> Understanding a sentence is much more akin to understanding a theme in music than one may think. What I mean is that understanding a sentence lies nearer than one thinks to what is ordinarily called understanding a musical theme. Why is just this the pattern of variation in loudness and tempo? Once would like to say 'Because I know what it's all about.' But what is it all about? I should not be able to say. In order to 'explain' I could only compare it with something else which has the same rhythm (I mean the same pattern). (One says

'Don't you see, this is as if a conclusion were being drawn' or 'This is as it were a parenthesis', etc. How does one justify such comparisons? – There are very different kinds of justification here.) (I: 527)

It is clear that if Nielsen were to cast doubt on 'pictures which say themselves', he would be casting doubt on huge domains of discourse. Among those pictures are religious pictures. Wittgenstein refers to them in his *Lectures on Aesthetics, Psychology, and Religious Beliefs*. He refers to Michelangelo's *Creation of Adam* and says that we will never understand how God could be in the picture if we think of the work as representational. But Wittgenstein also refers to catechisms and stories that tell of God. He calls these pictures too, but contrasts them with pictures of aunts and plants. The latter's representational character depends on a technique of comparison between the pictures on the one hand, and the aunts or plants on the other. But with pictures of God, the whole weight may be in the picture. There is no point in complaining, as Nielsen does, that we are not shown that which the picture pictures, since, as Wittgenstein said, we were not taught that technique of comparison in relation to these pictures.

I do not want Nielsen to say that he understands what he does not understand. Wittgenstein, on the other hand, says, 'For I *want* to apply the word "understanding" to all this' (I: 532). It is part and parcel of his contemplative conception of philosophy. I have been trying to show how, up to 1989, Nielsen's scepticism gets in the way of *his* saying this. As we shall see in Part III, where we discuss certain religious responses to our being in the world, for Nielsen, there is simply nothing to understand.

Notes

1 Both papers were published in *The Autonomy of Religious Belief: A Critical Inquiry*. Ed. F. J. Crasson, Indiana: University of Notre Dame Press 1981. Nielsen's paper was reprinted in his *God, Scepticism, and Modernity*. Ottawa: Ottawa University Press 1989.

2 My references to Nielsen in this chapter need some explanation. Where the material referred to has been incorporated into Chapters 1 and 3 of the present work, the first page reference provided refers to those chapters. The references also indicate the original home of the material, since the dates are important in tracing the ambiguities I find in Nielsen's use of 'Wittgensteinian Fideism' up to 1989.

3 See H. O. Mounce, 'Understanding a Primitive Society', *Philosophy* vol. 48 1973. For my response see 'Wittgenstein's Full Stop' in *Wittgenstein and Religion*, Basingstoke: Macmillan 1993.

4 See 'Voices in Discussion' in *Philosophy and the Grammar of Religious Belief*, ed. Timothy Tessin and Mario von der Ruhr, Basingstoke: Macmillan and New York: St Martin's Press 1995, p. 391. Nielsen is Voice H in the discussion.

5 For my discussion of this case, see 'One Priest, Two Sermons (Albert Camus)' in *From Fantasy to Faith*, Basingstoke: Macmillan 1991.

Bibliography

Brown, Stuart C. (1972), 'Fideism, Truth, and Commensurability', Presented at the Forty-Sixth Annual Meeting of the American Philosophical Association, Pacific Division, San Francisco, 23 March 1972.

Clack, Brian R. (2001), 'Wittgenstein and Magic' in *Wittgenstein and the Philosophy of Religion*, eds Robert L. Arrington and Mark Addis. London and New York: Routledge.

Conant, James (2005), Voice B in 'Voices in Discussion' in *Religion and Wittgenstein's Legacy*, ed. D. Z. Phillips and Mario von der Ruhr. Basingstoke: Palgrave.

Holmer, Paul (1978), *The Grammar of Faith*. San Francisco: Harper and Row.

Hughes, G. E. (1962), 'Martin's *Religious Belief*', *Australasian Journal of Philosophy* 40, August.

Mounce, H. O. (1973), 'Understanding a Primitive Society', *Philosophy* 48.

Nielsen, Kai (1967), 'Wittgensteinian Fideism', *Philosophy* XLII: 161, July.

—— (1973a), 'The Coherence of Wittgensteinian Fideism', *Sophia* XI: 3. Reprinted in *God, Scepticism, and Modernity*. Ottawa: Ottawa University Press, 1989.

—— (1973b), 'Does Religious Scepticism Rest on a Mistake?' *Scepticism*. London: Macmillan.

—— (1979), 'Reasonable Belief Without Justification', *Body, Mind, and Method: Essays in Honor of Virgil C. Aldrich*, eds D. F. Gustafson and B. L. Tapscott. Boston: D. Reidel Publishing Co. Reprinted in *God, Scepticism, and Modernity*. Ottawa: Ottawa University Press, 1989.

—— (1981), 'Religion and Groundless Believing', *The Autonomy of Religious Belief*, ed. F. J. Crosson. Indiana: University of Notre Dame Press. Reprinted in *God, Scepticism, and Modernity*. Ottawa: Ottawa University Press, 1989.

—— (1982a), 'Wittgensteinian Fideism I', *Introduction to the Philosophy of Religion*. London: Macmillan.

—— (1982b), 'Wittgensteinian Fideism II', *Introduction to the Philosophy of Religion*. London: Macmillan.

—— (1989), *God, Scepticism, and Modernity*. Ottawa: Ottawa University Press.

Nietzsche, Friedrich (1984), *The Anti-Christ*. Trans. R. J. Hollingdale. London: Penguin Books.

Phillips, D. Z. (1965), *The Concept of Prayer*. London: Routledge (Oxford: Blackwell, 1981).

—— (1970a), *Death and Immortality*. London: Macmillan.

—— (1970b), *Faith and Philosophical Inquiry*. London: Routledge and Kegan Paul.

—— (1986), 'Belief, Change, and Forms of Life' in *Belief, Change, and Forms of Life*. London: Macmillan.

—— *From Fantasy to Faith*. Basingstoke: Macmillan, 1991.

—— (1993), 'Wittgenstein's Full Stop' in *Wittgenstein and Religion*. Basingstoke: Macmillan.

Rhees, Rush (1959–60), 'Wittgenstein's Builders', *Proceedings of the Aristotelian Society, 1959–60*. Reprinted in *Discussions of Wittgenstein*. London: Routledge and Kegan Paul, 1970.

—— (1997), 'Religion and Language' in Rhees, *On Religion and Philosophy*, ed. D. Z. Phillips. Cambridge: Cambridge University Press.

—— (1998), *Wittgenstein and the Possibility of Discourse*, ed. D. Z. Phillips. Cambridge: Cambridge University Press, 1998 (a second edition to be published by Blackwell).

—— (2004), *Wittgenstein's 'On Certainty': There Like Our Life*, ed. D. Z. Phillips. Oxford: Blackwell.

Tessin, Timothy and Mario von der Ruhr (eds) (1995), *Philosophy and the Grammar of Religious Belief*. New York: St Martin's Press.

Wittgenstein, Ludwig (1966), *Lectures on Aesthetics, Psychology, and Religious Belief*, ed. Cyril Barrett. Oxford: Blackwell.

—— (1984), *Culture and Value*. Oxford: Blackwell.

—— (1993), *Philosophical Occasions*, eds James Klagge and Alfred Nordmann. Cambridge and Indianapolis: Hackett Publishing Co.

6. Wittgensteinian Fideism Revisited

KAI NIELSEN

Where does our investigation get its importance from, since it seems only to destroy everything interesting, that is, all that is great and important? (As it were all the buildings leaving behind only bits of stone and rubble.) What we are destroying is nothing but houses of cards, and we are clearing up the ground of language on which they stand.   Ludwig Wittgenstein

All that philosophy can do is destroy idols. And that means not making any new ones – say, out of 'absence of idols.'   Ludwig Wittgenstein

A common-sense person, when he reads earlier philosophers, thinks – quite rightly – 'Sheer nonsense.' When he listens to me he thinks – rightly again – 'Nothing but stale truisms.' That is how the image of philosophy has changed.   Ludwig Wittgenstein

I

So what is the divide between D. Z. Phillips and myself over what I baptized as 'Wittgensteinian Fideism'? It is not just a divide; it is a chasm. For Phillips, Wittgensteinian Fideism is like a kind of disease – indeed an intellectual or, perhaps better, an ideological plague that seems not to go away though it waxes and wanes. He thought for a while it was dying out but to his dismay he finds it has returned. Now at long last it is time to resolutely extirpate it from our cultural scene, hopefully forever. Our intellectual integrity and commitment to philosophical clarity requires this extirpation. Wittgensteinian Fideism, he has it, is an unscholarly term which is used to express a confused and deeply flawed conception.[1]

I, not unsurprisingly, have a very different view of Wittgensteinian Fideism. I think that Wittgensteinian Fideism is an important conception that a philosopher or other intellectual with integrity and sharpness of intellect might well avow. Phillips seems to think that I take 'Wittgensteinian Fideism' as a term of abuse or at least of censure and that I believe it is absurd to be a Wittgensteinian fideist. But Phillips badly misunderstands me. I do indeed argue, but with a full sense of my own fallibility, that powerful as the premises and the structure of argument of this Wittgensteinian conception is, say as exemplified in Norman Malcolm's and Peter Winch's work, it leads to *conclusions* that are deeply counter-intuitive – conclusions that (or so I claim) we cannot reasonably reflectively endorse. Indeed I have even said that many of the *conclusions* we are driven to by the force of Wittgensteinian Fideism's powerful arguments – or, if you will, the cluster of considerations it puts before us – are absurd. But here, as I also avowed, we need to have a good sense of our fallibility and more generally a recognition of the need for fallibilism. I think, of course, that my arguments are sound otherwise I would give them up. But I am not unmoved by the attitude expressed in Cromwell's remark to an opponent in the British Parliament: 'Think man, in the bowels of Christ, that you may be wrong.' I have spoken, and will here again speak, of the challenge of Wittgensteinian Fideism. I take it as a formidable challenge to my own naturalism and thorough-going secularism (Nielsen 1996; 2001). Like Phillips, I have little time for the standard philosophy of religion business. It is too complacently rationalistic and stuck with either a metaphysical realism or anti-realism or the dogmatism of Reformed epistemology. I think of the philosophy of religion as the slum section of contemporary philosophy and this considered judgement of mine has nothing to do with my atheism. This at least putative state of the philosophy of religion is all the more sad-dening given the human importance of religion.

Still, our somewhat shared attitudes to 'the philosophy of religion business' notwithstanding, Phillips and I are at loggerheads. He thinks Wittgensteinian Fideism a crude and ignorant error. I think it reflects a powerful and insightful stance that can understandably, though I think mistakenly, be a road to be taken in our trying to come to grips with religion.

II

Given this chasm there is little hope that we can find any significant common ground. I would, of course, like to be proven wrong, but I doubt that is on the cards. However, I think that *some* common grounds are actually there, but given his track record on Wittgensteinian Fideism, I doubt that he can acknowledge it.

That chasm separating us notwithstanding, I did find in reading the Introduction to his *Wittgenstein and Religion* key points of agreement with him, though the devil may be in the details. I disagree, of course, with what he said about what he regards as the ill-conceived notion of Wittgensteinian Fideism; I also disagree about philosophy consisting *only* in conceptual clarification, and with his ideas (taken from Wittgenstein) that *philosophy* should leave everything as it is. These are important disagreements that I shall return to. But for now I wish to focus on the extent of our at least apparent agreement. First, of language in relation to reality, of language as corresponding to or mirroring reality (Phillips 1993, xi). Indeed, in my own view, the very idea makes no sense. We should not talk about language and reality in that way. That is to be taken down the garden path. I also agree that metaphysical realism and anti-realism take in each other's dirty linen. We should be neither metaphysical realists nor anti-realists, but, if we speak benignly of realism at all, it should be of the kind of common-sense realism of which Hilary Putnam speaks and which, in my view, is an okay realism. But it is also utterly non-metaphysical (Putnam 1999).

Phillips and I are also both in agreement with Wittgenstein 'that language does not have the unity of a formal system' (Phillips 1993, xii). We engage in different language-games for different purposes and with different rationales in the same language, but there is nothing like one big language-game that covers our diverse language-games. Language-games are diverse, but neither they nor the modes of social life in which they are embedded are Balkanized, for there are relations between them, though Phillips thinks, mistakenly I believe, that the modes of social life are *incommensurable*. (Isn't this a kind of Balkanization?) Still, though there are relations between language-games, religious uses of language are often, and importantly, distinctive, reflecting the form of life (the mode of social life) that religion is. Religion, we again agree, like science or morality, is a form of life (Phillips 1993, xiii) or a cluster of practices embedded in a form of life.[2] I further in general, though not in specifics, agree with Phillips about the concept of practice both for its importance for Wittgenstein and more generally in philosophy. I agree that we 'cannot separate concepts from practice, from what we do, because it is only in practice, in what we do, that concepts have their life and meaning' (Phillips 1993, xiii).[3] Furthermore, we agree that to understand our religious concepts, which comes to understanding our use of religious terms, we must look at what we do with them: their functions in religious life. We are also agreed – to finish off the list of agreements – that the firmness of a religious belief or a belief rejecting a religious orientation may very well be 'the firmness of a whole way of regarding the world' (Phillips 1993, xiv).

With this extensive agreement, some might ask, and surely Phillips would ask, how can Nielsen take Wittgensteinian Fideism seriously? I would respond – perhaps revealing conflicting intentions – how could one not? (There we get a glimpse of the chasm facing us.) Part of the difficulty, I argue, comes from Phillips's caricature of Wittgensteinian Fideism. I try to show some of this in Chapter 3. Phillips responds in

Chapter 4 by saying that in talking about Wittgensteinian Fideism in the text I criticized that he was not talking about me. Yet I am, for good or for ill, the creator and author of such a conception and I know of no other very extensive characterization of it. It would be like – though not in respect to its importance – saying in criticizing justice as fairness that we were not talking about Rawls or in criticizing anomalous monism that we were not criticizing Davidson. Phillips repeats his mischaracterization of Wittgensteinian Fideism in a conveniently succinct form in his *Wittgenstein and Religion*. There Phillips says of Wittgensteinian fideists that they maintain that to speak of 'distinctive language games in relation to religion . . . is to claim that only religious believers understand religious belief, that religious belief of believers cannot be criticized, that *anything called* religion determines what is meaningful and that religions cannot be overthrown by any personal or cultural event' (Phillips 1993, xii, italics mine). Phillips, as we have seen, effectively argues against all *these* claims. This is roughly, Phillips claims, how Father F. C. Copleston conceives of Wittgensteinian Fideism, though he does not call it that (Copleston 1974). But, as we have also seen, this is not how I construe Wittgensteinian Fideism and indeed I agree with Phillips that all the claims in his succinct summary of Wittgensteinian Fideism are at best false. What I do claim is that Wittgensteinian Fideism is not those false claims. What, by contrast, I *do* claim can be usefully put in the following five propositions.

Wittgenstein Fideism

1 'Within a language-game there is justification and lack of justification, evidence and proof, mistaken and groundless opinion [and the same obtains for forms of life or for what Peter Winch calls modes of social life], but one cannot properly apply these terms to the language-game [or form of life or mode of social life] itself' (Malcolm 1977b, 208).

2 Our religions, for example, Judaism, Christianity, Islam, Buddhism, Hinduism, are either themselves forms of life or (as Phillips sometimes prefers to say) *in* forms of life, each with their own distinctive clusters of language-games and practices. But how 'the language-games . . . are taken depends on their connections with other things . . . This larger context of human life, in which we see how a language-game is taken, Wittgenstein calls a form of life' (Phillips 1986, 28).

3 Beliefs, utterances, conceptions, concepts 'are only intelligible in the context of ways of living or modes of social life as such' – that is in the contexts of forms of life or of being in forms of life (Winch 1995, 100–01).

4 Science is one such mode, morality another and religion still another

or they are each distinctive clusters of practices in a form of life. [See notes 2 and 3.] 'Each has criteria of intelligibility peculiar to itself . . . within science or religion actions can be logical or illogical', rational or irrational, reasonable or unreasonable, justified or un-justified, worthy of acceptance or not worthy of acceptance. 'But we cannot sensibly say that either the practice of science itself or that of religion is either illogical or logical; both are non-logical' (Winch 1995, 100–01).

5 Because of the above (1–4), it makes no sense, Wittgenstein has it, to try to justify modes of social life or forms of life or distinctive clusters of practices, for example, science or religion, as such. We cannot, for example, show or rationally establish that religion is rational or irrational, justified or lacking in justification, reasonable or unreasonable, worthy of acceptance or not. As modes of social life they are a cluster of practices that are just there like our lives. They either mean something to us (have significance for us) or fail to mean something to us. There is no bringing these clusters of practices constituting a mode of social life before 'the bar of reason' or to test them for reasonability; there are no canons of justification or vindication or rationality, such that we could intelligibly (sen-sibly, coherently) say that it is true or, for that matter, false that religion as such a mode of social life is an illusion or rests on a myth or merely has symbolic significance or is just a human projection. (No error theory of religion is possible.)[4] Christianity, Hinduism, Islam are a cluster of practices with their embedded language-games forming a mode of social life. They are just there like our lives and they either mean something to us (have some importance for us) or they do not, though for them to be either we must have at least a minimal understanding of the use of religious terms or sentences. But there is no showing that they *must* or even should mean some-thing to us – have some significance for us or value to us – if we are to be reasonable, not self-deceived or in bad faith. There is neither a showing nor establishing that religious beliefs must be taken to be true nor that they must be taken to be false. Neither is there, on the one hand, a showing or establishing that they must be, or even are, worthy of belief nor that, on the other hand, they are to be set aside, if we are to be non-evasive, as not being worthy of belief. Justification cannot, given what justification is, have such a reach, such a purchase.

Of such a conception Anthony Kenny says, 'Unfortunately Wittgen-stein's influence on the philosophy of religion has been disastrous' (Kenny 1975, 145). Taking as central the concept of language-game, and he could well have added the concept of forms of life, has, in his view, led us down the garden path in thinking about religion. Kenny, who certainly is no stranger to Wittgenstein's work, claims that 'the concept of language-game is an obscure and ambiguous one in Wittgenstein's writings: *in the hands of some of his religious admirers it has become a stonewall defence against any demand for a justification of belief in God*' (Kenny 1975, 145). And, I would add, if this is true of the concept of language-game, it is doubly true of the concept of form of life. Kenny adds, following Father F. C. Copleston, that one disadvantage of this is that 'any fruitful dialogue between religious belief and critical philosophy is excluded' (Kenny 1975, 146 quoting from Copleston's *Religion and Philosophy*, 1974).

Phillips, hardly surprisingly, will have none of this. I will comment on this later but I want now to turn to what I take to be the fundamental challenge of Wittgensteinian Fideism.

The Challenge of Wittgensteinian Fideism

In characterizing Wittgensteinian Fideism I did not raise the issue of externalism/internalism. Like Phillips, I think they feed off each other's deficiencies. I certainly do not regard myself as an externalist or, for that matter, an internalist either and I did not think of Wittgensteinian fideists as internalists ignoring external criteria, believing that 'what is and is not meaningful in religion must be determined by criteria *solely* determined by the religion in question' (Phillips 1986, 81, italics mine). Religious beliefs like all beliefs, or at least all non-technical beliefs, are 'interwoven with the surrounding features of human life' (Phillips 1986, 79). What I did assert, following Winch, is that all modes of social life, including religion, have criteria distinctive of them – though that does not mean that criteria come *solely* from them – and that if we ignore that distinctiveness we will misunderstand them and if we try to reduce or interpret religious belief without reference to these distinctive criteria, failing to take them as centrally determinative of what the particular mode of social life is, we will misunderstand our religious conceptions and in philosophically discussing them distort them, practise bad philosophy and fail to understand religion. This, I claimed, is a crucial thesis of Wittgensteinian Fideism as is the further thesis, also articulated by Winch, that these modes of social life cannot themselves be justified or shown to be unjustified or shown to be reasonable or unreasonable, but are themselves the crucial measure of what is justified or unjustified, reasonable or unreasonable for the mode of social life in question. There is no higher mode-of-social-life-neutral standard of reasonability or rationality that we can appeal to. Such a notion of a 'super-reasonability' or 'super-rationality' does not even make sense. We must acquire within our mode of social life, using its criteria, whatever sense of rationality or reasonability we have. Religion is one mode of social life and thus has its own distinctive criteria. This is not to say that other matters coming from practices in a different mode of social life cannot, and relevantly, effect religious belief and life. But it is to say that the practices that constitute the religious mode of social life are the most decisive thing – indeed the indispensable thing – concerning what can be *coherently* said, what is justified and what could count as a truth-claim in religious life or, if you will, the cluster of practices that are constitutive of it.[5] Of course all sorts of things could *cause* the demise of religion (or any mode of social life) – the cooling of the earth for example – but it would remain the case that what (if anything) establishes truth and falsity, justifiability and unjustifiability, reasonability or unreasonability in religion, as everywhere else, is principally set by the mode of social life in question. There can, of course, be criticism of religion and Phillips engages in it, but it comes, if Wittgensteinian Fideism is on the mark, to showing that *some religious* responses are superstitious and thus defective as religious responses or are metaphysical claims and are thus defective or clash in a way a more adequate religious response would not, with science or reflective morality, or are not themselves in accordance with criteria set by the distinctive mode of social life that religion is or, again if you will, *in* which religious life obtains. And it could also be a showing that some purely secular criticisms of religion are irrelevant. But what cannot be done, on a Wittgensteinian fideist view, is relevantly to criticize belief in God (where 'God' is properly conceived) or belief in his providential care of his creatures. What can be criticized, and is criticized from a religious point of view, are certain images of God or certain superstitious or anthropomorphic conceptions of God, but there is, Wittgensteinian Fideism has it, no intelligible way of saying that the very idea of God is incoherent or that belief in God rests on an illusion or that 'God exists' is false. This is a key notion of Wittgensteinian Fideism. It is accepted by Winch, Malcolm and (though less clearly) by Phillips. It is not an absurd, unscholarly notion and provides, if accepted, a challenge for someone who thinks, as I do, that we in our circumstances should be secularists all the way down and, as well, for what Phillips calls religious rationalists and non-religious rationalists. But Wittgensteinian Fideism does *shelter* religion; it makes, if correct, religious beliefs – the very core of religious beliefs – what Malcolm, following Wittgenstein, calls its framework beliefs – invulnerable to relevant critique and thus, looking at things normatively, to critique. Anthony Kenny very well calls it, as we have seen, *a stonewalling of religious belief from criticism*. It seeks to shelter belief in God, belief in his goodness and infinite love from refutation, from fundamental criticism and even from fundamental doubt. Belief in God and immortality (properly understood) is taken to be immune from critique. We can and often should reinterpret these ideas, but there is no way they can be shown or established to be either false or incoherent. This, or something very like it, is what fideism, of any kind, has always tried to do and this is what those I have called Wittgensteinian fideists (wittingly or unwittingly) have done, though with some important new twists. There is, for example, no longer talk of religious belief being a scandal to the intellect or talk of the necessity of believing what is intellectually absurd. Belief in God is not 'grounded in reason' but it is not taken by Wittgenstenian fideists as a stark existential choice for a knight of faith, or as something which cognitively speaking is absurd. Wittgensteinian Fideism, unlike much classical fideism, does not engage in such dramatics.

The question is, from my point of view, though not from Phillips's, is this a path we should take? Vis-à-vis religion, we are not or at least should not be – or so I argue – like Anselm, concerned – and indeed philosophically concerned, *except as a first step* – principally to understand what we really believe, but to ascertain, if we can, whether there is anything there truly worthy of belief, whether in Paul Tillich's often quoted phrase there is anything of intimate and ultimate concern, captured by religion, that in our time what Freud called a soberly educated person who is non-evasive could reflectively endorse. Perhaps in the Middle Ages or the sixteenth or seventeenth centuries an Anselmian way was the way to go, but for us, situated as we are and have been situated for a long time, it is not. Many people, some with considerable anguish, want to ascertain, if they can, what they should believe vis-à-vis religion and how they should try to live their lives. These are things they very much care about and want to get a handle on if they can. They, for example, may be pulled both in a Christian and in an atheist direction. Or it may well be instead the case that neither the Christian nor any other religious orientation nor secular alternatives grip them, or perhaps both religious and non-religious orientations grip them at the same time, though, both ambivalently, grip them or that what grips them is an atheism or Christianity of a *crude* kind, but with a coming to sense that it is crude, they try to ascertain, feeling such matters to be an important *life string* for them, if there are any coherent forms of Judaism, Christianity or Islam, on the one hand, or atheism, on the other, that are not crude (Nielsen 1962). They want reflectively to *think and feel* these matters through. But Wittgensteinian Fideism seems to block this at least on the *thinking* side and it seems to have powerful reasons for doing so. Should we reflectively endorse it? Is it, if we would be non-evasive, the way, everything considered, we ought to go? But Wittgensteinian Fideism also tells us that this is a senseless question. The very asking of such 'a question' – really 'a cluster of questions' – Wittgensteinian Fideism tells us shows that in such 'questioning' we do not know where to stop and we end up asking senseless questions. We are in reality like children who ask a question once too often. We are, as happens when things go metaphysical, asking senseless questions.

I should say here, *pace* what Phillips seems to think I think and feel, that I am not looking for the false comfort of a rationalism, religious or otherwise, including an updated version of Holbachian atheism.

I had hoped we would debate Wittgensteinian Fideism and particularly what I have called its challenge. I think, and have argued in detail, that Wittgensteinian Fideism is, notwithstanding that it is challenging, flawed, indeed very deeply flawed. I would have liked to have debated (reflectively discussed) that with Phillips and to consider what sort of challenge, if any, Wittgensteinian Fideism makes and how, if it succeeds in making a challenge, as at least taken at face value it does, it should be responded to. But that was not to be, for Phillips is largely preoccupied with who said what first and when and how their views changed. This seems to me, for the most part, a fruitless enterprise. I agree that if I had read the Phillips of 1986 I would have seen that his later views were not as compartmentalized as his earlier views, though given his views on incommensurability, I wonder how deep this change is. But that would have changed very little. The Wittgensteinian Challenge I have characterized above would still remain intact. On the other side, Phillips, if he had read me carefully or with even a minimal amount of charity, would have seen that I am not claiming for Wittgensteinian Fideism the thesis that 'only religious believers understand religious belief' or that '*anything called religion* determines what is meaningful' (Phillips 1993, xii). I would claim of Wittgensteinian Fideism that it holds that no personal or cultural event could *justifiably* or even *relevantly overthrow* religious belief, but *causally* speaking – and that is (or at least so it seems) what Phillips has in mind – of course it can (Phillips 1993, xii). Wittgensteinian Fideism is not a bit of the sociology of religion. I do not think, even at my worst, I ever said or implied anything like these Phillipsian theses he takes to be expressing Wittgensteinian Fideism. But if someone comes up with a passage in which I said, implied or presupposed any of these things, I would, admitting that they were lapses at least in draftsmanship and perhaps in thought as well, and, contending that they are not a part of the core claims of Wittgensteinian Fideism, disavow them. I do not pretend to be a historian of my own ideas. *Perhaps* once I did say and even thought something that ridiculous. What generally should be said is that if we are not intellectually dead our views will change over the years and we will upon occasion correct ourselves or just, without recognizing it, develop ideas that do not perfectly fit, or perhaps are even incompatible with, some of our earlier views. We hope our ideas will *develop*, but develop or not, they change. Someone would have to be very dogmatic or unreflective to not believe this to be so.

What I wrote in 1967 concerning Wittgensteinian Fideism I would now put somewhat differently, though I still think 'Wittgensteinian Fideism' was essentially right. But even what I wrote in 2001, which is my most developed and nuanced articulation of Wittgensteinian Fideism, I would not now put exactly as I did then. Donald Davidson's type of holism has taken a greater hold on me, but the crucial thing is not the exact articulation and critique of such an articulation. We should try to get a clear articulation that can be seen to have a point. But in such domains we will never get 'complete clarity'. Indeed I do not think we know, outside of formal matters, and perhaps not even there, what that looks like. I take this as a lesson I learned from Wittgenstein. What we should do, for starters, is get as clear as we reasonably can about something like Wittgensteinian Fideism or in other contexts for other purposes anomalous monism or justice as fairness and for Wittgensteinian Fideism its at least putative import and challenge (if any) and thus, coming to grips with such notions, look *ambulando* for what clarifications and modifications (if any) are needed or whether Wittgensteinian Fideism should be outright rejected. We should take Amartya Sen's advice and stop waiting for Toto. But Phillips does not do that. He sets up a straw Wittgensteinian Fideism and a straw Nielsen and then proceeds to beat on them.

III

I now turn to some of the specific criticisms of me made by Phillips in Chapter 5 and, more briefly, though somewhat distinctly, in Chapter 4. However, before I launch into an examination of his texts there are two things I want to say.

First, unless I am so ideologically blocked that I can't see what there is before me – something that can happen to anyone – much of the time Phillips gives a caricature of what I say, constructing straw Nielsens all over the place and then knocking them down. But this is not always true. There are places where Phillips's criticisms are to the point or at least more to the point. There are places where he refers politely to some things as having tensions, but these things may be worse than that. They may be outright inconsistencies. There are also places he points to where I have given a less than charitable reading of what I call Wittgensteinian claims – claims I take to be a part of Wittgensteinian Fideism – and that there are other perhaps better readings, which may free them from some of my claimed traps. In these places Phillips is not caricaturing me and I must, to be non-evasive, in one way or another answer to them. This I will endeavour to do in Section IV.

My second point is that there are two questions that need to be distinguished and held apart, which Phillips mixes together: (a) What, if anything coherent, is Wittgensteinian Fideism and is it really rooted in Wittgenstein or in any of the Wittgensteinians I have called Wittgensteinian fideists, or is it simply a creature, as Phillips thinks it is, of my own construction? and (b) Granted, at least for the sake of the discussion, that there is something identifiable and plausible called Wittgensteinian Fideism, are my criticisms of it, or at least some of them, well taken?

We have two issues here. (1) My characterization of Wittgensteinian Fideism could be on the mark and my criticism of it unsound. (2) My characterization of Wittgensteinian Fideism could be a caricature of what Wittgenstein and Wittgensteinians are about and my criticism of *that scapegoat conception* sound. I had hoped, as I remarked earlier, probably very unrealistically, that we could have agreed at least roughly on the creature – on what Wittgensteinian Fideism is – and then have gone on to consider criticisms with the aim of trying to ascertain whether Wittgensteinian Fideism should in some form be endorsed. But we seem, from my point of view unfortunately, for the purposes of our discussions here, to be stuck with the prior question. This is a pity for it seems to me that with Wittgensteinian Fideism we have a powerful, perhaps (*pace* me) even an, all things considered, compelling conception, which all the same, or so I shall argue, leads to what seems to me to be absurd conclusions (Nielsen 2001, 317–404). I would have liked to have been able to try to argue out whether this is so, and importantly whether the 'seems' is really an 'are' here, but alas that was not to be. Here there is little communication between me and Phillips.

To return to the centre of this section's concern – I shall first attend to what I believe to be Phillips's caricatures of my views. (Some are worse than others.) I won't attend to all of them for they are too numerous, but I will attend to what I hope is a fair and important sampling.

1. Consider what Phillips says about me and scepticism (Chapter 5, pp. 88–92). He takes it that I am referring to *epistemological* scepticism and am caught up in the grand Appearance/Reality distinction. But I was concerned in 'Wittgensteinian Fideism' and in my book *Scepticism* (Nielsen 1973) with a *religious* scepticism that did not rely on epistemological scepticism and I did not root my arguments in presuppositions about epistemological scepticism. There are plenty of sturdy metaphysical realists (J. J. C. Smart and David Armstrong, for example) who are also atheists. Moreover, like Wittgenstein and like Richard Rorty, I regard the metaphysical tradition from Plato to F. H. Bradley, making some grand, non-contextualist distinctions between Reality and Appearance, as nonsense up for therapeutic dissolution. Moreover, I never said nor implied, as Phillips claims, that language-games or forms of life are *appearances*. I don't even know what this means and I do not think that anyone else does either.[6]

2. Phillips accuses me of essentialism and of holding an 'essentialist thesis about the incoherence of religion' (Chapter 5, p. 76). In a later passage in Chapter 5 he speaks of something he mischaracterizes as my *essentialist* scepticism, claiming that I think I have 'grasped "the essence" of religion and ... exposed its *inherent* incoherence' (p. 88). It is, he says, essentialist scepticism that I hanker after. This mischaracterization surprises me for, like Wittgenstein and Rorty and a host of others, I have long held there are no essences or rather that such essence-talk is at best un-useful and at worse (and more likely) incoherent. His evidence for my essentialism is a quotation taken from 'Wittgensteinian Fideism II' where I say 'It will forever remain impossible to show that the believer's religious discourse and therefore his religious form of life and faith is *intrinsically* incoherent or unintelligible' (Nielsen 1982, 134). In using 'intrinsically', which Phillips later transforms, forgetting Georg von Wright's *The Varieties of Goodness*, into 'inherently', he assumes I am committed to essentialism, to the thesis that 'religious belief is inherently incoherent, that is not countered by Wittgenstein by the counter thesis that it is inherently coherent. We have to see how the language-game is played, what our practices are.' Exactly. And that is what I do and doing that, it seems to me, we have reason to believe that developed God-talk is incoherent. I make no claim to its being *inherently* incoherent. What I did say by using 'intrinsically' in the sentence Phillips quotes is misleading. And, if I were writing that sentence again, I would delete 'intrinsically'. But the whole context of my discussion of Wittgenstein makes it plain that I am not arguing for essentialism. Here Phillips is being uncharitable, making problems where there aren't any. While I am not concerned to argue that religious belief is intrinsically or inherently incoherent, I do give argument aiming to show that religious beliefs, and particularly belief in the God of Christianity, Judaism and Islam, as it has come to be standardly conceived, *turns out to be incoherent* and that careful examination of religious discourse shows that. Of course belief in a Zeus-like God or Wotan-like God – a thoroughly anthropomorphic God – is not incoherent. It is just plainly false, little more than a superstition and Braithwaite's and Hare's conception of God is a conception that is not substantively different from an atheist's rejection of God (Nielsen 1989, 172–89). But the concept of God in *developed* theisms is, I argue, incoherent (Nielsen 2001). But (*pace* Phillips) I make no claim that this is an a priori truth or that the concept of God is *inherently* incoherent.

3. When I start to refer to Phillips, Malcolm, Winch and Hughes as philosophers 'whom I have called – perhaps *tendentiously* – Wittgensteinian Fideists' rather than calling them, as I did in my 'Wittgensteinian Fideism', straight out Wittgensteinian Fideists, I was not in the least backtracking on what I had previously claimed. I was merely giving my readers to understand that my claim here had been contested. This (*pace*

Phillips) is not to indicate, or even suggest, any ambivalence on my part. It is just to acknowledge that my views had been contested and my fallibilism.

4. In characterizing Wittgensteinian Fideism as I did, I was claiming that Wittgensteinian Fideism had it that in our various modes of social life, to use Winch's way of putting things, the cluster of practices that religion, morality and science have or are (depending on how it is read), each has its own distinctive criteria of coherence. In making this claim there is a rejection of the claim that there is or that we can construct some ubiquitous super-criteria yielding some Archimedean point with which to assess our modes of social life or forms of life. But (*pace* Phillips) it was not at all a part of my brief in characterizing Wittgensteinian Fideism to say that these domains 'have nothing to do with each other' (Chapter 5, p. 85). The point was rather that each has distinctive criteria of significance (coherence, intelligibility) of their own and that it is a mistake, according to Wittgensteinian Fideism, to criticize religion or morality or science using criteria of any *other* of them, for example, we must not use the distinctive criteria of science to criticize the criteria of religion or vice versa. It, that is, is a mistake, Wittgensteinian fideists claim, to use the distinctive criteria of any *other* mode of social life to challenge the criteria of significance of any one mode of social life. This was what was meant by saying these distinctive criteria of social life are *sui generis* and this was what was meant by speaking of the *autonomy* of modes of social life or of forms of life. Does Phillips not, like Winch and Malcolm, accept that? And if he does, isn't it fair to characterize him as a Wittgensteinian fideist?

5. Phillips rightly sees that the idea of a form of life is a central notion in Wittgenstein's philosophy and not only for thinking about religion; yet it is also an obscure and illusive notion. But it is not so vague that it cannot point to a 'larger context of human life, in which we see how a language game is taken . . .'. This 'larger context of human life' is, Phillips tells us, what Wittgenstein calls 'a form of life' (Phillips 1986, 28). This is suggestive but still leaves us too much in the dark, for if we are puzzled about 'form of life' we are going to be very nearly equally puzzled about 'larger context of human life'. Yet it is hard to deny, and I would not deny, that there is something there. Phillips interestingly suggests how Rush Rhees, building on Wittgenstein and particularly in a way that makes it plain how we can come to see – going against any hint of compartmentalization – shows how language-games hang together and only are intelligible as part of a larger context of human life, that is of forms of life. (Here, though I do not know if it squares with Rhees's intentions, we see the beginnings of a *holism* that I would welcome.) Rhees is arguing against Wittgenstein that the analogy between language and games is not as tight or as useful as Wittgenstein takes it to be. 'All

games,' Phillips paraphrases Rhees as saying, 'do not make up one big game, all language-games occur in the *same* language' (Chapter 5, p. 86).[7] In *Philosophical Investigations*, Wittgenstein, reacting against his own earlier view of the calculus-like unity of language, went 'to the other extreme of holding that each language-game is "complete"' (Chapter 5, p. 86). What is important is not that stress, but Wittgenstein's conception that to imagine a language is to imagine a form of life and to see language-games and practices as being in a form of life. Phillips stresses, following Rhees, that it is crucial to see that discourse, unlike games, is not made up of 'logically distinct' domains 'which have nothing to do with each other' (Chapter 5, p. 85). Here Rhees and I are one and Phillips, dropping his earlier comparimentalized view, has come along. This idea fits well with Wittgenstein's perceptive slogan 'To imagine a language is to imagine a form of life' and, given the role that practices play in our use of language – our doing things with words – it also fits well with Rhees's repeated slogan 'Language makes sense if living makes sense.' Remembering Wittgenstein's builders, the point is that the utterance 'Slab' is only understood in the course of our living lives. Expounding Rhees, Phillips well says that it is in the course of lived lives that giving and receiving an order is intelligible.

> The order comes in the course of a day's work, work which itself has a place in people's lives; work to which people bring much that is not that work, and work which can be discussed, or reacted to, when it is over; work which stands in various relations to other aspects of life, a life which is part of a wider culture with its humour, art, music, social movements and so on. (see Chapter 5, p. 86)

Here Phillips well conveys the force of Wittgenstein's slogan to imagine a language is to imagine a form of life and Rhees's slogan language makes sense if living makes sense. We also catch on a little better to what we are talking about in speaking of forms of life or modes of social living. And we can also see the force of Rhees's 'correction' of Wittgenstein that it would be better 'to start from the notion of a conversation, than from the notion of a game', though it should not be forgotten that game: *language*-game (*sprachspiel*) brings out the essential link with action, with doing, in a way conversation does not. The latter makes the whole matter of using language sound too cerebral, but stress on language-games occludes too much the give and take of discussion and of deliberation. Even when one deliberates solitaire with one's imagined interlocutors, one gets what is in effect a conversation. It is never a one-man show. Wittgenstein and Rhees complement each other. Both accounts, without that complement, are one-sided. But Rhees's view is also both a criticism and an extension of Wittgenstein's. It could perhaps form a basis for a criticism of my own criticism of Wittgensteinian Fideism, but it would not show that my account of what I call Wittgensteinian Fideism was mistaken or un-Wittgensteinian or that my criticisms of *that* view were mistaken. It would, however, if Rhees's modifications are on the mark, provide a way out of some of the ills I have claimed Wittgensteinian Fideism is heir to.

Be that as it may, I claimed in characterizing Wittgensteinian Fideism that Wittgensteinian fideists asserted that our various modes of social life, the cluster of practices that religion, morality and science have or are, each has their own distinctive criteria of coherence. I further argued that Wittgensteinian fideists claim that there is no coherent making of the claim that there is or that we can construct some ubiquitous super-criterion or super-criteria – some Archimedean point – to assess our modes of social life or forms of life. No such skyhook is available or even coherently conceivable. But (*pace* Phillips) it was not at all a part of my characterization of Wittgensteinian fideists to say that they were claiming or assuming that these domains 'have nothing to do with each other' (Chapter 5, p. 86). That would be a silly view. The point was rather that each mode of social life has distinctive criteria of significance and that it was a mistake to criticize or try to assess religion or morality or science – the modes of discourse that they are – by using the criteria of one (say, morality) to criticize the very cluster of practices that constitute another mode of social life (say, science) or vice versa or to use the very cluster of practices that constitute science to evaluate the domain of discourse that constitutes religion. We cannot legitimately use one such domain (mode) of discourse to criticize another domain; we cannot legitimately use one mode of social life to challenge the criteria of significance of another. This was what was meant by speaking of the *autonomy* of modes of social life or of forms of life. Does Phillips not, like Winch and Malcolm, accept that? Does his reading of Rhees change that in any substantial way? And if he does accept such a characterization, isn't it fair to characterize him as a Wittgensteinian fideist?

6. Phillips in Chapter 4 claims my 1967 views conflict with my 2001 views. He points out that in 2001 I say that Wittgensteinian Fideism, neither as a matter of philosophy nor as a matter of life orientation, is 'a silly or shallow view or even an ideological one or a way of seeing things that no knowledgeable reflective human being, living here and now, could reasonably embrace' (Nielsen 2001, 16). But this, Phillips tells us, conflicts with what I said in 1967 when I said things like '*it seems* to me that the fideistic *conclusions* drawn by these philosophers [Wittgensteinian fideists] are absurd' or when I speak of such philosophers 'accepting beliefs which I find unintelligible' (Nielsen 1967, 202) or when I *think* that 'the very first-order discourse of . . . [the religious] form of discourse is incoherent or irrational' (p. 66). But Phillips doesn't get it.

In making remarks like that, I am attempting to make *reductio* arguments *against* Wittgensteinian fideists. Their arguments, I am saying, persuasive as they otherwise seem to me, seem at least to lead to absurd *conclusions*. And, if this is so, should not this lead to the rejection of Wittgensteinian Fideism? I am perfectly aware that they might reasonably respond either (or both) that *properly understood* (interpreted) the conclusions are arguably not absurd or that the putatively absurd conclusions actually do not follow from the premises. This is particularly pressing for me for some of the premises and the reasoning about and from the premises of Wittgensteinian Fideism, *seem* compelling to me or at least they seem strong candidates for being that. I back away from Wittgensteinian Fideism when I note its conclusions and on reflection take them to be genuine conclusions. I back away notwithstanding the persuasiveness of Wittgensteinian Fideism's premises and reasoning from those premises. But I should, if I am to be thoroughly non-evasive, ask myself if they really follow from the premises or whether the conclusions, supposing they do follow, are really as absurd as I take them to be. I signal this in the sentences Phillips quotes by such locutions as 'it seems to me'. D. Z. Phillips should have asked himself why I, perhaps even obsessively, write about him, Malcolm and Winch and not about Christian Science or fundamentalism or even not very much about Alvin Plantinga. Does he think I think the views of Malcolm et al. are stupid, utterly uninformed or *parti pris*? If I did I would ignore them as I ignore Christian Science or fundamentalisms – Christian, Jewish or Islamic. This was perfectly evident in 1967 as it was in 2001 when I wrote *Naturalism and Religion*. Anthony Kenny, in discussing me, clearly saw and acknowledged it (Kenny 2002). I sense in Wittgensteinian Fideism a real challenge I do not feel in Christian Science, fundamentalism, Thomism or even (rightly or wrongly) in views like Plantinga's or Swinburne's.

7. Phillips says I take practices in a *sociological* sense as simply referring 'to whatever happens, habits of ordinary life, including religious habits'. Taken in that way practices 'may be shot through with countless confusions ... [and] it is no part of Wittgenstein's account to say that ordinary habits can't be criticized' (Chapter 4, p. 67). But, he goes on to say, 'practice' for Wittgenstein has a *grammatical* use which is distinct from its sociological use. The grammatical use refers to a 'conceptually distinctive form of discourse'. But even it, Wittgenstein has it according to Phillips, is something which can be criticized. What can't be done, Phillips claims, is intelligibly to say of a practice, in this grammatical sense, that it is *confused*. But I do not see why not. We seem at least to have more arbitrary stipulation again.

'Practice', like 'language-game', 'form of life' and 'agreement in judgement', is a key concept for Wittgenstein, but all of these notions are poorly defined and characterized and they have been interpreted in various ways. They have, for some at least, including me, a powerful intuitive appeal, but not a few philosophers have been so frustrated by their illusiveness and ambiguity that they have abandoned philosophizing in Wittgensteinian terms. I am not one of those, but I certainly wish they were more carefully characterized. I regard Wittgenstein as a conceptual therapeutic philosopher and as not providing or wishing to provide a *theory*. But, all the same, we could do with a little more clarity here. I think Wittgenstein would counter that these conceptions are clear enough for his purposes. After all, he is not in the business of theory construction or tracking concept formation. He wants rather to take the fly out of the dusty fly bottle. And, we should not forget, there is no absolute context-independent criterion or criteria of clarity. It is always clarity relative to a certain purpose or aim.

Practices, as we have noted, for Wittgenstein are a conceptually distinctive form of discourse and a doing things with words. Or we could put it the other way around: distinctive forms of discourse are always conceptually distinctive practices or clusters of practices. Practices can't be identified with language-games though language-games are embedded in practices as practices are embedded in forms of life. Kjell Johannessen usefully points out that:

the concept of practice not only points to the ways in which the unity of our concepts are underpinned ... it also comprises the skills involved in *handling* the conceptualized phenomena, our prereflective familiarity with them, expressed in the *sureness* in our behaviour towards them, and the *judgemental* power in applying and withholding a given concept on a particular occasion. (Johannessen 1989, 357)

Practices are what we go by when we seek to understand concepts and other rule-governed notions. Following a rule is what Wittgenstein calls a practice. *But practices are what makes it possible to apply a rule without support of another rule.* The concept of practice is primarily concerned with the *activity* aspect of the use of 'practice'. *Practice for Wittgenstein gives words their meaning.* Wittgenstein remarks in *On Certainty* that 'there is always the danger of wanting to find an expression's meaning by contemplating the expression itself ... instead of always thinking of the practice' (Wittgenstein 1969, para. 601). Practice is rule following, but in establishing a practice not 'only rules, but also examples are needed ... Our rules leave loopholes open, and the practice has to speak for itself' (Wittgenstein 1969, para. 139). It is not going to have or need a foundation. Put otherwise, the practice has to look after itself. Johannessen remarks, taking it that he is expressing a central aspect of Wittgenstein's later views, '[t]he really important things in the life of human beings are not expressible in words; they take the form of deeds'.[8] That is also the reason why Wittgenstein quotes Goethe's *Faust* with such confidence: '*Im Anfang war die tat*' (Wittgenstein 1969, 402). In the beginning it was not the word but the deed. Language is an activity in which we are doing things with words for a plethora of purposes. We have language-games embedded in practices and in turn practices embedded in forms of life. There is no coherent possibility of standing outside of all of them and viewing the world independently of practices and forms of life. But that doesn't mean that, repairing the ship at sea, we cannot at least in a piecemeal way correct them, rejecting certain parts of them and showing them to be in certain ways confused. Nor is there any good reason to think language-games, practices or forms of life are *complete*. Indeed it is very unclear what it could even mean in this context to speak of their being 'complete'. There are all kinds of *lebensraum* for criticizing practices.

8. There is a surfeit of confusion in Phillips's remarks about what I say about truth-claims vis-à-vis religion. This shows itself in the use Phillips makes of parallels between Wittgenstein and Nietzsche. Phillips first quotes Wittgenstein:

Christianity is not a doctrine, not, I mean, a theory about what has happened and will happen to the human soul, but a description of something that actually takes place in human life ... I believe that one of the things Christianity says is that sound doctrines are all useless. They have to change your *life* (or the *direction* of your life). (Wittgenstein 1980, 28, 53, quoted by Phillips Chapter 5, p. 89)

Phillips then quotes Nietzsche:

It is false to the point of absurdity to see in a 'belief', perchance the belief in a redemption through Christ, the distinguishing characteristic of the Christian: only Christian *practice*, a life such as he who died on the cross *lived*, is Christian. *Not* a belief but a doing, above all, a *not*-doing of many things, a different *being* ... States of consciousness, *beliefs of any kind*, holding something to be true for example ... are *a matter of complete indifference* ... To *reduce* being a Christian, Christianness, *to a holding something to be true, to a mere phenomenality* of consciousness, means to negate Christianness. (Nietzsche 1990, 163, italics after 'being' are mine)

There are enough difficulties in the passage from Wittgenstein but they are compounded in the passage from Nietzsche. They are, of course, both right in saying Christianity necessarily and centrally involves a doing, a way of orienting and changing your life. But it is not *only* that; it, and equally, is a cluster of beliefs about how things are, can be and will come to be. Both *belief* and action – a changing of your life and a *certain* orienting of it – are essential.[9] Indeed you would not know how to orient your life if you did not have some beliefs – perhaps rather inchoate beliefs – about what you are like and might perhaps come to be, about what the world you live in is like and might come to be. And your religion (if you have one) could not direct your actions unless you know what at least your religion says and what it requires of you. All of these things inescapably involve beliefs.

Perhaps Phillips would follow Norman Malcolm and say, in an attempt to avoid the objection just voiced, that all religious beliefs are beliefs *in* not beliefs *that*. They are trustings or some other affective states and not conceivings that so and so. In the last section of my 1982 expanded version of 'Wittgensteinian Fideism' I argued, against Malcolm, carefully and I think conclusively, that, except for ideals, there can be no believing *in* without believing *that*. (And, after all, God is not *just* an ideal.) I cannot believe in Mandela unless I believe that he exists or at least once existed. Similarly I cannot believe *in* God without believing *that* he exists (Nielsen 1982, 92–7).[10]

Nietzsche and Wittgenstein are right in believing that Christianity is not a theory or a theoretical system. It is rather a way of life: a way of being and doing, a cluster of very ultimate commitments concerning how we should order our lives and relate to others. In that way it is like a morality. But it is a morality *plus* for it is also true that there are *no doctrineless* religions. Christianity is not a doctrine in the sense that it is a theory, but it has a number of doctrines that must be subscribed to or what we have would not be Christianity. And they are not just about subscribing to a certain moral orientation. These doctrines get variously interpreted, but they remain beliefs (believings in *and* believings that) that inform our various believings and doings. Christianity does not say (*pace* Wittgenstein) that sound doctrines are all useless. What it does say is that if they are not taken up and made a part of your life, a central element in your very way of being, they are useless. But without *accepting* certain doctrines you would not be a Christian and without *understanding* these doctrines you would not know as a Christian what to try to do and be. You would not know how to orient your life. And similar things would obtain for any religious person, Christian or otherwise. Religion *can't* just be a way of acting and being.

Nietzsche makes the same mistakes as Wittgenstein. But in addition he is mistaken in thinking that a belief in redemption through Christ or any kind of Christian belief is a matter of complete indifference, because these beliefs are *mere states of consciousness*, 'a mere phenomenality of consciousness'. Nietzsche's remarks here are completely off the mark. Holding something to be true is not a mere state of consciousness: it is not a mere phenomenality of consciousness. Belief in a redemption through Christ, for example, is not a mere state of consciousness. If I believe that but you do not and I suppose you are wondering if, after all, my belief is true, I do not think you are trying to ascertain the state of my consciousness, but what it is that I believe and my grounds for believing it. You are interested in my reasons for my belief. You would be interested in the state of my consciousness only if you either thought I was lying or if you were carrying out a psychological investigation of my belief states.

Neither *belief* in a redemption through Christ nor the Christian *practice* of living such as he who died on the cross lived is *the* distinguishing characteristic of Christians or, if you will, 'the Christian', whatever that is. There is no such thing as *the* distinguishing mark of Christians or of the Christian or perhaps even such a thing as '*the* Christian', though there are Christians and no doubt fewer of them are genuinely Christians than is usually thought. Both belief in a redemption through Christ and the Christian practice, the living of life such as he who died on the cross, are genuine markers of being a Christian. The latter austere one appeals strongly – and rightly so – to our religious sense, but it is also so demanding that there would, as Kierkegaard quipped, be no Christians in Christian Denmark, indeed there would be none – or at least very few – anywhere in the world. Perhaps Nietzsche, and Kierkegaard as well, would bite that bullet. But that marker is not only too austere, it is too harsh to be right. There are, of course, lots of 'fair weather Christians' – no doubt George Bush and Bill Clinton, for example – but there are plenty of humble and sincere Christians, people who try and largely succeed in living a Christian life, who are certainly not living a life such as he who died on the cross.

However, the most crucial error common to both Nietzsche and Wittgenstein is to argue that Christian practice is everything and Christian belief, belief that involves doctrines, is nothing. If Phillips is trying to embrace such a conception he is in error. Indeed he is not only in error, he has said something that is incoherent. Moreover, he has said – and so *here* has Wittgenstein – something that is in conflict with Wittgensteinian Fideism for he, and here Wittgenstein too, has not described how Christian language-games are played: given a perspicuous representation of them. But instead he has, condemning some of these Christian language-games, passionately *advocated* others, thus violating their own stress on what philosophy should be and even legitimately can be. We do not have philosophy 'in a cool place' here, but an engaging in a strong *advocacy* concerning what a Christian should be; not a neutral description or a perspicuous representation or an elucidatory description of Christian language-games or of its form of life, but a telling us, in effect utilizing a *persuasive* definition, what it is to be a '*true* Christian'. Passionate advocacy has here replaced careful elucidatory articulation. But it is the latter that Phillips thinks, with textual support from Wittgenstein, is the only legitimate philosophical task.

It may be thought paradoxical to say that Wittgenstein was failing *here* to be a Wittgensteinian fideist or a genuine Wittgensteinian. But it is not if we keep in mind Winch's remark that it is crucial to distinguish between Wittgenstein's philosophical remarks about religious discourse and his own religious remarks (Winch 1994, 133). Though, it should also be noted, some remarks are not clearly just one or the other just as *some* metaethical remarks can themselves be ethical. The passage Phillips cites is one of these 'not clearly just one or the other type'. But it is, with its *parti pris* advocacy, more of a religious remark than a remark about 'the logic of religious discourse' and, if it is taken in the latter way, it is surely a mistaken claim not only sociologically but, what is more to the point here, as I have argued above, philosophically and on Wittgenstein's and Phillips's own account of what philosophy is. I should note in passing that the quotation cited by Phillips is from Wittgenstein's *Culture and Value*. This is a collection of remarks taken from Wittgenstein's *Nachlass* and not even from extensive but unfinished or abandoned works, but from Wittgenstein's personal reflections. They sometimes are little more than 'wise sayings' of Wittgenstein and they are of a very uneven quality. Some are deep and perceptive but even these are usually one-sided. Others are *guru* remarks that fly in the face of Wittgenstein's and Phillips's conception of what good philosophy should be. Indeed on their own conception they are hardly philosophy. Perhaps Wittgenstein did not intend them as such, but then we need to face up to the fact that not a few of them are guru remarks of an embarrassing quality and even content (remember his remarks about Mendelssohn and Jewish music) for we admirers of Wittgenstein. *Culture and Value* should be used with considerable caution – keeping firmly in mind Winch's distinction – as a *supplement* to *Philosophical Investigations* and *On Certainty*, the key texts of Wittgenstein's in coming to try to gain an understanding of both what has been called 'the logic of religious discourse' and of what I have called Wittgensteinian Fideism. When we see someone writing on Wittgenstein and religion relying heavily on *Culture and Value* we should be suspicious.

9. Phillips has it that I ignore the logical roles of notions such as 'picture', 'form of life', 'language-game', 'agreement in judgements'. I do not ignore them, but treat some of them differently than he does. He might claim that I am not sufficiently contextual about them and do not heed their contextual lessons. That *might* be right, but it needs to be shown. Phillips himself seems to me to be 'so contextual' as to be lost in examples, including sometimes examples of doubtful relevance to the claims he wishes to make. Moreover, I, no more than Phillips, think that simply by staring at a word or thinking about a word, without

careful attention to its role in practices, will enable us to ascertain its use.

10. Phillips, and not without point, criticizes me for speaking of 'the overall structure of language by reference to which religious belief fails a reflective test' (Chapter 5, p. 68). He rightly complains that I am not clear enough about what I mean by '"the overall structure" which does not reintroduce the over-reaching conception of "reason" and "rationality" which he [Nielsen] wants to reject'. Well, we can speak of the overall structure of English, French, German and any other natural language, meaning by that the syntax, semantics and (perhaps) pragmatics of English, French, etc. And in doing that we need not invoke any over-reaching conception of 'reason' or 'rationality' and the like. But that is probably too thin a notion of 'overall structure' to do the work I wanted when I wrote those words. But perhaps not? We have language-games embedded in practices embedded in forms of life or – choose your vocabulary, Winch's or Wittgenstein's – modes of social life, but all of these activities are usually carried on in the same natural language (something Phillips himself stresses) and, as he also stresses, arguing against compartmentalist theses, these various activities are intertwined such that religious belief and other aspects of human life affect each other. But what is crucial to ask is *how they affect each other*. Phillips admits of *causal* connections. Evolutionary beliefs – beliefs taken from biological theory – may *cause* us to modify or even abandon at least certain religious beliefs or even moral beliefs. What Phillips rejects, as we have seen, is the idea that they could ever lead us *correctly* to abandon a belief in God or in God's providence or in the moral point of view. But the idea that God created us sits uneasily with the belief that we evolved from some simpler forms of life. Perhaps with supplementary arguments the at least putative challenge to a belief in a creator God can be saved from such a scientific challenge (pseudo-challenge) as perhaps claims to revealed Christian truths can be saved from the observations of cultural anthropologists, that, if we look at all the cultures of the world with their distinctive religions, many claiming access to revealed truths or their functional equivalents, most of which are conflicting, that such observations, if we would reflect, pose a genuine challenge to the claim of any religion, including Christianity, to revealed truth which should be authoritative for all humankind. 'Christ is the truth and the way' would be and should be without force, given that anthropological knowledge.

Considerations such as these seem at least to challenge the idea that a mode of social life such as religion cannot be justificatorily challenged from another mode of social life such as science. However, once we break with compartmentalism (as Phillips now agrees we should), and admit of intertwining beliefs and conceptions across modes of social life, it is hard to avoid, unless we stick our heads in the sand, *justificatory* arguments such as the ones I have just described. Moreover, even if I am mistaken and Phillips's argument is sound here, it strengthens Wittgensteinian Fideism rather than weakens it. But it does weaken my arguments *against* Wittgensteinian Fideism. Still Phillips's campaign against Wittgensteinian Fideism would also be weakened.

11. Finally, to conclude this section, at the end of Chapter 4 Phillips maintains whatever I may now think concerning Wittgensteinian Fideism that I should admit that I made 'extravagant claims in 1967 which should be retracted'. In short, Phillips claims that I need to face the following question: 'Can philosophy show that religious belief, in general, is incoherent, irrational or unintelligible? Does Nielsen still want to say that never in the past, not even for a moment, did he think it could?' My answer is straightforward. I thought that in 1967 and I think exactly that now. Or, more accurately, I thought both then and now that the basic concepts of developed forms of Judaism, Christianity and Islam are incoherent. Indeed this goes way back to my first extensively developed article on religion, 'On Speaking of God' (Nielsen 1962) and has remained constant with me, though exactly how I argued for it has, of course, in certain ways changed. Perhaps I am mistaken. Perhaps both early and late my arguments are unsound? Certainly people, including reasonable people, think so and that should give me and you pause. But that was and still is my considered judgement. I think it is only 'conventional wisdom', fear that we would have nothing to steer by, and *bad* philosophy, that holds this judgement extravagant.

I said above 'developed' vis-à-vis the Judaeo-Christian-Islamic religions, for in their earlier forms, as I always maintained early and late, where these religious beliefs – basic religious beliefs – are anthropomorphic, they are *not incoherent but false and plainly so*. Here with these anthropomorphic beliefs we have a considerable measure of superstition. I also said 'more accurately' for while I suspect that developed forms of Buddhism and Confucianism are also incoherent, it is, at least to me, less evident that this is so than for the Judaeo-Christian-Islamic religions. My suspicion that these other religions are incoherent is just a *conjecture*. I do not know enough about them to, with any fallibilistic confidence (the only kind I have), make such a claim. But if by religious belief in general Phillips is only thinking of developed forms of Judaism, Christianity and Islam as doing duty, for his purposes, for religious belief in general, then I would say religious belief, where these beliefs are developed, is incoherent or unintelligible and thus irrational.

My arguments for this, made extensively in many places, have in certain respects changed and have, I hope, grown stronger (Nielsen 1982; 1985; 1996; 2001). But the most basic arguments, though not in all their detail, I made in 1967 are among the same as I make now, though I have enlarged my repertoire.

To remind ourselves of a point made earlier, when I spoke, as Phillips notes, of what I have called *perhaps tendentiously* (I say) Wittgensteinian Fideism it was not to give to understand that I had come to be ambivalent about Wittgensteinian Fideism or to doubt that it has the force I claimed for it. It was merely to acknowledge, in the light of resistance to it, my own fallibility: what all of us, unless we are fanatics or overcome by *hubris*, should acknowledge. It was simply the fallibilistic acknowledgement that of course I could be wrong and that Wittgensteinians such as Malcolm, Winch, Rhees and Phillips heightened my sensitivity to the possibility that that might be so. In general we should follow Oliver Cromwell's advice mentioned earlier, 'Think man . . . that you may be wrong.' This fallibilist attitude, in this context, could go in at least two ways. I could, on the one hand, be wrong, as Phillips believes I am, in my very characterization of what I call Wittgensteinian Fideism; or, on the other hand, right (or at least roughly right) in my characterization of Wittgensteinian Fideism, but mistaken in my criticisms of it. And, of course, I could be wrong about both, making straw-men out of Wittgensteinian fideists and then giving bad arguments against Wittgensteinian Fideism. I, of course, think and argue I have done neither. Phillips thinks I have done both. But in both cases I come at this with the fallibilistic attitude that any reasonable person should have about their views. It is not that I think that anything in particular is wrong with my arguments, though I expect there is, for that is almost invariability true, particularly concerning arguments of large scope. If one is reasonable one expects at least large-scale philosophical arguments to be in one way or another mistaken or at least in need of qualification. It has always been true in the past so why should we expect a new dawn? What we can perhaps reasonably *hope* for is that philosophical accounts will sometimes get better. We can reasonably believe that Hume and Kant are at least in certain respects an advance over Plato and Aristotle and that Rawls and Wittgenstein are an advance over Hume and Kant and it is also not unreasonable to believe, if we don't blow ourselves up, that things like this will go on in the future. We are not at 'the end of history', but lest we become too Whiggish, we should also keep in mind that again and again there have been movements urging us to go back to Aristotle or back to Kant. One prominent philosopher even urged 'Back to the pre-Socratics!'

Perhaps I have failed to note the beam in my own eye and Phillips has managed to put his finger on some mistakes for mistakes are certainly there. I only wish I knew where they were. But I do not see that Phillips has fingered anything that is substantially wrong.

IV

I have in the previous section been principally concerned to refute what I regard as rather pointless as well as mistaken Phillipsian arguments against both my characterization of Wittgensteinian Fideism and some of my criticisms of it. They are, in my view, arguments that had he read my account more carefully or more charitably he would not have made or at least he would not have made them in the form he made them. To speak of charity here is not to beg for it, but to appeal to reasonableness and fairness. A view which you judge to have sufficient attraction to deserve your sustained attention you should try to state in a form which is the most accurate and acute form you can muster without, of course, distorting the account, but you should also where interpretation is in order, interpret the account in the strongest, most plausible form possible compatible with an accurate account of the relevant texts. That Phillips – or so it seems to me – has manifestly failed to do.

However these things that I would like to concern myself with what may not be dross in Phillips's critique of me. I would like to address what in it is powerfully challenging and to the point. He has, particularly in Section IV of Chapter 5, made some criticisms of me that I need to carefully consider and I must meet, if I can. If I cannot I must in some way backtrack on some of what seem to me important and correct claims. This is what I shall now turn to.

I should, however, note right at the beginning, that these arguments *do not even purport to show that Wittgensteinian Fideism is the poor confused thing Phillips takes it to be*, but pertain to *my criticisms* of Wittgensteinian Fideism. If they are on the mark my attempt with them to shipwreck Wittgensteinian Fideism is mistaken and Wittgensteinian Fideism is to that extent strengthened. This is surely something Phillips would not welcome for he wants to show that Wittgensteinian Fideism is utterly discreditable.

But now to a discussion of what I take to be Phillips's more substantial arguments or at least arguments which have a considerable prima facie force. Phillips argues plausibly that the verificationist strand in my thought conflicts with my more Wittgensteinian strand. The latter, he has it, drives me to believe that it is a mistake to treat religious beliefs 'as commensurable with non-religious beliefs'. Religious beliefs are not beliefs 'to be weighed against others in a common system of assessment' (p. 80). Phillips goes on to remark:

> Yet, early and late in his [Nielsen's] thought, we find him insisting that religious beliefs should meet criteria of meaning and truth which he has said do not apply to them. For example, he argues, 'It is a fact

there is a God; it is a fact that He created the world; it is a fact that
He protects me and the like. [Here I am reporting what I take it that
reasonably orthodox theistic believers believe. I am making no such
assertion myself. *My addition.*] Yet, how could we say what it would
be like for God to create the world, if it is impossible in principle to
say what would have to transpire for it to be false that God created
the world? Or to put this point in a weaker and more adequate way,
if we cannot even say what *in principle* would count as *evidence*
against the putative statement that God created the world, even "God
created the world" is devoid of factual content (Nielsen 1967, 203).
Here, Nielsen is treating the belief in God's creation as an empirical
hypothesis, and says that it constitutes a challenge unmet by Wittgensteinian Fideism. But, as we have seen, he also holds that such a
challenge misunderstands the nature of religious beliefs. (p. 80)

There are at least two errors here. I deny (and with good reason) that
'God created the world' is some kind of a priori statement ascertainable
by either pure theoretical reason or pure practical reason. And I do not
think that is something Phillips would contest. But I do not treat 'God
created the world' as an empirical hypothesis either. It is a sentence of
anomalous logical status. Yet *believers*, or at least reasonably orthodox
ones, claim it is *in some way* a factual claim. 'It is a fact that God created
the world' and factual claims, whatever their logical status, whether
hypotheses or not, require evidence for their validation. Only if we say
that 'five plus seven equals twelve' is a factual statement would we be in
trouble here. Some factual claims are so obvious, for example, 'In Maine
it snows in winter' or 'There are rocks on the earth', that we do not
bother to give evidence and think, and rightly, that it would be absurd
to do so. But if someone would ask for evidence we could, silly though
it would be, produce evidence. Only if there is something like synthetic
a priori claims, claims which are both a priori and synthetic and know-
able by pure reason do we have good reason to deny this. But that
rationalist claim is very implausible and it does not seem to be anything
with which Phillips would have any truck. Moreover I was, where this
objection came up, reporting the Wittgensteinian thesis that religious
beliefs are incommensurable with other beliefs, having a distinctive use,
with a 'logic' that is distinctive of this mode of social life. But it does not
follow from that, unless one is a *strict* verificationist and reductionist, that
the criteria of justification are unique to them. And far from accepting
incommensurability, in fact I believe, and have argued along Davidsonian
lines, that the very notion of incommensurability is incoherent. There are
no terms that are untranslatable and there are no concepts that are so
primitive that they cannot be compared (Nielsen 1991). Perhaps there
are no common principles of rationality that are not very thin, but we

can, and should, use wide and general reflective equilibrium in a way that cuts across modes of social life.[11] This is a notion that John Rawls, Norman Daniels and T. M. Scanlon have carefully developed and that I have developed in my *Naturalism Without Foundations* and my *Naturalism and Religion*.

I do not reject Wittgenstein's belief that 'there is no logical form that underlies all language and is its rational foundation' (Nielsen 1982, 110). I am (*pace* what Phillips claims of me) not looking for a common form for all kinds of assent and denial, but I am looking for, and argue, controversially, and without any great confidence, that I have found a common criterion for *factual* significance – for making a true or false claim about the world – and a general method for assessing beliefs of any kind, to wit, wide and general reflective equilibrium.[12]

It is not (again *pace* Phillips) that I think that God is an object among objects, but I do think – God being said by reasonably orthodox Jews, Christians and Muslims to be a person, someone who created the world, sustains it and protects his creation – that he must – in some very unclear sense – be taken to be a particular existent among existents though, of course, 'the king' among existents, and a very special and mysterious existent, but not an object, not a kind of object, not just a categorial or classificatory notion, but not a non-particular either. Though he is said to be infinite, he is also said to be a person, and these two elements when put together seem at least to yield a glaringly incoherent notion. He cannot be an object – a spatio-temporal entity but he is also a he – a funny kind of he to be sure – who is also said to be a person – again a funny kind of person – who is taken to be a person without a body: a purely *spiritual* being. This makes him out to be a 'peculiar reality' indeed. He gets even more peculiar when we are told he is an *infinite* person as well. But now language has really gone on a holiday. He is a person – an individual who is also not an individual; he is a person who is infinite but then he is not a person, not a particular, not something that can be individuated but still – or so it is said – acts in the world. God is said to be a mystery, a non-mysterious God would, of course, not be the God of Judaism, Christianity or Islam. But mystery is one thing – a contradictory nature is another, for example, 'an infinite individual', 'a being acting in the world but transcendent to the world'.

Such talk has the smell of incoherence.[13] When he (God) is said to be an infinite, all-encompassing, purely spiritual individual who is also a person, the incoherence is manifest. Phillips may again assert that this is not Nielsen at his best. But that on his part is little more than arm waving. What I have done here is just to follow the very logic of God-talk embedded as it is in our ordinary language and have seen where it leads us. The inconsistencies and other incoherencies are a part of the logic of that very talk. We gain a participant-like view of the use, attending carefully to that use, and see that this very use contains these (*pace* Wittgensteinian orthodoxy) incoherencies. This is what God-talk comes to when we attend to how it works. This in *some* ways is very un-Wittgensteinian, but isn't it so? *Note here that the claimed incoherence is independent of considerations of verifiability.* To see here how the language-game of God-talk is played is to see that such talk (and with it such concepts and conceptions) is incoherent. It is conflictual through and through, unsaying what it says. Moreover, my argument here – the reminders I assemble – does not rely on any claimed common form or a claimed unity of concepts for all kinds of assertion and denial. I think (*pace* Johannessen 1989, 357) that a good Wittgensteinian should be very wary of claims about the unity of concepts.

Phillips does not face such considerations, but contents himself by accusing me of a positivist essentialism. In much orthodox analytical philosophy of religion by way of a counter, I am reminded that 'God' is not a substance-word, but God is also said to be a person and 'person' on orthodox accounts is not taken to be metaphorical or in some way *just* symbolic. And it is also not just to say that God is personal (*pace* Putnam) as if we understood what that means. It surely looks like we have a nice incoherent mess here, but Phillips does not notice this, or at least does not advert to it, and it hardly seems enough to say, faced with the above considerations, that this language-game is played or that these are our practices, our spade is turned.

We do not need to have some Archimedean point beyond all practices to understand and see the point of what I have been saying; we just have to attend carefully – to carefully inspect – the practices we have and note, when we do so, that *some* are incoherent – indeed that a whole domain of discourse may be incoherent. In doing this we do not get beyond all practices. That should be perfectly clear from what I have said above. I am indeed, and controversially, denying the intelligibility of discourse about God – more accurately denying the intelligibility of non-anthropomorphic God-talk set, at least since the Middle Ages, in the practices of Judaism, Christianity and Islam. But in doing that I am not asserting, or giving to understand, that 'we can get beyond practices' whatever that means. I am saying rather that working with our practices, seeing how they hang together and how some of them fail to hang together, we see, or can come to see, how some of them are incoherent: how they are not in synch with a critical mass of the others. They could not *all* be incoherent or we would be lost: we would then be unable to understand anything. What I am claiming is that we have no perch beyond our practices by means of which to assess them, but we can, working within our practices, note conflicts between them and using wide reflective equilibrium arguments correct for conflicts by *forging* a more coherent view than that with which we started. Religious beliefs are very vulnerable here. They are often the odd man out. Moreover, we do not need a point of view exterior to practices to see that, we just need to show it what it would be to have a coherent set or cluster of practices with them included. My claim is that here we will fail unless we so adjust our religious vocabulary that it becomes naturalistic (and thus secular) in everything but name. But then we are no longer describing or elucidating any Judaeo-Christian-Islamic God-talk or belief. Phillips, though not very clearly, does that.

What Phillips thinks I should be doing is, by attending to the actual context of its use, to catch on to what it means to speak of God and in this way gradually come to understand what it is to do this. But Philips thinks that is not what I actually do. What I am actually doing, Phillips has it, is being an *epistemological* sceptic about God. But the issue here is how we can, if we can, intelligibly speak of God and that is logically prior to the question of whether we have good grounds for believing in God's existence, or denying his existence or whether we have good grounds for being agnostics. But (again *pace* Phillips) in making the claim that God-talk is unintelligible, I am not just uttering the platitude that *some* religious people sometimes say unintelligible things: make unintelligible utterances which *they believe* to be central to religion. Indeed some religious people, as some non-religious people, *sometimes* talk unintelligibly. Any religious believer, Wittgensteinian or not, can quite consistently acknowledge that, but my claim is that what Phillips takes plausibly to be the very 'logic of religious discourse' is incoherent. It was that that I was arguing above. It baffles me that Phillips does not see that. Moreover, it is not, again *pace* Phillips, the personal confession that religion does not mean anything to me. Of course it does. I see it as a desperate attempt, sometimes by very thoughtful people of great integrity, to make sense of their and our tangled lives. Why else would I like Dostoevsky and Kierkegaard so much? Again Phillips is in effect harping on what he takes, utterly mistakenly, to be my rationalism about religion: my belief that only a *religious* rationalism, if we could have it, would give us an acceptable view of religion. But that is not at all my view. Contrary to what Phillips says (to quote him): 'Nielsen's position does not allow him to say both: that religious talk is unintelligible and incoherent *and* that it has a point' (p. 82). My view does exactly that and I have just shown how it does. The point – or at least a central point – of religion is to make sense of our tangled lives. I see that very clearly, but I also see – or think I see – that God-talk is incoherent. It has a point – a very deep point – that even the most sceptical of persons – sceptical about whether talk of God even makes sense – can see and even be affectively attuned to what I have called the point, or if not *the* point, *a* central point, of religion while remaining utterly sceptical about the coherence of God-talk. Religion's aim, or one of its very fundamental aims, is to help us, in the moral wilderness and often human jungle in which we live, to make sense of our lives. But for those who would not crucify their intellects, religion fails in that task for what it tries to say is incoherent. But the *point* of it, what would give it a very fundamental value if only it did make sense, can be perfectly evident to a person who believes, and perhaps correctly, that God-talk is incoherent. And note here, again *pace* Phillips, that I have not in what I have said above assessed religious discourse in terms of some other mode of discourse, say scientific or moral discourse. I have only claimed that when we look at our various discourses crucial strands of religious discourse stand in conflict with much of our other talk and practice, talk and practice we could not abandon and still keep our sanity.

Phillips accuses me of having a verificationist strand. And indeed I do. Like Cheryl Misak, Elliott Sober and Bas van Fraassen I do not think all is dross in verificationism (Misak 1991, 1995, 2000; Sober 1999; van Fraassen 2002). Indeed, I think there is even a strain of verificationism in some of Malcolm's and even Wittgenstein's writings as has frequently been noted. And I think this is to the good. Phillips, like metaphysical realists (atheistic and theistic), has been blind to verificationism's import (Nielsen 2001, 424–95). But here I do not engage in such arguments at all or presuppose verificationism. I stick with Jewish, Christian and Islamic discourse and, against Wittgensteinian Fideism, display – or try to display – without an appeal to verificationism – incoherencies in it. Something that Wittgensteinianism has no conceptual space or resources to counter without considerable modification. It would, to have any chance at being successful here, have to go in a much more *holistic* direction, somewhat in the manner (themselves rather different but I think mutually supporting) of Donald Davidson, Richard Rorty and John Rawls, to perhaps counter what I have argued are incoherencies in Wittgenstein's accounts of religion. It cannot do so by taking the form it has in Malcolm, Winch and Phillips. Malcolm, I think, is the clearest here, and in being the clearest, he is the most clearly mistaken (Malcolm 1977a, 1977b; and see criticisms of Malcolm in Nielsen 1982, 92–110, Nielsen 1989, 111–37). (I do not mean to suggest that Davidson, Rorty or Rawls would support such a modified Wittgensteinian Fideism or any Wittgensteinian Fideism, but that a modified Wittgensteinian Fideism might try to utilize their holism to meet some of my criticisms of Wittgensteinian Fideism.)

Phillips taxes me for speaking of the 'overall structure of the universe of discourse of which it [religious discourse] is a part' as is scientific discourse or moral discourse. He thinks this commits me to some problematic metaphysical reification. *Au contraire*, I meant nothing more problematic than that religious discourse, moral discourse, scientific discourse, any domain of discourse at all that is non-formal occurs, and must occur, in some natural language and that this language has a syntax, a semantics and a pragmatics. Moreover, there are resources in such a language that enable us to talk about, including to compare and to criticize, the various domains of discourse. Something that is anathema to a Wittgensteinian fideist.

Phillips is on to something more substantial when he criticizes me for some remarks I made in my 'Wittgensteinian Fideism II' in my *An Introduction to the Philosophy of Religion*. Unfortunately he actually badly misquotes me (Chapter 5, p. 85). Even so, he may be on to something. I give the extended quotation he cites corrected, and then comment on what he says. The quotation runs as follows:

> when we reflect on the various 'forms of life' – the various linguistic activities that we actually engage in – we will find that some are 'ground floor', that is, determinative of what can be seen, after a careful reflection on one's language, as constitutive of or at least as an irreducible element in talk of what there is. The other forms of discourse are in various ways parasitic on it and if in trying to assert the existence of something we make assumptions which run counter to it we say something which is incoherent. (Nielsen 1982, 135)[14]

Perhaps Phillips is right that I have taken a wrong turn there, among other things, unwittingly starting to go down a foundationalist road, a road I certainly would not want to take. But the argument I just gave about natural languages and modes of social life does not depend on any kind of foundationalism. And my later practice-oriented wide-reflective-equilibrium-oriented way of arguing does not depend on it either. That latter approach of mine may indeed be better than the road taken in the above quotation. That may not be a road to be taken. That is why I said Phillips may be right. But let me hesitantly, and without any considerable confidence, say something in its favour – something that does not involve even a tacit foundationalism. We, whether we are speaking of religion, morality, art or science, speak of events occurring, things happening, of there being processes, and of rocks and lakes, of persons, of their being born, of building skills, of living together, fighting, being happy or unhappy, and the like. We could not understand religious, scientific, moral or aesthetic discourse if we did not understand such things, which means understanding the discourse of such things and the language-games that make them up. If we did not understand what it is for a mother to love her child we could not understand (assuming for the nonce we can) 'God loves us'. If we did not understand what it is for John to be a person we could not understand 'God'. In this way religious discourse is parasitic on what I perhaps mistakenly called 'ground floor discourse'. And so is scientific, aesthetic and moral discourse. Isn't this rather unproblematic?

However, I need not be stuck with this not uncontroversial claim.

What I could do more unproblematically – though, of course, still not beyond controversy – is to stick with, as I do, a practice-oriented, non-representationalist conception of language and make no claims or assumptions about what in that web of language and belief is more basic and less basic: more ground floor. Wittgenstein is right that to imagine a language is to imagine a form of life. Language is a rule-governed way of acting and doing. Where we have practices – rule-governed activities that give our uses of language the senses they have – they determine what is intelligible and what is not, but it is not the language-games and practices in isolation that do this, but the ensemble of practices which are forms of life and thus in a natural language. *It, that is, is not a practice taken in isolation but the cluster of practices which together constitute forms of life which are in some natural language, which, constituted as it is by its cluster of practices, is a way of doing, but also something which has a syntax and a semantics. Individual practices and clusters of practices forming whole domains of discourse, such as science, religion or morality, can be criticized by reference to their fit with the forms of language/forms of life taken as a whole.* And it is here where wide and general reflective equilibrium comes in by giving us a method for making our considered judgements best fit together into a coherent whole. Certain practices and, in principle at least, whole domains of discourse, can in this way be criticized, modified through criticism or even abandoned although we never step out of this ensemble of practices (Nielsen 1996; 2001).

We can make sense of that without making claims – claims bound to be controversial – about the overall structure of the universe of discourse or the unity of our concepts. The coherence we forge by the use of wide and general reflective equilibrium is enough. What does not fit with, conflicts with, a forgeable coherent (consistent) mass of practices constituting our forms of life is modified until it does fit or it is rejected (Nielsen 1996, 12–21, 115–205 and 2001, 69–70).

If our concepts have any unity it is the unity *forged* in wide and general reflective equilibrium (Rawls 1996, 393–94, note particularly note 16 on page 384 and page 388). What is intelligible (meaningful) to say is what has a use in our language. And we determine what words have a use in our language by noting what has a function in our practices, what is in accordance with their rules. The distinctive domains of discourse (e.g. science, religion, morality) *initially* give us our criteria of reasonability, justifiability distinctive to each domain of discourse, but domains are not unconnected and the form of life that is there with their practices can, and should, be appealed to where some practice or practices in one domain of discourse fits or fit badly with another. And here is where wide and general reflective equilibrium is important as a way of determining what constitutes the most coherent whole of these *sometimes*

conflicting practices and even domains of discourse. This is what Wittgensteinian Fideism does not allow with its conception of incommensurable
domains determining what constitutes a rational authority unique to each
domain of discourse. Rejecting along Davidsonian lines incommensurability and, given the wider scope of coherence of wide and general reflective equilibrium, we can assess whole domains of discourse. We can do
this without claiming that we can in some way stand free of all practices
and assess them with some sky-hook. We do not need this at best mythical
perch to criticize the at least seeming ethnocentrism and localism of
Wittgensteinian Fideism. We need not, that is, be stuck with just saying
that these are our practices and these are the language-games we play,
this is where we stand, this is what we do around here, these are the
rules we have and we can do no other. Here is a way without reification
or myth or postulating incoherent sky-hooks we can meet the challenge
of Wittgensteinian Fideism which, acknowledged or not, Phillips, Winch
and Malcolm well exemplify.

Notes

1 See Chapter 4, pp. 65, 67.

2 There is a *deliberate* ambiguity here for different Wittgensteinians go different
ways here and for the nonce I do not wish, or need for my purposes here, to take
sides on this issue.

3 There is an ambiguity here which I do not think is adverted to by Wittgenstein
or by Wittgensteinians (at least those whose work I know). Are religion, science,
morality, etc. forms of life or are they *in* a form of life as constituent parts?
Above I speak of religion as a form of life – something that is frequently done.
But we could just as well say it is in a form of life. I think it is *perhaps better*
thought of as a domain of discourse or a mode of social life *in* a form of
life. This is how I shall use it in the critically essential passages where I assess
Wittgensteinian Fideism.

4 For a characterization of an error theory of religion see Nielsen 2001, 29–55.

5 This is close to what Phillips takes a form of life to be. Phillips says, 'This
larger context of human life, in which we see how a language game is taken,
Wittgenstein calls a form of life' (Phillips, 1986, 28).

6 In the page reference Phillips cites as evidence of my reliance on an appearance/
reality distinction I was simply reporting Terence Penelhum's characterization of a
distinction he makes between conformist fideism and evangelical fideism. This is
another example of Phillips's often sloppy reading (Penelhum 1997).

7 That is a slip on Phillips's part for there are, of course, language-games in
English, French, Hindi, Greek, etc. I take it he meant to say that all language-
games occur in a language and that the language-games of a given language occur
in that language. (Even truisms can be true.)

8 See Johannessen 1989. This is at best a misleading way of putting this for the deeds must be characterizable in words. We do not get something that cannot be said but only shown.

9 Even if belief itself, à la Peirce, is a kind of action, it is a distinct kind of action. It is one thing to believe that socialism is a good thing. It is another to engage in militant struggle to try to bring it about.

10 We can believe *in* justice without believing *that* justice exists or believe *in* integrity without believing *that* there are people of integrity. If God were simply an *ideal* we could believe in God without a belief that God exists. But God is not taken simply as an ideal except on certain naturalistic accounts.

11 I am not even so sure that there are no substantive principles of rationality that cut across domains. I argued long ago for such principles in my 'Principles of Rationality', *Philosophical Papers* Vol. III, no. 2 (October 1974), 55–89. I abandoned such an approach – such a research programme – not because I became convinced that it was mistaken, but because I came to think the Rawls–Daniels type wide-reflective equilibrium achieved much the same results less controversially (Nielsen 1974).

12 I could, without fundamental change to my critique of Wittgensteinian Fideism, abandon my positivist-sounding claim about factual significance and stick just with my appeal to considered judgements in wide and general reflective equilibrium. I have come to have far greater confidence in the latter than in the former. Here is a considerable change in my views.

13 If we say we can only say what God is not, not what he is, we have gone the route of the *via negativa*. But if no positive predications can be made of God, we cannot say what he is not either. Positive and negative predications go together; we cannot have one without the other (Nielsen 1989, 190–207).

14 Phillips speaks of my being unscholarly about Wittgensteinian Fideism. He even claims – though he doesn't explain very clearly how – the very term is unscholarly. But such a charge is certainly the pot calling the kettle black. Such a gross misquotation as he made of me in Chapter 5 is, to understate it, something of a departure from being attentive to or respectful of scholarly standards.

Bibliography

Copleston, Frederick C. (1974), *Religion and Philosophy*. Dublin: Gill and Macmillan.
Johannessen, Kjell S. (1989), 'The Concept of Practice in Wittgenstein's Later Philosophy', *Inquiry* Vol. 31, pp. 357–69.
Kenny, Anthony (1975), 'In Defence of God', *The Times Literary Supplement*. 7 February, p. 145.
—— (2002), 'A Genial Solitude', *Times Literary Supplement*, 18 January, p. 281.
Malcolm, Norman (1977a), 'The Groundlessness of Belief' in Stuart C. Brown, ed., *Reason and Religion*. Ithaca, NY: Cornell University Press.
—— (1977b), *Thought and Knowledge*. Ithaca, NY: Cornell University Press.
Misak, Cheryl (1991), *Truth and the End of Inquiry*. Oxford: Clarendon Press.
—— (1995), *Verificationism: Its History and Prospects*. London: Routledge.

—— (2000), *Truth, Politics, Morality: Pragmatism and Deliberation*. London: Routledge.

Nielsen, Kai (1962), 'On Speaking of God', *Theoria* Vol. 28, pp. 110–37.

—— (1967), 'Wittgensteinian Fideism', *Philosophy* Vol. 42, no. 161, pp. 191–209.

—— (1973), *Scepticism*. New York: St Martin's Press.

—— (1974), 'Principles of Rationality', *Philosophical Papers* Vol. III, no. 2, pp. 55–89.

—— (1979), 'Religion, Science and Limiting Questions', *Studies in Religion* Vol. 8, no. 3, pp. 259–65.

—— (1982), *An Introduction to the Philosophy of Religion*. London: Macmillan.

—— (1985), *Philosophy and Atheism*. Amherst, NY: Prometheus Books.

—— (1989), *God, Scepticism, and Modernity*. Ottawa: University of Ottawa Press.

—— (1991), *After the Demise of the Tradition*. Boulder, CO: Westview Press.

—— (1996), *Naturalism Without Foundations*. Amherst, NY: Prometheus Books.

—— (2001), *Naturalism and Religion*. Amherst, NY: Prometheus Books.

Nietzsche, Friedrich (1990), *The Anti-Christ*. London: Penguin Books.

Penelhum, Terence (1997), 'Fideism' in P. Quinn and C. Taliaferro, eds, *A Companion to Philosophy of Religion*. London: Blackwell, pp. 376–82.

Phillips, D. Z. (1993), *Wittgenstein and Religion*. London: Macmillan.

—— (1986), *Belief, Change and Forms of Life*. Atlantic Highlands, NJ: Humanities Press.

—— (2001), *Religion and the Hermeneutics of Contemplation*. Cambridge: Cambridge University Press.

Putnam, Hilary (1999), *The Threefold Cord: Mind, Body, and World*. New York: Columbia University Press.

Rawls, John (1996), *Political Liberalism*, second edition. New York: Columbia University Press.

Rorty, Richard (1991), *Objectivity, Relativism and Truth*. Cambridge: Cambridge University Press.

Sober, Elliot (1999), 'Testability', *Proceedings and Addresses of the American Philosophical Association* Vol. 73, no. 2, pp. 47–76.

Van Fraassen, Bas (2002), *The Empirical Stance*. New Haven, CN: Yale University Press.

Winch, Peter (1994), 'Discussion of Malcolm's Essay' in Peter Winch, ed., *Wittgenstein: A Religious Point of View?* Ithaca, NY: Cornell University Press, pp. 95–135.

—— (1995), *The Idea of a Social Science*. London: Routledge.

Wittgenstein, Ludwig (1969), *On Certainty*. Oxford: Blackwell.

—— (1980), *Culture and Value*. Oxford: Blackwell.

7. Retrospective and Six Concerns in Logic

D. Z. PHILLIPS

At the close of Part Two of the book, I want first to make some retrospective remarks about the use of the term 'Wittgensteinian Fideism' and then raise six concerns that are issues in logic which have a bearing on Nielsen's methodology in the philosophy of religion.

I do not want to get involved in a dispute over the label 'Wittgensteinian Fideism'. Nielsen, in the previous chapter, accuses me of doing just that. I am reminded of Kierkegaard's story about the man who wanted his suit pressed. He took it to a shop which had a sign in the window which said, 'Suits Pressed Here.' But he came out with his suit unpressed. They were only selling the sign. I am not interested in the sign 'Wittgensteinian Fideism' as such. But Nielsen, as he admits, created it, and that creation has developed a life of its own in the literature. What is more, the phenomenon is ascribed over and over again to Wittgenstein and to the philosophers of religion influenced by him. To ask whether such an ascription is accurate hardly seems to be an unreasonable question. Even so, my purpose in asking it is because I believe that to see what Wittgenstein and others *are* saying furthers the central questions in the philosophy of religion. Interestingly, Nielsen's position is one in which he likes the Wittgensteinian arguments, but doesn't like the conclusions about religion. Is this a case of refusing to follow the *logos* because the conclusions are resisted for other reasons? Nielsen himself admits that he may be ideologically blocked where the conclusions are concerned. In the collection *Can Religion Be Explained Away?* Nielsen wrote a 46-page essay on 'Is Religion the Opium of the People? Marxianism and Religion' (Nielsen 1996). David McLellan wrote a 6-page reply called 'Is Religion the Opium of the People? A Reply to Kai Nielsen' (McLellan 1996), which, at the time, I found odd. But on reflection, the length of the reply had to do with a simple fact that he wanted us to remember, namely, that Marx had a tin ear as far as religion is concerned. Wittgenstein's term for this condition was 'aspect blindness' or 'meaning blindness'. In such cases, one cannot accuse the 'meaning-blind' person of misunderstanding the logic of the language in question. The language in question simply does not get off the ground for him or her. Is that what I'll end up saying of my disagreements with Nielsen? It is too soon to answer that question yet.

Despite Nielsen's frequent avowals of fallibilism, they play very little part in the actual expression of his arguments. He does not really entertain the thought that certain aspects of the language of religion simply do not get off the ground for him. He is clearly convinced that he *does* understand the primary language of religious belief. He has seen through it, and demonstrated, to his own satisfaction, its incoherence. His tone is not that of the fallibilists. He reacts strongly against atheists who are opposed to religion, but *not* on the grounds of its *incoherence*. He criticizes Nietzsche in the last chapter (see pp. 114–16) though, at other times, he says that his atheism is deep (see Chapter 5, p. 88).

Nielsen rightly does not want views attributed to his notion of Wittgensteinian Fideism that he does not hold. He complains in Chapter 3, that my use of the term in Chapter 2 is wider than his own. As I pointed out, I was talking there of a 20-year-old phenomenon wider than his own views. The fact that he created a label cannot control the views to which it has become attached. Furthermore, it is hard to believe that Nielsen is not perfectly aware of that fact. One can cite among many examples, Felicity McCutcheon's book, *Religion Within the Limits of Language Alone – Wittgenstein on Philosophy and Religion* (for an incisive criticism of these works, see Amesbury 2003 and Ashdown 2004a and b). More decisively, with respect to Nielsen, one need only refer to the collection *Wittgenstein and Philosophy of Religion* (Arrington & Addis 2001) to which Nielsen contributed along with Brian Clack and Mark Addis. In attacking Wittgensteinian Fideism, Clack and Addis include in it all the theses which, for Nielsen, have no place there (Clack 2001; Addis 2001). According to Nielsen, the claim that only believers understand religion should have no place in Wittgensteinian Fideism, but, describing its features, Addis says that these fideists hold that 'religious language is intelligible only to those who participate in the religious form of life' hence 'an atheist could not find religious belief intelligible much less criticize it' (Addis 2001, 85). Nielsen and I would agree that no Wittgensteinian philosopher of religion would recognize Addis's claim concerning them. But should it not give Nielsen pause for thought that no Witgensteinian philosopher of religion he refers to recognized the fideistic views which he ascribed to them? Rush Rhees, for example, was concerned about the term 'Wittgensteinian Fideism' and the discussions it led to because, in his view, it deflected one from Wittgenstein's *logical* concerns about language and reality in discussing religion. The result of such deflection is that philosophy degenerates into apologetics. In an effort to avoid deflection, I want, in the remainder of this brief chapter, to raise six concerns in logic relating to Nielsen's methodology.

*   *   *

First, does Nielsen think that there is some general form of language to which religion is answerable, and by which it is shown to be incoherent?

On the one hand, Nielsen says that he does 'not wish to attack Wittgenstein's claim that 'there is no logical form that underlies all language and is its rational foundation' (Chapter 6, p. 123). On the contrary, he calls it 'a profoundly correct philosophical insight'. We would not expect Nielsen, therefore, to criticize religion for not conforming to a logical form which he does not believe exists. Yet, this is precisely what he does when, on the other hand, he says that 'given the overall structure of discourse of which religion is a part, it may still be found that religious discourse, like discourse about fairies, is incoherent' (Chapter 1, p. 35). How can language which Nielsen says has no logical form be said by him to have an overall structure?

In Chapter 6, Nielsen recognizes the tension in his remarks and tries to ease it by saying, 'I meant nothing more problematic than that religious discourse, moral discourse, scientific discourse, any domain of discourse at all that is non–formal occurs, and must occur, in some natural language and that this language has a syntax, a semantics and a pragmatics' (pp. 126–7). This, of course, does not answer the question in logic being addressed to Nielsen. If he really agreed with Wittgenstein's insight, he would not say that domains of discourse *must* occur in a natural language, but that they *do*. Moreover, he would see that it is not the syntax, semantics, or pragmatics of a language which determines what *can* and *cannot* be said, but rather, it is what *is* or is *not* said which *shows* the syntax, semantics and pragmatics of the language. And what is shown does not take a common form. How can it when part of what is shown is conflict and criticism which, for some strange reason, Nielsen thinks that Wittgensteinianism cannot recognize? These criticisms are not simply those that some religious believers make of others. They also include criticisms of *any* form of religion from anti-religious or non-religious perspectives.

Second, if Nielsen recognizes Wittgenstein's logical insight discussed above, why does he find the notion of 'practice' in Wittgenstein so problematic?

Nielsen is led to speak of 'the overall structure of language' partly because he wants to avoid, as I do, a compartmentalization of language such that religion would be immune to criticism. A certain way of combining the notions of a 'language-game' and 'practice' would have that unfortunate result. A language-game, in Wittgenstein, refers to certain conceptually distinct activities, such as 'ordering', 'asking', 'reporting', etc. In this context, it makes no sense to speak of a confused language-game. If wider activities, called 'practices' are thought of as clusters of language-games, one reaches the unfortunate conclusion that no practice can be confused.

Clearly, the above conclusion is absurd. Equally clear is the fact that Wittgenstein never arrived at it. For example, at the time he wrote his 'Remarks on Frazer's *Golden Bough*', he thought it likely that most rituals were confused, and that some of these confusions are akin to metaphysical confusions. It would be absurd to attribute to him, or to any Wittgensteinian, the view that there are no confused practices.

The absurdity comes about from ignoring Wittgenstein's use of 'practice'. He thought that philosophy's descriptive task is to show the logical place of our words in *practice*; that is, to show their *grammatical* place. This, as I have said, is not the sociological use of 'practice', which simply refers to what goes on. What goes on may be riddled with all sorts of confusion. This is not an arbitrary stipulation, as Nielsen thinks, but simply a matter of being exegetically faithful to what Wittgenstein is saying. In the previous chapter there are plenty of indications that Nielsen *does* recognize Wittgenstein's use. In that case, however, he should withdraw the charge that this use of 'practice' in Wittgenstein is for defensive, apologetic purposes. What Nielsen should be arguing is that, given Wittgenstein's use of 'practice', there are no religious practices, only varieties of confusion. He should not say, as he does in Chapter 1, that someone can have an experience of 'God-talk where the "engine isn't idling"', while holding that such talk is the product of confusion (see p. 22). For Wittgenstein, if the talk is confused, 'the engine is idling'. Nielsen's position is that in religion language is always idling (apart from anthropomorphic beliefs which he holds to be false, not unintelligible).

Third, does the extension of Wittgenstein's work by Rush Rhees lead to a holism which shows the incoherence of religious beliefs?

Rhees argues that some of the ways in which Wittgenstein uses the term 'language-game', does make it look as though language is a collection of self-contained activities; a family of language-games. The games are seen to belong to the same language, by the fact that they have features that resemble each other, although there is no feature common to them all. On this view, the unity of language is still seen as a structural unity. It is the structure of the games which show their relation to each other. That is why Rhees says that it seems as though the structure of the proposition in the *Tractatus* has been replaced by the structure of the language-game in the *Investigations*.

As a corrective to this view, Rhees develops Wittgenstein's notion of a form of life, and the essential dialogical character of language. He says, again and again, that language makes sense if living makes sense. We do not first have language-games and then see that they are related to others by various features they possess. Wittgenstein's notion of 'family resemblances' does less than justice to his own emphasis on language as an activity; something the analogy with games was meant to bring out. Rhees is saying that but for the traffic of discourse, the ways in which people take things when speaking together, the language-games wouldn't *be* language-games in the first place. That is the point of Rhees's critique of Wittgenstein's claim that the order 'slab' could be the whole language of a tribe.

I have never been guilty of the kind of compartmentalism Nielsen ascribes to me. As I show, in Chapter 2, that is so from my earliest book, *The Concept of Prayer*, published in 1965. What is undoubtedly true is that not only have I come to realize the need to make this matter clearer, through the criticisms of Nielsen and others, but that editing Rhees's own work has shown me how logically far-reaching his own insights on this issue are. They show the inadequacy of the readiness of recent writers, including Nielsen, to settle for calling Wittgenstein a therapeutic philosopher. These insights are to be found not only in Rhees's explicit discussions of Wittgenstein in *Discussions of Wittgenstein, Wittgenstein and the Possibility of Discourse*, and *Wittgenstein's 'On Certainty'*, but also in his two-volume work on the Greeks, *In Dialogue with the Greeks: The Presocratics and Reality (Vol. I)* and *Plato and Dialectic (Vol. II)*. For Rhees, the question of the nature of reality remains central for Wittgenstein via the issue of the relation between language and reality.

Nielsen sees Rhees's remarks leading in the direction of a holism in terms of which, for Nielsen, religion could be shown not to fit with the rest of the culture. He admits that Rhees would probably not concur with these sentiments, and that is certainly the case. Rhees emphasizes, over and over again, that we are not all engaged in one big conversation, or in one all-inclusive enterprise. We did not learn to speak by talking to everyone about everything. We can certainly *try* to understand each other, and that is important. But, often, we fail. Rhees speaks of a hubbub of voices, conversations moving around each other, some close, others far from each other. Among these voices are religious voices, which Nielsen finds incoherent. Nothing Rhees says in his general remarks settles *that* issue one way or another. Questions of sense and nonsense are dealt with *as they arise*. Rhees's struggle with the sense and senselessness of religious beliefs is magnificently captured in his *On Religion and Philosophy*. Nielsen says that as they have arisen *for him*, religious beliefs have turned out to be incoherent. In any case, he will have to admit that the character of Rhees's thought is quite different from his own holism. We are brought up against the brute fact, once again, that Nielsen does not see sense where other philosophers, who include both believers and unbelievers, can acknowledge it. But this leads to further questions about the logic of Nielsen's methodology which has led him to these conclusions.

*   *   *

Fourth, does Nielsen think that the incoherence of religious belief in our culture is due to the fact that they cannot be verified in terms commensurable with those by reference to facts?

This is an issue on which it is extremely difficult to pin Nielsen down. On the one hand, he criticizes me for saying that religious beliefs are incommensurable with empirical beliefs. On the other hand, in his essay, 'The Coherence of Wittgensteinian Fideism', Nielsen defends me against the view that I should be able to verify whether God is in heaven, in a way commensurable with those by which we would verify the existence of objects in space. Nielsen says, 'Contrary to this, it is Phillips' intention – and it seems to me an entirely reasonable contention – that it shows an utter misunderstanding of what Christianity is all about to think that [the beliefs about the astronaut and God], could be possible utterances in that mode of discourse' (Nielsen 1973, 96). In Chapter 3, we find him saying, 'Someone who asks these questions shows that he does not understand such religious discourse' (p. 55). But when Nielsen discusses the story of God speaking to Job out of the whirlwind, he asks, 'So how did he do it? Nobody, or at least nobody who matters, believes any more in a sky God up there, who might have done it in a very loud voice' (Chapter 1, p. 33). On his own account Nielsen is asking a question which he says no one who understood anything about religion would ask, since it misrepresents the nature of the religious belief. Is Nielsen's position this: he knows religious belief can't mean x, but he can't see any alternative to x?

Fifth, does Nielsen simply assume that religious beliefs are metaphysical beliefs?

According to Nielsen 'Wittgensteinian Fideism' is as opposed to metaphysical beliefs as he is. We are supposed to be on the same side of the fence in this matter in our criticisms of contemporary philosophy of religion. So what is the point of reiterating *to me* his objections to forms of religious beliefs which he construes as metaphysical? In respect to my work, I compared his situation to that of Albert Camus in relation to Simone Weil. Camus found that Weil attacked everything about religion that he attacked. Yet he acknowledged that she was deeply religious. He was beginning to explore these other possibilities at the time of his untimely death. Nielsen recognizes that I contrast the religious beliefs I am discussing with both empirical beliefs and metaphysical beliefs. Isn't Nielsen's position that he sees no alternative other than calling religious beliefs something like 'morality touched with emotion'? For me, his thinking stops short of a thorough exploration of other possibilities. This throws light on his admission that he is attracted by Wittgenstein's arguments, but draws back from their conclusions with respect to religion.

*   *   *

Sixth, does Nielsen believe that religious discourse is incoherent simply on the grounds that it is different from, or analogically related to, other aspects of discourse?

Sometimes Nielsen seems to be saying this, at other times not. At times he is mindful of G. E. Hughes's caution 'that it is possible to show any category of statements or expressions to be conceptually confused if one is allowed to insist that they must conform to the logic of some other category or categories of statements or expressions if they are to be said to make sense' (Chapter 1, p. 23). So if the presence of differences were sufficient, *all* relations between different aspects of discourse would, in Nielsen's terms, be fideistic. At other times, Nielsen says that the trouble with religious beliefs lies precisely in their being *distinctive*. This is odd. If there were no distinctiveness there would be no analogies. One would only have identities. So do all analogies fall under the accusation of fideism? I do not think there is a way out of this impasse for Nielsen. Is not the real situation this: Nielsen sees clearly that religious beliefs claim to be distinctive, but he cannot make anything of what that alleged distinctiveness amounts to? On examination, it turns out to be incoherent.

So at this stage of our discussion, my six concerns in logic prevent further progress in our philosophical discussion. Yet, I want to repeat, that from early on it could have been otherwise. I quoted from Nielsen's 'The Coherence of Wittgensteinian Fideism' in Chapter 5. We seemed to have reached a promising agreement on the grammar of the conflict between belief and unbelief; that it need not be a conflict between com- mensurable beliefs within a common system. We seem to agree that, though not identical, the conflict between belief and unbelief is more like a conflict between two conflicting moral perspectives than a conflict between conflicting empirical hypotheses. Nielsen says, 'There is some- thing here which is important and has, I am convinced "a ring of truth about it"' (see p. 79). Had we pursued that 'ring of truth together' we could have explored the grammar of forms of belief and atheism without calling *either* incoherent. For me, that is an essential part of philosophy's contemplative task – illustrated by Rhees's multi-faceted reflections in *On Religion and Philosophy*. Nielsen, unfortunately, did not go in that direction. Instead, he says, 'yet, I am also convinced, it should be looked at with a jaundiced eye' (see p. 79). This, for me, is to look with a jaundiced eye at the tasks facing philosophical contemplation. I would say to Nielsen, 'Relaxez vous' – let beliefs and atheisms be themselves. The next part of the book shows what happens between us when we try to do this with respect to the religious belief that God is beyond human understanding.

Bibliography

Addis, Mark (2001), 'D. Z. Phillips' Fideism in Wittgenstein's Mirror' in *Wittgenstein and the Philosophy of Religion*, eds Robert L. Arrington and Mark Addis.

Amesbury, Richard (2003), 'Has Wittgenstein Been Misunderstood by Wittgensteinian Philosophers of Religion?' *Philosophical Investigations* 26: 1.

Arrington, Robert L and Mark Addis (eds) (2001), *Wittgenstein and the Philosophy of Religion*. London and New York: Routledge.

Ashdown, Lance (2004a), 'A Tragic Tale of Magic and Philosophy', *International Journal for the Philosophy of Religion* 56: 2–3.

—— (2004b), 'Much Ado About a Point of View', *Dialogue* 43.

Clack, Brian R. (2001), 'Wittgenstein and Magic' in *Wittgenstein and the Philosophy of Religion*, eds Robert L. Arrington and Mark Addis.

Hughes, G. E. (1962), 'Martin's *Religious Belief*', *Australasian Journal of Philosophy* 40, August 1962.

McCutcheon, Felicity (2001), *Religion Within the Limits of Language Alone – Wittgenstein on Philosophy and Religion*. Aldershot: Ashgate.

McLellan, David (1996) 'Is Religion the Opium of the People? A Reply to Kai Nielsen' in *Can Religion be Explained Away?* ed. D. Z. Phillips. Basingstoke: Macmillan.

Nielsen, Kai (1973), 'The Coherence of Wittgensteinian Fideism', *Sophia* XI: 3. Reprinted in *God, Scepticism, and Modernity*. Ottawa: Ottawa University Press, 1989.

—— (1996), 'Is Religion the Opium of the People? Marxianism and Religion' in *Can Religion be Explained Away?* ed. D. Z. Phillips. Basingstoke: Macmillan.

Phillips, D. Z. (1965), *The Concept of Prayer*. London: Routledge (Oxford: Blackwell, 1981).

Rhees, Rush (1970), *Discussions of Wittgenstein*. London: Routledge.

—— (1997), *On Religion and Philosophy*, ed. D. Z. Phillips. Cambridge: Cambridge University Press.

—— (1998), *Wittgenstein and the Possibility of Discourse*, ed. D. Z. Phillips. Cambridge: Cambridge University Press (second edition, Oxford: Blackwell, 2005).

—— (2003), *Wittgenstein's 'On Certainty'*, ed. with an afterword by D. Z. Phillips. Oxford: Blackwell, 2003.

—— (2005a), *In Dialogue With The Greeks* Vol. I: *The Presocratics and Reality*, ed. with an introduction by D. Z. Phillips. Aldershot: Ashgate.

—— (2005b), *In Dialogue With The Greeks* Vol. II: *Plato and Dialectic*, ed. with an introduction by D. Z. Phillips. Aldershot: Ashgate.

Wittgenstein, Ludwig (1993), 'Remarks on Frazer's *Golden Bough*', in *Philosophical Occasions*, eds James Klagge and Alfred Nordmann. Cambridge and Indianapolis: Hackett Publishing Co.

PART THREE

Religion and Understanding

8. Can Anything be Beyond Human Understanding?

KAI NIELSEN

I

The answer to the question of my title, if anything could reasonably count as an answer, depends in large part on how we take 'can' and 'beyond understanding'. I will come to this. But my discussion also takes place against the background of D. Z. Phillips's remarks about 'the vicissitudes of human life being beyond human understanding' and about the 'limits of human existence'. All, in turn, take place against the background of thinking about religions in a non-rationalistic Wittgensteinian manner. I will argue that there are senses in which Phillips is right in his claim that there are vicissitudes in human life which are beyond human understanding, but that these senses are of little philosophical interest. In the senses that might deliver philosophical gold, the claim is at best false.

Phillips is a charter member of the club which I have called Wittgensteinian fideists.[1] I am still inclined to believe that my criticisms of Wittgensteinian Fideism were essentially correct. That notwithstanding, I have considerable sympathy with what Phillips says about theodicies and towards what he takes to be the key division in the philosophy of religion: a division not between believers and unbelievers, but between rationalistic believers and unbelievers, on the one hand, and non-rationalistic believers and unbelievers on the other. The rationalists think it important to formulate theodicies or anti-theodicies, to examine what 'miracles' can show, and to examine the proofs for the existence of God with an eye to determining whether any of them could after all be sound. By contrast, a non-rationalist approach takes such rationalistic philosophical questions as questions which tend to distract us from serious thinking about religion. Here I am in agreement with Phillips. But for reasons I will make clear in this chapter, I do not wish to characterize the non-rationalists (whether believers or not) as people 'who recognise that the limits of human existence are beyond human understanding' (I, 153).[2]

It should be noted, however, that the *Weltgeist* has gone against both of us. I had hoped 20 years ago that the discussion of religion – including the deliberations between belief and unbelief – would take a broadly Wittgensteinian / Kierkegaardian / Feuerbachian / Barthian turn. Instead, such non-rationalism was short-lived, going along with the rise and fall of Oxford linguistic philosophy. The dominant trend is now towards the pre-Wittgensteinian and pre-Kierkegaardian issues and questions: towards a kind of religiosity which discusses the traditional metaphysical questions of natural theology making use of analytical philosophy and modal logic, but still proceeding as if only Geach, Dummett and Kripke – but not Wittgenstein, Quine, Putnam, Davidson and Rorty – ever existed. We get foundationalist arguments for or against realism rather than a sense that the dispute between realists and anti-realists is a pseudo-issue better dissolved than resolved. Rather than leaving such metaphysical issues to benign neglect, most analytical philosophers of religion rush in to take either a staunch metaphysical realist stance, as in the case of William Alston, or, with Dummett, they adopt a firm anti-realist stance. Insisting on 'ontological seriousness', they take such metaphysical theses at face value and try to resolve them. Davidson, Putnam and Rorty have, by contrast, shown us the way to go here; and more generally, they have set aside metaphysical issues as unanswerable without falling into positivist dogma. With Putnam there is from time to time a nostalgic looking back, but there is also a firm understanding that metaphysics is a house of cards which neither requires nor stands in need of answers. But contemporary analytic philosophy of religion, seemingly unaware of these developments, is deep in the metaphysical mud. Phillips sets his face against this as firmly as I do. This is all to the good. But he unwittingly tangles himself in some metaphysical issues which stand in the way of a perspicuous understanding of our forms of life, and with this, of our lives.

II

Phillips has written voluminously on what I should characterize as a Wittgensteinian approach to the philosophy of religion. In years past I have come to grips with roughly the first half of Phillips's corpus on this broad topic. As I remarked initially, I have not changed my views in any essential respects about what I called Wittgensteinian Fideism. But in the last decade my disinterest in the philosophy of religion has become so great that I have read very little of the literature, and except for the following two essays I have not studied Phillips's later work at all. Here I shall concentrate on two recent essays germane to my topic: his 'On Not Understanding God' and 'From Coffee to Carmelites'. I shall argue that in these essays Phillips surely wants to get out of the fly bottle, but that he has not succeeded and that this failure carries a salutary lesson.

III

I now turn to his arguments and to his narrative. Phillips claims that in philosophy, and in our Enlightenment culture generally, there is a reluctance – rooted, he believes, in prejudice, or at least in confusion – to admit 'that there is anything which passes beyond human understanding' (II, 131).[3] There are many things, of course, that we do not understand – ignorance and self-deception are widespread. Even when we work at them in a careful and disciplined way – as scientists, logicians or philosophers – there are things we fail to understand. There is wide cultural agreement about this.

However, this is still something which just happens to be the case. It does not at all mean, or even suggest, that what we fail to understand 'is something which is beyond understanding'. What we fail to understand remains in principle, the orthodox claim goes, within the reach of human understanding. There is nothing that is *necessarily* beyond human understanding. 'That something could be necessarily beyond human understanding seems to be an intolerable thought, the denial of a philosophical vocation' (I, 153). Phillips takes the belief that this is so to be a pervasive philosophical prejudice flying in the face 'of what is platitudinously obvious: that there is much that passes beyond human understanding' (II, 131). He believes that a philosopher might, and a fully perceptive philosopher *will*, come to understand that there is something – *necessarily* – beyond human understanding. And a crucial bit of this is 'that the limits of human existence are beyond human understanding' (II, 131). It is surely evident that if accepted this would give consolation both to the Kierkegaardian knight of faith and to the Camusian-Sartrean existentialist atheist. But this is not a fine brash philosophical thesis to be affirmed or denied, but a philosophical muddle which rests on a failure to command a clear view of our language. It is a claim which should be up for dissolution rather than resolution.

Let me turn now to an explanation of why I say this. What is it to say that when 'one is reacting to the vicissitudes of human life . . . one is reacting to something which is beyond human understanding' (I, 160)? And what does it mean to say, as it is standardly said by religious people, that 'the ways of God are beyond human understanding' (I, 163)? Put otherwise, the ways of God are said to be inscrutable. If, as I think, it is a right move in philosophy to begin thinking about God by exploring 'the grammar of talk about the ways of God, given in our language, instead of assuming *ab initio* standards by which such talk *must* be assessed', then we will start our exploration by simply acknowledging that religious people say that God is inscrutable and that his ways are beyond human understanding (I. 166). That is just how we play, if we play such language-games at all, the language-game of Christian, Jewish and Islamic God-talk.

So why does Phillips say 'that there is something necessarily beyond human understanding' (I, 168)? According to Phillips, what is crucial here is to recognize that we are up against, not *limitations* to human understanding which might be overcome, but the very *limits* of human understanding. Whether your reaction to a recognition of the limits, rather than the limitations, of human understanding is religious or non-religious, if it is not confused it will be a recognition that *there is nothing to be understood*, nothing to be put right by understanding or action (I, 168). Samuel Beckett says it, with a succinct translation into the concrete, when he has his character Hamm say, 'You're on earth: there's no cure for that' (I, 168; S. Beckett, *Endgame*, Faber & Faber, 1976, p. 37).

What sorts of things does Phillips say are necessarily beyond human understanding and can take no relevant explanation, for there is nothing to understand? He tells us that there are certain facts of human existence which can typically be given mundane causal explanations, but where our *reactions* to them show us, if we reflect, that even when perfectly correct these explanations are plainly not to the point. They are, that is, not what is to the point when we react to these facts of human existence: facts of what Phillips obscurely calls the limits of human existence. Here we are talking about the vicissitudes of human life. As I noted, in some ways they are explainable, or at least in principle could be, but in an important respect they are still necessarily beyond human understanding. (I would think, since in the relevant respect they are not a matter of understanding or knowledge at all, they would be beyond superhuman understanding, if such there be, as well. They would be beyond God's understanding as well as ours, and since there is nothing to be known, that would be no limitation on God's omniscience or omnipotence.) The characteristic facts in question are the 'blind forces of nature, the unpredictable visitations of disease and death, the transitoriness of fame, treason by friends and kin . . . [and] the limitations of time and place' (I, 161).

Suppose a writer, caring much about her work and struggling against odds to achieve something of merit and insight, is, unknown to herself, about to receive the Nobel prize for literature. But the day before the announcement was to come to her, she suddenly and unexpectedly has a heart attack and dies without ever knowing that she has received the award. It is natural in such circumstances to lament 'Why did it have to happen to her just then, on just that day?' As Stephen Toulmin has noted with his conception of a limiting question, this 'Why?' is not a request for an explanation but a verbal expression of a cry of anguish.[4] We characteristically ask it when we have good causal explanations of why something happened. We are not looking for more information; indeed, unless we are metaphysically befuddled, we are not asking for any bit of knowledge or any explanation at all. We recognize, causally explainable though it is, that we are just up against one of those brute contingencies that happen for no rhyme or reason. There is no justifying it or blaming anyone for its happening; we are here outside the domain of what is justifiable and what is not. (If it cannot be justified, it makes no sense to say it is unjustified either. Such normative terms have no hold or application here.) Why it happened, *looking at it normatively*, is beyond understanding. And it is a plain example of things that happen again and again and are to be contrasted with a child's death from starvation – one of the 35,000 that so die everyday – or people dying of AIDS brought about by a transfusion of tainted blood. These latter things could, with care and commitment, be prevented. They are things for which certain people are responsible, and they are unjustifiable in that wrongs are done to people that can and should be prevented. But the writer dying just then, dismaying as it is, is nothing that is up before the bar of moral or otherwise normative assessment, criticism or deliberation; it is not the sort of thing that with foresight and resolute action could have been prevented or ameliorated. Questions of neither justification nor exculpation are in order; there is nothing normatively relevant to be known.

While it is at least plausible to believe that in the order of causes a principle of sufficient reason is at work, it is altogether implausible to believe that such a principle is at work in the domain of good and bad such that there is a justifying or excusing reason for every bad or good thing that happens. Some bad and some good things happen to us for no reason, and where they are horrendous enough we may cry out against them. What is puzzling is not that these things happen but that Phillips makes such a hue and cry about them. If we like we can talk about the 'limits of human existence', 'the limits of understanding', of something being necessarily beyond knowledge or understanding. But this is just a grandiloquent way of saying what could be expressed more prosaically and less misleadingly by saying that these matters are important to us, and that they are not matters of knowing or failing to know, of understanding or failing to understand, of reason or lack of reason, but things to which the notions of knowing and understanding, for God or man, are not applicable.

IV

To sum up: The vicissitudes of human life are often understood well enough, in the sense that we know their causes. We also know that they happen for no rhyme or reason; and because of this the notion of justifying them, or failing to justify them, makes no sense. But there is no need to make a mystery out of that. There is no intolerable thought here, making mish-mash out of the 'life of reason', that something is, or even could be, necessarily beyond human understanding in that sense. It is simply the case that in the domain of the normative the principle of sufficient reason does not apply. Horrible things happen for no reason, with no one to blame, with no injustice being done.

Is there, however, perhaps some more significant sense in which something could be said to be *necessarily* beyond human understanding? We – meaning people who are likely to read this chapter and people from a similar social stratum who share, in a general way, a similar way of life – find certain other cultures utterly alien to us such that we cannot, or so we believe, understand them. These other people live in 'an alien society' which we cannot understand from within the mode of understanding we possess. There is sometimes, or so it has been claimed, a radical *incommensurability* between two societies (II, 133). Phillips accepts, plausibly enough it seems to me, the Wittgensteinian point that 'language gets its sense from the way it enters human life' (II, 132). But when people have radically different lives there will 'be as many differences in their languages as there are in their lives' (II, 132). As a result, they do not just *fail* to understand each other; they *cannot* understand one another.

This is H. O. Mounce's view, which Phillips is criticizing in part, but also partially endorsing – though not very plainly. It appears, that is, that Phillips is endorsing the radical incommensurability just characterized. Sometimes there are societies, say A and B, in which there are some things in A which the people in B cannot understand: they necessarily pass beyond understanding for them. This, Phillips seems to agree, can and does sometimes happen.

But such an incommensurability claim misses the quite different, though mutually supporting, points made against it by Donald Davidson, Isaac Levi and Charles Taylor.[5] If in saying that the beliefs, conceptions and concepts of society A are incommensurable with those of society B, we are saying that there are beliefs, conceptions and concepts expressible in the language of B which are untranslatable into the language of A, then we have said something which is at best false. Where we treat meaning holophrastically and go moderately holistic, as do Quine and Davidson, there is no indeterminacy of translation. There are, as a matter of fact, no languages that are mutually untranslatable.[6] This is true even of the radically different languages of radically different cultures. (This was even stressed, paradoxically, by the articulators of what came to be called 'the Whorf-Sapir hypothesis'.) Moreover, given the resources for mutual comprehensibility between radically different languages of radically different cultures, there are no good reasons, if we go holophrastically, to think that there are even terms in one language that cannot be understood in the terms of the other language. Where the one culture is very alien to the other, and where it is very difficult to understand a concept in the language of the one culture by utilizing the resources of the other, there is a temptation to speak of incommensurability. But we cannot reasonably ask for term-by-term translation. We need to go holophrastic, and moderately holistic, and still we will make mistake after mistake, and perhaps never *in fact* get the translation of the alien language just right.

A good example of what I am contending is that of E. E. Evans-Pritchard's and Peter Winch's treatment of the Azande concept of witchcraft, a concept that certainly does not, to put it minimally, match our own.[7] But Winch, in correcting Evans-Pritchard's errors and at the same time building on him, gave us an understanding of the Azande concept. Moreover, if we *necessarily* could have no understanding of the concept, such that in principle no attempt to characterize or elucidate it in our language or any other language could succeed, then for reasons Davidson has forcefully argued we could never know whether or not that was so.[8] We would understand nothing at all here. But that is very different from saying there is some belief, concept, conception, term, sentence or truth that passes beyond the understanding. We would at least have to know enough about it to understand what it was that passes beyond our understanding. Let us fabricate some language and suppose there is in that language a term 'uzad'. Suppose I master the language but still do not understand 'uzad'. All my efforts to get a grip on it fail. But to say that it is logically impossible for me, starting from my native tongue, to translate or understand it, as distinct from saying that so far all attempts at translation have failed, makes no sense. At least to know that 'uzad' is part of the language in question, I must understand it as a word, a phrase or perhaps a sentence in that language. I see that it fits or fails to fit with other grammatical sentences in the language. I catch something of its syntax. If I do not understand anything like that, then I am in no position to say that there is a term, concept, conception or belief in the language of that culture that I cannot – necessarily cannot – understand. The thesis that there are concepts of an alien culture that necessarily pass the understanding of the people of another culture is an incoherent conception, probably a product of the Kantian scheme/content dogma criticized so effectively by Davidson.

We can escape these difficulties by dropping talk of 'necessarily' or 'necessity'. Doing so leaves us with the banality that it is often difficult in certain particular respects to understand others both within our own culture and, even more obviously, in different cultures.[9] Sometimes they have notions we do not understand very well at all, notions that thoroughly baffle us. Moreover, it is not only the people in New Guinea that I have a hard time understanding. The skinhead with the shaved head with a red stripe painted across it, his arms and chest almost completely tattooed, with long earrings and a strange gait, is nearly as strange to me. I observe him as he gets on the same bus as I do and then the same metro, and I wonder what he is thinking, what ambitions, hopes and fears he has, what sense of himself he has and why it is that he so decks himself out. I feel at a considerable distance from such a person: his life seems, and no doubt is, alien to me; and mine to him, no doubt. But there are also all the familiar ways in which I could learn about the life of such a person. There is no logical or otherwise conceptual barrier of incommensurability here, or, as far as we can discover, anywhere else either, which justifies, or even gives sense to, the belief that there are, for a person in a given culture, other people in the same or in another culture, with conceptions so alien to this person that they are necessarily incommensurable, that is, untranslatable, such that this person can have no understanding of what they mean when the others speak: each being immersed in a different conceptual scheme such that both are conceptually imprisoned in their own perspective with no possible understanding of the other.

Suppose we say (*pace* Davidson) that incommensurability should not come to untranslatability but either to non-comparability or to the lack of shared standards of rationality, making common acceptance and assessment impossible. The response to this should be that once untranslatability is abandoned, there is no reason to believe that comparability is impossible or that we have so little common toehold in rationality that some sharing in understanding and common acceptance of what is rational and what is not is even in principle impossible. Of course, people, over time and place, will have different standards of rationality.[10] But to say, as Phillips does, that there is no common rationality which people can appeal to, is to say more than that standards of rationality differ. To establish this claim, we would need to know not only that standards differ, but also that they have no central features in common. The platitudinous truth is that in some respects they differ and in some respects they are the same. With that sameness, even if it is rather thin, we have some common starting point from which we could reason and deliberate about our differences, using something like what John Rawls and Norman Daniels have called the method of reflective equilibrium.[11] To think, as did Lucien Lévy-Bruhl, that there is something like a primitive mentality that leads primitive people to think utterly differently than we do, is at best a groundless claim. Our wiring is very similar and with our large brains (something cutting across cultures) we can, if other things do not go too badly, think. Moreover, we all have beliefs, desires, intentions and plans. We wish to realize our desires, to see whether our beliefs and desires fit, or fail to fit, reasonably well, and the like. And if they hang together reasonably well, we will seek a better fit. (If this is folk psychology, make the most of it.) With these capacities and resources we can, and do, deliberate about what it is reasonable to think and do. It is not plausible, perhaps not even intelligible, to think that we will run up against points where what we take to be reasonable to believe or think is *so different* from what people in other cultures take to be reasonable, that it is *necessarily* the case that any cross-cultural deliberations and comparisons will be fruitless, or will break down, revealing a radical incommensurability of perspective. It is more plausible to believe that than to believe in incommensurability as untranslatability. And if there are common resources of rationality, there will also be common resources for comparability. To put the point more modestly, if such deliberation and such comparisons are *necessarily* impossible across cultures, such that the disputants even in theory cannot understand one another or deliberate together, then (a) give some evidence for that, and more fundamentally, (b) show how it is that we can know, or even coherently believe, that this is so. There is the empirical fact that understanding, fruitful argument, agreement, and so on, across cultures, and even within cultures, is difficult. But we must not, if we wish to remain relatively clearheaded and reasonable, slip from that fact to the claim that they and we are conceptually imprisoned in utterly incommensurable frameworks. There is no good reason to believe that mutual incomprehension and bewilderment are so intractable and so deep.

V

So the fact that there are cultures alien to each other, and that even within a single culture there are very different people with very different perspectives (say a Hamann and a d'Holbach, a de Maistre and a Condorcet), gives us no toehold for the belief in a radical incommensurability whereby some people necessarily pass beyond the understanding of some other people. But Phillips also considers, critically following Mounce, whether 'there are things which pass beyond the understanding of *all* human beings: things which human beings can never come to understand' (ll, 136; my italics). The kinds of cases Mounce presents, and Phillips considers, are our trying to understand the condition of a dog, what it is like to be a bat, or whether fish can feel pain. Mounce works with these

examples in order to 'illustrate the difference between that which we fail
to understand and that which passes beyond human understanding' (II,
131). Phillips argues, cogently I believe, that the bat, the dog or the
fish cases do not show us that 'there are things which pass beyond the
understanding of all human beings; things which human beings can never
come to understand' (II, 136–41).

There are also, it is claimed, things that one class of human beings can
never understand about another class. The rich, Mounce has it, can never
know what it is like to be poor, to live on the dole for example. But
(*pace* Mounce) the rich can see, indeed observe rather systematically
(travel with their eyes open, as de Beauvoir and Sartre did); they can read
social scientists' accounts of poverty, extend their understanding by the
reading of imaginative literature, and the like. Like George Orwell and
Simone Weil they can even live and work with the poor, taking jobs the
poor take, living with the poor as the poor live. But Mounce would say
'that no matter how much understanding of the poor the rich have, they
do not know *exactly* what it is like to be poor' (II, 141–2). Even Orwell
could not know what it is like to be poor, even after living and working
with them and writing *Down and Out in Paris and London*, for he was
not poor and did not have the same inescapable vulnerability as the poor.
On Mounce's account, to really know what it is to be poor comes to
saying that you must be poor. Since the rich do not have to live with
poverty, they do not know, and cannot – really – know, what it is like to
be poor. But this is to turn something by means of an implicit, persuasive
definition into a tautology that on normal readings or understandings it
is not. It is very likely true that most of the time the poor know more
about poverty than the non-poor. But the non-poor can know a great
deal about poverty; and in some cases someone like Orwell or Weil, who
acutely observed and reflected on what they saw, might very well come
to know more about poverty and being poor than do many of the poor.
At least we cannot rule this out by conceptual fiat. Similar things can,
and should, be said about paranoia and schizophrenia. Harry Stack
Sullivan probably knew more about what it is like to be schizophrenic
than most, perhaps all, schizophrenics. We cannot justifiably identify
'understanding a way of life' with 'living a way of life'. These examples
do not show that there are some things for some human beings which
necessarily pass beyond their understanding.

The dog, bat and fish cases may seem to show that there are some
things which pass beyond the understanding of all human beings. But I
think Phillips shows that those familiar claims are mistaken. I do not
know whether fish feel pain or not; but by studying carefully their nervous
system and the like, and watching carefully their behaviour, I, and others,
could come to a reasonable understanding of what is likely the case here.
Similar things obtain for understanding what it is like to be a bat or a

dog. A dog to which you are very close and know very well might, when you look at him reflectively, come to seem enigmatic to you. You wonder what is going on in his head, how he perceives the world. And this is even more so with bats, with whom most of us do not live in very close contact. Phillips shows how we could come to understand such animals reasonably well. There is not some conceptual gulf between what they are and how they react such that we could not understand them at all. What Mounce, and in this case Thomas Nagel as well, show is that we can never know from the inside, as it were, what it is like to be a dog or a bat, but this is only, again by the use of an implicit persuasive definition, to identify knowing what it is like to be a bat or a dog with being a bat or a dog. But this works no better for these cases than for the others. Dog trainers and some dog lovers know a great deal about dogs without being dogs, and bat specialists can know a great deal about bats without being bats. In general, to understand or know x is not the same thing as being x or even, in some tendentious sense, experiencing x.[12] We have no plausible or even firmly coherent model for saying that there are some things – a bat, a dog, a god, God, a Martian, a computer, or what not – that human beings *necessarily* cannot know so that these things are beyond human understanding. And this is not hubris, but a reasonable grasp of how our language-games are played.

VI

Mystical experience, and mystical awareness of the inscrutable, God in particular, is sometimes used as an example of what few special people who have had that experience can know, and that others cannot understand – necessarily cannot understand. Those of us who have not had mystical experiences cannot understand what the mystic can. It is sometimes claimed that this religious case will yield a genuine example of understanding something that for most people passes beyond the understanding.

There are, of course, problems about the very intelligibility of talk of mystical experience, for the mystic as well as non-mystic. But that aside, there is, at least on the face of it, much that can be learned about mystical experience from those who have not had it but have carefully studied and reflected on it. William James, W. T. Stace and Ninian Smart have, without having had mystical experience, written about it with care, and sometimes insight; and some people have, to some extent at least, understood them.[13] To say that what the writers and readers understand is not really to understand mystical experience, for to understand the experience it is necessary to have it, is to make the unjustified claim of identifying understanding x with having x. We have already seen that there is no justification for that claim. Thus it cannot be correct to say that the mystical experiences, spiritual exercises and more generally contemplative practices must pass beyond our understanding if we have not had mystical experience. Mystics were not, of course, born mystics. They came, typically after rigorous self-discipline, to experience something which at one time was beyond their understanding. Phillips claims that what they came to experience came about as the result of a transformation, not an extension, of their prior understanding. The claim is that only by such a transformation of the understanding can such experiences be understood (II, 143).

Suppose it is claimed that reading these accounts of mystical experience, including the writings of someone like St John of the Cross, will not convey real understanding until the reader has had the experience itself. Those readers who have not had mystical experience, the argument goes, are to St John's reports like the blind are to the sighted. To this we should respond that the analogy is apt. The blind can understand what sight is; they just cannot see. The mystical experience case seems to be fully analogous. Moreover, even if the understanding requires a transformation of experience, the transformation is rooted in something we already have and is familiar to us, and we could not have such a transformation, with the changed perspective on life it brings, without it. It is a necessary background condition for the transformation. Indeed, extension and transformation slide into one another. In those ways the stress on a sharp contrast between extension and transformation is in error.

St John of the Cross thought that what he was saying would only be fully understood by those specially prepared to receive it. But this 'being specially prepared' was to have received a certain spiritual training; and this is, as Phillips remarks, 'a matter of building on, extending, ordinary religious practices' (II, 146). There is a transformation that takes place in mystical experience, but it is a transformation that is essentially connected with the religious practices and conceptions which preceded it. Mystical experience does not come about as a result of some unmediated initiation. The belief that it does, Phillips writes, is itself 'a magical view of mysticism' (II, 146). So mystical experience is not inherently inexpressible, the mystic's claims are not self-authenticating, and they are not something that can be understood only by someone who has them. Again we have nothing that necessarily goes beyond understanding.

VII

It has not been shown that it is the case, or even can be the case, that the experiences or understanding some people have *necessarily* pass beyond the understanding of all human beings. Contingently, of course, there are many things that some people know and others do not and cannot know. Children, to say nothing of infants, do not know many things that normal adults do. Primitive peoples know some things that we do not know and we know some things they do not. In both cases some things *contingently* pass beyond the understanding of some people. These things are the merest truisms, but true for all that. They are only worth reminding ourselves of because of certain philosophical confusions.[14]

It is only slightly less truistic to say that if there are gods, or if God or intelligent Martians exist, these beings (if that is what God is) will know things that no human being as a matter of fact can know. But this is like saying that human beings cannot hear certain sounds that dogs can, as when we blow a whistle that we do not hear ourselves but dogs do. There is no conceptual, or logical, ban on our hearing these sounds; it is just the case that, as a matter of fact, we cannot hear them. But what the Martians or gods, if such there be, and what God, if he is even possible, can know that we cannot is just like that. This, however, is not the kind of 'failing to understand' in which Phillips is interested. It is not the model he wants for trying to understand what 'passing beyond one's understanding' amounts to. Moreover, philosophers, like everyone else, have not been at all reluctant to admit that things can and sometimes do pass beyond our understanding in these – philosophically speaking – trivial ways. However, where we stick with 'in principle' and 'of necessity' in trying to model the understanding of something passing beyond human understanding, we run into trouble teasing out a coherent sense for these claims. If a Martian can understand it, why is it logically impossible for us? If an adult can understand it, why is it logically impossible for a child? If God understands it, why is it logically impossible for us? There seems to be no answer to these questions. At the very least Phillips has suggested none.

Suppose we drop the qualification 'human' and say instead, including even God in our scope, that 'there may be something beyond understanding; not something accidentally or temporarily beyond it, but something necessarily beyond understanding'. It is a tautology to say that if something is not a matter of knowledge or understanding, so that there is nothing to understand or fail to understand, then it cannot be understood. But it is extravagant rhetoric to say that we have here something which passes beyond understanding. This is more like bad poetry than philosophical description and analysis. To say that we understand something which it makes no sense to understand is a contradiction; to say that we should not try to understand what in principle is not a matter of understanding is a truism – though it is perfectly true that as a *second-order* matter we can come to understand that some things are not matters of understanding or knowledge at all. But as we have seen, we get into trouble when, as Phillips does, we add 'human' to qualify 'understanding'. If understanding is logically impossible, then it is logically impossible, period. Bringing God in will not make the slightest difference. What we have seen is that in a trivial, philosophically uninteresting sense, Mounce is right that it is 'platitudinously obvious that there is much that passes beyond human understanding', but that in the philosophically interesting ways of construing that claim it is at best thoroughly problematic.

We talk in an inflated and obscurantist way when we talk of the limits of human existence or the limits of understanding. In both instances, if it means anything, it means, as Phillips shows, that in certain situations there is nothing to understand: not for us, for Martians, for computers or for God. So if there is nothing to understand then there is no object of, or proper occasion for, wonder or perplexity over the fact that there is something that passes beyond understanding that we could not set right by understanding. That is about as evident as anything can be. Consider an example. People age and sometimes their powers – physical, intellectual and on occasion even moral – fail. There are reasonable causal explanations of why this happens. But there is no mystery here, nothing to wonder or be perplexed about, or to reflect on with an eye to making sense of it. It is just a brute fact of the world, one of the contingencies of the world that matters to us. It does not pass beyond understanding in the sense that we do not know *why* it happens; neither does it pass beyond understanding in the sense that God or a Martian could see the justification for it while we cannot. There is no justification for it: not because it is unjustified, but because it could be neither justified nor unjustified. Such normative notions have no hold here. (Not seeing this is, in part, what is the matter with theodicies.) In that sense they are not a matter of knowledge. Suppose a great poet grows senile and comes to write drivel. Faced with this we may say 'Oh, why did it have to happen to him? Why? Why?!' This is our old friend the limiting question again, expressing our lament and anguish and our sense of regret that the world is such. The 'Why?' does not ask for an explanation, for more knowledge, for a rationale, excuse or justification to be supplied, or anything like that. It gives vent to our feelings. It is an expressive use of language. To say that it points to something that passes beyond understanding is misleading at best, for it suggests that something like understanding is at issue, when what is at issue are human reactions and deliberations in the light of these brute facts on what are the more appropriate reactions in such circumstances, if this can ever be reasoned out or reasoned *and* felt out. (That we can in some instances deliberate on what are the most appropriate feelings does not mean that feelings themselves are a form of cognition or a form of knowledge or understanding.)

VIII

What has all this to do with divine inscrutability? Phillips, wanting to avoid theodicies, wants as a 'philosopher . . . to understand what is meant by saying that God's ways are beyond human understanding'. What he has perhaps succeeded in showing us, or at least given us some understanding of, is what can sensibly be meant by 'God's ways are beyond understanding *sans phrase*'. But then he has in effect also shown us that there is nothing to be understood except that the whole matter should be set aside. Moreover, even if we do somehow get, against what I have argued, some appropriate understanding of what it is for God's ways to be beyond human understanding, this does not mean, as Phillips is quick to point out, that we understand God (I, 168–9). But we then fall into still other difficulties. The hope was that by coming to some understanding of 'the place that the belief that God's ways are beyond understanding has in the lives of believers', we could gain a foothold on what it is to believe in God and what it would be to encounter God (I, 169; II, 149). But if this does not help us to understand God, then, we should ask, what does? It seems that the very concept of God, in developed forms of Judaeo-Christianity and Islam, is incoherent. The idea of God as an 'infinite individual transcendent to the universe' has at least the appearance of a contradiction; and the definite descriptions used to teach the meaning of 'God', where these descriptions are supposed to specify a non-anthropomorphic reality, all seem so problematic as to yield no tolerably firm sense of what we are talking about. We seem to have no more than human reactions to a something, we understand not what. Divine inscrutability is so inscrutable that we do not even have a sense of what it is to scrutinize here.[15] If God is utterly beyond human understanding, then there is nothing to be said, nothing to be thought, nothing to be perplexed about, nothing to wonder at. Accounts of encounters with God, of coming to know and love God, of living or standing in the presence of God, of sensing or feeling the grace of God, are what Axel Hägerström called 'empty phrases' without sense.[16]

Phillips claims that the mystics do not give reports, flawed or otherwise, 'or descriptions which fall short of the mark, but expressions of their encounter with God' (II, 149). He also says that this encounter with God, if genuine, must be an experience which passes beyond all human understanding (II, 149). Given the other things he says, it must be an experience that necessarily, and not just contingently, passes beyond human understanding. But we have seen that this is an incoherent notion, and this being so, that the very notion of an encounter with God, at least on this reading, must also be incoherent.

Phillips might respond, as he does to Mounce, that like most philosophers I place too much weight on *understanding*. I worry about the coherence or truth of the belief that, where God is concerned, we need to understand that it is something that passes beyond our understanding, 'at least while we are on earth'; and, over-intellectualizing things, I try to see if any coherent sense can be made of that. Phillips remarks that 'religious reactions . . . are very different. When they speak of that which passes beyond understanding, they invite us to consider the possibility of reacting to human life in a way other than by understanding' (II, 149). One reaction that Phillips takes to be religious, and appropriately so, is that of wonder. But it is to wonder in such a way that we can think of the grace of God. It is not the speculative wonder of the Greek philosophers. Phillips thinks that this is a natural way for wonder to go for the person of faith. But we – including in the 'we' the person of faith – need some understanding of 'God' to see how the 'gifts of nature can be seen as gifts of grace', God's grace (II, 150). But then we cannot just be reacting to human life in a way other than by understanding. The very possibility of so reacting requires some understanding, and we cannot have that if God is necessarily beyond human understanding.

Phillips might respond that the language of the mystic, like religious language more generally, is in our midst and 'language gets its sense from the way it enters human life'; so that 'the language of walking with God, meeting God, gets its sense, if it does anywhere, from the way this language entered the life of St John of the Cross' (II, 151). That language, which is one paradigmatic strand of religious language, involves talk of God being beyond human understanding as well as talk of the importance in the religious life of 'dying to the understanding'. Phillips would no doubt claim that in saying that such talk is incoherent, that it does not make sense, I must be importing standards of rationality or intelligibility from outside the religious language-games actually played; and it is unclear where these standards could come from, what authority they could have, why we should appeal to them, or why the religious person, or anyone else, should pay any heed at all. They seem, Phillips could say, like news from nowhere, arbitrary impositions from out of the blue.

I agree with Phillips that language gets its sense from the way it enters human life. This is a lesson we have rightly taken from Wittgenstein. But language must be taken more holistically than Phillips takes it. We must not take one language-game or linguistic practice, or even a localized cluster of them, standing by themselves. It is not enough to say, 'This language-game is played'. We need to look at the language more broadly and try to gain a perspicuous representation of how various language-games in various domains of our talk and thought, of our discoursing with each other, go, or fail to go, together. Thus we might come to recognize that religious talk ('God-talk' as I call it, as distinct from other religious talk, such as the Buddhist might engage in) could have the grammar – the logic, in Phillips's extended sense of 'logic' – that he says it has and still be incoherent because of the way it stands with other parts of our talk. That something like this is the case is what I think. But I can think that, while still taking it that language gets its sense from the way it enters human life, because I look at language more holistically than does Phillips – thinking that a moderate holism, such as we find in Donald Davidson and Richard Rorty, squares better with how our language and thinking works than any Balkanized or molecular view of language.

I think, and indeed hope, that God-talk, and religious discourse more generally, is, or at least should be, dying out in the West, or more generally in a world that has felt the force of a Weberian disenchantment of the world. This sense that religious convictions are no longer a live option is something which people who think of themselves as either modernists or post-modernists very often tend to have. It may even be partly definitive of being such a person. For Alasdair MacIntyre, and presumably for Phillips as well, this is a distressing, or at least a saddening, matter. For me, firmly modernist as I am, it is a hopeful sign. As Richard Rorty puts it, perhaps we can at last get the Enlightenment without the Enlightenment's *rationalism*. Among the intelligentsia such attitudes of disenchantment are widespread; and these attitudes, given a moderate amount of security and wealth, can reasonably be expected to trickle slowly down to the rest of society. The view from North America is that the view has not trickled down extensively to the population more generally. There has, however, been a lot of such trickling down in the securer, more prosperous and better educated Scandinavian societies.

This Weberian and Habermasian sense of how modernity can be expected to evolve under conditions of security and abundance could go with a view like Phillips's that language gets its sense from the way it enters human life. Simon Blackburn has stated, though rather as an aside, what many philosophers who have been touched by modernity or post-modernity think, including such Wittgensteinians as Richard Rorty. Blackburn remarks:

> Practice alone rules whether the choice of a mathematical or physical or psychological or modal or moral religious language stands us in good stead. The philosopher may, as a lucky amateur, make a contribution to recognising the excellence or the infirmity of some discourse, but there is no profession of being lucky. And when a discourse or way of life dies, as the religious way has effectively done in the West, this is never because it could not stand the scrutiny of Minerva, but because the consolations and promises it offered eventually lost their

power to animate us. The philosopher can only ride the hearse declaiming that he thought the patient dead before the rest did.[17]

There is a little hyperbole here, but not much. It seems to me that this is the situation we are in. Perhaps this is a superficial way of looking at or reacting to religion, a way that has not looked at it carefully enough, sympathetically enough or long enough; but then again, perhaps not. Phillips tries to exhibit sources of animation, but he has in reality afforded more of a reason for thinking that the discourse is, or at least should be, dead. He has tried, by assembling reminders, to show us that there are some sources in our lives and language that will reveal how the consolations and promises of Christianity, and religion more broadly, still have the power to animate us. But he has, I think, failed. It is time, if we have an impulse to do any declaiming at all, to ride the hearse.

Notes

1 The original article, 'Wittgensteinian Fideism', *Philosophy* XLII, no. 161 (July 1967), 191–209, appears in a somewhat expanded form and with a follow-up chapter, in my *An Introduction to the Philosophy of Religion* (London: Macmillan, 1982), 65–133, along with my direct discussion of Wittgenstein on religion, 43–64. I pursue the twistings and turnings of Wittgensteinian Fideism in my *God, Scepticism, and Modernity* (Ottawa, Ontario: University of Ottawa Press, 1989), chapters 5–11, in my *Scepticism* (New York: St Martin's Press, 1973), 23–40, in my *Contemporary Critiques of Religion* (New York: Herder and Herder, 1971), 94–112, and in my *Philosophy and Atheism* (Buffalo, NY: Prometheus Press, 1985), 77–106, 211–27. See, as well, Michael Martin, 'Wittgenstein's Lectures on Religious Belief', *Heythrop Journal* XXXII (1991), 369–82.

2 The essays by D. Z. Phillips that shall be the object of my attention are his 'On Not Understanding God' and 'From Coffee to Carmelites'. All references to Phillips will be given in the text. 'On Not Understanding God' will be referred to in the text by I, followed by the page number, and 'From Coffee to Carmelites' will be referred to by II, followed by the page number. The two essays are in *Wittgenstein and Religion*, Macmillan and St Martin's Press, 1993.

3 See H. O. Mounce, 'The Aroma of Coffee', *Philosophy* 64, no. 248, 159–73. This essay is the object of Phillips's attention in 'From Coffee to Carmelites'.

4 Stephen Toulmin, *An Examination of the Place of Reason in Ethics* (Cambridge: Cambridge University Press, 1950), 202–21. I discuss limiting questions in my 'Religion, Science and Limiting Questions', *Studies in Religion* 8, no. 3 (1979), 259–65, my 'The "Good Reasons Approach" and "Ontological Justifications" of Morality', *The Philosophical Quarterly* 9, no. 35 (April 1959), 2–16 and in my *Justification and Morals* (unpublished doctoral dissertation, Duke

University, 1955), 63–72 and 216–45. See here, as well, Robert C. Coburn, 'A Neglected Use of Theological Language', *Mind* 72 (1963).

5 Donald Davidson, *Inquiries into Truth and Interpretation* (Oxford: Clarendon Press, 1984), 181–242 and his 'The Myth of the Subjective' in Michael Krausz, ed., *Relativism* (Notre Dame, IN.: University of Notre Dame Press, 1982), 159–81; Isaac Levi, 'Escape From Boredom: Edification According to Rorty', *Canadian Journal of Philosophy* XI, no. 4 (December 1981) and his 'Conflict and Inquiry', *Ethics* 102 (July 1992), 314–34; and Charles Taylor, *Philosophy and the Human Sciences* (Cambridge: Cambridge University Press, 1985), 15–59, 116–51.

6 Hilary Putnam, 'Meaning Holism' and W. V. Quine, 'Reply to Putnam' both in Lewis Edwin Hahn and Paul Arthur Schilpp, eds, *The Philosophy of W. V. Quine* (La Salle, IL.: Open Court, 1986), 405–32 and W. V. Quine, *Pursuit of Truth* (Cambridge, MA.: Harvard University Press, 1990), 13–16, 50–9.

7 E. E. Evans-Pritchard, *Witchcraft, Oracles and Magic Among the Azande* (Oxford: Oxford University Press, 1939) and Peter Winch, 'Understanding a Primitive Society' in D. Z. Phillips, ed., *Religion and Understanding* (Oxford: Basil Blackwell, 1967), 9–42.

8 Davidson, *Inquiries into Truth and Interpretation*, 183–98; Børn T. Ramberg, *Donald Davidson's Philosophy of Language* (Oxford: Basil Blackwell, 1989), 116–40; and Simon Evine, *Donald Davidson* (Stanford, CA.: Stanford University Press, 1991), 134–71. If there is a verificationist streak here so be it. Not everything in verificationism is wrong, not every application mistaken.

9 See Richard Rorty on the import of dropping talk of necessity. Richard Rorty, *Consequences of Pragmatism* (Minneapolis: University of Minnesota Press, 1982), 19–36 and Rorty, *Objectivism, Relativism and Truth* (Cambridge: Cambridge University Press, 1991).

10 Charles Taylor and Isaiah Berlin (his talk of incommensurability notwithstanding) make it clear why in spite of different standards of rationality we still have overlapping criteria of both rationality and what is taken to be humanly acceptable. Taylor, *Philosophy and the Human Sciences*, 116–33 and Isaiah Berlin, 'Reply to Ronald H. McKinney, "Towards a Postmodern Ethics"', *The Journal of Value Inquiry* 26 (1992), 557–60. Taylor goes on to show, in ways that mesh with the method of wide reflective equilibrium, how we can reason our way out of ethnocentric traps.

11 John Rawls, *A Theory of Justice* (Cambridge, MA.: Harvard University Press, 1971), 19–21, 48–51, 571–87; John Rawls, 'The Independence of Moral Theory', *Proceedings and Addresses of the American Philosophical Association* 47 (1974/75), 7–10; Norman Daniels, 'Wide Reflective Equilibrium and Theory Acceptance in Ethics', *Journal of Philosophy* 76 (1979); Norman Daniels, 'Reflective Equilibrium and Archimedean Points' in J. Angelo Corbett, ed., *Equality and Liberty* (London: Macmillan, 1991), 90–109; Kai Nielsen, *After the Demise of the Tradition* (Boulder, CO.: Westview Press, 1991), 195–248; and Kai Nielsen, 'Rawls and the Socratic Ideal', *Analyse & Kritik* 13, no. 1 (1991), 67–93.

12 Alice Ambrose, 'The Problem of Linguistic Inadequacy' in Max Black, ed., *Philosophical Analysis: A Collection of Essays* (Ithaca, NY: Cornell University Press, 1950), 15–37.

13 William James, *The Varieties of Religious Experience* (New York: Paul R. Reynolds, 1902), Lectures XVI, XVII and XX; W. T. Stace, *Mysticism and Philosophy* (Philadelphia: Lippincott, 1960); and Ninian Smart, *Reasons and Faiths* (London: Routledge & Kegan Paul, 1959).

14 Anthony Kenny cites Wittgenstein as remarking in an unpublished manuscript (the Big Typescript): 'A common-sense person, when he reads earlier philosophers thinks – quite rightly – "Sheer nonsense". When he listens to me, he thinks – rightly again – "Nothing but stale truisms". That is how the image of philosophy has changed'. Anthony Kenny, 'Wittgenstein on the Nature of Philosophy' in Brian McGuinness, ed., *Wittgenstein and His Times* (Oxford: Basil Blackwell, 1982), 22.

15 This claim about the incoherence of the concept of God in the developed forms of Judaeo-Christianity and Islam is articulated in the works of mine cited in note 1. David Ray Griffin, in a clearly formulated and fairminded review of my *God, Scepticism and Modernity*, has succinctly stated the core of my account, setting it out usefully in the form of seven propositions. He then argues that both my argument against theism and for atheism are incomplete. I argue that non-anthropomorphic concepts of God are incoherent (E), anthropomorphic concepts of God may be coherent, but they are superstitious and plainly involve false beliefs (F) and that concepts of God that are neither incoherent nor anthropomorphic are essentially atheistic (G). My case against theism is not exhaustive, Griffin has it, because the concepts of God referred to in the above theses (E, F and G) would have to be exhaustive but they are not. The non-anthropomorphic conceptions of God of *traditional* theism are, Griffin seems at least to agree, incoherent, but I fail to consider subtler forms of anthropomorphism in non-traditional theisms such as Tennant's or Whitehead's, which also reject the conceptions of God of traditional theism as incoherent without falling into a *crude* anthropomorphism or into atheism. Hence my case against theism is incomplete. I agree that it is not complete and that a complete case would have to consider such accounts and no doubt others as well. My suspicions here are (for now, they are no more than that) that if I did consider them I would find that (a) the God of such philosophers was at a very considerable distance from the God of Judaeo-Christianity and Islam, (b) that where their views are coherent they will reveal (as Spinoza's conception of God does) an atheistic substance, and (c) that their distinctively metaphysical strands are, as in all such speculative philosophy, at least as incoherent as traditional non-anthropomorphic theism. It is just such metaphysical thinking that we need, à la Rorty (a former Whiteheadean), to get rid of. Arthur Murphy's 'Whitehead and the Method of Speculative Philosophy' is insightful here. See his essay by the same title in Paul Arthur Schilpp, ed., *The Philosophy of Alfred North Whitehead* (New York: Tudor, 1941), 351–80 and set it, as well, alongside his 'Moore's "Defense of Common Sense"' in Paul Arthur Schilpp, ed., *The Philosophy of G. E. Moore* (New York: Tudor, 1942), 299–317 and his 'Can Speculative Philosophy be Defended?' *Philosophical Review* LII (1943), 135–43. My case for atheism is also incomplete, Griffin contends, for I do not argue but simply assert that non-theistic accounts of the world are adequate. But that is not true for I do argue for their adequacy in my *Equality and Liberty: A Defense of Radical Egalitarianism* (Totowa, NJ: Rowman & Allanheld, 1985), my *Reason and Practice* (New York: Harper & Row,

1971), my *Why Be Moral?* (Buffalo, NY: Prometheus Books, 1989), my *Ethics Without God*, revised edition (Buffalo, NY: Prometheus Press, 1990), and in my *God and the Grounding of Morality* (Ottawa, Ontario: University of Ottawa Press, 1991). In *Reason and Practice*, pace Griffin, I also argue that the efforts of natural theology have failed. See part III and, more indirectly, but still crucially, part VI, chapters 31, 36, 37 and 38. See also in this connection Michael Martin, *Atheism* (Philadelphia: Temple University Press, 1990). My arguments, no doubt, are in one way or another defective. That is not surprising in any event, but it seems to me that in the last three centuries there have been varied and *cumulatively* very strong arguments for the adequacy of non-theistic (i.e. naturalistic) accounts. Taken together they present a very formidable case. It is little wonder that so much of the defence of religion has turned fideistic. Moreover, and vitally, what is reasonably taken to be 'adequate' or not varies with what the alternatives are (what the live options are). If the God of traditional theism is incoherent, and Wittgensteinian Fideism is at best obscurantist, and the God of crude anthropomorphism is something yielding beliefs which are just plainly false, and non-crude anthropomorphism is (where non-atheistic) metaphysical moonshine, there is, if these things are really true, little in the way of an alternative to a pragmatic thoroughly non-metaphysical naturalism such as that articulated (though differently) by John Dewey, Jürgen Habermas and Richard Rorty. I have also turned my hand to that in my *After the Demise of the Tradition* (Boulder, CO.: Westview Press, 1989) and I have, as well, a bit in the tradition of Murphy and a bit in the tradition of Rorty, sought, without reliance on positivist assumptions, to undermine the claims of metaphysics (most particularly revisionary metaphysics). If metaphysics is a non-starter, then the very theological enterprises which rely on it, such as Paul Tillich's or Reinhold Niebuhr's or that (to quote Griffin) of such 'nontraditional theists, such as Pfleiderer, James, Tennant, Whitehead and Hartshorne', cannot, relying as they do on the constructions of speculative metaphysics, get off the ground. If I am right about the impossibility of metaphysics, there is little point in looking at the details of such views which are plainly metaphysical constructions. That is to say, key parts of their accounts rely on such constructions. I have argued for the impossibility of metaphysics in my 'Broad's Conception of Critical and Speculative Philosophy', *Dialectica* (forthcoming), 'Reconsidering the Platonic Conception of Philosophy', *International Studies in Philosophy* (forthcoming), 'Jolting the Career of Reason: Absolute Idealism and Other Rationalisms Reconsidered', *The Journal of Speculative Philosophy* (forthcoming), and 'What is Philosophy? The Reconsideration of Some Neglected Options', *History of Philosophy Quarterly* (forthcoming). See David Ray Griffin, 'Review of *God, Scepticism and Modernity*', *Journal of the American Academy of Religion* 59, no. 1 (1992), 189–90. In this setting aside of metaphysics (to return to the beginning of my essay) Phillips and I, and Wittgensteinians generally, are one, though they are usually loath to put things so bluntly. But Phillips, while abandoning metaphysics, and still seeking to keep the God of Christianity, or any other God for that matter, has only left us something akin to morality touched with emotion and obscurity.

16 Axel Hägerström, *Philosophy and Religion*, trans. from Swedish by Robert T. Sandin (London: Allen & Unwin, 1964), 224–59.

17 Simon Blackburn, 'Can Philosophy Exist?' in Jocelyne Couture and Kai

Nielsen, eds, *Reconstructing Philosophy? New Essays in Metaphilosophy* (Calgary, Alberta: University of Calgary Press, 1993). The exaggeration there that needs questioning is that the scrutiny of Minerva can have no causal impute. It cannot have the grand causal impute that philosophers are self-deceived into assuming. But that it has none at all would take a lot of showing. I doubt that Blackburn really wants to make such a strong claim.

9. Understand or Else

D. Z. PHILLIPS

I Problems of an Intermittent Dialogue

In Chapter 5, I discussed Nielsen's views on Wittgensteinian Fideism from 1967 to 1989. In Chapter 7, I presented the logical difficulties that remain despite Nielsen's response in Chapter 6. The present chapter looks at his attitude to it in 1993 as found in Chapter 8. Nielsen writes there, 'I am still inclined to believe that my criticisms of Wittgensteinian Fideism were essentially correct' (p. 143).

Part of the difficulty in responding to this claim is Nielsen's admission that having lost interest in the philosophy of religion for almost a decade, he read very little of its literature. More particularly, apart from the two papers discussed in Chapter 8, he had not studied my later work at all. On my side, given the absence of any response by Nielsen to the material presented in Chapter 2, I did not add to my criticisms of 'Wittgensteinian Fideism', although I drew attention to that misleading label often enough. After my first presentation of the refutations in Chapter 2, in 1986, the use of the term abated, only to return in the 1990s. As a result, I presented a shortened version of the textual evidence in *Religion and the Hermeneutics of Contemplation* (2001).

I mention the fact that Nielsen had not studied my work, not to lament that fact, but to point to a practical difficulty in responding to Chapter 8. My response needs, as its background, the logical claims in my work which, as I have indicated, I do not think Nielsen has addressed. Furthermore, I am unclear, by this time, what the phenomenon of Wittgensteinian Fideism is supposed to amount to. In 1973, Nielsen describes that work as a paradigm case of Wittgensteinian Fideism, but in 1978 he wonders whether it was tendentious to so describe me. In Chapter 5, I said, 'In the course of the present dialogue my philosophical status, with respect to fideism, may well change again' (p. 74). And so it turned out. In Chapter 8, Nielsen's 1993 view is that 'Phillips is a charter member of the club which I have called Wittgensteinian fideists' (p. 143). As I have shown, the contemporary use of the label refers to theses which Nielsen and I agree are absurd. So the general use of the term is certainly unscholarly. But is it a scholarly exposition of Wittgenstein's views *at all*?

So what is Wittgensteinian Fideism if not my reading of the theses I rejected in Chapter 2? Is it the paradoxical thesis that modes of life cannot be appraised as logical or illogical ascribed to Wittgensteinian fideists by Nielsen in Chapter 3 (p. 57)? Nielsen advanced this thesis because he believed that '"form of life" is a term of Wittgensteinian art and [that] it is too minimally articulated to bear the great weight Wittgenstein, Winch, Malcolm, Cavell, and Phillips put on it' (Nielsen 1982, 131). Rhees agrees that the notion of 'forms of life' needs further development, but the charge of 'minimal articulation' is far too strong in the light of the logical issues that surround, issues that have been discussed extensively. These discussions involve the terms 'pictures' and 'practices', which are, along with 'forms of life', key logical terms in Wittgenstein's thought. If one is going to criticize them in the name of Wittgensteinian Fideism, it is that *logical* role which has to be discussed. Nielsen is diverted from that task by his apologetic concerns. He contents himself, too often, with simply saying that he finds the terms problematic. It is the neglect of these terms in my own work too, by Nielsen, which accounts for a lack of preparation, in the present context, for the two papers from my collection *Wittgenstein and Religion* that Nielsen discusses, namely, 'On Not Understanding God' (1988) and 'From Coffee to Carmelites' (1990). Had he discussed other papers in the collection, he would have come across the key logical notions mentioned above, notions which would have thrown light on the religious claim that God is beyond human understanding. In the next section, I try to indicate why I make this claim.

II   Logic and Language

In 'Sublime Existence' (1990), I argued that Anselm was concerned with conceptual elucidation of belief in an eternal God. This is misunderstood by philosophers who think Anselm is trying to penetrate the impenetrable 'since, being human, we can have no understanding of ultimate reality' (Phillips 1993, x). Nielsen agrees that the belief in a God who passes human understanding faces philosophers with the task of conceptual elucidation:

> If, as I think, it is a right move in philosophy to begin thinking about God by exploring 'the grammar of talk about the ways of God, given in our language, instead of assuming *ab initio* standards by which such talk *must* be assessed', then we will start our exploration by simply acknowledging that religious people say that God is inscrutable and that his ways are beyond human understanding. That is just how

we play, if we play such language-games at all, the language-game of Christian, Jewish and Islamic God-talk. (pp. 145–6)

In 'Searle on Language-Games and Religion' (1989), I argued that the notion of an 'Archimedean point outside all language games by which we assess the adequacy of language in relation to reality . . . is a chimera' (1993, xi). As we have seen, Nielsen wants to agree with this view. I went on to argue that one cannot say, in Wittgensteinian terms, as Searle wants to, 'that we would not engage in religious language games unless we *first* believed in the existence of God, [since] this "belief" cannot be the external justification of the language games, since it is only in the context of the language games that belief in God has any meaning' (1993, xi). Nielsen wants to hold on to Wittgenstein's insights about logic and language, without drawing this conclusion. As a result, he has to claim that in talking of a God who passes beyond human understanding, Wittgensteinians are unwittingly searching for the Archimedean point outside language, which Wittgenstein showed to be a philosophical chimera. So despite my pointing out this confusion throughout my work, I am said to fall foul of it.

In 'On Really Believing', in an attack on philosophical or metaphysical realism,

I show how these issues take us to the heart of disputes . . . in contemporary philosophy of religion. In saying that no-one would worship unless he first believed that God exists, the realist assumes that we are *all* realists with respect to religion, believers and atheists alike. This assumption hides the fact that so far, *no* conceptual elucidation has been provided of what this *prior* belief in the existence of God amounts to. No intelligible account could be given of it. The realist will not allow any appeal to religious worship in elucidating the belief, since to do so, he claims, is to confuse religious belief with its fruits. The religious life, he argues, is the fruit of the belief in God's existence which is its foundation. And so we have a search for a minimal, basic belief in the existence of God, one which involves no affective response. Such a search ends up with a marginal phenomenon far way from the realities of religion. (1993, xi)

Nielsen says that we are both on the same side of the fence in our opposition to metaphysical realism. But his attack on a belief in a God who is beyond human understanding depends on reading it in a metaphysically realist way. What is more, in criticizing my emphasis on the affective responses in religious worship, his criticism depends on something which he regards as asking for the impossible, namely, that these responses be subsequent to a prior metaphysical belief in God's existence.

What is odd is that Nielsen should attribute to me the metaphysical realism he says we oppose. When he does not, his alternative is to accuse me of reducing religion to 'morality touched with emotion'.

The real problem is that Nielsen sees no alternative for the analysis of religious belief – either metaphysical realism or morality touched with emotion. This is failure, on his part, to see what concept-formation comes to in this context. For example, when I refer to the notion of 'grace' to illustrate the internal conceptual relations between 'hiddenness' and 'God', Nielsen thinks that 'grace' must be a subsequent ascription to a conception of God already known. He does not see that talk of grace is part of the *formation* of that very concept.

In 'Wittgenstein's Full Stop' (1981), I discussed the importance of knowing where to stop in philosophical enquiry. As we have seen in appealing to the Wittgensteinian notion of 'practice', Nielsen thinks I stop far too soon. In Chapter 1, he says, 'to start at this point is one thing, to end there is another' (p. 34). I discussed the concern that 'if practices are clusters of language-games it seems that no practice can be confused' (1993, xii). My solution, at the time, was to emphasize the diverse relations between language-games: 'In this traffic, distinctive language-games may lose their character; they many become distorted or confused' (1993, xiii). I now think, as I showed in Chapter 5, that these issues are answered better in the distinction between Wittgenstein's use of 'practice' and a sociological use of this term.

Given this distinction, it is clear that I recognize that in practice, in the sociological sense, talk of something being beyond human understanding may be confused. It may invoke a 'something', or 'a place' where that description obtains. In that case, the assumption would have to face Nielsen's critical questions: if such matters pass beyond human understanding, how are we able to identify them, or to know that we are in contact with them?

At times, Nielsen recognizes that reactions to the vicissitudes of life may not be reactions in terms of 'the understanding'. People ask, 'Why must things be like this? Nielsen's reaction, however, is to say that if the responses have nothing to do with the understanding, they cannot be said to go beyond it. What this ignores is that the responses are reactions to bewilderment at the impotence of reason in this context. These responses may take the form of stoical resignation, saying 'That's life', 'That's fate', 'Life is pointless', or 'That's the will of God.' Despite his commitment to conceptual elucidation, Nielsen pays little attention to these responses, among them being belief in a God who passes human understanding. I have suggested, in this section, that his neglect of issues concerning logic and language, and his desire for apologetics, explain why.

III   Looking for a 'Something' Necessarily Beyond Human Understanding

Why does Nielsen compare my papers, 'From Coffee to Carmelites' and 'On Not Understanding God'? In discussing the first, he wants to give a qualified support to my criticisms of H. O. Mounce, who claims that it is platitudinously true that there are many things that necessarily pass beyond human understanding.[1] Nielsen's claim is that I do not learn from these criticisms in 'On Not Understanding'. Instead of seeing that it is confused to say that *anything* passes beyond human understanding, I, having rejected Mounce's examples, come up with an example of my own, namely, God.

The discussion, in Chapter 9, has, at its centre, the notion of incommensurable modes of discourse. The differences between Mounce, myself and Nielsen can be understood in terms of what we say about this notion. All of us agree that modes of discourse are incommensurable when they cannot be understood in terms of a common logic or grammar that they share. If one fails to understand a mode of discourse, in this context, it would not be a case of making a mistake within an agreed discourse, but a case of a certain kind of discourse failing to get off the ground for one; one cannot find one's feet with it. For Mounce, when this is the case, 'one has no idea even in principle, how that understanding might be acquired' (Mounce 1989, 162–3). The understanding is *necessarily* beyond one. For myself, while agreeing that there are such cases of incommensurability, I deny that the situation is *necessarily* unalterable. Mounce misses this possibility because he 'does not recognise . . . that not every acquiring of understanding is a matter of succeeding within the same mode of understanding within which one had previously failed. One's understanding may be extended or transformed' (Phillips 1993, 134). We may come to an understanding of rituals in a remote society, by an extension of our understanding of rituals in our own. But even '[a]n extended understanding is not simply the old understanding corrected' (Phillips 1993, 134). But what if, like Frazer, one has a tin ear for rituals while thinking one understands them? If Frazer could be brought to see what Wittgenstein showed could be found there, it would involve a transformation of his understanding, and a renunciation of his earlier condescension. Mounce seems to argue that if this happens, it simply shows that the alien society and its rituals had not passed beyond human understanding after all. Nielsen agrees with my view that 'in that case all Mounce presents us with is a rather unilluminating tautology: if X passes beyond understanding Y, and Y does not change, there is no way even in principle by which X can be understood in terms of Y' (Phillips 1993, 135). But Y can and does, sometimes change, not by correcting its mistakes, but by being transformed by something new.

By contrast, Nielsen does not believe that there are any incommensurable modes of discourse. He argues: 'The platitudinous truth is that in some respects they differ and in some respects they are the same. With that sameness, even if it is rather thin, we have some common starting point from which we could reason and deliberate about our differences, using something like what John Rawls and Norman Daniels have called the method of reflective equilibrium' (p. 150). But this seems pure dogma. I see no reason why 'thin' agreements should take us, necessarily, beyond what is thin, especially when the trouble lies in thick disagreements. In discussing his paper, Nielsen writes,

> Some disagreement is benign, but much of it is not. This fact with all its cultural and social consequences has to be faced. Of course, reflective equilibrium does not work in any context. It certainly is not going to be effective with Nazis! But within the context of democratic institutions we can reflect on the basic goods we need. Certain public civic concepts enable us to move from one form of life to another and to ask what kind of difference it makes. We can ask where religious reasons come from; where they get their sense from.[2]

Winch responded, 'I am not so impressed as you are with the notion of "reflective equilibrium". You mention that not all disagreement is benign. But not all agreement is benign either. It can suffer from an intolerable smugness which ignores or distorts real differences.'[3] In *Religion Without Explanation* (1976) I argued that early anthropological, sociological and psychoanalytic accounts of religion are guilty of just such distortion. I showed this in greater detail in *Religion and the Hermeneutics of Contemplation* (2001), but I also emphasized that the aim is not to ignore religion's deep confusions, but to deny the essentialist claim that that is all there is to be found there.

In his late paper, 'Can We Understand Ourselves?' Winch argues that we should be flexible enough to recognise how indeterminate a notion 'understanding' is. If we are, we will not ask, in general terms, whether anything passes beyond human understanding. Much will depend on the context, and what is being claimed. Consider, for example, Mounce's claim that only the poor understand what it is to be poor. Sometimes, there is a point in saying this, for example, in emphasizing that only those who are poor have to face a life of poverty, understand what comes their way in that situation. To counter this with Nielsen's assurance that one shares this understanding because one has 'read social scientists' accounts of poverty' (p. 152) would not be very convincing. What of Orwell who lived with the poor and wrote about them? But the poor don't live together in order to write about poverty. Evans-Pritchard said that when he lived with the Azande, he chose to organize his life in their way, and found it worked well. But the Azande are not choosing to organize their lives; or finding it works well. Rush Rhees used to say that Evans-Pritchard had his return air-ticket in his pocket. In such circumstances, there is some point in saying that we can't acquire the understanding possessed by the poor or by the Azande; that is, we do not face up to life in the ways they do. But, in other circumstances, we may want to deny that poverty, as such, brings about a special understanding of itself. Attitudes among the poor vary. Poverty can make one self-centred. A poor person may be so absorbed in his own plight that he is prepared to take advantage of his fellow poor. 'Contrast such a man with a rich person who learns that a former employee of his has fallen on hard times. He seeks him out, gives him money, helps him to find another job, etc.' (Phillips 1993, 141). If we ask which person has the greater understanding of poverty, is it clear how one should answer? Again, think of someone who gives up all her riches to live among the poor. Do the poor have her understanding, including those who dream of being rich? Saint Peter Claver, who worked among lepers, prayed to become one of them. His request was granted. Do I understand his love of lepers? Did the lepers, including those who would pray to be cured?

Reflecting on examples such as these leads us to recognize the indeterminacy which may be involved when we ask whether we do or do not understand something. In 'Can We Understand Ourselves?', Winch corrects the impression he may have given in 'Understanding a Primitive Society'[4] that radical difficulties of understanding exist, essentially, between different cultures. Winch points out, and as we have seen, such difficulties may occur within one's own culture. As Winch says, someone working on medieval manuscripts may feel more at home with that culture, remote though it is, than with certain aspects of his own culture. Winch says he cannot understand the kind of violence associated with sport. He refers to an incident, in a South American soccer match, when a player was shot because he scored an own goal. Nielsen, too, says, 'it is not only the people in New Guinea that I have a hard time understanding. The skinhead with the shaved head with a red stripe painted across it . . . is nearly as strange to me. I observe him as he gets on the same bus as I do . . . and I wonder what he is thinking, what ambitions, hopes and fears he has, what sense of himself he has . . . I feel at a considerable distance from such a person: his life seems, and no doubt is, alien to me; and mine to him, no doubt' (p. 150). Nielsen says, 'But there are also all the familiar ways in which I could learn about the life of such a person' (p. 150). But would they understand each other? Is it clear that we must seek one kind of answer here?

There are two reasons why Nielsen does not give the indeterminacy in the notion of understanding the attention it deserves. Both are connected with the *general* way in which he discusses whether there is anything beyond human understanding. In the discussion of his paper, Nielsen says, 'I do not believe that there are any sentences which fall into this category.'[5] His attempt to show this reminds me of the way Feuerbach tried to replace 'God', in human esteem, with 'the human species'.[6] He had the problem of finding a parallel to God's perfection in the perfection of the species. How could he, given the frailty of human beings? Feuerbach's answer was that people sin as individuals in their particular ways: one is a liar, a second a lecher, a third covetous, and so on. These deficiencies cancel each other out, and, when subtracted from each other, leave the species as such as a perfection to be esteemed. By comparison, we have seen that there are all sorts of proximities and distances between people, as between cultures and within the same culture. What one understands, another doesn't. Instead of remaining with this ragged scene, we may be tempted to argue that as long as *someone* understands, that cancels out the one who doesn't, so allowing us to say that *nothing* passes beyond a generic something called 'human understanding'. Aren't both arguments equally weak?

The second reason takes a more substantive, but no less dubious, form. At times, Nielsen speaks as though philosophy sets rules by which the comprehensibility or otherwise of anything can be determined. At other times, Nielsen argues against this view. But in discussing his paper, Nielsen says that philosophy is concerned with second-order statements which 'are statements which assert the conditions of sense for sentences. Religion seems to fall foul of these conditions.'[7] James Conant responded, 'Sentences aren't nonsensical. It is people who fail to mean something by the sentences. But before we can reach that conclusion we must pay attention to the contexts in which they speak.'[8] Something similar may be said about Nielsen's use of Davidson-like appeals to translatability as proof that nothing is beyond our understanding. One may be able to translate a prayer, or the words of a ritual, without understanding them. One has only to think of countless television programmes on ancient civilizations in which such words are translated, only to be followed by 'explanatory' glosses of staggering banality.

What we have been saying has far-reaching consequences for a philosophical enquiry in which we seek to do conceptual justice to the world in all its variety. This contemplative task involves the formidable problem of understanding, not simply perspectives we appropriate personally, but those perspectives which are very different from them. If a philosopher's range of understanding is too narrow, he or she will be unable to do so.

In one's personal life, one may have thought little of religion. If that life is transformed religiously, we have a special word for it. It is called conversion. Conversion is not a correction within a direction, but a change of direction. If a philosopher has a tin ear for religion, but then comes to an appreciation of it, he or she may be said to have 'the possibility of belief' in them. This 'possibility' does not refer to the likelihood of their becoming believers. It refers, rather, to an ability to understand the *kind* of belief it is; appreciating what is involved in seeing the world in that way. This philosophical 'coming to see' may well involve an imaginative transformation of one's previous narrower powers of understanding.

IV 'God' as Necessarily Beyond Human Understanding

Nielsen's view is that despite my criticisms of Mounce's examples of things that necessarily pass beyond human understanding, I try to come up with an example of my own, namely, God. I do so, he argues, in an attempt to give an answer to a question people often ask faced by the vicissitudes of life. By the vicissitudes of life I mean such things as the blind forces of nature, the transitoriness of fate, sudden sickness or death, broken relationships, betrayal by friends. People have asked why things have to be like this. Nielsen recognizes my opposition to religious apologists who have sought to give explanatory answers to this question, theodicies which explain and justify God's ways to human beings. Nielsen agrees with these criticisms by saying that they 'tend to distract us from serious thinking about religion' (p. 143). In fact, my criticisms have been far stronger than that. I have accused theodicies of distorting notions of moral responsibility and of embracing a consequentialism that allows no logical space for moral refusals to indulge in it. For me, theodicies have done great harm and are one of the saddest spectacles in the philosophy of religion. It is encouraging to see the revulsion of countless believers when they hear them. Neither is it any defence to distinguish between the intellectual problem of evil and what is called the pastoral problem of evil. By the latter is meant the problems people have in actually facing up to evils in life. I call these *real* problems. If the intellectual arguments distort them of what use are they?[9]

There are philosophers who offer, not theodicies, but defences of God in face of evil. A theodicist claims to know why God allows evil, but a deviser of defences does not. All that is claimed is that God has good reasons for allowing evil, but that we have no idea what they are (see Davis 2001). Further, though God has his reasons, it is said that he has no obligation to divulge them to us (see Plantinga 2000). On this view, it is not that God's reasons are logically inscrutable. On the contrary, we'll get to know what they are after death when God divulges them to us (see Adams 1996). God's ways are only inscrutable to us while we are on earth.

I have criticized defences as well as theodicies. They do not overcome their fatal instrumentalism. Further, although theodicies offered reasons, horrific though many of them are, defences refuse to do so while claiming that good reasons exist. It leaves no logical space for the moral reaction that says that to withhold a good reason from a mother who has lost her child is not a defence, but an added indictment. The real difficulty in revealing the reasons is that they would turn out to be as unsatisfactory or horrific as those theodicies make explicit. All this is powerfully endorsed by Herman Tennessen in the paper I discuss in 'On Not Understanding God'.[10] I question the basic assumption that knowing that reasons exist always makes things better. After the mother has been told that her child died of meningitis, is she supposed to be comforted by the thought that, furthermore, it was allowed to do so to fulfil someone's plan which will be shown to her some day? Does it not make sense, at least, to say that this would make things infinitely worse rather than infinitely better?

In any case, as Nielsen points out, these arguments do not yield any sense for 'that which necessarily passes beyond human understanding', since there is no conceptual or logical ban on knowing God's reasons; it is just the case that, as a matter of fact, we do not (see p. 155). As Nielsen says, 'This, however, is not the kind of "failing to understand" in which Phillips is interested' (p. 155). That being so, however, Nielsen thinks that I can find no coherent context for talk of anything which passes beyond human understanding. On the other hand, he admits to knowing full well the context I have in mind. It is worth quoting Nielsen at length on this point.

> Phillips shows that in certain situations there is nothing to understand ... So if there is nothing to understand then there is no object of, or proper occasion for, wonder or perplexity over the fact that there is something which passes beyond understanding that we could not set right by understanding. That is about as evident as anything can be. Consider an example. People age and sometimes their powers – physical, intellectual and on occasion even moral – fail. There are reasonable causal explanations of why this happens. But there is no mystery here, nothing to wonder or be perplexed about, or to reflect on with an eye to making sense of it. It is just a brute fact of the world, one of the contingencies of the world which matters to us. It does not pass beyond understanding in the sense that we do not know *why* it happens; neither does it pass beyond understanding in the sense that God or a Martian could see the justification for it while we cannot. There is no justification for it: not because it is unjustified, but because it could be neither justified nor unjustified ... Suppose a great poet grows senile and comes to write drivel. Faced with this we may say 'Oh, why did it have to happen to him? Why? Why?!' ... The 'Why?' does not ask for an explanation, ... for a rationale, excuse or justification to be supplied, or anything like that ... To say that it points to something

which passes beyond understanding is misleading at best, for it suggests that something like understanding is at issue. (p. 156)

Let us *begin* with the last claim. Nielsen begins by admitting that I make it clear that I am talking of situations where 'there is nothing to understand', but ends by saying that I suggest 'that something like understanding is at issue'. My discussion in 'On Not Understanding God', gives him no reason for this conclusion. When I say there that reactions to the vicissitudes of life, including religious reactions, go *necessarily* beyond human understanding, the 'beyond' has a grammatical force. The responses are something other than forms of understanding. But why *necessarily* 'other than'? For precisely the reason Nielsen provides, namely, that it makes no sense here to speak of anything that could be set right by understanding. We are confronted by the brute contingencies of life. Nielsen is wrong, however, to say that this is not an occasion for wonder and perplexity, since it often is. Moreover, the understanding *is* involved, but not in the way Nielsen suggests. It is involved in the sense that our bewilderment and anguish, expressed in the question 'Why?' are themselves a reaction to the *impotence of the understanding* in the situation. This is what Wittgenstein called the riddle in time and space. And as Nielsen acknowledges, these things matter to us. The question 'Why?' is not a request for an explanation. It is asked even when all explanations have been provided. Maybe the question 'Why?' will cease to be asked one day, maybe not. Nielsen recognizes that this is the issue: one of human reactions in the light of these brute facts.

Where Nielsen and I differ is in his philosophical unwillingness to allow the intelligibility of religious responses to these brute facts, including the belief that we are in the hands of a God who passes beyond human understanding. He cannot see how this can mean anything, because we are *both* claiming to know something, and call that something unknowable at the same time. It is as though language has a boundary, but that in religious experience, we are privileged to look over the edge, and have, what Conant has called a 'glimpse of comprehension into that which is incomprehensible' (Conant 1995, 292). Again, Jamie Ferreira has expressed the kind of worry Nielsen has when she says that 'one cannot keep pointing "as if knowingly" to the reality which one cannot describe. It is not that one cannot describe exhaustively – one cannot know how or even if what one says applies' (Ferrera 1995, 124). It is considerations such as these that make Nielsen reluctant to let me invoke, without objection, the fact that religious believers do wonder at the vicissitudes of life 'in such a way that we can think of the grace of God. It is not the speculative wonder of the Greek philosophers. Phillips thinks that this is a natural way for wonder to go for the person of faith. But we –

including in the "we" the person of faith – need some understanding of "God" to see how the "gifts of nature can be seen as gifts of grace", God's grace' (p. 158). But according to Nielsen we cannot have that understanding 'if God is necessarily beyond human understanding' (p. 158).

In reply to these objections I think Wittgenstein would say, 'Don't ask how religious believers *can* react in this way. Concentrate on the fact that they *do*.' I would add: don't think that before you can understand 'grace' you need first to understand 'God'. Consider, rather, that in understanding 'grace', you will understand one use of 'God'. I am speaking here of philosophical understanding; a grasp of the grammar of these concepts. Nielsen recognizes that if this understanding is achieved, it does not mean that we would have understood God or grace – to say that is ruled out in religious discourse. What we would appreciate is the role played by 'God's grace is beyond human understanding' in religious belief. Instead of turning his attention to that task, Nielsen settles for generalities stating that the intelligentsia find religion incoherent and how, given a certain amount of security and wealth, this attitude to it will slowly trickle down to the rest of society. With a bit of luck we'll all end up like Scandinavia. I do not know how these armchair exercises in futurology are supposed to bear on the philosophical issues we are supposed to be discussing. Nielsen's hopes are encouraged by my analyses, since they fail, in his eyes, to show that religion still has the power to animate us. As far as religion is concerned, he claims, it is time for us all to ride the hearse. No doubt, many will find in these remarks the same condescension that Wittgenstein found in Frazer, but I have no interest in pursuing that further. My main regret is that Nielsen pays so little attention to the many examples I provide in my work, examples which are meant to animate, not religious belief, but philosophical appreciation. I shall end this chapter, therefore, by calling attention to some of these.

First, let us begin with the attitude of a fellow atheist to the vicissitudes of life. Herman Tennessen's reading of the Book of Job as a work of existential blasphemy that has fooled the faithful is bizarre, but immensely interesting. Like Nielsen, he sees that the reactions to life's contingencies he wants to discuss are not a matter of the understanding. He recognizes that there is a radical caprice in human life. Interestingly, he is not content simply to express that in that secular way. He sees the caprice as divine, or, perhaps, sees divinity in it. Tennessen characterizes Job as discovering that God has *no* reasons for what happens to human beings. In this discovery, what is revealed to him is not God's quantitative greatness, but his qualitative smallness. Tennessen says:

> We can easily imagine Job's boundless astonishment at this tangible appearance by Jehovah ... Job [thought he was dealing with] ... a

god of such holiness and purity that even his indictment would release exultation! Only to find himself confronted by a ruler of grotesque primitivity, a cosmic cave dweller, a braggart and a rumble-dumble, almost congenial in his complete ignorance about spiritual refinement. (Tennessen 1973, 8)

Tennessen asks, 'But this god in the Book of Job, does *he* concern us? Is the whole of it any more than a poetic game with an alien and out-dated concept of the divine? Do we *know* this god?' (1973, 10). Nielsen would reply, 'Of course not. We're on the road to Scandinavia.' Tennessen, on the other hand, replies, 'Yes, we know him from the history of religion; he is the god of the Old Testament, "the Lord of Hosts" or, as we might put it the Lord of Armies: the jealous Jehovah' (1973, 10). But this is not the end of Tennessen's story. He asks,

But does he live only in the history of religion? No, he also lords it over our own experience, today as many milleniae ago. He represents a familiar biological and social milieu: the blind forces of nature, completely indifferent to the human need for order and meaning and justice ... the unpredictable visitations by disease and death, the transitoriness of fame, the treason by friends and kin. He is the god of machines and power, of despotism and conquest, of pieces of brass and armoured plates. There are other men than Job who counter him with weapons of the spirit. Some of them are trampled down in heroic martyrdom. Others recognise the limitations of martyrdom, then yield on the surface, but hide the despair in their hearts. (Tennessen 1973, 10)

Would not Camus have found echoes of his own emphasis on unending protest in Tennessen? Surely, he would. Neither will it do to accuse them of anthropomorphism, as Nielsen might, since it would make no sense to account for the divine role of caprice in human terms. It is not an additional being of any kind, but the element in which people live and move, although they have their being in a relation of protest to it. Absurdity is seen as divine.

Hume, in his *Dialogues Concerning Natural Religion* criticizes attempts to form hypotheses about the creation of the world. He argues that any hypothesis is as good as any other, which amounts to saying that they are not hypotheses at all. His conclusion is that so wild and unsettled a system of theology is surely not preferable to none at all. But, in the course of his arguments, he imagines the world as the work of an infant deity who has lost all interest in it, and has left it to run unattended. Alternatively, he imagines it to be the work of a superannuated deity, a kind of basket-weaving among the gods. Again, I think it would be foolish to dismiss this as anthropomorphism. It is another instance of absurdity seen as divine.

Think, now, of a different example, in which caprice and chance are called 'the ways of the gods', something we ignore at our peril. Oedipus is convinced that he cannot be the cursed one, the person who has killed his father and married his mother, while, on the other hand, the Chorus is telling us of his misplaced confidence – 'O foolish man!' Despite all our plans, all our endeavours, there is always the inscrutable way of the gods, to deny which is to be guilty of hubris.[11] Lucretius suggested that these ways are rendered irrelevant. Science will give a better explanation of those thunderbolts which miss their intended guilty targets and carry the innocent away in flames. Convinced of the explanatory irrelevance of religion, Lucretius issues his challenge: show me Jupiter thundering from a clear sky. Horace, in one of his odes, takes up the challenge. He speaks of a king who is confident that his reign is secure, nothing can touch him. Suddenly, fate, with a great whirling of her wings snatched away his crown and gave it to another. Jupiter thundered from a clear sky.[12]

It may be said that there is a parallel in Christianity in the central idea that we all stand in need of grace, and that to deny that is to deny God. Peter was confident that no matter what the other disciples did he would stand by Jesus. Looking at him sadly, Jesus predicts his denial of him, not once, but three times. It is difficult to believe that the confident Peter took him seriously. When Jesus is taken captive, he follows at a safe distance. In the temple courtyard a maid accuses Peter of being with Jesus. He replies immediately, 'I never knew him.' Jupiter thundered from a clear sky. If one is asked when Peter denied Christ, the popular answer is: when he broke his promise. Simone Weil's answer is: when he made it. The confident promise was a denial of grace. Peter weeps after his denial of Christ, yet this is said to be the rock on which the Church is built. The Church has, as part of its foundation, a realization that Jupiter can thunder from a clear sky.[13]

The religious view of grace does not seek an explanation of why some people are able to believe in their dependence on it and others not. This is not to say, of course, that religious apologists do not often suggest otherwise. Richard Swinburne has suggested that atheists fail to acknowledge the probabilities of God's existence which are there for all to see, because, despite their intelligence, they are afraid of the demands on their lives acknowledging the evidence would involve. Alvin Plantinga and Nicholas Wolterstorff have explained their inability in terms of the malfunctioning of their God-given faculties. There is a danger of phariseeism here: 'I thank thee that my faculties are not those of others.' But it has its parallel in atheistic talk, not always absent in Nielsen, of how atheism is the obvious outcome for those educated enough, intelligent enough, and sensitive enough, to appreciate that fact. By contrast, Augustine comes to realize a way to God which is not 'a way of knowing', but a 'way of unknowing'. In the first nine books of his *Confessions*, he elucidates a spiritual method which he thinks he possesses, a way of ascent by which he moves, step by step, from knowledge of corporeal things to a knowledge of God. But in Book Ten, he confesses that he does not know himself in the way he had claimed. It is grace itself which, in ways beyond any methodical understanding, grants or creates conditions of its own acceptance (see Thompson 2002). Therefore, no believer has any reason to boast. I wrote: 'the first admission necessary to receive such grace, however, is the admission that one does not possess a way of knowing how to ascend to God, but that one comes, empty-handed, to receive the grace that descends on the poor in knowledge'. (Phillips 2003)

Nielsen will no doubt object to all my examples, demanding a prior knowledge of God as a precondition of ascribing grace to the divine. It is as though philosophers insist on prefacing any 'way of unknowing' with 'a way of knowing'. In this respect, it is worth recalling Feuerbach's brilliant critique of any attempt to separate God as 'the metaphysical subject' from the divine predicates.

> God is love: but what does that mean? Is God something besides love? a being distinct from love? Is it as if I said of an affectionate human being, he is love itself? Certainly; otherwise I must give up the name God, which expresses a special personal being, a subject in distinction from the predicate. Thus love is made something apart . . . it receives both in theory and in feeling, both objectively and subjectively, the rank simply of a predicate, not that of a subject, of the substance; it shrinks out of observation as a collateral, an accident; at one moment it presents itself to me as something essential, at another, it vanishes again. God appears to me in another form besides that of love; in the form of omnipotence, of a severe power not bound by love; a power in which, though in a smaller degree, the devils participate. (Feuerbach 1967, 52)

One recalls Feuerbach's famous conclusion,

> What theology and philosophy have held to be God, the Absolute, the Infinite, is not God; but that which they have held not to be God is God: namely, the attribute, the quality, whatever has reality. Hence he alone is the true atheist to whom the predicates of the Divine Being, – for example, love, wisdom, justice, – are nothing. And in no wise is the negation of the subject necessarily also a negation of the predicates considered in themselves. (Feuerbach 1967, 14–15)

As we know, however, Feuerbach was not as free from 'the metaphysical subject' as he supposed. As a result of rejecting it, he concluded that we come to recognize that the so-called divine predicates are human attributes. His aim, perhaps one shared by Nielsen, but one Van Harvey thinks looks naïve after the experiences of the twentieth century – not to mention horrific events in our own (Harvey 1997) – was 'to transform friends of God into friends of man, believers into thinkers, devotees of prayer in to devotees of work, candidates for the hereafter into students of this world' (Feuerbach 1967, 285). But Feuerbach realized full well that no being in addition to human beings, and certainly not one thought of as a super-human being, could fill the logical space the divine is said to occupy. No individual can be the element, the light, the spirit, in which we live, and more and have our being, if only because one wants to ask, 'And what about the life of that individual?' After all, Jesus prays. There is a parallel difficulty in saying, 'All things are atoms' or 'All things are water.' One wants to ask, 'What about the reality of the atoms and the water? They call for an account of themselves.' As we know, Feuerbach tried to substitute 'the human species' for 'God' with somewhat comic results.

But, Nielsen will say, 'Grace and other predicates can't just float around unattached. They must be predicates of something, and that is the God we can give no account of.' At that point, however, we need to remind ourselves of Rhees's analysis of divine identity, and his point that 'grace', 'love' and other divine attributes are related to 'God' as 'hands', 'feet', 'arms', 'face' are related to 'human being'.[14]

Wittgenstein, in different ways, argues against various metaphysical attempts to get 'behind' our forms of life. Philosophically, he says that these are given and what must be accepted. Their logic needs no apology from us. I have been talking of religion as one reaction among many to 'the given'. At one level, it is an instance of it, one language game among others. At another level, it is a reaction to the givenness of these things, since it is a reaction to life itself, and in that way, not so much a matter of the standards one finds in morality. There is a comparable, yet different wonder in philosophy, expressed by Rush Rhees as follows:

Wonder is characteristic of philosophy anyway, as it is of the thinking of less corrupted peoples. Wonder at death – *not* trying to escape from death; wonder at (almost reverence towards) madness; wonder that there should be the problems that there are, and that they should have the solutions that they do. (Pythagoras treating the 'discovery' that any triangle inscribed in a semi-circle is right-angled, as divine revelation, as a word to be reverenced.) Wonder at any natural scene that is beautiful. Wonder at the beauty of human actions and characters when it appears in them. And in the same way, wonder at what is terrible and what is evil. (We cannot say 'wonder at what is mediocre', and there may be something important in this.) Wonder – treating as important – what is terrible just *because* it is terrible; as primitive peoples may celebrate it in rites: the burning of human figures, perhaps of children, in effigy; treating what is terrible as a sacrament. If someone can think these practices only as 'morbid' or as 'perversions' – or if he can think of them only as methods to *ward off* the terrible things they celebrate – this means he cannot imagine how people might wonder at terrible events because of what they are (as opposed to: wondering what neglect should have allowed them to happen, how they might be avoided, etc.). (Rhees 1994, 578)

O. K. Bouwsma used to joke that over every university there is a hidden sign which reads 'Understand or else.' In this chapter I have been urging, in more than one context, the importance of the grammar involved in saying that some things necessarily pass beyond human understanding.

Even when Nielsen recognizes the different reactions to life's vicissitudes I have been talking about, he thinks we can deliberate (in the name of philosophy?) 'on what are the more appropriate reactions in such circumstances'. I look forward to hearing what form such deliberation is supposed to take. He assures us that the fact 'That we can in some instances deliberate on what are the most appropriate feelings does not mean that feelings themselves are a form of cognition or a form of knowledge or understanding' (p. 156). Whether or not this does justice to 'feelings', what odds that religious feelings do not make the grade? 'Understanding', it seems, has the last word after all.

Notes

1 H. O. Mounce, 'The Aroma of Coffee', *Philosophy* Vol. 64 No. 248. Page references for Mounce's remarks are from his paper. References in my criticisms come from my paper, 'From Coffee to Carmelites' in *Wittgenstein and Religion*.

2 See 'Voices in Discussion' in *Philosophy and the Grammar of Religious Belief*, eds Timothy Tessin and Mario von der Ruhr, Basingstoke and New York: Macmillan and St Martin's Press 1995, p. 391. In the discussion, Nielsen's views are represented by Voice H.

3 'Voices in Discussion' in Tessin and von der Ruhr 1995, p. 392.

4 In *Ethics and Action*, London: Routledge 1972.

5 'Voices in Discussion' in Tessin and von der Ruhr 1995, p. 375.

6 See Feuerbach, *The Essence of Christianity*. New York: Harper 1957. For my critique of Feuerbach see *Religion and the Hermeneutics of Contemplation*, chapter 4 'Feuerbach: religion's secret?'

7 'Voices in Discussion' in Tessin and von der Ruhr 1995, p. 375.

8 'Voices in Discussion' in Tessin and von der Ruhr 1995, p. 376.

9 For my criticism of theodicies see 'The Problem of Evil', a symposium with Richard Swinburne in *Reason and Religion* ed. S. C. Brown, Ithaca: Cornell University Press, 1977; 'On Not Understanding God' in *Wittgenstein and Religion*; 'Theism Without Theodicy', along with my critiques of John Roth, John Hick, Stephen T. Davis, David Griffin, and my replies to their criticisms in *Encountering Evil*, ed. Stephen T. Davis, Louisville: Westminster John Knox Press 2001; for related criticisms see *The Concept of Prayer*, Oxford: Blackwell 1981 (Routledge 1965), Chapter Five; and *Death and Immortality*, London: Macmillan 1970, Chapter Two. See also my *The Problem of Evil and The Problem of God* (SCM Press).

10 Herman Tennessen, 'A Masterpiece of Existential Blasphemy: the Book of Job', *The Human World* No. 13, November 1973.

11 For my discussion see *Religion and the Hermeneutics of Contemplation*, Chapter 1.

12 For my discussion see *Religion and the Hermeneutics of Contemplation*, Chapter 1.

13 See my 'On Not Understanding God' in *Wittgenstein and Religion*. Basingstoke: Macmillan 1993.

14 See Rush Rhees, 'Religion and language' in Rhees, *On Religion and Philosophy* ed. D. Z. Phillips. Cambridge: Cambridge University Press 1997, p. 48. See the discussion of Rhees in Section VI of Chapter 4 in this volume.

Bibliography

Adams, Marilyn McCord (1996), 'Evil and the God-Who-Does-Nothing-In-Particular' in *Religion and Morality*, ed. D. Z. Phillips. London: Macmillan.

Conant, James (1995), 'Putting Two and Two Together' in *Philosophy and the Grammar of Religious Belief*, eds Timothy Tessin and Mario von der Ruhr. New York: St Martin's Press.

Davis, Stephen T. (2001), 'Free Will and Evil' in *Encountering Evil: Live Options in Theodicy*, ed. Stephen T. Davis. Louisville: Westminster John Knox Press.

Ferreira, M. Jamie (1995), 'Religion and "Really Believing"' in *Philosophy and The Grammar of Religious Belief*, eds Timothy Tessin and Mario von der Ruhr. New York: St Martin's Press.

Feuerbach, Ludwig (1967), *The Essence of Christianity*. New York and Evanston: Harper and Row.

Harvey, Van A. (1997), *Feuerbach and the Interpretation of Religion*. Cambridge: Cambridge University Press.

Mounce, H. O. (1989), 'The Aroma of Coffee', *Philosophy* 64: 248.

Nielsen, Kai (1982), 'Wittgensteinian Fideism II', *Introduction to the Philosophy of Religion*. London: Macmillan.

Phillips, D. Z. (1965), *The Concept of Prayer*. London: Routledge (Oxford: Blackwell, 1981).

—— (1970), *Death and Immortality*. London: Macmillan.

—— (1976), *Religion Without Explanation*. Oxford: Blackwell.

—— (1993), *Wittgenstein and Religion*. Basingstoke: Macmillan.

—— (2001), *Religion and the Hermeneutics of Contemplation*. Cambridge: Cambridge University Press.

—— (2001), 'Theism Without Theodicies', Criticisms, and Replies to Criticisms in *Encountering Evil: Live Options in Theodicy*, ed. Stephen T. Davis. Louisville: Westminster John Knox Press.

—— (2003), 'Negative Theology and Post-Metaphysical Thought', *Archivio di Filosofia*, ed. Marco Olivetti. CFDAM-CASA Editrice Dott Antonio Milani.

—— (2004), *The Problem of Evil and the Problem of God*. London: SCM Press.

Plantinga, Alvin (2000). *Warranted Christian Belief*. New York: Oxford University Press.

Rhees, Rush (1994), 'The Fundamental Problems of Philosophy', ed. Timothy Tessin. *Philosophical Investigations* 17:4, October.

—— (1997), 'Religion and Language' in *On Religion and Philosophy*, ed. D. Z. Phillips. Cambridge: Cambridge University Press.

Richard Swinburne (1977), 'The Problem of Evil' in *Reason and Religion*, ed. Stuart Brown. Ithaca, NY: Cornell University Press.

Tennessen, Heiman (1973), 'A Masterpiece of Existential Blasphemy: The Book of Job', *The Human World* 13, November.

Tessin, Timothy and Mario von der Ruhr (eds) (1995), *Philosophy and the Grammar of Religious Belief*. New York: St Martin's Press.

Thompson, Caleb (2002), 'Wittgenstein, Augustine, and the Fantasy of Ascent', *Philosophical Investigations* 25: 2.

Winch, Peter (1972), *Ethics and Action*. London: Routledge and Kegan Paul.

—— (1997), 'Can We Understand Ourselves?' *Philosophical Investigations* 20: 3, July.

Wittgenstein, Ludwig (1993), 'Remarks on Frazer's *Golden Bough*' in *Philosophical Occasions*, eds James Klagge and Alfred Nordmann. Cambridge and Indianapolis: Hackett Publishing Co.

10. On Anything Being Beyond Human Understanding

KAI NIELSEN

I

If something is beyond human understanding then we could never know what that was, understand what it was being said about, get a faint glimpse – as through a glass darkly – of what it is, or even have any understanding of what it is that might be the case if this were so. As the man said, 'Whereof one cannot speak one must be silent' and his sidekick added, 'If you can't say it you can't say it and you can't whistle it either.' If something is unutterable you can't utter it, if it is unknowable you can't know it, if it is not comprehensible you can't comprehend it, and it makes no sense even to try to do these things. Moreover, if it is unutterable, inexpressible in any language or alternatively in any system of notation (say, a musical or mathematical notation) there is nothing for us to understand or fail to understand. What used to be called 'knowledge by acquaintance' is logically dependent (if intelligible at all) on 'knowledge by description'. There is no just brute inexpressible experience which can give us an understanding of anything (Ambrose 1950). What is ineffable must remain ineffable and if ineffable it is unknowable, it is beyond comprehension. We do not even have an understanding of what the 'it' is. If something is beyond human understanding we could never know what that 'it' is or come to in any way, direct or indirect, understand or grasp what that is. Such talk is completely meaningless. And to say that if such talk is meaningless so is its negation is just to drive home the thesis that anyone who wishes to be intelligible, who wishes to make sense, must be silent here. She knows that there is nothing that can be said or known or grasped. We are not going in any way to be able to comprehend the incomprehensible.[1] And the silence is not a deep mystical or unsayable understanding of what cannot be said, but something that if we insist on warbling here we warble nonsense.

To say this is not *hubris*, a positivist or any other kind of dogma, a rationalist belief that understanding is everything or a demand to 'understand or else'. It is rather just paying attention to an obvious bit of the 'logic of our language', or, to speak less metaphorically, to attend to how our language-games are played when language is not idling. If some things, as Phillips keeps on reiterating, 'necessarily pass beyond human understanding' then we are not going to understand *what* they are. This is so no matter how indeterminate or context-dependent understanding is and it survives the truth of the fact that both understanding and clarity admit of degrees: sometimes we only more or less understand someone as when someone speaks to me in German and then asks me in English if I understood and I reply 'More or less'. Even partial or inadequate understanding is understanding. But if we don't and can't come to understand at all, as when someone utters 'Trees converse in crimson', then that is the end of the matter. The rest should be silence.

Phillips in effect responds as follows:

> When I say ... that reactions to the vicissitudes of life, including religious reactions, go *necessarily* beyond human understanding, the 'beyond' has a grammatical force. The responses are something other than forms of understanding. But why *necessarily* 'other than'? For precisely the reason Nielsen provides, namely that it makes no sense here to speak of anything that could be set right by understanding. We are confronted by the brute contingencies of life. Nielsen is wrong, however, to say that this is not an occasion for wonder and perplexity, since it often is. Moreover, the understanding *is* involved, but not in the way Nielsen suggests. It is involved in the sense that our bewilderment and anguish, expressed in the question 'Why?' are themselves a reaction to the *impotence of the understanding* in the situation. (Chapter 9, p. 175)[2]

Phillips acknowledges that the question 'Why?' here is not a request for an explanation and he should have added it is not a request for understanding, elucidation or justification either. It is, as I said, following Stephen Toulmin on 'limiting questions', a cry of anguish (Toulmin 1950, 205–22; Nielsen 1979). Understanding is involved in seeing why (causally why) they cry out in anguish, but not in some justificatory way, deep or otherwise, of why this happened. There is nothing to be justified or shown to be unjustified. There is no *rationale*, good or bad, for why this happened. It is just a brute response to one of the terrible contingencies of life. There is a *cause* why things happened but no *reason*. There is no rationalizing such things though there is a grieving them. Phillips is right in saying people not only anguish over such things but sometimes *feel* bewilderment over such things. But this bewilderment is not a reason for wonder or perplexity over such things, but 'a reaction to the *impotence of the understanding* in the situation'. Anguish and grief are exactly the right way to describe such reactions but bewilderment, perplexity and wonder are not. (Just as one can *feel* guilty without *being* guilty so one can *feel* bewildered without actually *being* bewildered as when one feels that way when there is nothing one can be bewildered about. We cannot be bewildered where nothing could possibly count as an answer to that bewilderment.) No doubt, all the same, many would describe their reactions as 'bewilderment' and no doubt they *feel* they are bewildered, but that is indicative of a deep though understandable confusion on their part, an inability to see the world clearly. What Phillips describes as 'the impotence of the understanding in the situation' can be less emotively described as 'that there is nothing to be understood in such situations'. Once this is clearly recognized we will recognize that there can be nothing to be wondered at or about or be bewildered by. It is on a par with trying to answer a question which one recognizes to be unanswerable – necessarily unanswerable, not just contingently so. Seeing this, if she or he is at all rational and reasonable, they will just take their anguish and grief straight without obfuscation. We can *wonder* at why the world is as it is, but not (*pace* Wittgenstein and presumably Phillips) *that* it is. *Here* Carnap is a far better guide than Wittgenstein. Here, unless one really wants to go around being confused, at least being tough-minded is better than being tender-minded. And this is not to say or to give to understand that the only way to react to the world is by way of understanding. Anguish and grief is the right way to react to many of the terrible contingent vicissitudes of life. Phillips is right in the scorn he has for theodicies: of attempts to justify God's way to humans or, for that matter, other animals. But then don't take it all back by speaking of wonder or bewilderment here. Only the metaphysically confused – people trying to answer unanswerable questions – could see these things in these lights. Just take your anguish and grief straight.

Does this mean that 'understanding' has the last word or that I am assuming that? Well, yes and no. *Yes* in the sense that if you did not understand the use of 'anguish' or its equivalent in some other language and (among other things) have some understanding of how it differed from 'fear' or 'terror' you could not in any full sense be anguished. It is *not* like being in pain. You can be in pain without knowing what pain is. Think of an infant. But the same does not hold for being anguished. To have that very reaction (though the reaction is not a form of knowledge or understanding) you must have an understanding of the use of 'anguish' in our language-games. *Not* in the sense, as I just said, that these reactions themselves are not a form of knowledge or understanding, though you could not have such reactions without having some understanding of the concepts involved. But to be in anguish is not a *cognitive* response to the world but an *affective* one. Being in anguish is not a way, or at least not a direct way, of knowing or understanding. Something could 'be beyond human understanding' in the trivial sense that an affective reaction is not a matter of understanding, though without some understanding we could not have that (or any) affective response. After all, affective responses are not just grunts and groans.

So there are terrible vicissitudes of life, for example, that a writer who struggled all her life to create something of lasting value should die just the day before she would have received notice of being awarded the Nobel Prize for Literature; that two small children are left parentless by the death of their parents in an automobile accident for which neither their parents nor anyone else was in any way responsible; or that a person is struck down with cancer before she could complete a project of importance to herself and others. Things like this happen. There is no *reason* for these things though there are *causes* of their occurring. And they are neither justifiable or excusable nor unjustifiable or inexcusable. Such notions have no grip here for what happens in such cases is neither done intentionally nor do they have a rationale. They just happen; they are just there like our lives.

Where we are aware that they have the character that they have and where we have an affective attunement to our fellows, they grip us very powerfully. But Rush Rhees is mistaken in thinking that people so gripped or, for that matter, anyone aware of these vicissitudes, will, if she is at all clear-headed, wonder about them, for there clearly is nothing to wonder about. She may dwell on them in her anguish but that is another matter. There is nothing that would count as having your wonderment satisfied. Where they are not wonderable there is nothing that can be wondered about. People can say they 'wonder about them' or are 'perplexed about them', but if there is nothing that even in any way can serve as resolving their wonder or their perplexity, they are misusing the word 'wonder' or 'perplexity' if they say they 'wonder' or are 'perplexed'. Their very behaviour belies what they say. We do not have to engage in nonsense in order to be sensitive and caring and to recognize and grieve that there are these terrible human vicissitudes.

Perhaps Rhees goes wrong because he strangely equates 'wonder' with 'treating as important' (quoted by Phillips in Chapter 9, p. 181). But, if that is what Rhees does, that is clearly a mistake. The deaths mentioned in my three examples do not cause wonderment or even cause us to *feel* as if we were wondering or perplexed, if we are reasonably clearheaded, but they do cause sadness and sometimes grief and perhaps for *some* religious people something like a rebellion against God that things go this way, a stance that might, if it persists, drive them away from religion altogether, though I conjecture that with such attitudes they would remain in the shadow of it. Still the central point here is that we treat what happened as important, but not as something, if we are rational, to be wondered at or about, to be perplexed over. Being important and being a matter of wonderment do not always coincide. Things that are important need not be something to be wondered about or even something that can be wondered about. Moreover, Rhees is clearly mistaken in thinking we cannot wonder at what is mediocre. Fred gives his whole life to playing concert music, had every opportunity from early on to develop his talents in a perfect environment, used that opportunity to the full to develop his talents, had the best teachers during the considerable time he spent at Julliard, developed near technical perfection, yet he still turned out, despite all his efforts and opportunities, to be a mediocre pianist. It is perfectly natural both to wonder about this and to feel sad about it given how deep his commitment is. So we can and often do wonder at or about what is mediocre.

There is a big difference between God and a complex big-brained extraterrestrial and it is very likely it is a difference that makes a difference, as the pragmatists like to say. Consider this: We can understand why it is that in general our cognitive powers exceed those of chimps by – among other ways, but importantly in this way – inspecting human brains and chimp brains. When the appropriate scientists make such an examination of why human cognitive powers are greater than those of chimps, it can be known that there are some things we as a matter of fact can know that chimps can't know. But parallel lines of reasoning work between us and the complex big-brained extraterrestrials. Suppose such a big-brained extraterrestrial lands on earth and in a few days dies. Our brain scientists naturally are very curious and they dissect the brain and, given their knowledge of brains and evolution, they conclude with the reasonable conjecture that with that brain the extraterrestrial animal had cognitive powers superior to ours. There is nothing mysterious or problematic in that. It fits into our web of belief. Working with the scientific knowledge we have, we animals, with lesser cognitive powers, can come to have good scientific reasons to conclude that that animal probably, perhaps very probably, had greater cognitive powers than ours. There is nothing mysterious in that.

But God is a different kettle of stew. Brain scientists have nothing comparable to go on here nor does anyone else. Our understanding that the extraterrestrial has greater cognitive powers than ours is rooted in knowledge of brains and of evolution. It is an understanding that is well captured by wide reflective equilibrium. But we have nothing like that to go on in the case of God. However intelligent we believe God to be, he still, being a purely disembodied being, is brainless. We have nothing to go on to give us even a clue as to what it *means* to say he has greater cognitive powers or any cognitive powers at all. We are plagued with all the familiar difficulties of understanding: What is it for something to be a purely spiritual – an utterly disembodied – being, thinking without a brain and superlatively thinking at that? And we top it off with talk of his cognitive powers passing beyond our understanding. We do not understand what it is for him to think, of how he can be intelligent at all without piling unintelligibility on top of unintelligibility by saying he has an understanding that surpasseth our understanding not to again add incoherence to incoherence by saying it is an understanding that surpasseth all possible human understanding. Here language is idling. We have something that is as bad as all the houses of cards that Wittgenstein destroys.

This is not on our part – if you will on our bloody secularist's part – *hubris*, arrogance or an allegiance to scientism, but just a disposition not to be gulled: to hold on to our brains and our common understanding.

The above matter notwithstanding, if what obtains is not a matter of reasoning – is not something that as a *vicissitude* of the sort that Phillips and I have described can have a rationale – then it is something not having a reason. This being so God could not know the reason for it. There can be no reason for something that doesn't have a reason. (Truisms can be true.)

The usual picture is of us with our puny finite reason and of God with his infinite all-knowing reason having with his 'infinite reason' reasons we cannot know. We have just seen, however infirmly, that if God exists, and is as Jews, Christians and Muslims take him to be, there are some things he knows that we as a matter of fact cannot know. But if there really is nothing to know – if it is not a matter of reason, of something there could be a rationale for – then even God could not know it: know, that is, its rationale when it does not have any. He could, of course, know that that was so, but he could not know that something without a rationale really has one. And this is not in conflict with God's omnipotence for even an omnipotent being cannot do or know what is *logically* impossible, for example, create a round square or understand 'a colourless shade infinitely expanding'. But that, as has been known since the Middle Ages, is no limitation on God's omnipotence.

In spite of what I said above, it makes no sense to say that we are 'in the hands of a God who passes beyond human understanding' *where in saying this*, as Phillips puts it himself, 'we are *both* claiming to know something, and call that something unknowable at the same time' (Chapter 9, p. 175). Phillips mentions this as an objection to his own account, but as far as I can ascertain he never gets around to responding to it, let alone refuting it or showing that it is in any way mistaken. If it is meant as a response (though I can't see how it could be) to say that there is no understanding 'grace' without understanding 'God' and vice versa, that is something (*pace* Phillips) I do not deny. That grace comes from God and that without God there would be no grace just as there would be no grace without the Jewish, Christian or Islamic God is what Wittgenstein and Phillips call grammatical remarks just as 'God loves us and protects us' and 'God is eternal' are grammatical remarks. But acknowledging that is compatible with claiming there are no eternal realities or claiming that talk of 'eternal realities' is incoherent or that there is no God who loves us. Similarly 'grace' and 'God' (the Christian God) go together, but it still could be the case that neither term makes sense either taken together or taken separately when we carefully reflect on the logic of God-talk. But if there is a perplexity about how we could know that there is a God who surpasseth human understanding, an understanding of 'grace' and of 'God' will not help us.

Phillips does take it as a response of kinds to say 'I think Wittgenstein would say "Don't ask how religious believers *can* react in this way. Concentrate on the fact that they *do*"' (Chapter 9, p. 176). This is, he has it, the way to come to grasp the grammar of these religious concepts and *where we have an established use we cannot have incoherence*. We would then, if we did this, come to appreciate the roles played by 'God's grace is beyond human understanding'. But this conflicts with Phillips's claim that religious language-games are not compartmentalized and must be understood in relation to other language-games in our forms of life. However, as my above remarks show, or at least begin to show, when we take these diverse language-games together and try to show how they hang together we get a conflicting jumble; for example, we end up both claiming to know something and calling that something unknowable at the same time and seemingly at least in the same respect. It is not enough (*pace* Wittgenstein and Phillips) to say this language-game is played or to say this is in fact what religious people do. To say 'Don't ask how religious believers *can* react in this way. Concentrate on the fact that they do' is too much like saying 'Don't ask how intelligence testers can know that it is intelligence they are testing. Concentrate on what they do. Intelligence is whatever intelligence testers test.' Analogously, if religious believers *say*, in engaging in religion, that God is necessarily beyond human understanding, then God is necessarily beyond human understanding. If physicists tell us they have built a perpetual motion machine, then they have built a perpetual motion machine. Moreover, to say, as Phillips does, that grace is beyond *methodological* understanding is not to say it is beyond understanding. 'Methodological understanding' is not pleonastic. There very well may be for certain things an understanding which is not methodological and in certain circumstances it may even be superior to methodological understanding or at least the only kind of understanding we are likely to have in certain domains. But still an understanding.

What is incoherent in such situations is to say that what is beyond understanding *altogether* is still something we can somehow grasp, i.e. that it is something we can gain in religious experience, come to have a 'glimpse' of comprehension of: that is to say, come to have a comprehension of that which is incomprehensible or to point 'knowingly' at what is indescribable and in that way – keeping in mind the indeterminateness of understanding – gain in some way an understanding of what is beyond understanding. It is here where we get nonsense just as we get nonsense in claiming to wonder at or be perplexed by that which is not and cannot be a matter of understanding. That is like asking someone to wonder at what is not understandable. There you cannot, where this obtains, even intelligibly wonder at what it is you are supposed, some say, to wonder at or about. And here (*pace* Phillips) we do not get the imposing of a dogma or doctrine but we get something we come to understand in trying to understand how, if they do, our diverse practices hang together. It is not (again *pace* Phillips) that I neglect or miss the logical character of these Wittgensteinian views I oppose – the grammatical status claimed for them – but seeing their logical character I see, or at least I think I see, how they generate incoherencies. It is very likely a rationalistic bias on Wittgenstein's part and on Phillips's as well to think all of our language-games hang together (must hang together?) and make sense. This, of course, sits badly with the general temper of Wittgenstein's mind. Perhaps here a rationalistic bias is sneaking in. But remember I said 'perhaps'.

II

The above I take to be my response to the central core of issues raised by Phillips in Chapter 9. I will in the remainder of this chapter concern myself with some relatively important but disparate odds and ends.

1. I agree with Phillips and Wittgensteinians generally that we should pay careful attention to the uses of our language, including religious talk, as they occur in our actual language-games, which in turn occur in our practices, which in turn are integral parts of our forms of life. I further agree that there is no Archimedean point outside of our practices and forms of life in accordance with which we can describe them, perspicuously represent them or assess them rendering judgements about their adequacy. We can have no such perch, though I do argue, starting with our practices and working from inside and never trying to bust out of our practices (something which is impossible) we can repair the ship at sea using *wide reflective equilibrium* to criticize and amend our practices seriatim and upon some occasions set some practices and even some forms of life aside as incoherent or otherwise inadequate as the practices of astrology and witchcraft in our liberal Western societies have been set aside.[3] (I do not speak of the Azande.) It is a bootstrapping operation but is still something that is possible and often desirable. But we must

start with an understanding of our uses of language *and* our considered convictions. But plainly, indeed definitionally, for religious people God is mysterious: a non-mysterious God, if it is the God of the Judaeo-Christian-Islamic religious strand that is at issue, is a contradiction in terms. And with that religious people say that God is inscrutable and his ways are beyond human understanding. I have considered that and giving it a strong reading, trying both to take the claim literally and in ways that might have some religious significance, I have argued that it is incoherent. We cannot say his ways are 'beyond our understanding' for if they are literally beyond understanding we cannot even identify *his ways*. We cannot say, or even gesture at, stutter about, *what* his ways are. So we are in no position to say they are beyond our understanding. If they are utterly beyond our understanding we have no idea what (if anything) are his ways or even whether he has any ways with respect to us. Again, as so often is the case with God-talk, we are in the swamp.

That can't be right, a Wittgensteinian will respond, for it is the very uses of religious language that are our *given* and are our *yardstick* for what it makes sense to say, think and do in the context of religion. Moreover, sentences like 'God is inscrutable and his ways are beyond human understanding' stand in need of interpretation. We have seen in the previous section that Phillips and I have interpretations that are partially, and importantly, divergent. But still I end up saying that such God-talk is incoherent. This, Wittgensteinians would say, must be wrong given that our actual uses are our given and are *normative* for our understanding. What I want to say is that taken in a *strong, literal way these* bits of God-talk are incoherent and to see this is important for making a philosophical point about whether we can understand or somehow grasp anything that is taken to be literally and completely beyond human understanding. This is what I have been concerned with. But it is also important to see that this attempt at a literal reading need not be how these bits of God-talk are taken by most religious people who make such religious utterances – use them in the course of their lives. Perhaps an interpretation can be given of such utterances that frees them from such claims of incoherence. Perhaps we can go this way. We can say that 'God is inscrutable and his ways are beyond human understanding' can, and should, be taken as hyperbolic.[4] It is a dramatic way of saying that this very mysterious God does not yield easily to understanding, that our understanding of him is fleeting and fragile and there is much that confronts our understanding such that we have no even remotely clear conception of what we are talking about and to whom we speak to or of when we talk to or of God. And that that should be so is exactly right given the relation of God to us. But if we are concerned to be as literal as we can be, we can question whether we have no understanding at all when we speak *to* or *of* God. When we try to construe the sentence literally that God is beyond our understanding, we get, or at least seem to get, incoherence, but not on the more hyperbolic interpretation. It yields sense where otherwise we would get nonsense. This being so, is not the more charitable hyperbolic reading the more reasonable reading? That way of looking at things seems to me to be right and it also allows us to claim that the stronger putatively literal reading, or attempt at a literal reading, which is also the more philosophically interesting reading, is incoherent without violating the givenness of our language-games as a crucial, indeed an indispensable, point of departure for our thought: the *first* word but not necessarily the last world. (Here we should remember J. L. Austin.)

2. Phillips charges some philosophers of religion, including some prominent analytical philosophers of religion, other than Wittgensteinian ones, with having an *apologetic* agenda that takes them (including me) away from *genuinely* doing philosophy and into engaging in unphilosophical polemics for or against religion: for example, Swinburne for, Mackie against or Hick for, Hook against. And I do it against religion with my desire to show that all religious forms of life, practices and pictures are inherently incoherent.[5] But it is not only we atheists who, moving away from genuinely philosophically significant practices, engage, Phillips has it, in polemics in the name of philosophy, but staunch theists such as Richard Swinburne, Alvin Plantinga and Nicholas Wolterstorff are also so characterized – all major analytical philosophers of religion. It seems that only Phillips and his fellow Wittgensteinians (actually a certain sect of Wittgensteinians) do what is genuinely philosophy of religion.[6] But this only follows from his arbitrary stipulative and persuasive definition of 'philosophy of religion', and 'philosophy' generally, as consisting only in the attempt to give a description of 'the logic of our discourses' and for philosophy of religion specifically as a description of the 'logic of religious discourse'. I, Swinburne, Plantinga, Wolterstorff and most philosophers of religion attempt, as well, or sometimes unfortunately just alternatively, to give substantive normative arguments concerning religion. It is arbitrary for Phillips to circumscribe philosophy as he does and doubly arbitrary to label such substantive normative arguments as *apologetics*. The intellectuals or scholars (they can, of course, be both) in question reason carefully, clearly and at least some of them gain some reasonable measure of impartiality. They are not doing apologetics but, among other respectable intellectual things, they can be doing philosophy. John Rawls and Thomas Scanlon are exemplars. If they are not doing philosophy without apologetics, who is? Phillips and Ilham Dilman? Rawls and Scanlon *perhaps* are mistaken,

perhaps they are even badly mistaken and doing philosophy in the wrong way, as I think Plantinga does, but they are doing philosophy – and indeed paradigmatically – all the same. Moreover, we again have the pot calling the kettle black here for, if there ever was an apologist, Phillips is it. He so construes religion that it is immune from the very possibility of serious challenge. If, he has it, we have clearly seen what religion is and do not confuse it with metaphysics, idolatry, crude anthropomorphism or superstition, it is immune from fundamental criticism. Clearly articulated there is no coherent or appropriate challenging belief in God. In so shielding religion from critique, he has engaged, whether he is aware of it or not, in apologetics. Phillips, as all Wittgensteinian fideists do, does that. In addition Phillips's very tone – what Gilbert Ryle calls logical tone of voice – oozes religiosity. We have here apologetic polemics deceiving itself as pure description and perspicuous representation. Phillips's philosophy in a cool place is anything but that. What he should do instead of so dancing around is come out and carefully argue for the substantive and normative beliefs that he is committed to. Instead of charging Swinburne with apologetics, he should carefully and impartially articulate his own religious commitments and show why it is a good thing to have those commitments or, if like Kierkegaard, he thinks it all is, when push comes to shove, a matter of decision, of arbitrary choice, he should argue that and why this is so and, why this being so, we should so commit ourselves to an inescapably *groundless* commitment. If he does not do either of these things, or at least something like them, he fails – or so it seems to me – in his very vocation (Weber's sense) as a philosopher and engages in *apologetics by insinuation*.

3. Phillips and I agree – and this is an important agreement – that it is only in the context of certain language-games, which taken together constitute certain distinctive practices, that belief in God can have meaning. But without any grounds Phillips contends that I deny this. He says, 'Nielsen wants to hold on to Wittgenstein's insights about logic and language, without drawing this conclusion' (Chapter 9, p. 167). Fortified by that false conclusion about my views, he proceeds to claim, 'As a result, he [Nielsen] has to claim that in talking of a God who passes beyond human understanding, Wittgensteinians are unwittingly searching for the Archimedean point outside language, which Wittgenstein showed to be a philosophical chimera' (Chapter 9, p. 167). Where do I say that or even suggest that? I think this is a figment of Phillips's imagination.

Building on this figment, or putative figment, of his imagination, he maintains that my 'attack on a belief in a God who is beyond human understanding depends on reading it in a metaphysically realist way' (Chapter 9, p. 167). But that is not at all my 'attack'; instead right or wrong, it depends on careful attention to what Wittgensteinians call 'the logic of our language'. Like Richard Rorty and Hilary Putnam, I reject both metaphysical realism and anti-realism as metaphysical constructions that take in each other's dirty linen. I am only a realist in the Putnamian sense of a common-sense realist, namely that I believe there were rocks before there was talk or thought of rocks or even truths about rocks. Likewise I believe there were elephants before there was talk of elephants and stars before there was talk of stars, etc., etc. and, if Christians are right and God created the world including us, there must have been this God before there was talk of God. If there is a Jewish-Christian-Islamic God at all, he could not be *a social construct* as chess or football or Judaism, Christianity and Islam are social constructions: *things that did not exist before and independently of our practices.* These are mere truisms (though some of them might be differently put), but still they are unassailably true all the same. Any philosophy that denies them thereby discredits itself. They have a greater claim to being true than any philosophical claim. But this common-sense realism is very distant from metaphysical realism (Putnam 1999, 12–20, 48, 54–6, 111, 164–5).

4. Phillips contends that I just assume that in an analysis of religious discourse – say, in analysing 'God is our creator and loving father' – that I can only allow for a *metaphysically* realist construal (which both Phillips and I agree is incoherent) *or* go to a Braithwaite–Hare-like analysis which is an *expressive* account in which religious beliefs are simply moral beliefs linked with *narratives* in which the religious believer may or may not believe, for example, the gospel narrative of Jesus' crucifixion. Put crudely, the latter alternative comes to treating religion as morality touched with emotion (Nielsen 1989, 172–89). But I do not assume these are the only alternatives. There are others, but aside from the expressivist and error-theory ones, they all run afoul of metaphysics (Nielsen 1996, 27–43 and 49–50). Wittgensteinians, including presumably Phillips, reject metaphysics and do not want to take the Braithwaite–Hare line which after all is *substantively naturalistic* and *thus* atheistic (Nielsen 1996). But Phillips's actual talk here seems to me just an *obscurantist* version of something like the Braithwaite–Hare thing – a thoroughly naturalistic theory – put in moralistic religiose terms. It is one of the places where Phillips substitutes apologetic moralizing, indeed preaching, for elucidation and clear description. If Phillips, without embracing some metaphysics, has an alternative to morality touched with emotion he needs to explain it clearly. (See here importantly, for other putative alternatives acknowledged by me, my long note 8 in Nielsen 1996, 423–4.)

5. Phillips contends (rightly I think) that to understand what I call God-talk properly – to understand the language-games we play that count in our and similar cultures as religious – we will have to come to an understanding (for example) of 'God's grace is beyond human understanding' in the role(s) it plays in live religious contexts.[7] We need

to understand the use of that bit of religious discourse in the following contexts: (1) A person lost in the far north in killing cold temperatures gets through it and says 'But for God's grace I would never have gotten through it'; (2) Another struck down with cancer says 'God's grace falls on all of us as he wills. Whatever happens to me, it is God's will and is to be accepted and acknowledged as good. His will is beyond our understanding and certainly beyond our judgement.' We, if we understand God-talk at all, know that these are not deviant utterances. It is not like saying 'God's feet are large.' And we understand, as Phillips likes to reiterate, that 'God' and 'grace', like 'bachelor' and 'unmarried', are internally related. If we understand 'God' we understand 'grace' and if we understand 'grace' we understand 'God'. We can't understand one without the other. But still both terms, when we try to go beyond anthropomorphism – for example, Herman Tennessen's monstrous creature – what we say may (I think *will*) turn out to be unintelligible and we (believers and sceptics alike) may not have the foggiest idea of what even counts for or against 'God's grace being with us no matter what happens' or 'God's grace being beyond human understanding.'

Phillips writes, 'My main regret is Nielsen pays so little attention to the many examples I provide in my work, examples which are meant to animate, not religious belief, but philosophical appreciation' (Chapter 9, p. 176). But I have pondered his examples and I have not found them doing any philosophical work: animating *philosophical* appreciation; though some of them, *for people with certain inclinations*, may animate religious belief or cause a religious response. That is why I find, whatever his intentions, Phillips more of an apologist, more of a preacher, than a philosopher describing and clarifying our religious discourse in a cool place. (Is this, on my part, the pot calling the kettle black?)

After saying he regrets I ignore his many examples aiming to enlighten us about our religious language-games and supposedly specifically about the use of 'God's grace is beyond human understanding', Phillips provides us with some additional examples. Consider his cases. Herman Tennessen's Job remarks are *good fun*. He is almost always good fun. Read some time his 'Happiness is for the Pigs' (Tennessen 1966). But how do remarks Tennessen makes concerning Job aid our understanding of 'God's grace is beyond human understanding'? Phillips does nothing to enlighten us here. The same obtains for his Hume example and his Lucretius–Horace example. Fine literary stuff but little elucidation of how God-talk works. The closest he gets, setting aside for the moment his Simone Weil example, with his examples to yielding some philosophical illumination is in his comments on some things the Chorus says in *Oedipus Rex*. There we can see the force of 'Despite all our plans, all our endeavours, there is always the inscrutable way of the gods to deny which is to be guilty of hubris.' This *may* help us understand the central claim that 'we all stand in need of grace, and that to deny that is to deny God' (Chapter 9, p. 178). But what is that but to realize our lives are fragile, subject to all the vicissitudes of life, that we stand in need of luck and that to deny this is to deny our fragile contingency? We may not wake up tomorrow. That possibility is always with us, sometimes more insistently than others, but it is always there. If we go in for high fallutin' talk we can speak of the inescapable human condition. But here, while catching the need for religious people of grace-talk, we still have something that is utterly secular. But Phillips will tell us with his typical irrelevance that we are on the road to Scandinavia.

His best example is that about Simone Weil's comment on Peter's denial of Christ. Phillips writes, 'If one is asked when Peter denied Christ, the popular answer is: when he broke his promise. Simone Weil's answer is: when he made it. The confident promise was a denial of grace' (Chapter 9, p. 178). Weil's remark indeed has insight. Its force strikes us immediately on reading it even when we are not confident we properly understand it. It brings vividly to us our *hubris*, our confusion about ourselves, the fragility and the utter contingency of our lives, how deeply we can, and not infrequently do, deceive ourselves and our vulnerability to how things go and how we will react to them and our need of good fortune. We often *schmaltz* it up when we express it in religious terms trading on the emotive force of the terms and on obfuscation. Still both the secular way and the religious way of putting things (if it is stark) are good warnings against *hubris* and rationalistic overconfidence. And Weil's religious response was stark and not at all religiose. (Perhaps this is why she is often such a compelling figure.) Still, put less obscurely in a secular mode, we should say that we stand in need of luck; we stand in need of good fortune and, if we are lucky enough to have it, we should not preen ourselves over it or take pride in our good fortune. As luck and good fortune it was not our doing. It may be gone tomorrow and it (to repeat) will not be any of our doing, for, if it were, it would not be good luck or good fortune. We need to recognize and acknowledge the vicissitudes of life, for good or ill, as something we must just accept without being persons who as agents intervene in the world to try to realize our various projects without ever failing to acknowledge and accept how fragile we are and how fragile these projects are.

Phillips *seems* to *want* to say more than what I have given in this utterly secular account, an account which seems to me appropriately stark, but what more does he say? What more is there to say? What more does he add but something with (for some people) a greater emotive wallop and in a religiose tone for those people who, having been conditioned in a certain way, are religiously inclined? (They may be those who bend their knees and those who ambivalently want to – like some of Dostoevsky's characters – but cannot bring themselves to do so.)

Phillips writes, 'It is grace itself which in ways beyond any methodical
understanding, grants or creates conditions of its own acceptance . . . the
first admission necessary to receive such grace, however, is the admission
that one does not possess a way of knowing how to ascend to God, but
that one comes, empty-handed, to receive the grace that descends on the
poor in knowledge' (Chapter 9, p. 179). Whatever, if any, philosophical
clarification – a better understanding of religious language-games – this
may yield, it is also a bit of *apologetics*, indeed a bit of *preaching*,
precisely the thing that Phillips chastises me, Swinburne, Plantinga and
Wolterstorff for. He cannot, given his Wittgensteinian commitments concerning what proper philosophy is, let this stand as a bit of philosophy.
Still, some ride the hearse; others mount the pulpit.

Phillips remarks, 'Nielsen will no doubt object to all my examples,
demanding a prior knowledge of God as a precondition of ascribing
grace to the divine' (Chapter 9, p. 179). I have already pointed out that
I do not do anything of the kind. 'God' and 'grace' are internally related,
as 'equilateral triangle' and 'equiangular triangle' are internally related,
without being identical. But if we have trouble understanding 'God',
and if 'God' is unintelligible, as I claim it is, where 'God' is not used
anthropomorphically, we will also have trouble understanding 'grace'
and since 'God' and 'grace' are internally related, we cannot use the one
term to understand the other at least if we are seeking to gain something
more tangible, something clearer, à la Peirce, than what he took to be the
empty Leibnitzian way of making our ideas clear (Peirce 1992, 124–41).

Religious people say 'God is love'. This would normally be taken by
religious people – perhaps Phillips would say by naïve religious people –
to be that God is a loving person. Indeed God is a person who has infinite
love for all His creation. But Phillips, in a good Feuerbachian spirit, will
have no truck with that. God, for Phillips, as for Feuerbach, is not a
supernatural being, a super-human being, the Absolute, the Infinite, an
ineffable being beyond space and time, a or the being – Being – transcendent to the world or any such offending metaphysical pseudo-reality. All
such talk for Phillips is nonsense. He likes Feuerbach's famous conclusion, 'What theology and philosophy have held to be God, the Absolute, the Infinite, is not God; but that which they have held not to be
God is God: namely, the attribute, the quality, whatever has reality.
Hence he alone is the true atheist [we have Feuerbach here giving us a
fine implicit persuasive definition] to whom the predicates of the Divine
Being – for example, love, wisdom, justice are nothing. And in no wise
is the negation of the subject necessarily also a negation of the predicates
considered in themselves' (Phillips quoting Feuerbach (*The Essence of
Religion*, 285), Chapter 9, p. 179). Phillips likes this for it gets rid of the
incoherent conception of the God of metaphysical realism and it points
to the centrality of moral and other normative considerations vis-à-vis

Christianity. But now he asks 'God is love; but what does that mean? Is God something besides love? A being distinct from love?' Before I continue the quotation from Phillips something immediately needs to be said. God is not distinct from love in that the Christian God is necessarily a loving God. He is not Tennessen's malicious, vengeful, arbitrary embodied Jehovah. 'Love' like 'grace' is internally related to the Christian 'God'. But it is not (*pace* Rhees) like 'hand' is related to 'human being' for a being without hands is still a human being, but a putative God who is not loving cannot be the God of the developed Judaeo-Christian-Islamic strand. So in that way God is not a being distinct from love. But God is distinct from love in the sense that God is not *identical* to love. To deny that may not be what Feuerbach calls '*true* atheism', but it surely is atheism for to make such an identity claim is to claim that if there are loving people then there is a God and if there is a God then there are loving people. But 'God' and 'love' are neither intensionally nor extensionally equivalent. There being loving people is neither a necessary nor a sufficient condition for God's existence. So, though God is love, he is also something, if he exists at all, besides love. But then we have hoving into sight again that pesky notion of a supernatural being that Phillips is determined to junk. Metaphysical religiosity is coming in the back door. What Phillips wants to junk returns like the repressed.

So what does Phillips do? Next he engages in one of his not infrequent obscurities. He asks in saying that 'God is love', 'Is it as if I said of an affectionate human being, he is love itself?' (Chapter 9, p. 179). He responds resoundingly, 'Certainly!' But then Phillips, pure and simple, is an atheist or, like Braithwaite and Hare, an utter reductionist to the secular, which is to be an atheist in poor disguise with some additional emotive and expressive effects. All we have, Phillips's denial to the contrary notwithstanding, is morality touched with emotion along with a dash of obscurity. We have a thoroughly naturalistic and secularist view, which is not a representation – let alone a perspicuous representation – or a description of the language-games of Judaism, Christianity or Islam. We have *stipulation*, not *description* here. But this is flatly opposed to Phillips's conception – accurate conception – of what philosophy is for Wittgenstein.

Notes

1 It might be said that if it is utterly incomprehensible it could neither be asserted nor negated. But the plainest incomprehensible nonsense can have a negation sign placed before it. If we utter the nonsense sentence 'Trees converse

in crimson' we can also utter 'It is not the case that trees converse in crimson'.
But in neither case have we made an assertion or its negation. Even a random
bunch of words 'trees your or' could have a negation mark before it but nothing
that counts as an assertion or denial obtains.

2 This is a fine begging of the question. See my comments on this later in the
body of the text.

3 Phillips, and Winch as well, show a very impoverished understanding
of reflective equilibrium. (See Phillips, Chapter 9, with his reference to Winch.)
To see how impoverished it is compare Rawls 1999a 286–302; Rawls 1999b,
18–19, 42–3, 507–08; Rawls 1996, 8, 28, 45, 72, 392–94; Rawls 2001, 26–31,
55–72, 134–6; Daniels 1996, 1–178, 333–53; Daniels 2003, 241–76; Scanlon
2003, 139–67; Rorty 1991, 175–96; and Martin 2002, 73–110. Martin's accurate account of wide reflective equilibrium is interesting in that it is both very
un-Wittgensteinian and un-Rawlsian – after and including 'Justice is Fairness,
Political not Metaphysical' – by tying his (Martin's) justification of wide reflective
equilibrium with metaphysical, epistemological, normative, ethical and meta-
ethical theories, forgetting Rawls's remark that justice as fairness is a *political*
conception of justice and should travel *philosophically light*. One can and should
use wide and general reflective equilibrium not only as a method of justification
in ethics and politics but in science and religion as well without taking on the
baggage and all the contestability of that baggage of metaphysical et al. theorizing. That should be welcomed by atheists for then one can argue for atheism and
an utterly secular morality without such trips into metaphysics, meta-ethics,
etc. and thus avoid unnecessary and problematic arguments and, as well, meet
Wittgensteinian fideists on their own ground about what good philosophy consists in. The person employing wide reflective equilibrium however need not even
agree with the Wittgensteinian conception of what good philosophy consists in
to effectively use wide reflective equilibrium against Wittgensteinian Fideism.
Note also that someone who Rawls-like appeals to wide reflective equilibrium
need not, like a Wittgensteinian, say that these metaphysical, epistemological,
normative ethical or meta-ethical considerations are houses of cards, but only
that he can and should treat them with benign neglect in seeking to get *objective*
justification in matters moral, political and social. That is the power of wide
reflective equilibrium and it shows how much deeper Rawlsians go over these
matters than do at least the Swansea Wittgensteinians. It is also useful to compare
my atheistic account with that of Martin's. I generally in my later writings follow
Rawlsian methodological restrictions and avoid commitment on metaphysical
and epistemological issues while Martin thinks they are vital to an adequate
defence of atheism (Nielsen 1996; Nielsen 2001; Martin 2002).

4 It might be responded that there is no non-contextual understanding of the
cut between what is literal and non-literal. The claim that what we are saying is
literally true needs always to be taken contextually. But the cut is not sharp.
This, I think, is right. But in many situations we have no difficulty in drawing
the distinction, e.g., 'Hitler had a black moustache' is literal but 'Hitler had a
black soul' is not. A hyperbolic remark – an exaggeration not intended to deceive
– is somewhat on the non-literal side and need not be taken to be literally true.
I say a more philosophically interesting reading for if we stick with the hyperbolic
reading we have with the very notion of 'an exaggeration not intended to deceive'

the need to understand an exaggeration of *what*? And then we are back with the putatively literal use and thus with our original difficulty. Hyperbole cannot take us to 'the bottom' of the issue, to what we really want to ascertain if we can.

5 Of course that is not literally true and Phillips as usual distorts my position. I repeatedly have said of religion, and over the years, where it is anthropomorphic, that its claims are false not incoherent. And this is not trivial for the non-anthropomorphic ones grow out of reacting to the evident falsity of the anthropomorphic ones. This earlier use gives us the false sense, as a carryover, that the non-anthropomorphic ones make sense when they do not, and are true or illusory when they are not. They are, rather, nonsense. I have made this point on numerous occasions.

6 'Genuinely' tips us off to a *persuasive* definition at work here. Attention to how persuasive definitions work tells us something important about how our language functions (Stevenson 1944, 206–26).

7 I use 'God-talk' not, as it is often presumed, to be provocative, aggressive or iconoclastic, but to cover with one term 'talk of God', 'talk to God', 'talk about God' and the like as well as first-order talk and second-order talk and talk which is indeterminate with respect to that distinction.

Bibliography

Ambrose, Alice (1950), 'The Problem of Linguistic Inadequacy' in *Philosophical Analysis: A Collection of Essays*, edited by Max Black. Cambridge: Cambridge University Press.

Daniels, Norman (1996), *Justice and Justification: Equilibrium in Theory and Practice*. Cambridge: Cambridge University Press.

—— (2003), 'Democratic Equality: Rawls's Complex Egalitarianism' in *The Cambridge Companion to Rawls*, edited by Samuel Freeman. Cambridge: Cambridge University Press, pp. 241–76.

Mandle, Jon (2000), *What's Left of Liberalism? An Interpretation and Defense of Justice as Fairness*. Lanham, Maryland: Lexington Books.

Martin, Michael (2002), *Atheism, Morality and Meaning*. Amherst, NY: Prometheus Books.

Nielsen, Kai (1967), 'Wittgensteinian Fideism', *Philosophy* Vol. XLII, no. 161, pp. 191–209.

—— (1973), *Scepticism*. New York: St Martin's Press.

—— (1979), 'Religion, Science and Limiting Questions', *Studies in Religion* Vol. 8, no. 3, pp. 259–65.

—— (1982), *An Introduction to the Philosophy of Religion*. London: Macmillan.

—— (1985), *Philosophy and Atheism: In Defense of Atheism*. Buffalo, NY: Prometheus Books.

—— (1989), *God, Scepticism, and Modernity*. Ottawa: University of Ottawa Press.

—— (1996), *Naturalism Without Foundations*. Amherst, NY: Prometheus Books.

—— (2001), *Naturalism and Religion*. Amherst, NY: Prometheus Books.

Peirce, C. S. (1992), *The Essential Peirce, Vol. I*, edited by Nathan Houser and Christian Kloesel. Bloomington, IN: Indiana University Press.

Putnam, Hilary (1999), *The Threefold Chord: Mind, Body, and World*. New York: Columbia University Press.

Rawls, John (1996), *Political Liberalism*, second edition. New York: Columbia University Press.

—— (1999a), *Collected Papers*. Cambridge, MA: Harvard University Press.

—— (1999b), *A Theory of Justice*, revised edition. Cambridge MA: Harvard University Press.

—— (2001), *Justice as Fairness: A Restatement*. Cambridge, MA: Harvard University Press.

Rorty, Richard (1991), *Objectivity, Relativism and Truth*. Cambridge: Cambridge University Press.

Scanlon, T. M. (2003), 'Rawls on Justification' in *The Cambridge Companion to Rawls*, edited by Samuel Freeman. Cambridge: Cambridge University Press, pp. 139–67.

Stevenson, Charles (1944), *Ethics and Language*. New Haven, CT: Yale University Press.

Tennessen, Herman (1966), 'Happiness is for the Pigs: Philosophy versus Psychotherapy', *Journal of Existentialism* Vol. VII, no. 26 (Winter), pp. 181–207.

Toulmin, Stephen (1950), *An Examination of the Place of Reason in Ethics*. Cambridge: Cambridge University Press.

11. On Human Understanding

NANCY BAUER

Why is it that in this case I seem to be missing the entire point?
(Wittgenstein 1967, 53)

My initial goal is to make clear why this chapter is called 'On Human Understanding' when the title originally *assigned* to me was 'Is There Anything *Beyond* Human Understanding?' I confess that when I saw the duelling pistols on the poster for the conference for which this chapter was written, a conference assessing the breadth and nature of the distance separating Kai Nielsen and D. Z. Phillips on the issue of 'Wittgensteinian Fideism', I started looking for ways to dodge bullets. And an obvious strategy – indeed a time-honoured one among philosophers of a certain stripe – was to refuse the terms in which Nielsen and Phillips frame the matters I was to discuss. Aside from my natural cowardice and an argument from authority, I have three principled reasons for ducking my calling and, thereby, the intellectual shrapnel. The first is that Wittgenstein, who is as important to me as he is to Phillips and, in various moments, Nielsen, is among those philosophers I admire who show us how to make philosophical progress by subjecting the ways we are inclined to speak philosophically to critical reflection. Second, there is a certain irony in the way this particular stage of the duel has been set up, since in their writings on the nature and limits of human understanding both Nielsen and Phillips seem at various junctures to reject either the coherence or the importance of the question I was assigned to address. And the third is that it strikes me, after thinking about the papers assembled for this volume and related others, that the notion of 'human understanding' and not what may or may not be 'beyond' it, whatever we might be able to agree that word means, is precisely what stands in need of further illumination.

A devotee of Wittgenstein, however, will warn you that you cannot make good sense of any notion when it is wrenched from those contexts that are, as he puts it, its natural home. And one problem with the phrase 'human understanding' is that it's hard to think of a natural home for it apart from those circumstances in which our powers to grasp what is going on are lumped together as a type and are explicitly or implicitly contrasted with a superior type – with, if you are religious, that of a deity. You might be tempted to think that the contrast might also or instead work implicitly downwards, as it were, so that the concept 'human understanding', used in the way it is ordinarily used, might invoke a contrast with, say, dog understanding. But think about the fact that we ordinarily don't talk about types of understanding – or about anything, for that matter – being 'beneath' human understanding. And when in a specific instance we say that, for instance, a dog is incapable of understanding something, we are not suggesting that a dog's powers to understand things are of an incomprehensibly inferior *type*. If and when we find ourselves speaking of what a dog cannot understand – as when, for instance, we must regrettably subject Fido to a painful operation to save his life – what we are observing is that it is impossible for us to make ourselves and our reasons for doing what we are doing as intelligible to the dog as we can in principle make them to each other. This does not mean that we can do nothing: we can pet Fido and reassure him and give him drugs to ease his pain and anxiety. We might be able to make the pain we are causing him *somewhat* intelligible, given that his capacity to understand is not an incomprehensibly different type from ours but rather is simply *limited* in comparison with ours. We refrain from reading a book to Fido and then quizzing him on its contents, not because Fido's way of understanding things is completely different from ours but because Fido is not *smart* enough to grasp concepts.

But when we use the phrase 'human understanding', we seem to be suggesting that the difference between our powers to grasp the way things are and those of some hypothetical or real superior being are separated by more than our respective capacities for intelligent thought. We seem to be imagining that our capacities to grasp what is going on are *in principle and in general* different in type from the comparable capacities of some radically different sort of cognizing being. And yet how are we to make sense of *this* idea? Well, we might say that to speak of human understanding is in effect to put ourselves in the position of Fido: we might be hypothesizing that the superior being to which we are implicitly or explicitly alluding can only do so much to make its ways intelligible to us – to give us to understand why, for example, we must undergo the painful experiences we undergo without understanding why we have to undergo them. But if we suppose that this being is, as most gods are conceived to be, omnipotent, then it will be hard for us to understand why it keeps us in a state of intellectual subjection. (I can't imagine anyone who has had to bear the suffering of a beloved pet, let alone a young child or senile parent, who would not jump at the chance to snap her fingers and grant or restore the sufferer's power to understand what is going on.) If we have a certain doctrinal religious understanding of what happens to us after death, we might be inclined to imagine that

God *will* or at least could in principle explain his plan to us, could justify our suffering to us, once we get to heaven. But notice that at the heart of this explanation, if it is to count as an explanation, will have to be God's reasons, given his omnipotence, for failing to give us to understand what was going on at the time we were suffering. And it may be difficult for us to imagine in our present state how God would go about making these reasons intelligible to us.

The moral I want to draw from these preliminary considerations is twofold. First, it appears that, unfortunately for me, we will not be able to make good sense of the concept of 'human understanding' apart from thinking about what I have been suggesting is the logically prior idea of something's being *beyond* human understanding. And, second, it strikes me that when we are talking about human understanding we are at least in principle worrying about how and why things can be made intelligible both to us and by us.

Reluctantly enough, then, I am going to turn to the question as originally posed to me and to look for help in grappling with it from Phillips and Nielsen. Is there anything beyond human understanding? Both Phillips and Nielsen try to understand this question with respect to our ordinary experience. They both acknowledge, specifically, that the 'vicissitudes of life' tend to strike us as beyond our understanding and that when tragedy strikes seemingly out of the blue it's natural and understandable that we are inclined to ask the unanswerable question 'why?' Of course, we can often provide sufficient *causal* explanations in the face of life's vicissitudes. We understand the course of fatal diseases, the odds of winning the lottery, and the fact that stray bullets can put an early end to children's lives. But what we can't explain is why tragedy befalls some people and not others, why some of us seem cursed and others blessed.

Phillips and Nielsen are as one in rejecting the idea that what are unfortunately sometimes called 'acts of God' lend themselves to simplistic, rationalistic attempts at explanation: they both respond with revulsion to the suggestion that sudden catastrophes *are* acts of God, that we should take comfort in the idea that they are part of God's plan. But Phillips's reasons for resoundingly condemning this response in the face of life's vicissitudes are radically different from Nielsen's. On Phillips's view, the claim 'it was part of God's plan' is not a genuinely religious idea but rather a misguided 'philosophical abstraction', one that's positively immoral in so far as it belittles human suffering and positively blasphemous in so far as it entails the idea that God would plan for human beings to suffer (Phillips 1994, 166). Phillips believes that it is confused to talk about God's plan, at least in simplistic ways, since to be a Christian in the best sense of the term is not to *convince oneself* that God has a plan but to *experience* God's grace – which of course is not to suggest that

206 NANCY BAUER

part of this experience, at least, will involve certain sorts of beliefs. 'Both trials and blessings,' to use Phillips's words, remind the Christian that 'everything is ours by the grace of God' (Phillips 1994, 167) and that 'we are in the hands of a God who passes beyond human understanding' (Chapter 9, p. 175). That God's ways and the vicissitudes of life are beyond human understanding are instances of what Phillips calls 'the limits of existence', and these limits are experienced by the Christian in terms of the notion of divine grace (Phillips 1994, 160f.).

For Nielsen, on the other hand, it is confused to talk about 'God's plan' not because God's ways are beyond human understanding but because all God-talk is either false or incoherent. It is false when it is indulged in by people who have a crude conception of the deity as some kind of paradoxical big man in the sky – and these are of course the same type who tend to intone platitudes about 'God's plan' in the face of the horrible contingencies of life. And it is incoherent when it is uttered by the likes of Phillips – that is, someone who, on Nielsen's construal, wants on the one hand to say that 'the ways of God are beyond human understanding' and on the other hand to insist that we can in fact understand at least some general features of God's ways – such as, I take it, the idea that they are beyond human understanding. 'If God is utterly beyond human understanding,' Nielsen reasons, 'then there is nothing to be said, nothing to be thought, nothing to be perplexed about, nothing to wonder at' (Chapter 8, p. 157). The 'vicissitudes in human life' are beyond human understanding not because they make us mindful of the power of God's grace but because they 'happen for no rhyme or reason' (Chapter 8, p. 147). They are not subject to the workings of the understanding, that is to say, the concept of 'understanding' is irrelevant when it comes to these vicissitudes. It is not that some other sort of being, with some other sort of understanding (whatever that could mean, given that 'understanding' is a thoroughly human concept) could make any sense of life's vicissitudes beyond the sense, or lack thereof, that we ourselves can make. It is that the concept of 'understanding' reaches the end of the line at those junctures at which we can make no sense of things.

The disagreement between Phillips and Nielsen on the question of how to understand the limits of human understanding is of course an offshoot of their broader clash on the subject of what Nielsen has since 1967 called 'Wittgensteinian Fideism'. By 'fideism' Nielsen means the claim, proffered as a piece of philosophy, that religious faith is a matter of the heart rather than the head and is thereby immune to philosophical criticism. Nielsen's own work in the philosophy of religion turns on the negation of this claim, for on his view first-order religious utterances, in their falseness or incoherency, are crying out for philosophical rebuke. One can imagine how disturbing it must have been to the Nielsen of 1967 that fideistic philosophers (though he did not at this time mention

Phillips) could find and, on his judgment, were finding new fodder for their views in Wittgenstein's *Philosophical Investigations*, the ink on the pages of which was still damp. For Wittgenstein can be seen in that book to be exempting human ways of being in the world – 'forms of life', in his argot – from rational criticism. 'Philosophy,' as he famously says at *Investigations* §124, 'leaves everything as it is.' It has the power to destroy nothing more substantive than houses of cards (*PI* §118). Wittgenstein seems to argue that philosophy's powers of criticism are drastically more attenuated than we might have thought they are in so far as the practice of philosophy requires detaching words from the forms of life that give them what intelligibility they have. If we add to this the (as far as I can tell) non-Wittgensteinian but apparently uncontroversial assumption that being religious is a 'form of life', then we arrive at the conclusion that religion need not justify itself in the face of philosophical scepticism, and Wittgenstein's philosophical views can be taken to underwrite a form of fideism. Although Nielsen has endlessly stressed that he finds Wittgensteinian Fideism more plausible and interesting than other attempts to protect religion from rational criticism (perhaps, as Nielsen acknowledges, because he is in other contexts an admirer of Wittgenstein's later philosophy), he has also been relentless in his attack on those who on his view subscribe to it, including Phillips.

Phillips was not identified as what Nielsen deems a 'charter member' of the club of Wittgensteinian fideists for some years after the coining of the term.[1] Membership in this club is something that all philosophers Nielsen identifies as enjoying it disavow. Phillips's reasons for attacking the very idea of Wittgensteinian Fideism, as far as I can tell, have to do with what he takes to be Nielsen's misreading of, on the one hand, Wittgenstein and, on the other hand, religious utterances. (These two issues blur for Phillips when it comes to Wittgenstein's *Nachlass*, in which Wittgenstein occasionally has things to say about religion.)[2] When it comes to Wittgenstein, the main thing that Nielsen doesn't get, on Phillips's view, is that on Wittgenstein's understanding of things the question of the *justification* of our various ways of talking about the world cannot coherently be formed. Of course – and Phillips thinks that Nielsen is especially thick on this point – we can and often should say that certain *instances* of a way of talking about the world are wrong or incoherent or unjustified. But we have no criteria for attacking *überhaupt* the various ways that we speak. To put the point in a way that I'm not sure Phillips would find congenial, we might observe that even if we could make sense of the idea of some super-discursive way of speaking – one we might be tempted to identify with the discourse of philosophy and whose job would be to justify our ordinary linguistic practices – that superdiscourse would itself stand in need of justification. The ensuing regress suggests that the notion of justification makes no sense when it comes to our verbal practices.

Furthermore, religious utterances, Phillips thinks, are in order as they are not because they are to be understood, Wittgensteinian-fideist-style, as walled off from criticism but because they are not *beliefs* on the rationalistic philosophical understanding of the term. They are not sterile cognitions accepted one by one on the basis of ample evidence. One does not first decide that there is a god and then that this god is a god of grace and then that our fate is in this god's hands. Rather, one *reacts* – cognitively as well as emotionally – to the *experience* of God's grace by acknowledging it. And these acknowledgements might take the form of various professions of faith, such as the claim that we are in God's hands, the ways of which are beyond our understanding. To accuse Phillips and others, as Nielsen does, of exploiting Wittgenstein's writing in an attempt to ward off philosophical scepticism about the plausibility of the idea that there is a god is to fail utterly, at least on Phillips's view, to appreciate the role that professions of faith play in our language games.

Both Phillips and Nielsen are clearly indebted to Wittgenstein – and, of course, both have repeatedly acknowledged this fact – in their writings on the limits of human understanding. Phillips appeals to Wittgenstein in attempting to make intelligible to Nielsen the idea that the language-games we use to express our religious faith, games that give point to concepts such as 'belief' and 'faith' and 'grace' and even 'God', are not exercises in making foundationalist *claims* about what the world is like. To suggest, as Phillips thinks Nielsen does, that some sort of garden-variety cognition, some non-linguistic 'belief' in God, for example, under-writes religious discourse is to misconstrue radically the nature of religious belief in a way that on Phillips's view but not, to his mind, Nielsen's, is utterly unintelligible. Nielsen's debt to Wittgenstein in his discussions of the limits of human understanding is perhaps less obvious. But he displays it amply in (1) his worrying about how we can speak of, for instance, 'religious belief' apart from considerations of other uses of the word *belief* that look for all the world to be, as Wittgenstein would say, grammatically connected with the religious instance and (2) his challenging the likes of Phillips to make intelligible to him and the world why we should imagine that there is some special, rarefied notion of belief that cannot at least in principle be grasped via cognition alone.

But doesn't it say something rather disturbing about the coherence of Wittgenstein's writing in *Philosophical Investigations* that two intelligent and sincere people could come away from the book with such profoundly different readings of its ramifications when it comes to religious utterances? We get an answer to this question if we return to Wittgenstein's observation that philosophy leaves everything as it is. One corollary of this claim is that even an airtight philosophical argument will not, except by coincidence, perhaps, persuade a non-believer to drop his pen and follow Jesus, nor will it have an atheistic effect on someone who has found himself drawn to do so. Such arguments can't persuade the atheist to become a believer or the believer to abandon his faith. They can't, in other words, make us intelligible to one another. Philosophy on Wittgenstein's understanding of it makes a kind of progress – one that takes the form of the philosopher's attaining a sense of peace that allows him to stop doing philosophy for the nonce – only when the philosopher can admit to himself that when he finds himself wanting to talk about the essence of things, about How Things Are With the World, he is obliged to own up to the unintelligibility of his words, to see that what he wants to say is not what he is saying, and to stop feeling inclined, at least temporarily, to say what he cannot intelligibly say, to himself and others.

If we were to trace the steps of the debate, if you can call it that, between Phillips and Nielsen back to its origins, we would arrive at the first sentence of Nielsen's 'Wittgensteinian Fideism', the first shot in the ongoing salvo: 'Wittgenstein did not write on the philosophy of religion' (Chapter 1, p. 21). Nielsen goes on immediately to suggest that, nevertheless, there are 'certain strands of his later thought' that 'readily lend themselves' to what he is going to call Wittgensteinian Fideism. But suppose Nielsen had taken a different tack. Suppose he had been inclined to wonder about the fact that Wittgenstein did not write on the philosophy of religion. (I hope it is clear that I am not suggesting that Nielsen *should* have taken his inquiry in this direction.) Why did Wittgenstein, though he has things to say about religion in his *Nachlass*, fail to prepare such remarks for publication or to do anything we could in good conscience call 'philosophy of religion'? I find it helpful in thinking about this question to turn to a claim of Phillips's. Somewhere Phillips writes, 'A philosopher tries to understand what is meant by saying that God's ways are beyond human understanding.' Of course, Phillips is not suggesting that anyone who does not undertake this project is not a philosopher. But he does seem to be saying that the only correct *philosophical* response to the sentence 'God's ways are beyond human understanding' is to try to understand what it means. So we can ask: why didn't Wittgenstein, take an interest in *this* project? Why didn't he try to understand what this sentence and others like it mean?

There is ample evidence in his *Nachlass* that in fact Wittgenstein *was* interested in understanding what it would mean to say something like 'the ways of God are beyond human understanding'. But it is also evident that he saw that no *philosopher*, himself included, was going to be able to make this claim fully intelligible to him. This is because there is nothing *philosophically* untoward about the idea that the ways of God are beyond human understanding. There is nothing to be made intelligible, at least by the procedures of philosophy. It turns out, Wittgenstein indicates again and again, that the intelligibility of religious faith is not something that we can *dope out* philosophically. (And we can extend this claim to all sorts of things that we are inclined to say, in all sorts of discursive domains. Think about whether a philosopher could do a better job than anyone else of making intelligible the idea that we should – or should not – bomb a country that might harbour terrorists. Of course, some people think that philosophers are positively obliged to weigh in on such issues in an authoritative way, but I am arguing that Wittgenstein was emphatically not one of them. This leaves for another time the question of how a philosopher inspired by Wittgenstein's methods ought to construe the relationship between philosophy and politics or, more broadly culture. That question is at the heart of my own work, but I must leave it aside here.) Over and over again in his writings, Nielsen rebukes Phillips, sometimes in painfully strong terms, for failing to take up the challenge to make himself more intelligible. At one juncture Nielsen writes of Phillips that 'what he should do instead of . . . dancing around is come out and carefully argue for the substantive and normative beliefs that he is committed to' (Chapter 10, p. 194). He should 'carefully and impartially articulate his own religious commitments and show why it is a good thing to have those commitments' (Chapter 10, p. 194) or he should argue that his commitment is groundless and yet nonetheless something to which we should commit ourselves. If he does not do this sort of thing, Nielsen concludes, then Phillips fails 'in his very vocation . . . as a philosopher' (Chapter 10, p. 194). Phillips has never said exactly this about Nielsen, but his repeated attacks on Nielsen's capacities as a reader have a similar effect.

Perhaps the polite thing for me to do here would be to throw up my hands and talk of 'incommensurability of modes of discourse' or 'indeterminacy in the notion of "understanding"' as both Phillips and Nielsen do in their writing on this subject. I find I can't do that, however, and for several reasons. The first is that I find both of these notions to be deeply in tension with Wittgenstein's philosophical writing, which, like Nielsen and Phillips, though in a different way, I find directly pertinent here. And one reason that I find these notions in such tension is because they both strike me as teetering on the edge of unintelligibility: I can understand the idea of *explanations* or *theories* being incommensurable, but I cannot understand how we can talk about 'modes of discourse' not sharing, in numerous particular instances, a common logic or grammar, as Phillips as done (Chapter 9, p. 169). In the specific case of the concept 'belief', for example, I am not prepared to say that the religious use of this word has nothing in common grammatically, in Wittgenstein's sense of that term, with the scientific use. And to employ the Quinean term 'indeterminacy' to characterize the concept 'understanding' seems to me a needlessly complicated and potentially confusing way to express the idea – one that Phillips insist upon even in the face of Nielsen's apparent acceptance of it – that what counts as 'understanding' varies from case to case. And that brings me to a final reason for not acceding here to the notions of 'incommensurability' or 'indeterminacy' in my attempt to say something useful about human understanding: these concepts are at best at the periphery of what creates what Phillips has called the 'ragged scene' of his duel with Nielsen – or so I believe (Chapter 9, p. 172).

What then, do I think is controlling this scene? Let me rephrase the question. Why does Phillips's refusal to defend his religious faith, what Nielsen perceives as his damnable and intellectually irresponsible fideism, so exercise Nielsen? And why does what Phillips must perceive as Nielsen's perverse lack of desire and ability to understand the nature of religious faith so exercise Phillips? Both Phillips and Nielsen seem to think that the other is not making a serious effort to understand his views. And each seems to think that he himself is trying desperately, and in perfect faith, to understand the other's views through engaging in something they would both call 'philosophy of religion'. Each, to be more specific, is committed to the project of putting forth philosophical arguments, arguments that are as perspicuous and easily surveyable as each can possibly construct, in order to try to get through to the other. But what each seems to me to be failing to do is to scrutinize philosophically, first, his failure to make himself intelligible to the other, second, his fantasy that the way to achieve this intelligibility is through philosophical argumentation and, finally, the verbal violence with which he is willing to respond in the face of the other's failure to understand.

Both Nielsen and Phillips have good reasons for wishing that the other would come around to his way of thinking about things. Nielsen is among those convinced that religion, or at least our indulgence of religious ways of talking, is responsible for many of the evils in the world. There is superficial evidence that this conviction is not entirely off base (though, in my view, the evidence is decidedly superficial: what do we make of the United Methodist Church's vehement condemnation of George W. Bush, one of its card-carrying members, for his announcement that God was (is, as I write) somehow underwriting his aggression against Iraq? (see, for example, Bloom 2004)). And Phillips is out to show naysayers that one can be thoroughly rational and impeccably philosophical and still be deeply religious. One need look no further than the history of philosophy to find ample support for this view. And yet I don't think we have done enough work to conclude that it's a mere coincidence that a very large number of thoughtful and morally righteous philosophers and intellectual fellow-travellers find themselves unable or unwilling – or, in the case of Thomas Nagel, afraid – to adopt a religious perspective on their lives (see Nagel 1999).

I concluded early on in this paper that considerations of how we tend to use the phrase 'human understanding' suggest that what is at stake is the question of how and why things can be made intelligible both by us and to us. I then suggested that, despite its investment in making things perspicuous, philosophy may not offer a direct route to our mutual intelligibility. Does that mean that I don't think that philosophy has any role to play in, as it were, fostering human understanding? I find that to address this question I have to take an entirely different tack.

On 18 January 2003, while I was in the thick of reflecting on the question, 'Is there anything beyond human understanding?' a child in my son's elementary school went to sleep with a mild stomach bug and never woke up. His father found him dead in his bed the next morning and called the mother, who happened to be more than 1,000 miles away, visiting her parents. As the news spread the next day, everyone had the same question: why? Part of what we wanted to know would be answered within a couple of days via an autopsy. It turned out that Jordan had had asymptomatic, undiagnosed juvenile diabetes, the end stage of which looks like a stomach flu. But of course this news – that there was a rational explanation for why Sara and Marcus Weiss's son had died while the hearts of the rest of our children, including my two, were still beating – hardly quelled the chorus of 'why's. Why did this have to happen, if it did have to happen, when only one parent was in town? Why did Jordan's older brother, Jared, have to suffer this anguish? Why this wonderful family? Why would a human being get only nine years to live? Adults, of course, did not expect answers to these questions, which is not to say that they have yet to let them go. But the children of our community understandably were afraid of their own beds in the wake of them. If Jordan could have had undiagnosed asymptomatic diabetes and gone to bed and not woken up, why not them? One night my eleven-year-old daughter came into my bedroom, crying, at a very late hour. 'I just don't understand, Mommy,' she sobbed. 'Why did Jordan die?'

I could not and did not want to say to Anneliese what my father, a sophisticated, deeply compassionate Lutheran minister whose integrity I have always admired, would have said to me had he been in my slippers and I in my daughter's, namely, that we cannot understand the ways of God, who no doubt hurts for all of us. My parents' orientation in and toward the world has not been mine since my early adulthood, when my religious faith disentangled itself from my sense of moral rectitude and, like an old skin, simply sloughed off bit by bit. I still cannot say exactly how or why this happened, and I doubt a full story would be of much general interest. But I can say what did not happen: I did not lose my faith as a result of someone's advancing a philosophical demonstration of its inherent irrationality. When I was in my mid-20s and pretty much faith-free, I became interested in what was then the newly emerging field of medical ethics. At that time (and, I suspect, to this day) the most experienced medical ethicists were hospital chaplains, and an acceptable place to get a degree in the subject was in a divinity school, one of which, despite my lack of religious orientation, I attended. To study at a seminary is inevitably to be confronted not just with positive theology but also with writers bound and determined to prove, via what they construe as rational argumentation, that religious faith in any form is by nature irrational, self-delusional and even dangerous. Positivistic theologians, even systematic ones, have a certain audience in mind and evince no more interest in convincing their readers to believe in the existence of God than biologists, also with a certain audience in mind, evince in convincing their readers to believe in the existence of scientific truths. But people who wish to evangelize on behalf of atheism appear to be convinced, unlike the theologians they disdain, that reason itself works in mysterious ways.

I don't know if my daughter, or my daughter in a parallel universe brought up in a religious household, would have felt comforted on the night she woke me up by what my father would have said to me in the same circumstances. Perhaps she would have reacted the way I did when I was ten years old and suffering from a terrible bout of juvenile depression, and my father told me that God was crying for me. This is one of the most vivid memories of my childhood. I was sitting in my father's lap, completely miserable, in his little office in the basement of our house, and when he said this I burst into fresh tears, largely because I felt bad that my own sadness was making God, who had felt so far away during those days, feel so bad. I am not sure whether it was my despair or my father's sense that he had failed to convey to me what he had meant to convey by saying that God was crying for me that caused his tears to well up and overflow. But I have always been deeply grateful for that moment, in which I came to grasp the value – the gift – of a fatherly being's tears, something that no argument could have brought me to understand. This was not a gift that I was able to give to my daughter the night she came to me sobbing. All I could do was to scoop her into my lap and try to let it be a space in which she could express her despair, could come to terms with the fact that her mother the philosopher had absolutely nothing helpful to say.

Notes

1 Nielsen identifies Phillips as a charter member of this club in Chapter 8, p. 143.

2 See, e.g., the collection of remarks I've cited in my epigraph, L. Wittgenstein, *Lectures and Conversations on Aesthetics, Psychology, and Religious Belief*, Berkeley, CA: University of California Press, 1967.

Bibliography

Bloom, Linda (2004), 'Religious Leaders Criticize Bush Administration Over Iraq', General Board of Global Ministries News, United Methodist Church: http://gbgm- umc.org/globalnews/fullarticle.cfm?articled=2417.

Nagel, Thomas (1999), *The Last Word*. New York: Oxford University Press.

Wittgenstein, Ludwig (1967), *Lectures and Conversations on Aesthetics, Psychology, and Religious Belief*, ed. by Cyril Barrett. Berkeley, CA: University of California Press.

12. The Grammar of 'Beyond Understanding'

D. Z. PHILLIPS

In the first sentence of Chapter 8, Nielsen says that the answer to the question, 'Can Anything be Beyond Human Understanding?' depends on what we mean by 'beyond understanding', or, as I would say, on the grammar of that expression. I couldn't agree more.

It seems also, at times, as though Nielsen and I are agreed on what that grammar does not amount to, namely, the postulation of a metaphysical 'something' beyond the reach of the language of finite human beings. Nancy Bauer concurs. If we *are* agreed on this, there is little point in reiterating, in *this* discussion, that 'God' cannot be so understood. Nielsen does so because, while not wanting to attribute metaphysical beliefs to me that he knows I do not accept, he thinks my alternative account runs into metaphysical difficulties I do not recognize. So I end up having metaphysical views attributed to me after all. The only alternative Nielsen offers is settling for religion as 'morality touched with emotion'. Those are the parameters within which he argues. I, on the other hand, suggest that we have to move outside these parameters, since they are conceptually limiting.

I have argued that we speak of things being 'beyond understanding' in certain circumstances where 'understanding' is impotent as a response to them. Nielsen responds, 'I will argue that there are senses in which Phillips is right in his claim that there are vicissitudes in human life which are beyond human understanding, but that these senses are of little philosophical interest. In the senses that might deliver philosophical gold, the claim is at best false' (Chapter 8, p. 143). I find this conclusion incredible. How does Nielsen arrive at it?

The kind of responses I have in mind exist in abundance in people's lives in both religious and secular contexts, and great literature is unimaginable without them. The responses go 'beyond understanding', not simply in announcing its impotence, but in going on to speak of resources of different kinds that have helped people to face such situations. The responses come to terms with the anguish Nielsen refers to. He recognizes that they give 'consolation both to the Kierkegaardian knight of faith and to the Camusian–Sartrean existentialist atheist' (Chapter 8). But Nielsen will have none of it. Such cases, he asserts, depend on 'a philosophical muddle which rests on a failure to command a clear view of our language. It is a claim which should be up for dissolution rather than resolution' (p. 145). If Nielsen merely wanted to reject the responses of Camus and Sartre, that would be his privlege, but he wants to *dissolve* them by showing that they are philosophically confused. To do this would need, of course, a detailed discussion of Camus' notions of 'absurdity' and 'rebellion', Sartre's notion of 'existential choice' and Kierkegaard's notion of 'patience' in religion. What exactly is Nielsen claiming? Is he saying that were philosophy to do its work properly, we would see that there is only one rational response to the vicissitudes of life, all others having been shown to be confused?

This is connected with my criticisms of philosophy as advocacy. Nielsen thinks that I have to deny that, as a matter of biographical fact, philosophical clarifications may help us in the course of arriving at a substantive moral or religious point of view. Of course, I do not deny that for a moment. But that is not the high claim of religious apologetics that I am attacking. That claim, in the history of philosophy, has argued that philosophy can determine the nature of the good life, the most desirable political organization, and whether there is a God or not. It does not allow *real* differences in these contexts to be themselves, but regards them as preliminary data on which philosophy will work. That apologetic aim is prominent in philosophy. Nielsen objects to my criticism of such apologetics, but philosophy is a critical activity, and its history has been obsessed with the issue of its own character. That is no accident. It is not that I *begin* with a persuasive definition of philosophy, as Nielsen claims, and simply rule out apologetics. Rather, in the course of philosophizing, I come to see and show that the high claim of philosophical apologetics is confused. It will not be taught differences.

For example, one of the weakest claims in Bernard Williams's *Shame and Necessity*, is that, for us, politics replaces belief in fate. A similar claim may be made for the achievements in medicine. As I argued elsewhere, the trouble with this suggestion is that politics and medicine can and have contributed to the very bewilderment at life they were meant to allay:

'If only the cure had been available then . . .', 'We had hopes of what the revolution would usher in, and then look what happened . . .', 'All those people who passed their lives under evil regimes; the millions lost without trace' . . . This is not to say that everyone does, or must, experience this bewilderment. It *is* to say that one cannot argue that there is something confused about it. Neither is it to deny that there are various responses to this bewilderment. Among these are religious responses which, I want to say, cannot be shown philosophically, to be the product of confusion and illusion. (Phillips 2001, 45)

What is Nielsen's response? He writes, 'Some bad and some good things happen to us for no reason, and where they are horrendous enough we may cry out against them. What is puzzling is not that these things happen, but that Phillips makes such a hue and cry about them' (Chapter 8, p. 147). Like a latter day Euripides, Nielsen is saying that all this amounts to is 'simply a banal truth that human affairs are likely to prove unpredictably ruinous' (Phillips 2001, 44). That personal reaction, again, is Nielsen's privilege, but not his philosophical claim that he can reduce the responses I discuss to these terms.

Had things been different, Nielsen and I could have proceeded from this point to discuss *different* responses to life's vicissitudes, exploring their character, the nature of inter-criticism between them, and what is meant if an adherent to any of them calls his or her response 'true'. This cannot happen, since, for Nielsen, all religious responses are either false or incoherent. By contrast, in my collection *From Fantasy to Faith* (1991), I discuss a range of religious and secular responses via 20 writers in twentieth-century literature, in which I discuss depth and shallowness on *both* sides of the fence. This is different from a philosophical apologetics that sees its task as determining which response to the vicissitudes of life is the right one.

Interestingly, Nancy Bauer sees both Nielsen and myself as engaged in a kind of apologetics. She suggests that though we both admire Wittgenstein, a real appreciation of the spirit of his work would take both of us outside the terms of our debate, since she sees me as attempting to get Nielsen to accept the sense of the religious response to the vicissitudes of life, and sees Nielsen as attempting to get me to acknowledge that that response is meaningless. For Bauer, we both argue as though philosophy can determine whether the response makes sense or not. But we need to turn in another direction. Bauer writes,

> There is ample evidence in his *Nachlass* that in fact Wittgenstein *was* interested in understanding what it would mean to say something like 'the ways of God are beyond human understanding'. But it is also evident that he saw that no *philosopher*, himself included, was going to be able to make this claim fully intelligible to him ... It turns out, Wittgenstein indicates again and again, that the intelligibility of religious faith is not something that we can *dope out* philosophically. (Chapter 11, p. 209)

Thus, it was not philosophy that brought it about that Bauer lost her father's faith, and it was not want of philosophy that made it impossible to repeat her father's comforting words to her as a child, when she could not offer that comfort to her own daughter, bewildered at the sudden death of a schoolfriend. Abandoning this role for philosophy, she says that a positive account of philosophy's relation to our culture must be left for another time (p. 210). That is a pity, since it is that very question, it seems to me, which would reveal a misunderstanding of my contemplative philosophical method.

I do not think for one moment that philosophical justifications bring about the personal appropriation of religious or atheistic responses to the vicissitudes of life. That appropriation, for the most part, has its roots in other sources. On this matter, I agree entirely with Bauer. But my concern is with responses that *already exist*. We may be philosophically puzzled about what they amount to. Or we may be responding to philosophical accounts which we think distort these responses. In ethics, as well as in religion, Wittgenstein is always reminding us of other possibilities if we are inclined to say that people *must* respond to life in a certain way. As in literature, philosophy asks us to do conceptual justice to responses other than our own. As we shall see later in our discussions, the difficulty of philosophical contemplation is that our own strongly held beliefs may get in the way of our doing justice to different beliefs. Clearly, what we elucidate (and recognize as unconfused) is far wider than what we appropriate personally. Reading any great work of literature makes the same point. We see how human life can be seen in a certain way, without, necessarily, being able to see our own lives in that way. Bauer lost the sense of the religious words with which her father comforted her. Philosophy's contemplative task would ask her to strive to regain a *sense* of what his words amounted to, but this need not entail that she could *say* those words herself to comfort her child. So if Bauer asks how philosophy is related to culture, I'd reply, 'As the contemplator of it.'

Nielsen does not treat my examples contemplatively, nor does he think I do so. He writes in Chapter 10,

> But I have pondered his examples and I have not found them doing any philosophical work: animating, *philosophical* appreciation; though some of them, *for people with certain* inclinations, may animate religious belief or cause a religious response. That is why I find, whatever his intentions, Phillips more of an apologist, more of a preacher, than a philosopher describing or clarifying our religious discourse in a cool place. (p. 196)

The problem with remarks of this kind is that they give a verdict without showing the road by which it is reached. Surely it is *this*, not the use I make of examples, which constitutes the avoidance of philosophy.

If Nielsen thinks that the examples do no philosophical work, he must show where he agrees or disagrees, with Tennessen's discussion of Job, for example, and the same holds for the other literary examples. Actually, Nielsen's own comments give the game away. Speaking of Lucretius, Horace, Sophocles, Nielsen says, 'Fine literary stuff but little elucidation of how God-talk works' (p. 196). But suppose we ask Nielsen what he means by 'fine literary stuff', if it is not what the examples show with great power. If they do this, is it a puzzle why they should be used to counter the generalities of philosophers about, say, religion or ethics? In this respect, it is useful to compare the remarks of Bernard Williams and Peter Winch on Greek tragedy. Williams writes

> I have said, more than once, that we do well to remember that tragedy is a form of art [Nielsen's 'fine literary stuff'?]: there is no suggestion here of anyone behaving as a tragic hero. (That remember can only be reinforced by bearing in mind the extent to which Sophoclean necessities of fate are themselves the product of art). (Williams 1993, 165)

By contrast, Winch writes,

> I shall ... take it for granted that these stories are not merely told for the entertainment value (though that is of course, sometimes, a significant element), but are intended to convey important insights about the nature of human life, about 'the human condition.' (Winch 2001, 420)

Notice, Winch speaks of important *insights*. Nielsen wants to rule out religious responses as either false or incoherent. The point of my literary examples is their power to show insight in the contexts where Nielsen finds nothing. For example, Horace's verses show how responses to life's vicissitudes can be religious, and must not always take the form of scientific explanation, as Lucretius thought. It is because Lucretius is in the grip of that assumption that Lucretius concludes that religious beliefs are an irrelevance. Horace had thought likewise, until he retraced his steps to realize that 'Jupiter thundered from a clear sky' can have a very different meaning. I tried to bring out parallels with *Odeipus Rex* and Peter's denial of Christ. Nielsen, too, needs to retrace his steps to reflect on the insights shown in these works.

Because I use some examples which may animate religious belief in *some* people, Nielsen calls me an apologist for religion. But my examples of atheistic thought in *From Fantasy to Faith* may animate atheism for *some* people. Does that make me an apologist for atheism? In the world of philosophical apologetics, the view is that philosophical reflection will show us whether there is a God or not. In this sense, Nielsen is an apologist, but I am not. I want to do conceptual justice by belief and atheism. I am not *advocating* either. That should be clear from the following:

> But why the gods? Why not settle, as Euripides suggests we should, for saying that life is unpredictable? What I offer in reply is not a proof that one cannot or should not settle for this, but simply the reminder that one does not have to. (Phillips 2001, 49)

Why are these examples a closed book for Nielsen? Partly because he believes Greek beliefs in the gods to be anthropomorphic and empirically false. Does Nielsen really believe that people discovered that there were no gods on Olympus by climbing it? In that case, why didn't they stumble over Pan who remained in the Grove? Contrast Nielsen's charge of anthropomorphism with Winch's discussion of *Prometheus Bound* (Winch 2001).

Another obstacle to Nielsen's appreciation of the religious beliefs, is his assumption that while one can wonder at *why* the world is as it is, one cannot wonder at the fact *that* it is. A little reflection shows that this is not so. Not all cases of 'wonder' are cases of 'wondering why' or 'wondering whether'. One does not need examples of aesthetic wonder at great works of art and literature to point this out, plentiful though they are. One need only listen to Louis Armstrong singing, 'I see trees of green, red roses too ... and I say to myself, What a wonderful world!' He is wondering *at* the green trees and the red roses, not wondering how they came to be green and red. Nielsen has an impoverished, positivistic distinction between 'the cognitive' and 'the affective'. If we had an interest only in how things are, there is much that we would never see. Could one wonder at the coming of the dawn, or at a sunset, if one were interested only in a scientific explanation of how they occur? Religious rites at the coming of a day, or at the end of it, contribute to people's conception of the day, what the day is, the spirit in which it is to be accepted, and the sense of being answerable for how one has spent it. Are 'love', 'hate', 'friendship', 'magnanimity', cognitive or affective? What of the wonder at them which any of them may occasion? If 'wonder' were as limited as Nielsen suggests, we would earn the chastisement by Wittgenstein that Szabados quotes in his Introduction: 'People who are constantly asking "Why?" (or "What?") are like tourists, who stand in front of a building, reading Baedeker, and through reading about the building's construction etc. are prevented from seeing it' (p. 1). Notice, prevented from *seeing* it.

Nielsen thinks that Carnap is a better guide than Wittgenstein in these matters. Carnap and his fellow positivists longed for a notion of 'pure seeing' (the purely cognitive) which would be the ultimate constituent in any analysis of a perceptual proposition. Rhees has pointed out that the notion of 'pure seeing' cannot play this role, since the notion of 'seeing' itself stands in need of analysis (Rhees 2003, Chapter 4). In the *Investigations* Wittgenstein shows why such an analysis is needed (Wittgenstein 1955, Part II xi). He provides a whole range of examples of 'seeing', bringing out grammatical differences between them. He considers cases such as seeing *this*, now *that*, as the apex of a triangle; seeing the triangle as standing upright, or as having toppled over; the duck–rabbit example; seeing a white cross on a black background, but then seeing a black cross on a white background; two people drawing exact copies of two faces, but only one of whom sees a similarity between them; and a person wishing he could see what was going on in another person's head. Wittgenstein's point is that all these are proper uses of 'seeing'.

The point of citing such examples is to show how impoverished is the positivistic distinction between the cognitive and the affective. Such examples cannot be dismissed in terms of Nielsen's language of 'high fallutin talk', or of 'science touched with emotion plus obscurity'. They are familiar features of human life.

Consider, in this context, my discussion in Chapter 5, section VII, of what it is to see something in a picture. Sometimes, as in representational pictures, to see is to see what it represents, such as the crowning of Napoleon. But Wittgenstein also discusses genre pictures, where he wants to say that the picture says itself. The important point is that Wittgenstein insists that, in relation to language, the analogy with *both* kinds of pictures has a place. Nielsen finds 'the picture says itself' to be a dark saying, but if someone claimed to see something of God in Michelangelo's 'Creation of Adam', I find it hard to believe that Nielsen (J. L. Mackie (1982) notwithstanding) would think he is thereby committed to thinking that Michelangelo's picture is a portrait, or a representational diagram! As Wittgenstein says, the picture must be used in an entirely different way.

When the Israelites came out of Egypt, they are said to have travelled as people who had *seen the invisible*. What does that mean? In the films of the Invisible Man, he appeared now and again. When he did so, he was, of course *visible*. But when the Israelites saw the invisible, they did not see it as visible. There is meant to be a contrast with visible earthly concerns. 'The invisible' refers to the things of the spirit. To travel in that spirit, for a believer, is to travel with God, for God is Spirit. It is that element in which believers live, and move and have their being. This reference to 'the element' in which they live, has overlap with Wittgenstein's concern with the 'elements' of our thinking in *On Certainty*. I shall be concerned with this in the last part of the book.

Nielsen is quite right in pointing out that religious wonder is different from the wonder to be found in philosophy. The latter, in our present context, is wonder at the different ways in which people respond to the world, the different answers they give to problems, the different conceptions they have of what constitutes a 'problem' or an 'answer' in the first place. This is a very different conception of philosophy from that which concerns itself with fixing things, seeking answers, and so on. Whereas the great philosophers gave priority to understanding the world, the present age sets greater store on seeking solutions and arriving at answers. It was partly this emphasis on progress which led Wittgenstein to say that perhaps he was writing for another generation. Wittgensteinian philosophers of religion feel similarly isolated in a world dominated by the apologetic concerns of philosophical theism and philosophical atheism.

Bibliography

Mackie, J. L. (1982), *The Miracle of Theism*. Oxford: Oxford University Press.
Phillips, D. Z. (1991), *From Fantasy to Faith*. Basingstoke: Macmillan.
—— (2001), *Religion and the Hermeneutics of Contemplation*. Cambridge: Cambridge University Press.
Rhees, Rush (2003), *Wittgenstein's 'On Certainty'*, ed. with an Afterword by D. Z. Phillips. Oxford: Blackwell.
Williams, Bernard (1993), *Shame and Necessity*. Los Angeles: University of California Press.
Winch, Peter (2001), 'What can Philosophy say to Religion?' *Faith and Philosophy* 48: 4. Ed. D. Z. Phillips.
Wittgenstein, Ludwig (1955), *Philosophical Investigations*. Oxford: Blackwell.

PART FOUR

Wittgenstein and Religion

13. Wittgenstein and Wittgensteinians on Religion

KAI NIELSEN

I

Wittgenstein once remarked, 'I am not a religious man: but I cannot help seeing every problem from a religious point of view' (Rhees 1984, 79). Though he wrote very little about either religion or ethics, it is true that a sensibility to and concern for broadly speaking ethical and religious matters is pervasive in almost all of his work. He wrote extensively about language, meaning, intentionality, mind, consciousness, the self, logic, mathematics and necessity, but woven into all these considerations, which have been central to the main historical tradition of philosophy, is a religious and ethical concern. Perhaps it is better characterized as an intense ethico-religious concern, for when he speaks of ethics it is always in a distinctively religious way. But this would be badly understood if it were taken, after the fashion of Richard Braithwaite and R. M. Hare, to be a reductive view of religion in which religion is viewed as morality touched with emotion associated with certain traditional narratives which may or not be believed (Braithwaite 1975; Hare 1973). Wittgenstein linked ethics and religion tightly. But, as we shall see, his thinking here was very different from that of the reductive, basically straightforwardly ethical accounts of religion of Braithwaite and Hare.

It should also be noted that Wittgenstein did not write treatises or even articles on either ethics or religion and that he did not even discuss the topics that moral philosophers normally consider. Moreover, it is clear that he would have regarded both philosophy of religion and ethical theory with great suspicion and even with disdain. John Hyman rightly observes that 'Wittgenstein's influence in the philosophy of religion is due to scattered remarks, marginalia, and students' notes. He never intended to publish any material on the subject, and never wrote about it systematically' (Hyman 1997, 156). But all of that, as I will try to make plain, does not gainsay the import of my opening quotation from him.

In understanding what Ludwig Wittgenstein has to say about religion
or indeed about anything else, it is crucial to understand how Wittgenstein proceeded in philosophy and why he proceeded in that way. Here
we must see that and how Wittgenstein was remarkable in generating and
carrying out two revolutions in philosophy, the latter one dismantling the
philosophical practices, techniques, and conceptions of the former while
keeping a very similar metaphilosophical conception of the aim of philosophical activity.[1] It is not an exaggeration to say, as P. M. S. Hacker
does, that 'Ludwig Wittgenstein . . . was the leading analytical philosopher of the twentieth century. His two philosophical masterpieces, the
Tractatus Logico-philosophicus (1921) and his posthumous *Philosophical Investigations* (1953), changed the course of the subject' (Hacker
1999, 538). Hacker goes on to observe that 'the first was the primary
origin of the "linguistic turn" in philosophy, and inspired both logical
positivism and Cambridge analysis in the interwar years. The second
shifted analytic philosophy away from the paradigm of depth-analysis
defended in the *Tractatus* and cultivated by logical positivists . . . and
Cambridge analysts toward the different conception of "connective
analysis," which was a primary inspiration of Oxford analytic philosophy' (Hacker 1999, 538). However, this remark of Hacker's while
saying something importantly on the mark is also in a way misleading,
for not only in tone and attitude, but in method and aim Wittgenstein
was very different from Rudolf Carnap or Hans Reichenbach (positivists)
on the one hand and Ryle or Peter Strawson (Oxford analysts) on the
other. Wittgensteinian would have rejected the 'scientific philosophy' of
Carnap and Reichenbach and the 'descriptive metaphysics' (more
descriptive than metaphysical) of Strawson as well as the avuncular complacently confident tone of Ryle's ordinary language philosophy. Both
positivism and Oxford analysis would have struck him as scientistic –
though Carnap's and Reichenbach's plainly more overtly so. Moreover,
the system-building of Carnap and Strawson would have been regarded
by him as impossible (more 'houses of cards') and, even if possible,
unnecessary and indeed harmful.

Through both revolutionary turns, Wittgenstein held a therapeutic and
antiscientistic conception of philosophy with a deep underlying ethico-
religious intent. (Hence the word 'harmful' in the previous sentence.) But
it is important that we do not misunderstand Wittgenstein here. It is not
at all that he wanted to replace logic, metaphysics, epistemology, or
semantical analysis with moral philosophy, reformist moralizing, or some
lebensphilosophie. Nothing could be further from his intent. Rather he
thought *philosophy itself*, as a particularly bad species of intellectualizing,
was bad for human beings since it stands in the way of our coming to
grips with our lives. This coming to grips with our lives – something
which he took to be supremely important – had, in his view, as well as

in Kierkegaard's, nothing to do with philosophy. Philosophy just gets in our way here. Philosophical perplexities, both traditional and those arising in contemporary 'scientific philosophy', arise from the often obsessively gripping but still misleading pictures of the workings of our language that we come to have when we reflect on it, though often we do not recognize that it is certain pictures of our language that are generating our perplexities. And it is where that happens that we get in philosophical trouble: we catch the philosophical disease. We do not command a sufficiently clear view of the workings of our language when we try to think about (for example) consciousness, thought, sensations, truth, warrantability, intentionality, and the like. The idea is not to provide some general descriptive account of our language (Strawson) or some formal scientific account of the semantics of our language (Carnap), but to provide, at our conceptual trouble spots, where we are experiencing mental cramps, a sufficiently clear representation of how our language works to break that perplexity. It will not, of course, cure all perplexities forever, but it might cure the particular one that is befuddling us and so we proceed on from case to case. In this way philosophy is to be therapeutic. It does not (*pace* Carnap or Strawson) yield a theory of any kind – the search for one is perhaps *the* philosophical illusion – but is an activity which, where successfully pursued, yields a sufficient understanding of the workings of our language and with that of our practices and forms of life to break the spell that a misleading picture of the workings of our language at some particular spot exerts on us. Philosophy is taken by Wittgenstein to be an activity and not something which constructs some theory to explain our language or the forms of life in which our language is embedded.

There has been a tradition in philosophy (extending even to Gottlieb Frege and Bertrand Russell) which regards philosophy, in contrast with the empirical sciences, which investigate the domain of contingent truth, as the a priori science which investigates the domain of necessity. Wittgenstein argues in the *Tractatus* that this 'view' is nonsensical. The propositions of logic are either tautologies or contradictions. They are not in any sense descriptions or characterizations of anything substantive. They neither (*pace* Frege) describe timeless relations between abstract objects (meanings) nor (*pace* Russell) do they describe the most general features of the world. Both Frege and Russell failed to see a crucial radical difference between the propositions of logic and empirical propositions. They thought that the propositions of logic, like empirical propositions, *say* something. Logical propositions, they thought, say very different kinds of things than what empirical science does, but they still say something. Wittgenstein denied this. The propositions of logic (tautologies or contradictions) say absolutely nothing and thus are degenerate propositions. They give no information whatsoever about the world or 'the structure

of the world' or about some '*noumenal* world' (assuming such a notion
is even intelligible). So-called logical truths are simply tautologies. Wittgenstein remarks in the *Tractatus*, 'I know nothing about the weather
when I know that it is either raining or not raining . . . All propositions
of logic say the same thing, to wit nothing' (Wittgenstein 1921, 4.461,
5.43). Neither tautologies nor contradictions are bipolar (capable of
being true and capable of being false). They have no truth-conditions
or assertability-conditions. Tautologies are 'unconditionally true' and
contradictions 'unconditionally false'. A tautology is true under every
possible assignment of truth so it excludes no possibility. A contradiction,
by contrast, is false under every possible assignment of truth and thus it
excludes every possibility. They both have zero sense and say nothing at
all. But this vacuous logical necessity is the only a priori necessity that
we have. There is no argument at all for a claim common to Descartes,
Wolff, Kant, Husserl and many other traditional philosophers that while
the empirical sciences investigate the domain of contingent truth philosophy, by contrast, is an a priori science or a priori theory which investigates the domain of necessity. Pure reason cannot attain knowledge about
reality, for to know the truth of a tautology is not to know anything
about how things are or how things stand in reality or even about how
in some substantive sense things must be. (There is no substantive a priori
necessity.) In the philosophy of religion it is sometimes claimed we can
obtain such a knowledge of God – that there are some necessary but still
substantive religious propositions (Copleston 1956, 1957, 1975). But
that belief rests on an illusion.

Wittgenstein famously in the *Tractatus* asserted that 'what can be said
can be said clearly, and what we cannot talk about we must pass over in
silence' (Wittgenstein 1921, 3). He went so far as to assert that 'the whole
sense of the book might be summed up' in those words (Wittgenstein
1921, 3). Propositions according to what is *Tractarian* doctrine (assuming for the nonce that he was serious about there being such doctrine
and not purposefully for therapeutic purposes leading us down the garden
path) can only describe facts, neither philosophy nor anything else can
be used to explain how sentences must be related to the states of affairs
they represent, for to do so is to try to do more with words than merely
describe the facts (Wittgenstein 1921, 4.12). But when we try to do so –
that is, when we try to do philosophy – we end up talking nonsense.
Wittgenstein recognized that this claim entails that his own philosophical
propositions in the *Tractatus* are nonsensical. But here he bites the bullet
and remarks in a famous passage at the end of the *Tractatus*: 'The correct
method in philosophy would really be the following: to say nothing
except what can be said . . . and then, whenever someone wanted to say
something metaphysical to demonstrate to him that he had failed to give
a meaning to certain signs in his propositions' (Wittgenstein 1921, 6.53).

And then Wittgenstein goes on to say, 'My propositions serve as elucidations in the following way: anyone who understands me eventually recognizes them as nonsensical, when he has used them – as steps to climb up beyond them. (He must, so to speak, throw away the ladder after he has climbed up it.)' (Wittgenstein 1921, 6.54). Moreover, it is not just philosophy and metaphysics that are nonsensical, but religion, talk about the meaning of life, talk about making sense of life, talk about the meaning of the world, talk about God, ethics, and aesthetics. All such talk is nonsense – lacking in all propositional content – having no cognitive force. Such talk, Wittgenstein has it, belongs to 'the mystical' and that is also something which is nonsensical.

On the standard reading of Wittgenstein, such talk – something identified with the meaning of life, which Wittgenstein understood as the meaning of the world – could not be just plain old nonsense, but must be deep nonsense hinting at *unsayable ineffable truths*. Something, that is, that can be *shown* but not *said*. It was, so this reading has it, Wittgenstein's belief at the time of the *Tractatus* – and before and way down to and through his 'Lectures on Ethics' (1929–1930) – that all such talk – talk vital to our sense of life – could not be put into intelligible form. (Think, to feel the force of this, that 'intelligible talk' should be pleonastic.) Nothing that touches on matters of value can be captured by words. People, of course, try to do so, but they end up, though unwittingly, talking nonsense. Any attempt to even articulate, let alone answer, 'the problems of life' must be in vain. All thought, including philosophical thought, is useless here. And when 'the answer cannot be put into words [then] neither can the question be put into words' (Wittgenstein 1921, 6.5).

Most straightforwardly understood we have here – once we take away the rhetoric about *das Mystische* – what James Conant has called a 'collapse into positivism', though (*pace* Hilary Putnam) it is not at all evident that *here* this is a bad thing (Conant 1989; Putnam 1995). That is to say, the importance we attach to religion, along with aesthetic experience, ethics, and metaphysics, is the result of an illusion. Hard as it is to face, we have, when we cut through the disguised nonsense, just plain nonsense. And, as Frank Ramsey famously said, if it can't be said it can't be said and it can't be whistled either. Wittgenstein quite unequivocally said such talk was nonsensical, but he would paradoxically just as clearly not say that religion and ethics were of no importance. For him they were of supreme importance though not as bits of philosophy or intellectualizing. He was very far from being a secularizer. So where are we here? It looks at least like we are in a very bad muddle.

The (as I mentioned) standard and pervasive interpretation of the *Tractarian* Wittgenstein (one I subsequently will resist) has it that the idea that we have nonsense full stop is not at all what Wittgenstein thought. Not even in that respect would he make one with positivism. Talk of a collapse into positivism here is off the mark. Rather, it is typically thought, what Wittgenstein felt was that what can be said – what can be put into words – is piddling by comparison with what cannot – *with what can only be shown*. Wittgenstein himself in a letter written to a friend in 1919 says of the *Tractatus* that it 'consists of two parts: of that which is under consideration here and of all that I have not written. And it is precisely this second part that is the important one' (Luckhardt 1979, 94). The claim – certainly paradoxical – is that Wittgenstein believed during the *Tractatus* period, and at least up to 1929, that there are things that *can be shown that cannot be said*. As Hacker, for example, reads Wittgenstein,

> What is shown by a notation cannot be said. Truths of metaphysics are ineffable and so too are truths for ethics, aesthetics, and religion. Just as Kant circumscribed the bounds of language in order to make room for faith, Wittgenstein circumscribed the bounds of language in order to make room for ineffable metaphysics. (Hacker 1999, 344)

Pace positivists, this standard reading goes, there are truths here and presumably sometimes insight into these truths. They are things that, though only with heroic difficulty, can be grasped but not said. They show themselves to us if we have insight. Among them (on such a reading) are the 'ineffable truths' of religion that, Wittgenstein has it, for people who are genuinely attuned, form a passionately grasped system of reference. Still, given the traditional interpretation of Wittgenstein, these truths are ineffable and what the system of reference is is unsayable. But, for all of that, the traditional interpretation goes, they are of powerful significance.

Wittgenstein did indeed remark in the *Tractatus* 'How things are in the world is of complete indifference for what is higher. God does not reveal himself *in* the world' (Wittgenstein 1921, 6.432). In the very next sentence Wittgenstein goes on to remark, 'It is not how things are in the world that is mystical, but *that it* exists' (Wittgenstein 1921, 6.44). But he ends up – or so it seems – with another 'unsayability' here. For, as he also says, 'the fact' that the world exists is 'the fact' that 'there is what there is' (Wittgenstein 1961, 86). But 'there is what there is', unless 'is' in its two occurrences is used equivocally, is a tautology, so there is no fact at all and we have something on Wittgenstein's own *Tractarian* conception that is impossible to state. Remember that Wittgenstein stresses that tautologies say nothing. Yet the standard interpretation has it that Wittgenstein also believes that here is another supposed showable but not stateable something that reveals to us, in a way that cannot be said, a deep but ineffable truth. If the 'is' in its first occurrence in 'There is what there is' is used differently than the 'is' in the second occurrence, then we also have something that is nonsensical. We simply have no understanding of what we are saying: nothing can be made of such remarks. Either way, it is here, *if* this is how we are to understand Wittgenstein, where, for all his concern with clarity, the charge of obscurantism seems at least to have force. He appears at least to be trying to say – or to gesture at – that there is something of which we must say that we can only show it but not say it. But trivially we cannot say what the 'it' is that we are supposed to understand. But what then can understanding come to here? And how can 'There is what there is' be the least bit significant? But then again what can understanding possibly come to here? How can there be an it which we are supposed to understand if we can't *say* what this *it* is? It would surely appear to be – against the standard interpretation – *nothing*. But nothing is not a strange kind of something. We just do not understand what we are talking about – or trying to think – here. Put even more strongly, we cannot know or understand what we are talking about or trying to think here for there is no *what* or *this* for us to be talking about or to somehow conceptualize or grasp as an ineffable something we know not what. It is better – shows more integrity and clarity of thought – to say that we have just plain nonsense here on Wittgenstein's *Tractarian* conception of language and not some 'deep nonsense' taking us to some profound 'ineffable truths' about the meaning of life, fate and the meaning of the world itself (Wittgenstein 1961, 73).

There is a persistent tendency in our thought, both philosophical and religious, to believe that language cannot capture our deepest thoughts and feelings (Ambrose 1950). But that is nonsense and indeed Wittgenstein in his arguments in effect establishes this or, put more cautiously, at least gives us reason to question this claim of depth. We should just, without vacillation, acknowledge that Wittgenstein shows that it is nonsense full stop and that there is an end on it.

Still this doctrine of the unsayable but somehow showable with its supposed deep significance is the standard reading of Wittgenstein of the period of the *Tractatus*. And with *that interpretation* goes the not unfounded charge of obscurantism. But there is a minority view concerning Wittgenstein, with which my last remark in the last paragraph is attuned, represented powerfully by Cora Diamond and James Conant, which sees things differently (Diamond 1991; Conant 1989, 1990). On this interpretation, Wittgenstein is not even giving one to understand or hinting at obliquely in indirect discourse, let alone trying (but failing) to assert, that there are things that can be shown that cannot be said, including the claim that what is shown by a notation cannot be said in that notation. And that among these 'unsayables' there are deep 'ineffable truths' that cannot be said, but, ineffable though they be, can still be known or at least grasped. Wittgenstein indeed does say that such remarks are nonsense. Any interpretation of Wittgenstein will acknowledge that. But in addition this minority view denies that the gnomic remarks in the *Tractatus* that get highlighted by Wittgenstein as nonsensical are 'deep nonsense' pointing at something profound but unsayable. Rather they are just plain old nonsense – gibberish, though gibberish that tends to be disguised from us. And further, the claim is, Wittgenstein so regarded them. But the very conceptual work that Wittgenstein does should enable us to see that. That we typically do not understand that that is so is due to the fact 'that we do not *command a clear view* of the use of our words – our grammar is lacking this sort of perspicuity' (Wittgenstein 1953, para. 122).

My aim here is not to try to adjudicate which reading most accurately represents Wittgenstein's thought. My hunches are with the second one and a principle of interpretative charity would push us, I believe, in that direction. But I will not try to argue that. However, I will argue that if Wittgenstein did not take that latter way he should have. This way of reading him saves him from obscurantism and, as I shall attempt to show, it still allows him to take the respectful attitude toward religion, or rather some parts of it, that he was so concerned to take.[2]

James Conant, in a subtle though somewhat overblown article, probes carefully what needs to be said here (Conant 1989). The standard interpretation, as we have seen, takes it that Wittgenstein is telling us – and some of his interpreters think that that is something very profound on Wittgenstein's part – that there are things he cannot say but which he can and is gesturing at. There are some particular things, some of them very crucial to our lives, that can be shown but cannot be said. Conant, *au contraire*, argues that Wittgenstein is giving us to understand, and rightly so, that 'there is no particular thing that cannot be said. The "what" in "what cannot be said" refers to nothing' (Conant 1989, 244). The *Tractatus* ends as it does because of Wittgenstein's understanding that 'beyond what can be said there is nothing more to say or offer except more silence' (Conant 1989, 244). But at least some of the standard interpreters would respond in alarm that, so read, 'Wittgenstein would become indistinguishable from Carnap' (Conant 1989, 244). On the standard view 'Wittgenstein only agrees with Carnap insofar as he holds that the positions of ethics and religion are nonsense. However, [the standard view has it] they are supposed to be deep and significant forms of nonsense whereas for positivism they are void of any cognitive content whatsoever' (Conant 1989, 244). Conant, in a fine fit of reasonable common sense, wants to reject such a claim both as a correct reading of Wittgenstein and as an important bit of philosophy in its own right. And I want to reject it too for at least the last reason. If this is what it is to be Carnapian then we should all in that respect be Carnapians. It makes no sense to speak of something being 'nonsensical yet significant' or 'meaningless but *not* void of cognitive content'. Those conjunctions are unintelligible. They could only be *made* intelligible by some arbitrary stipulative *redefinition* of some of the constitutive terms. They are not intelligible as they stand. And the arbitrary stipulative definitions are just that.

However, as Conant worries out, what, if we do not resort to bald assertion, are we to say to a standard interpreter who retorts 'What kind of sense do you wish to make here?' Conant remarks,

> They are willing only to concede that these conjunctions were, strictly speaking, nonsensical. Nevertheless, they would say, they were *not* incoherent, admittedly they could not be coherently expressed, but they are not unintelligible. Indeed, for these commentators, it was the possibility of making such conjunctions intelligible that was the singular achievement of such works as the *Postscript* and the *Tractatus* to have delimited. (Conant 1989, 245)

Both Conant and I wish to dig in our heels here and reject this as good philosophy, good sense, good thinking about religion, and as a way to make the maximal sense out of Wittgenstein.

What argument can be made for such a digging in of one's heels? I will proceed indirectly by first intensifying our sense of what is at issue here. The standard interpreters maintain that for the *Tractatus* the propositions of ethics and religion – as well as all the important propositions of the *Tractatus* itself – are both nonsensical *and* deeply significant. They seem to lack cognitive content and still in some mysterious way have cognitive content, though an 'ineffable cognitive content'. Their significance is reputed to lie either in the fact that they do, or at least attempt to, *show the unsayable, exhibit in some unsayable way the ineffable.* This, Conant remarks,

> requires a conception of language as possessing capacities for exhibiting meaning over and above its ordinary capacities for conveying the sense of a proposition. Such a conception is required even if one only wants to maintain that Wittgenstein's deeply nonsensical propositions are only *trying* (but failing) to say something that cannot be said. For one needs an account of how one can so much as recognize what it is that a piece of nonsense is even just trying to say. (Conant 1989, 248)

The standard commentators wish to claim that there are *kinds* of nonsense leading to a *hierarchy* of nonsense. It is not only that we need to distinguish between intelligible nonsense as opposed to gibberish or gobbledygook, but we must go further and attribute to Wittgenstein the view that there are certain forms of intelligible nonsense, culminating at the top of the hierarchy of kinds of nonsense, in something which consists in certain ways of transgressing the syntax of our language which are ways that are 'deeply revelatory of the nature of certain matters that lie beyond the scope of language' (Conant 1989, 246). In the case of religion, the deep nonsense at the top of the hierarchy of nonsense – the 'profound intelligible nonsense' – is (in its generalized form) the claim that the deepest ineffable truths are revealed in mystical experience – the very paradigm of the (so-called) unsayable and inexpressible but still revelatory of 'ultimate reality'.

In his *A Study in Wittgenstein's Tractatus*, Alexander Maslow remarks that 'mysticism is an important part of Wittgenstein's view. Mysticism becomes the last refuge for the most cherished things in life, in fact for all values, for all that cannot be discussed and yet is of the utmost importance to us' (Maslow 1961, 160). Commenting on this passage, Conant remarks 'that Wittgenstein views mysticism as some form of "last refuge" and that he has the greatest respect for the impulse to seek such refuge, both strike me as correct perceptions' (Conant 1989, 276). But he adds significantly that the claim that Wittgenstein wishes to condone mysticism as a refuge is without textual support. Wittgenstein says in the *Tractatus* that 'the feeling of the world as a limited whole is the mystical feeling' (Wittgenstein 1921, 6.45). Wittgenstein wished to give a diagnosis of the source of the feeling. What he wished to diagnose was the claim that mystical experience, as it is understood by William James and others, is experienced as something utterly ineffable and yet seems to those who have had such an experience that it has (a) a distinctive *noetic* quality but is also (b) felt by them not to be identical with pure states of feeling. They are, or seem to be, states of feeling *and* states that seem to those 'who experience them to be also states of knowledge unplumbed by the discursive intellect' (James 1935, 380). This is a rather standard characterization of mystical experience. Wittgenstein was not concerned to reject such descriptions of how things *seem* to the mystic, but was concerned to diagnose it: to diagnose, that is, what James, who gave a careful account of it, took mystics to be trying to say of their experience. But in doing that Wittgenstein was not at all acknowledging that there was or even could be such knowledge or understanding.

A crucial error in the traditional interpretation is 'to mistake the views that are under scrutiny in the *Tractatus* for the views the author wishes to espouse' (Conant 1989, 248). Wittgenstein's diagnosis of our situation is as follows. The only alternatives to silence are (1) plain ordinary effable speech including scientific extensions of it; (2) *actually* unintelligible though *apparently* in some way intelligible talk; and (3) mere gibberish. Conant remarks, correctly, that (2) and (3) 'differ only in their psychological import: one offers the illusion of sense where the other does not. Cognitively, they are equally vacuous' (Conant 1989, 249). There is, he goes on to say, no fourth alternative, as the standard interpretation would have it, namely the possibility of speech that lacks sense but still yields deep, unsayable, ineffable truths (Nielsen 1973). That, when we take away the obscurantist rhetoric, is just the contradictory claim that these mystical utterances both – and in the same respect – are void of cognitive content *and* somehow have it. When we inspect with an unclouded eye these oracular utterances, we go from an obscurity to a contradiction. Sometimes we are conceptually confused and *mistakenly* think a sentence has cognitive content – makes sense – when it does not. Here Wittgensteinian philosophical therapy can sometimes help. 'The only distinction between deep nonsense and mere nonsense ... that the *Tractatus* allows is between pieces of gibberish that *appear* to have sense and those that don't. In neither case does the book countenance the possibility of a piece of irreducible nonsense' (Conant 1989, 268).

This is not gainsaid by the famous ending of Wittgenstein's 'Lecture on Ethics' – still very much in the *Tractarian* mode – where he says that religion 'springs from the desire to say something about the ultimate meaning of life ... What it says does not add to our knowledge in any sense. But it is a document of a tendency in the human mind which I personally cannot help respecting deeply and I would not for my life ridicule it' (Wittgenstein 1993, 44). This shows clearly enough Wittgenstein's respect for human beings and his sense of what deep needs such religious utterances and the experiences that go with them answer to, but it does nothing to show that there is any error in our claim that, on his *Tractarian* account, religious conceptions – what Wittgenstein regards as *das Mystiche* – must be just nonsense: straightforward nonsense. Seen clearly, that is, they are seen to be what they are, namely just nonsense though where seen through a glass darkly – seen confusedly – they remain *disguised* nonsense. But disguised nonsense is all the same nonsense and not something obscurely pointing to some deep 'ineffable truth', some deep reality we cannot otherwise grasp. We never have 'intelligible nonsense' or 'ineffable knowledge' for there is and can be no such thing.

Conant *might* be thought to be blurring the austerity of the above conclusion when he says that the '*Tractatus* ... does hold that we can always breathe life into a piece of language by finding a use for it in our lives' (Conant 1989, 260). However, we cannot do this without engaging in arbitrary stipulative redefinition of the religious utterances that Wittgenstein is most concerned with – the supposedly 'deep foundational ones' that he has in mind, the ones that on his view make religion religion. They *have* no sense and the sense that we can *give* them in an attempt to breathe life into them renders them into empirical trivialities or at least empirical utterances that no longer meet religious needs – that no longer could serve as a last refuge for people with religious impulses.

Take, for example, what Wittgenstein in 'The Lecture on Ethics' regards as the key paradigm religious experience. It is the experience a person has when he wonders at the very existence of the world – at *that* the world is, not *how* it is. It is the experience people have when it strikes them 'how extraordinary that the world should exist' (Wittgenstein 1993, 41). Wittgenstein flat out, says that the verbal expression 'we give to these experiences is nonsense' (Wittgenstein 1993, 44). He remarks

> If I say 'I wonder at the existence of the world' I am misusing language. Let me explain this: It has a perfectly good and clear sense to say that I wonder at something being the case, we all understand what it means to say I wonder at the size of a dog which is bigger than any one I have ever seen before or at anything which, in the common sense of the word, is extraordinary. In every such case I wonder at something being the case which I *could* conceive *not* to be the case. I wonder at the size of this dog because I could conceive of a dog of another, namely the ordinary size, at which I should not wonder. To say, '*I wonder at such and such being the case has only sense if I can imagine it not being the case . . .*' But it is nonsense to say that I wonder at the existence of the world, because I cannot imagine it not existing. I could of course wonder at the world round me being as it is. If for instance I had this experience while looking into the blue sky, I could wonder at the sky being blue as opposed to the case when it's clouded. But that's not what I mean. I am wondering at the sky *whatever* it is. One might be tempted to say that what I am wondering is a tautology, namely at the sky being blue or not blue. But then it's just nonsense to say that one is wondering at a tautology. (Wittgenstein 1993, 41–2)

Suppose we say instead that in wondering (thinking one wonders) not *how* the world is but *that* it is we are still wondering about something that is the case, namely *that* the world is, and in doing that I am all the same making a non-vacuous contrast. I am wondering instead why there is not instead nothing. In wondering at that, I am wondering in every case at something actually being the case which I *could* conceive not to be the case. I can wonder in every particular case that could possibly be brought to my attention why it could not be the case and I understand clearly that, as far as logical possibilities are concerned, it could not be the case. In wondering at the existence of the world I am wondering why there is not nothing rather than anything at all. Why could not all *empirical* existential statements be false and, if they were, then there would be nothing. But some empirical statements must be true for it even to be *possible* for us to know this or understand what is being said. And this makes the statement itself nonsense. Moreover, 'nothing' does not stand for a something that might be the case but just doesn't happen to be. It is, to put it mildly, an opaque notion to try to conceptualize what it would be like for all empirical existential statements to be false at once. What we could say distributively of each statement taken by itself entails nothing of what we could collectively be taken to be saying about them. Wondering – trying to wonder – about why there isn't nothing is nonsense. It is like trying to say there might be nothing which is also some kind of something. It would be like saying 'There is an is which is an isn't.'

We might give, following Conant's instructions, 'I wonder at the existence of the world' a sense by saying it is equivalent to 'I wonder why people must die.' But now we have turned a pseudo-question into an obvious empirical triviality. If we are wondering why people must die there are empirical answers to that. We have given – rather far-fetchedly – the religious pseudo-proposition a use by turning it into a straightforward, perfectly secular, perfectly empirical remark. We have given it a use all right, but not a religious use or even a use which has much in the way of a religious significance.'[3]

Suppose we say instead, in saying 'I wonder why people must die,' I mean 'Why could people not be made of such a hard metal that they would never wear out and thus never die?' But again there are, to the extent that we can make sense of that, as perhaps we can in some science-fiction way, empirical answers to it and, even if there were not, what we have said, in so speaking, has no religious significance. It is not a reasonable candidate for giving a use to 'I wonder at the existence of the world.'

Suppose we say that in wondering why people wear out – don't just have endless duration – we are wondering why they are not immortal, why they do not have life eternal. But to have life eternal is not just to have endless duration, but to have a life such that the question of our dying cannot arise. Here we have a question that is religious all right, but we have simply substituted one form of nonsense for another (Nielsen 1989b and 2001 chapter 3). (Remember that 'endless duration' is one thing, 'eternity' is another [Malcolm 1960].)

II

I turn now from an examination of the so-called saying/showing distinction and remarks about *das Mystische* in the work of the early Wittgenstein and its relevance for his and our thinking about religion to what I take to be more fruitful and more interesting considerations for religion emerging from Wittgenstein's later work, work which again, now for the second time in contemporary history, revolutionized philosophy. In my view, a view I share with Conant and Diamond, Wittgenstein continued to view philosophy as conceptual therapy, but his method for dissolving conceptual confusions – centrally the metaphysical confusions that stand in the way of our understanding – radically changed. In this way there was in his later work a radical dismantling of the *Tractatus* along with a continuity in his conception of the role of philosophy. I think this shift in method leads to a much more valuable way of doing philosophy and yields a much more adequate account of religion. (The fascination with – I'm inclined to say fixation on – the work of the early Wittgenstein rather than the later reflects for many philosophers a continued hang-up with metaphysics. They see the *Tractatus* for all its anti-metaphysical thrust as the last great work, Wittgenstein's intentions to the contrary notwithstanding, of metaphysics.)

I shall very briefly say a bit more about what Wittgenstein's second revolution consists in and then turn to a detailed consideration of what it comes to for religion. Again there is a paucity of material directly on religion; during this later period, as well as in the earlier, Wittgenstein wrote nothing for publication specifically and in detail about religion. But there are many things, though often only indirectly, that are very suggestive for thinking about religion in quite different ways than has traditionally been done – in ways which I think cut through or rightly bypass much of the cackle that goes for 'the philosophy of religion'. Fortunately, as far as texts go, we have in a recent work written by a former student, close friend, and well-known interpreter of Wittgenstein, Norman Malcolm, a work (*Wittgenstein: A Religious Point of View?*) which provides a detailed collection of remarks on religion made by Wittgenstein along with an analysis by Malcolm of those remarks followed by a substantial critique of Malcolm's account by Peter Winch. In this account of Wittgenstein on religion by two prominent Wittgensteinians, who are also philosophers of importance themselves, we have a perceptive and faithful account of Wittgenstein's views on religion, plus, particularly on Winch's part, the beginnings of a probing critique of them. (Winch is less of an uncritical disciple than Malcolm is.) I shall build on this material seeking to etch out (a) a portrayal of Wittgenstein on religion in his later philosophy and (b) an account of some Wittgensteinian emendations provided by Wittgensteinians (principally Winch) that will not only bring out the force of Wittgenstein's later account, but will, pointing to its vulnerabilities, enable us better to assess its soundness and import, both in its pristine form and in its critical Wittgensteinian reformulations. Here we can hopefully examine Wittgenstein's account of religion at its full strength. I shall attempt to do something of this.

But first a thumbnail general account of what the later Wittgenstein was up to. In *Philosophical Investigations* (1953), the central work of his later philosophy, as well as in work beginning as early as 1930 and in work following *Philosophical Investigations*, and most particularly in his last work, *On Certainty* (1969), Wittgenstein articulates his changed conception of how to proceed in philosophy and applies it to a range of philosophical problems. Propositions are no longer construed as having a fixed logical form and, more generally, language is no longer construed as having a fixed and timeless structure, but is viewed as changeable, and not infrequently changing, in which these forms of language are now seen as our historically and culturally contingent forms of life. The picture account of meaning is completely abandoned in his later work. The conception that words stand for simple objects that are their meanings is now regarded by Wittgenstein as a bit of incoherent philosophy. (On the Diamond–Conant reading of the *Tractatus* that was true of it too.) Instead the notions of language-games and practices are introduced. In being socialized – in learning, as we all must if we are at all to navigate in the world, to be human – we come to have practices in which words and actions are interwoven. In this activity, in learning to play these language-games, we come to understand words by coming to know their uses in the stream of life, and with this we come to know how to use words in the course of our various practice-embedded activities.

With this Wittgenstein abandoned his earlier formalist *Tractarian* demand that language, if coherence is our goal, requires determinacy and exactness and that the sole function of language is to describe. Rather language is seen as an activity that has many different functions, is embedded in different practices which answer to and structure our different needs, interests, or purposes. For someone to understand a word it is not sufficient to bring the learner face to face with its putative referent while repeating the word. In many cases nothing like this is possible and in all cases, or at least almost all cases, the learner must come to understand what *kind* of word he is being taught; to grasp this an extensive training needs to have taken place in which the learner comes to be at home with the everyday activities – the social practices – of which remarks using the word are a part. As Wittgenstein put it in an oft-quoted remark from his *Philosophical Investigations*, 'For a large class of cases – though not for all – in which we employ the word "meaning" it can be defined thus: the meaning of a word is its use in language' (Wittgenstein 1953, 43).

There is on Wittgenstein's account no standing free of our practices and forms of life or escaping the context, including the historical contexts, in which they are embedded. Both the *Tractarian* (on the traditional reading) and metaphysical realist conception of an independently articulated world are incoherent on Wittgenstein's later account. We have no coherent conception of a world that we can describe by accurately copying it or mirroring it or even representing it in our thought. There are no referents 'out there' that simply force our concepts on us. We rather understand our concepts by coming to understand their use in our life activities. Concepts are aspects of our forms of life. They are not items forced on us by the world. To understand a concept is to understand the use of words expressing it as they function in our language and in our lives. And these will be various things, depending on the particular concept, as part of the varied contexts and the various purposes we have. These varied activities and ways in which we talk form our practices and they build together into our forms of life. We have no concepts or conceptions which stand independently of them.

Wittgenstein's earlier views – more accurately his meta-views – on religion, at least on the standard interpretation of the *Tractatus*, could not withstand his changed conceptions about language. As I have noted, the idea of a general propositional form is illusory. There is no common property or set of common properties that all and only propositions have. There are many different kinds of structures that we call propositions. As P. M. S. Hacker has put it, many things count as 'propositions':

> avowals of experience (such as 'I have a pain' or 'It hurts'), avowals of intent, ordinary empirical propositions, hypotheses, expressions of laws of nature, logical and mathematical propositions, 'grammatical propositions' (in Wittgenstein's idiosyncratic use of this term) which are expressions of rules (such as 'red is a color' or 'the chess king moves one square at a time'), ethical and aesthetic and so on. (Hacker 1999, 545–6)

In the regimented, austere conception of the *Tractatus*, religious utterances are pseudo-propositions lacking bipolarity. They are, that is, not capable of being true or capable of being false. They on that conception describe nothing, are without any cognitive content at all, and thus are nonsensical. By contrast, given Wittgenstein's later philosophy, they are not, at least on these grounds, nonsensical. On Wittgenstein's later, more relaxed and more realistic conception of propositions many of them are propositions. 'Bipolarity is a feature of an important member of the family, but not a defining property of propositions as such' (Hacker 1999, 546). Moreover, Wittgenstein's earlier conception that it was the sole function of a proposition to describe is mistaken and importantly so. The 'roles of many kinds of propositions, such as logical propositions and mathematical propositions are not to describe' (Hacker 1999, 546).[4] Yet for all of that, they are in order. We cannot take such a short way with dissenters and simply rule out religious utterances *carte blanche* as expressions of pseudo-propositions and thus nonsensical because they fail to have the general form of a proposition. The shoe is on the other foot. The error – the illusion – is to believe that there is such a general propositional form: that there is something that propositions essentially are.

Wittgenstein continues, the above notwithstanding, to believe that religious beliefs are very different from factual beliefs. Surface appearances to the contrary, quite ordinary religious propositions are unlike factual propositions. They function very differently. But they are not, Wittgenstein now has it, any the worse for all of that. They are not therefore nonsensical.

A pervasive and, Wittgenstein believes, a pernicious error of our scientistic culture is to try to assimilate key uses of religious language (e.g., declarative sentences such as 'God created the world.') to those of hypotheses, predictions or theoretical explanations. To do that, he has it, is to completely misunderstand their use. It is to be fettered by one kind of use of language and to try to read it into other uses. When, for example, a religious person says 'I believe that there will be a last judgement,' it is a complete mistake, according to Wittgenstein, to take that utterance to be making a prediction. That is not the use, or even anything like the use, it has in religious language-games. In believing in the last judgement a person is not, Wittgenstein maintains, thinking that there will be, or even that it is probable that there will be, a certain kind of extraordinary event which will occur sometime in the future. The religious person – or at least Wittgenstein's religious person – is not thinking any such thing (Nielsen 1982, 43–64). He is not trying to make any kind of prediction at all (Wittgenstein 1969, 56). Rather, Wittgenstein equates having religious beliefs with (a) using affirmatively certain religious concepts and (b) having the emotions and attitudes that go with these concepts. He remarks, as we have seen, 'that a religious belief could only be something like a passionate commitment to a system of reference' (Wittgenstein 1980, 64). But these beliefs – beliefs such as a belief in the meaning of life or the meaning of the world – can be neither true nor false. The question of their truth or falsity cannot even meaningfully arise. Moreover, they are beliefs which are neither reasonable nor unreasonable. But what Wittgenstein does regard as unreasonable are apologists either for or against religion who assume that religious beliefs can in any way be tested: can be shown to be either true or probably true or, false or probably false by evidence or by argument or 'grasped by reason' to be so. Views like that he regards as ludicrous (Wittgenstein 1969, 58).

Now with something of Wittgenstein's later conception of how to proceed in philosophy before us, I shall turn to an examination of *Wittgenstein: A Religious Point of View* starting with some central considerations by Norman Malcolm. They consist in a rather orthodox but still well thought out articulation of a Wittgensteinian point of view.

A *leitmotif* of Malcolm's discussion of Wittgenstein on religion is

Wittgenstein's remarks in his *Philosophical Investigations* that 'philosophy simply puts everything before us, and neither explains nor deduces anything' (Wittgenstein 1953, 126). Concerning this Malcolm remarks:

> Wittgenstein is here proposing a radical change in our conception of what philosophy should be doing. To say that philosophy does not seek to explain anything is certainly not a true description of philosophy as it has been, and still is, practiced. Many philosophers would be dumb-founded or outraged by the suggestion that they should not be seeking explanations. The traditional aim of philosophy has been to explain the essential nature of justice, right and wrong, duty, the good, beauty, art, language, rules, thought. A philosopher may well ask: 'What am I supposed to do if not explain?'
> In Wittgenstein's later thinking there is an answer. The task of philosophy is to *describe*. Describe *what*? Describe *concepts*. How does one describe a concept? By describing the use of the word, or of those words that express the concept, that is what philosophy should 'put before us.' (Malcolm 1994, 74)[5]

There is no language-independent access to concepts, Wittgenstein is at pains to maintain in *Philosophical Investigations*, and Malcolm follows him here. Malcolm continues, 'The description of the use of a word is called by Wittgenstein describing the "language-game" with that word' (Malcolm 1994, 74). Then, without highlighting the therapeutic side of Wittgenstein's conception of philosophy, but in effect remaining faithful to it all the same, Malcolm remarks that it is not the task of philosophy to describe the use of a word in its *totality*, as if we had an understanding of what it would be like to do that, but only those features of the word that in certain determinate contexts give rise to philosophical perplexity. We assemble reminders to break a certain perplexity where we have mental cramps concerning the workings of our language. (Here again we see how very different Wittgenstein is from Strawson.) Describing the use of an expression is called, rather eccentrically but harmlessly by Wittgenstein, describing the grammar of the expression. But this, as by now should be evident, is not just giving an account of sentence-construction or syntax. The point of speaking of language-games is to bring into focus, and clear prominence, 'the fact that the *speaking* of a language is part of an activity or a form of life' (Wittgenstein 1953, 23). Malcolm, uncontroversially and rightly, takes this to mean 'that in describing the language-game, or some part of the language-game with a word, one is describing how the word is embedded in actions and reactions – in human behavior' (Malcolm 1994, 75). 'Words,' Wittgenstein remarks in his *Zettel*, 'have meaning only in the flow of thought and life' (Wittgenstein 1967, 173). 'Our talk,' he adds in *On Certainty*, 'gets its sense from the rest of our actions' (Wittgenstein 1969, 229). Our language-games embedded as they are in forms of life provide us a place for explanations, for giving reasons and for justifications inside the framework of these language-games or forms of life. But there is, *Malcolm* has it that Wittgenstein has it, neither explanation nor justification for the existence of these forms of language or language-games themselves.

Illustrating the way language-games work and their links with forms of life, Malcolm comments on our use of 'motive'. We not infrequently wonder about the motives of people. Normally the quickest and surest way to find out is to ask them. 'Now of course he may not reveal it: perhaps he himself does not understand it, or perhaps he misrepresents it both to himself and to others' (Malcolm 1994, 76). But then Malcolm goes on to observe, 'what is highly interesting is that if he does disclose his motive, typically his acknowledgement of it will not be based on any *inference* from the situation, or from his own behavior or previous actions – as would be the conjecture of others. He *tells* us his motive *without* inference' (Malcolm 1994, 76, first italics added).

We can, when we reflect about how this language-game works, just be struck by its sheer existence and contingency. And this is true not only with the language-games we play with 'motive' but also with 'intention' or with any other language-game (Malcolm 1994, 75–7). We have contingency here, not necessity. Gone are the supposed necessities of the *Tractatus* and indeed of the whole philosophical tradition. Reflecting on how Wittgenstein is reasoning and how Wittgenstein thinks we should reason if we would be realistic, Malcolm remarks, we 'cannot explain why this use of language exists. All we can do is describe it – and *behold* it' (Malcolm 1994, 76). He quotes from *On Certainty* where Wittgenstein makes a general comment about language-games. 'You must bear in mind that the language game is, so to speak, something unforeseeable. I mean it is not based on grounds. Not reasonable (or unreasonable). It stands there like our life' (Wittgenstein 1969, 559).

Religions, that is Judaism, Christianity, Islam, Hinduism, Buddhism, etc., etc., are ancient and complex forms of life that over time change in a myriad of ways with their distinctive but purely contingent language-games.[6]

Within these language-games there can be the giving of reasons, explanations, and justifications, but for the language-games and forms of life themselves, as we have noted, there can be no explanations or justification and no foundations for them either. They are human activities that are just there and religious forms of life like other forms of life are neither reasonable nor unreasonable. They do not rest on some deeper metaphysical or theological foundations or any kind of grounding theory. They neither have some foundationalist epistemological grounding nor any other kind of grounding nor do they stand in need of such grounding,

rationalization or theorizing. They are, Wittgenstein argues, in order just
as they are. They are just there, as we have already noted Wittgenstein
saying, like our lives. There can, and indeed sometimes should, be *internal*
criticisms within religious language-games. Some expressions of faith are
less adequate than others, less adequately capture the aspirations of a
particular religion, but there can be, Wittgenstein has it, no intelligible
standing outside these forms of life and assessing them. Justification
comes to an end when we come up against them. This is true for all
forms of life, religion included. As Malcolm puts it, giving what he takes
to be Wittgenstein's account, 'Wittgenstein regarded the language-games,
and their associated forms of life, as beyond explanation. The inescapable
logic of this conception is that the terms "explanation," "reason," "justification" have a use exclusively *within* the various language-games'
(Malcolm 1994, 77, italics added). Or again, 'An explanation is *internal*
to a particular language-game. There is no explanation that *arises above*
our language-games and explains *them*. This would be a super-concept
of explanation – which means that it is an ill-conceived fantasy' (Malcolm
1994, 78). What we can and should do as philosophers is observe and
describe language-games; and, with hard work and luck, we will come
to see more clearly, by a perspicuous representation, the use of the terms
of our language-games and the role they play in our lives. Philosophy,
the kind of therapeutic philosophy that Wittgenstein, Conant, Diamond,
Malcolm, Rhees and Winch practise, enters when we become entangled
in our concepts – the use of our terms. There, in such particular situations,
philosophy can, by assembling reminders for a particular purpose, enable
us to command a clearer view of our use of these terms and it can
dispel our confusions about them. Philosophy, Wittgenstein has it, as do
neopragmatists as well, 'cannot explain why anything happens or exists'
and 'it cannot reveal the essential nature of anything' for there are no such
essential natures. Its way of proceeding is descriptive and elucidatory,
elucidatory in the service of dispelling the confusion we almost invariably
fall into when we reflect on our concepts. We normally can operate *with*
them without difficulties, but we often fall into confusions – suffer from
mental cramps – when we try to operate *upon* them.

   All of this, of course, applies to our religious concepts, as much as to
any other concepts. When the engine isn't idling; when we work with
them – operate *with* them rather than *upon* them – we understand them,
Wittgenstein gives us to understand, well enough, if we have been enculturated into such forms of life, but when we think about them, as when
we think about other concepts as well, we almost irresistibly fall into
confusion about them. The task of philosophers, for themselves as well as
for others, is to dispel such confusions by providing *in situ* a perspicuous
representation of these concepts. We move about, usually effortlessly, in
our grammar, in our everyday practices. But in thinking *about* what we

do with words we not infrequently fall into perplexity. In order to remove our misconceptions, Malcolm has it, no *theorizing* is called for, neither scientific nor philosophical. What is required is only that we *look* carefully at the grammar which is at our command. We can think with it even if we stumble, while still thinking with it, when we try to think about it. But in doing this Wittgenstein's counsel is 'Don't think, but look!' (Wittgenstein 1953, 66; Malcolm 1994, 79–80).

Philosophy, that is good philosophy, should replace our age-old metaphysical theorizing and its ersatz scientific replacements in a so-called scientific philosophy bent on formulating theories about the nature of meaning, thinking, reference, belief, knowledge, mind, good and God. By contrast, good philosophy – therapeutic philosophy practised after the fashion of Wittgenstein – cannot interfere with the actual use of language. For it, *elucidation* comes to accurate description in the service of dispelling confusions *about* our use of language. We have a mastery of our language – of the use of our terms – but we fall into confusion when we try to think about them; when we reflect about our use and try to grasp 'the essence' of our concepts expressed by these terms. Wittgenstein remarked in his *Philosophical Investigations* that our 'mistake is to look for an explanation where we should see the facts as 'primary phenomena [*Urphänomene*]'. That is, where we should say: *this language-game is played*' (Wittgenstein 1953, 176). Or again, 'The question is not one of explaining a language-game by our experiences, but of observing a language-game' (Wittgenstein 1953, 176).

A language-game, as Malcolm well puts it, 'is an employment of language that is embedded in one of the innumerable patterns of human life' (Malcolm 1994, 81). *Some* forms of life are forms of life that not all people in all cultures share (Malcolm 1994, 82). We cannot, Malcolm has it, explain why this is so: that is why some people have them and others do not. He remarks, 'Neither philosophy nor science can explain this. What philosophy can do is to correct our inclination to assume, because of superficial similarities, that different language-games and forms of life are really the same' (Malcolm 1994, 82). Some words refer to or stand for something. They have a reference. But 'Hans', 'blue', '2', 'the Empire State Building', 'grace' and 'God' do not all refer in the same way. We must, in particular, not assume that 'God' refers like 'Hans' or 'the Empire State Building'.

Wittgenstein, and, for that matter, Norman Malcolm and Peter Winch both following Wittgenstein, are as much set against the idea that there could be a one true description of the world or some ultimate explanation which would show us what reality really is as are neopragmatists such as Richard Rorty and Hilary Putnam. Such notions, they all believe, are without sense. Natural theology and natural atheology, as much as metaphysical realism, are incoherent. We can have no such knowledge and we do not need it. Religious beliefs neither can have any backing from metaphysics or natural theology or science, nor do they need it. (Here there is no difference between the earlier and the later philosophy of Wittgenstein.) But, by parity, atheological metaphysical theories or so-called scientific theories of a so-called scientific philosophy or a 'scientific world-view', which are really metaphysical theories in disguise, are also incoherent and can provide no intelligible ground or basis for *rejecting* or *criticizing* religion. Such activities – theology and atheology – take in each other's dirty linen. Both should be set aside as houses of cards.

However, Malcolm is quick to remind us that Wittgenstein's account is not a form of irrationalism or nihilism which says goodbye to reason or reasonableness, though Wittgenstein, as much as does Paul Feyerabend, says farewell to Philosophical Reason or Scientific Reason. ('So-called Philosophical Reason or Scientific Reason' would be more apt.) But to be against Reason is not to be against reasoning and justification *within* language-games and to the reflective effort to make sense of our lives and to be reasonable. And that reasons, falsifications, explanations come to an end 'does not mean that there are no reasons, justifications, explanations for anything' (Malcolm 1994, 82).

Within many of our language-games, when we are operating with them, and reasoning and reflecting inside their parameters, reasons, justifications, explanations often can be given and often are perfectly in place. What, however, Wittgenstein does stoutly claim, and Malcolm and Winch follow him here, is that the giving of reasons, justifications, and explanations come to an end *somewhere*.

> Where is that? It is at the existence of the language-games and the associated forms of life. There is where explanation has reached its limit. There reasons stop. In philosophy we can only notice the language-games, describe them, and sometimes wonder at them. (Malcolm 1994, 82)

There we see what has been called Wittgenstein's *quietism*. Quietism or not, for us here it is a key question whether, and if so how, it applies to religion – to Christianity, Hinduism, Islam, Judaism and the like. What is at least initially unsettling in this context in thinking about Wittgenstein and Wittgensteinians such as Malcolm and Winch is that it seems that, if their way of characterizing how to proceed in philosophy is correct, this means that no philosophical or any other kind of reasonable criticism, or for that matter defence, is possible of forms of life or indeed of any form of life, including Hinduism, Christianity, and the like.[7] Is this where we are? Is this the end of the line?

III

It can be responded to such Wittgensteinianism that religions, and most strikingly Christianity with which Wittgenstein and Malcolm are most concerned, are *inescapably in part metaphysical religiosities* (Hägerström 1964). Moreover, the part that is metaphysical cannot be excised from the rest leaving the rest intact. Without a metaphysical part as a settled element (component) in that form of life, the form of life will not even be recognizable as Christianity, Hinduism, Judaism or Islam. There are no doctrineless or creedless religions. Religion is indeed a doing, a committing yourself to act or try to act in a certain way, but it is not *only* that. In Christianity, for example, God is said to be the ultimate spiritual being – the very ground of the world – transcendent to the world and, in being so, is eternal and beyond space and time. And it is an essential part of that very religion to believe that human beings have immortal souls such that they – that is we – will not perish or at least will not perish forever when we die: when, that is, we lose our earthly life. And in addition there is what Kierkegaard called the scandal of the Trinity, but still, he believed, a scandal to be accepted trustingly on faith. These are central beliefs for Christianity and without them Christianity would not be Christianity. It, of course, is not *only* a belief-system. It is also, as Wittgenstein and Kierkegaard stress, a demanding way of life that requires of believers – genuine believers – a reorientation of their lives. But it is also, and inescapably, a belief-system with a set of doctrines.

This belief-system is a metaphysical belief-system and Christianity integrally is a metaphysical religiosity. It simply comes with the religion. But, if what Wittgenstein, Malcolm, Winch and the neopragmatists say is so, metaphysical belief-systems are all incoherent: 'houses of cards', as Wittgenstein said. But then that very form of life, *metaphysically infused as it is*, should be said by Wittgenstein and Wittgensteinians to be incoherent. But that is not at all what they say.

Still, that anti-metaphysical strain is central to their accounts. But, on another equally central part of Wittgenstein's account, Christianity can't be incoherent, for Christianity, as other religions as well, consists in a more or less integrated cluster of distinctive language-games – employments of language embedded in a pattern of human life – and thus a form of life. But forms of life and language-games cannot on Wittgenstein's account be incoherent or illusory or even in any central or crucial way in error. Such notions have no application with respect to forms of life. So we can see here that something has to give. Two central points of Wittgenstein's account – or so at least it seems – are incompatible with each other. Religions are metaphysical schemes and metaphysical schemes are incoherent, but religions are forms of life and it makes no sense to say of a form of life that it is incoherent.

Wittgenstein, I think, would respond, and here I think Kierkegaard would respond in the same or a similar manner as well, that these doctrinal elements – these metaphysical or metaphysical-theological beliefs as important as they have *historically* been to Christianity and other religions as well – are nonetheless incoherent and should be set aside while still keeping other elements which are vitally important to those religions. These religious metaphysical beliefs are not what is really important in religion and religiously sensitive people have – though sometimes inchoately – always recognized that.

What Wittgenstein saw as important in religion is that, if one could have faith – if one could trust in God – that that will turn around one's life enabling one to be a decent person and to without vanity or arrogance do good in the world. He took *faith without works* to be utterly vain. Indeed it should not, as he saw it, properly speaking even be called 'faith'. Moreover, as he says in his *Notebooks* of 1916, 'to pray is to think about the meaning of life' and that 'to believe in God means to see that life has a meaning' (Wittgenstein 1961, 73; Malcolm 1994, 10). These remarks are, against most of the philosophical temper of Wittgenstein, utterly reductionistic. If what they say is so, it would make, by implicit stipulative redefinition, many reflective and sensitive atheists into believers in God. By verbal magic all sensitive, reflective, caring people become religious believers. It is to take what may very well be a *necessary* condition for genuine religious belief and turn it into a *sufficient* one. Is this the end of the matter? Perhaps not quite. Let me proceed indirectly by first recording some of Wittgenstein's specific comments about religion. Moreover, it is important to keep in mind the fact that historically religions have changed over time and that there is no reason to believe 'history has come to an end' and to think that they will not continue to change.

Wittgenstein had, as I have remarked, scant patience with philosophical theology or the philosophy of religion, but throughout his life he read and reread the gospels, thought at one time seriously about becoming a priest, and was deeply taken by the ancient liturgical prayers of the Latin rite and their translation in the Anglican prayer book, remarking that they 'read as if they had been soaked in centuries of worship' (Malcolm 1994, 17). Speaking to his close friend, Maurice Drury, who had formed the intention to be ordained as a priest, Wittgenstein remarked

> Just think, Drury, what it would mean to have to preach a sermon every week. You couldn't do it. I would be afraid that you would try and give some sort of philosophical justification for Christian beliefs,

as if some proof was needed. The symbolisms of Catholicism are wonderful beyond words. But any attempt to make it into a philosophical system is offensive. (Malcolm 1994, 11)

It was the *activist*, life-orientation involving, *not* the speculative-cosmological side of Christianity that appealed to Wittgenstein. What gripped him was Christianity's call to radically alter the manner of one's life – to be just and caring with one another, to clearly see what a wretched person one was, to atone for one's sins, and to struggle to be a decent human being.

The influence of Kierkegaard on Wittgenstein was very deep. It shows itself in the above remarks about guilt and sin and, again quite differently, in his attitude toward the historical claims of Christianity and in what he thought philosophy could achieve vis-à-vis religion. Wittgenstein (echoing Kierkegaard) wrote, 'Christianity is not based on a historical truth; rather it gives us a (historical) narrative and says: now believe! But not, believe this narrative with the belief appropriate to a historical narrative – rather believe, through thick and thin, and you can do that only as the result of a life' (Wittgenstein 1980, 32; Malcolm 1994, 32). Wittgenstein, again like Kierkegaard, saw religion not only as something that makes extreme demands on one, but as something which answers to the needs of genuinely religious people – people who not only see themselves to be extremely imperfect but as wretched. 'Any halfway decent man,' Wittgenstein wrote, 'will think himself extremely imperfect, but a religious man believes himself *wretched*' (Wittgenstein 1980, 45; Malcolm 1994, 17). Somewhat earlier in his *Miscellaneous Remarks*, Wittgenstein wrote 'faith is faith in what my heart, my soul needs, not my speculative intelligence. For it is my soul, with its passions, as it were with its flesh and blood, that must be saved, not my abstract mind' (Wittgenstein 1980, 33; Malcolm 1994, 17).

He, given his sense of what religion really is, is fully, intellectually speaking, on the fideist side coming down to us from Tertullian, Pascal, Hamann and, most fully, from Kierkegaard. But in his very conceptualization of fideism there was also for religious persons an intense activist side very distinct from his Quietism in *philosophy*. This comes out strikingly in a remark he made in 1946:

One of the things Christianity says, I think, is that all sound doctrines are of no avail. One must change one's *life*. (Or the *direction* of one's life.)
   That all wisdom is cold; and that one can no more use it to bring one's life into order than one can forge *cold* iron.
   A sound doctrine does not have to *catch hold* of one; one can follow it like a doctor's prescription. – But here something must grasp one

and turn one around. – (This is how I understand it.) Once turned around, one must stay turned around.

Wisdom is passionless. In contrast faith is what Kierkegaard calls a *passion*. (Wittgenstein 1980, 53)

For Wittgenstein, as for Tertullian, Pascal, Hamann and Kierkegaard, religion was not a question of proving anything or even the articulating of doctrine, even a doctrine that orders one's life.

[Wittgenstein] objected to the idea that Christianity is a 'doctrine,' i.e., a theory about what has happened and will happen to the human soul. Instead, it is a description of actual occurrences in the lives of some people – of 'consciousness of sin,' of despair, of salvation through faith. For Wittgenstein the emphasis in religious belief had to be on doing – on 'amending one's ways,' 'turning one's life around.' (Malcolm 1994, 19)

He came to have, mixed together with this striving to turn his life around and his realizing that this was what religion was about, an intense desire for purity together with an equally intense sense of his own impurity, his sinfulness and guilt, his standing under divine judgement, his need for redemption and forgiveness. He had a keen sense of a judging and redeeming God, but the conception of a creator was foreign to him and, as Malcolm put it, 'any cosmological conception of a Deity derived from the notion of cause or of infinity would be repugnant to him' (Malcolm, 1994, 10).

In spite of Wittgenstein's statement that 'I am not a religious man,' I think that it is, as Malcolm puts it, 'surely right to say that Wittgenstein's mature life was strongly marked by religious thought and feeling' (Malcolm 1994, 21). Kierkegaard has percipiently shown how difficult it is to be religious, how many people are deceived in thinking they are religious when they are not, and that some people who would honestly say they are not, and even some – say, some militant atheists – who would vehemently assert that they are not, are nonetheless religious and indeed deeply so. It is also the case that with his clarity of intellect, together with his deep religious sensitivity, Wittgenstein is likely to have had a keen sense of what a religious form of life is. I have claimed, as have many others, that there is no doctrineless religion and that religion inescapably involves making cosmological (metaphysical) claims (Nielsen 1989a, 1999). Wittgenstein firmly rejects this. Is he right to do so?

IV

Concerning what we discussed in III and what we shall continue to discuss here, it will be necessary, as Winch reminds us, 'to observe the distinction between Wittgenstein's own religious reflections and his philosophical comments on religious discourse' (Winch 1994, 133). I shall be concerned centrally with the latter and shall show concern with the former principally to help us, if it can, to gain a purchase on how we should think and feel about religion. I want to try to see what kind of form of life it involves, what kinds of language-games are integral to it, what role it can and should play in our lives, and what philosophically we are justified in saying about these matters.

Pursuant to this I should say something about Peter Winch's discussion of Wittgenstein on religion and about his reservations concerning Malcolm's account. Malcolm's account of how Wittgenstein understands religion and how he understands philosophy in relation to religion is an important one. That notwithstanding, Winch, I believe, has brought out some key ways in which Malcolm's account is flawed. I want to highlight them and then comment on them.

1. As we have seen, Malcolm claims, and claims for Wittgenstein, that there is no explanation for the existence of language-games or forms of life. Winch says that this is misleading. I think he actually shows something stronger, namely, that, taken straightforwardly, the claim is just false. Still, though false, taken straightforwardly, we can give it a very specialized reading in which it is not false and, so understood, it makes an important point that is frequently lost sight of in thinking about what religion is.

Winch does not disagree with the general understanding that Wittgenstein firmly maintained that explanation has an end and that explanatory theories are inappropriate in philosophy (Winch 1994, 100). Good philosophy, he agrees, should be descriptive in the way Malcolm, following Wittgenstein, characterizes. That is not at all in dispute between them or between me and them as being something that Wittgenstein firmly maintained. Moreover, Winch, like Malcolm, thought that Wittgenstein was right about this. But Malcolm overlooks, Winch has it, 'the very different issues that are at stake in various of the contexts in which Wittgenstein insists that "explanation has an end"' (Winch 1994, 100). Winch writes that it 'is misleading to say that "Wittgenstein regarded the language-games and thus associated forms of life, as beyond explanation." Language-games are not a phenomenon that Wittgenstein had discovered with the peculiar property that their existence cannot be explained!' (Winch 1994, 104–05). Malcolm maintains that neither the 'hard' sciences nor the 'soft' sciences can explain why various practices exist. But, as Winch points out, that is simply false. There are many cases, he observes, 'in which historians, anthropologists, or linguists give well founded explanations of the existence of this or that practice. Why ever not! The important question for us [that is for we philosophers] to ask is: what relevance would such explanations have to the resolution of philosophical difficulties?' (Winch 1994, 106). What Winch takes it that (*pace* Malcolm) we should *not* maintain is that language-games are *intrinsically* beyond the power of these sciences to provide explanations of, but rather what we should say is that any explanation they might offer would turn out to be quite uninteresting, and useless *as far as the philosopher's characteristic puzzlement is concerned* (Winch 1994, 106).

Wittgenstein, Winch has it – and it seems to me correctly as a bit of Wittgenstein interpretation – was not concerned to deny that there was any reasonable sense in which explanations of practices could be given. He was concerned, rather, 'with the peculiar pseudosense in which philosophers seek "explanations"'. Spinoza, for example, thought, as Winch remarks, 'that because explanations have come to an end there must be something which has no further explanation, a *causa sui*' (Winch 1994, 104, quoting Spinoza). Wittgenstein was concerned to combat that, to show that that kind of rationalism is senseless: that it makes no sense to say that there is something beyond explanation – something intrinsically unexplainable – on which all ordinary explanations depend or that there is, if we push matters resolutely, some *ultimate explanation* – some super-explanation as it were – which finally explains everything and brings enquiry to an end. Wittgenstein does not think, Winch observes, 'that explanations come to an end with something that is intrinsically beyond further explanation. They come to an end for a variety of quite contingent and pragmatic reasons, perhaps because of a practical need for action, perhaps because the puzzlement which originally prompted the search for explanation has evaporated (for one reason or another)' (Winch 1994, 104). There are many situations, perhaps most situations, in which we have no need 'at all' to explain a practice. The practice seems to us – and sometimes rightly so – unproblematic. But then, as C. S. Peirce and John Dewey stressed, circumstances might arise in which we need, or at least want, an explanation for one or another specific pragmatic purpose – political, moral, sociological, or some combination of them – or perhaps because the practice does not seem for some reasonably specific reasons to be working so well and indeed might not be working well. Such situations do arise and there is no reason to think such explanations, answering to such problematic situations, are impossible, always or even generally undesirable, or that they will invariably, or even standardly, degenerate into philosophical pseudo-explanations. Moreover, we do not have good textual grounds for thinking that Wittgenstein thought that.

Suppose, however, we stop talking about explanation and talk of *justification* instead. Wittgenstein also famously said that justification must come to an end or it would not be justification. Malcolm has stressed as a view which is both Wittgenstein's and right 'that reasons, justifications, explanations, reach a terminus in the language-games and their internally related forms of human life' (Malcolm 1974). Let us set aside explanation and just concentrate on the giving of reasons and the justifying (if such is in order) of a form of life. Winch takes it, correctly, as a bit of Wittgenstein exegesis, 'that the expression of religious belief is itself a language-game for which it makes no sense to ask for . . . rational justification' (Winch 1994, 111). *Within* a form of life, a justification of particular beliefs or particular conceptions in accordance with the constitutive norms and conceptions of that form of life can sometimes be given. But a request for a justification of the constitutive norms and conceptions – the very framework beliefs of a religious form of life – is another matter. Wittgenstein has it that to ask for justification here is senseless. Job's seeking to require God to answer to him is seen to rest on a mistake for one who has faith. The showing of why God's will is sovereign and should never be questioned – the challenging of the whole framework – is, given Wittgenstein's conceptions, out of place. Indeed, not simply out of place, but incoherent. Malcolm had remarked, Winch reminds us, that even in this technological and materialistic age, there are people who are inside the practices, the language-games of, say Christianity or Judaism, who pray

> to God for help, asking him for forgiveness, thanking him for the blessings of this life – and who thereby gain comfort and strength, hope and cheerfulness. Many of these people would have no understanding of what it would *mean* to provide rational justification for their religious belief – nor do they feel a need for it. (Malcolm 1994, 84)

And indeed Wittgenstein has it – and here both Malcolm and Winch follow him – justification here is not possible and, moreover, even if it were, there is no need for it. Asking for it is not only obtuse but is wrong, morally wrong.

There are at least three issues here. First, it seems fair enough to say that a plain, untutored person – say a minimally educated person living in an isolated community of believers – is being reasonable – or at least not unreasonable – in so believing. Moreover, it would, in most circumstances, be sadistic to challenge such a person's faith – a faith that that person regards as an undeserved *gift* from God. It would be unnecessary and pointless cruelty causing, if it was at all psychologically effective, unnecessary and pointless suffering. *Second*, there is the question that, if that person began to feel – say quite without wishing it – the irritation of doubt, whether (a) there are considerations available to an honest, reflective person sufficient to still, without subterfuge or self-deception, those doubts or (b) this is even an intelligible or legitimate possibility: whether it makes sense to have such doubts? They *may* themselves rest on philosophical confusions. Moreover, perhaps concerning something so basic – something so much a part of the life of some people – we have something that does not admit of such rationalization, such a reasoning out of things? *Third*, whether, that isolated person aside, for anyone in our modern cultures there are considerations which that person, or several persons reasoning together and sensitively feeling through the matter, could articulate which would show that such beliefs were not only coherent but not unreasonable? Or which would show the opposite conclusion? Are these, as it seems Wittgenstein and Wittgensteinians believe – *must* believe? – bad questions? But if that is claimed, it seems to be in order for us to ask just *why* are these bad questions. Or are they really bad questions? Do we just have, in maintaining they are, Wittgensteinian dogma here?

I think any Wittgensteinian would respond to this last query and the second one as well by rejecting them out of hand. It is *practices* which give the intelligibility and coherence to talk – words as they are used in their living contexts, in this case the context of a living engaged faith. *If theorizing, he would say, makes the talk seem incoherent or unreasonable, then so much the worse for the theorizing.* Moreover, and in addition, religion is something special for it is not a matter, except peripherally, of the intellect but of the heart. The intellect in this context can only dispel bad philosophical reasoning that gets in the way of faith. There is in such fideistic reasoning a great distance between the confident doing of natural theology by Aquinas and Scotus and the fideistic reasoning of Kierkegaard and Wittgenstein: between the confident claim that if we reason carefully and attend to the facts we can see that it is irrational not to believe in God, to the acceptance of God simply on faith – on a faith, or a trust, that eschews all search for or recognition of the appropriateness or even the very possibility of justification, except in the purely negative sense of showing the mistakes of those who would say that without justification your faith is in vain. For to say that – to demand justification here – is not only unjustified but unjustifiable. Philosophical clarity, Wittgensteinians will argue, shows such argumentation is at best mistaken. If Wittgenstein and Wittgensteinians such as Norman Malcolm, D. Z. Phillips, Rush Rhees, Peter Winch, Stanley Cavell and James Conant and neopragmatists such as Hilary Putnam and Richard Rorty are right about the incoherence of metaphysics and foundational epistemology, then the rationalistic arguments of the philosophy of religion or natural theology or atheology cannot get off the ground. Then isn't the conclusion we should come to about religion such a Wittgensteinian one? Though this, of course, does not mean that we ourselves should become religious, but that we should desist from making philosophical claims about religious belief resting on a mistake. That is itself, they would argue, a mistake – a very big philosophical mistake. We might continue perfectly appropriately, if we are, to remain atheists. But we should not engage in atheology – philosophical arguments for atheism. Philosophy has nothing to say here either for or against religious belief. Isn't this the conclusion we should be drawn to?

2. Perhaps what has been said above should be sufficient to put such matters to rest, to lead us, if we would be reasonable, to react and view things in such a manner. Still such an equilibrium is seldom the case in philosophy over something so fundamental. So let us look at things from another angle. Malcolm, correctly catching something that Wittgenstein stresses, remarks that what for Wittgenstein is 'most fundamental in a religious life is not the affirming of creeds, nor even prayer and worship – but rather, doing *good deeds* – helping others in concrete ways, treating their needs as equal to one's own, opening one's heart to them, not being cold or contemptuous, but loving' (Malcolm 1994, 92). Surely someone with any religious sensitivity – or indeed with just plain human sensitivity – will feel the force of that. That said, Winch's cautionary remarks are very important here. Winch says that the link between faith and works 'is by no means as straightforward as Malcolm's discussion may suggest' (Winch 1994, 121). There are people with just the doings and feelings described above – people having exactly those attitudes – who lack religious sensibility who, as Malcolm himself in his seventh chapter reminds us, 'take a serious view of religion, but regard it as a harmful influence, an obstacle to the fullest and best development of humanity' (Winch 1994, 121). Are we, to return to something mentioned earlier, to turn them into religious believers – people with religious faith – by *stipulative redefinition*? Wittgenstein remarked to Drury that it was his belief 'that only if you try to be helpful to other people will you in the end find your way to God' (Malcolm 1994, chapter 1). Winch tersely and correctly remarks,

> It is important because Wittgenstein did *not* say that being helpful to other people *is* finding one's way to God, nor that it is a *sufficient condition* of doing so. He said it is a *necessary condition* of doing so. One cannot live a godly life *without* 'good works'; but all the same there is more to the godly life than that. (Winch 1994, 121)

Moreover, as Winch also stresses, we cannot, as Malcolm sometimes seems to think, understand the 'works' Wittgenstein stresses – understand the role they play in the believer's life – independently of their connections 'with a particular faith on the part of the doer' (Winch 1994, 124). The doing of good, the being loving and humble, are for the religious believer *internally* connected to the 'use of the language of faith in the life of the believer' (Winch 1994, 124). This seems to me, but *perhaps* not to Winch, to imply that such ways of being cannot in the thought and actions of a believer be disconnected from certain doctrinal strands and the creedal expressions of a particular religion. But this at least seems to run against Wittgenstein's own setting of doctrines aside as not being what religion is or anything essential to religion.

It is not difficult to surmise how Wittgenstein, and Kierkegaard as well, would respond. 'There you go again,' they would no doubt snort, 'with your stubborn and even arrogant intellectualism, turning religion into a *theory* – failing to see what is there before your eyes that gives religion its importance. It is not doctrines or creeds that count but commitment and concern turned into action on yourself, though at the same time with a certain inwardness, and *for* others. Religion is ultimate commitment and concern. Brush aside all this sterile intellectualism. Theorizing about religion is not the way to God: thinking of great intellectual mansions while you live in a little moral shack' (Kierkegaard's comment on Schelling and Hegel).

Theorizing about religion is, indeed, not the way to God, if there is a way to God. The way is in your action on yourself and for others, but, if it is done religiously, it is embedded in words integral to a form of life that would not be the form of life it is without the doctrines and the creeds. Religions are for the sake of life – for the very things Wittgenstein stresses – but genuine religious believers, immersed in those forms of life, see and feel their commitments and concerns and deeds in terms of these very forms containing, and inescapably, these doctrines and creeds. *They do not have religious feelings which swing loose from religious concepts.* Both their very understanding and deepest reactions are tied up (internally linked) with doctrines and creeds and the distinctive concepts that go with them. And their reactions and understanding here cannot be split apart (as if there were a 'cognitive' and a 'noncognitive' side to them). *There is no religious understanding without the reactions and no reactions which are intelligibly religious without that understanding.*

To try to reduce religion and religious belief to some basic deep commitment and a concern to be a decent human being, to really care about others and do good, even if we add – probably with very little understanding – 'ultimate' to 'commitment' and to 'concern', just takes what, as we have already observed, is a *necessary* condition for being genuinely religious (note the implicit *persuasive* definition here) and turns it into a *sufficient* condition. On such a view of things Marx, Engels, Luxembourg, Durkheim, Freud, Dewey, Weber, Gramsci all become religious. But that is a *reductio*.

3. Wittgenstein, under the influence of William James's *Varieties of Religious Experience*, came to recognize that the way in which people express their religious beliefs differs enormously (Winch 1994, 108). Even within a given confessional community there are 'vastly diverse forms of religious sensibility. And these different forms of diversity criss-cross in bewilderingly complex ways' (Winch 1994, 109). Even if we avoid any attempt to so define 'religion' such that it captures all and only the great historic religions and those group activities and beliefs anthropologists firmly regard as religious activities of recognizable religions, for example, the religion of the Dinka or the Nuer, and concentrate only on those religions – Christianity and Judaism – in which Wittgenstein took the most interest, we still get very diverse forms of religious sensibility and conceptualization and interpretation of doctrine and even of doctrine itself.

Wittgenstein saw life as a 'gift' from God for which one should be grateful, but life, he firmly believed, was something that also imposes inescapable obligations. He also thought that in his work and in his life he required help: some 'light' from above, as he put it. These attitudes, Winch observes, unlinked as they are with specific confessional commitments, are from the 'point of a developed theological doctrine' inchoate (Winch 1994, 109). But this, as Winch is perfectly aware, would not have bothered Wittgenstein one bit. He set himself, as we have seen, against theological and religious *doctrine*. More worrisomely, from Wittgenstein's point of view, there are considering the above attitudes – the above expressions of religious sensibility – some serious and reflective people whose very seriousness manifests itself in opposition to such attitudes (Winch, 1994, 110). Some people will have an attitude that accepts 'one's fate as "the will of God," an attitude which neither pretends to provide any explanation of that fate nor seeks to find one' (Winch 1994, 110). This attitude characteristically goes along 'with an attitude of *gratitude* for life' (Winch 1994, 113). But Wittgenstein remarks, commenting on the expression of a very different attitude,

> We might speak of the *world* as malicious; we could easily imagine the Devil had created the world, or part of it. And it is *not* necessary to imagine the evil spirit intervening in particular situations; everything can happen 'according to the laws of nature'; it is just the whole scheme of things will be aimed at evil from the very start. (Wittgenstein 1980, 71)

But the reference to the Devil here is, of course, no more an explanation – nor does Wittgenstein think that it is – than is a reference to the will of God. Either viewed as attempts at an explanation would be what Wittgenstein called an unnecessary and stupid anthropomorphism

(Wittgenstein 1980, 71). But faced with all the horrible contingencies of life, the suffering, cruelty, indifference, pain, jealousy, hatred, failures of integrity, the breaking of trust – the whole bloody lot – some would speak neither of God nor of the Devil nor of the world nor of the goodness, in spite of it all, of the world or of the malignancy or maliciousness of the world. Indeed they would think (*pace* William James) that such talk makes no sense. Some would say, as I would, ' "That's how things are" without reference to God or the Devil' (Winch 1994, 114). I think (to abandon for a moment a Wittgensteinian commitment to description and to speak normatively) this austere approach reflects a more proper frame of mind. We see that the plague is always with us, though sometimes rather dormant but at other times raging, and always as something that will return and we resolve to fight the plague. (Recall this was Albert Camus' figure of speech and his resolve as well.) But again this expression of attitude makes no more an attempt at an explanation than the expression of attitude that goes with speaking of God's will does or of the Devil having created the world does. Winch remarks perceptively that one 'might want to single out the reference to the will of God as the only one that expresses a religious attitude; or one might want to single out "that's just how things are" as the only attitude among these particular attitudes genuinely "free of all superstition" ' (Winch 1994, 114). Our language-games and forms of life, he observes, let us do either. And people, of course, do either. People, including reflective people of integrity, often differ here. And, as Hilary Putnam stresses, this is something to take to heart (Putnam 1995, 27–56). Moreover, it is not at all evident, to put it minimally, that there would be anything even approaching a consensus about which attitudes are the more appropriate or which run the deepest. Indeed not a few will think there is no answer to such 'questions' and indeed no genuine questions either. And others would think that, even if in some sense there were, it would be inappropriate to ask them.

'It's God's Will,' 'It's the work of the Devil' and 'That's how things are' are all non-explanatory and in some language-games are not only where explanation stops, but where, Wittgensteinians would have it, justification and the giving of reasons stop as well. I think myself 'That's how things are' is by far the more adequate way of viewing things. It is cleaner with less mystification and comes closer to – or so I think – telling it like it is. However, it should be immediately sceptically queried: how can I consistently say anything even remotely within that ball park, given my pragmatist and Wittgensteinian perspectivism and contextualism with its rejection of the idea that there can be a one true description of the world and my arguments to the effect that it makes no sense to say that one vocabulary is closer to reality than another or that we can coherently speak of standing outside all our practices and assessing them or that there is some unifying comprehensive practice that, like the Absolute, encompasses everything? (Putnam 1992, 80–107). I could say that for certain purposes 'That's how things are' is the more adequate response and for other purposes other ways are better, but I could not consistently, it is natural to respond, flat out say 'That's how things are' is the more adequate conception. I could not say this because some non-contextualist conception of 'That is how things are' is unintelligible. And, even more plainly and less controversially, I cannot even consistently say that that is so because it comes closer to telling things like they are and is less mystificatory and obfuscating. There is no way things are *überhaupt* or even if there is, even if such talk somehow makes sense, we have no way of knowing or even plausibly conjecturing when this is so. So we are back with my pragmatic contextualism and how Wittgenstein sees things.

I think I can consistently have my pragmatist perspectivism *and* my claim about the greater adequacy of what I call my more austere 'That's how things are' way of viewing things. I will now argue that this is so: that it is not a case of having my cake and eating it too. We have genuine descriptions and explanatory practices which are nonconflicting alternatives to each other. For example, the giving of a physiological description of bodily movements or a description in terms of actions and intentions. Or, to take another example, the giving of a common-sense description of tables, bits of mud, water flowing, the moon being pink on a given night, in contrast to giving a scientific physical description where we will say different things about solidity, colour and the like. These are alternative descriptive and explanatory practices utilized for different purposes. But none of these descriptions are 'closer to reality' or more adequate *sans phrase* than any other. We can only say that for different purposes one is more adequate than another; not that one is a more adequate or a better telling it like it is than another *period*. There the story about my perspectivism and contextualism is perfectly in place. It is also the account that Richard Rorty and Hilary Putnam would give of things.

To say (1) 'That's God's will,' (2) 'That's the Devil's work,' (3) 'That's how things are' do we not also have, in a way similar to describing things in terms of bodily movements and describing things in terms of human actions, different perspectives answering to different interests with none of them being in some general, 'perspective neutral' sense, more adequate? We can and should retort by remarking that with 'That's God's will' or 'That's the Devil's work' we have *metaphysical* utterances penetrating into our common life. They are metaphysical conceptions. And they, being metaphysical conceptions, are nonsensical, as Wittgenstein, and both Malcolm and Winch following him, contend, and, as we neopragmatists do as well. They are, when expressed, utterances which, in being metaphysical utterances, are incoherent, yielding pseudo-descriptions and pseudo-perspectives from which no intelligible descriptions, interpretations or explanations could flow. Premises (1) and (2) but not (3) yield nonsense, but not 'intelligible nonsense' somehow conveying 'cognitive depth' as traditionalist interpretations of the *Tractatus* claim Wittgenstein obliquely hints at. If Wittgenstein, the Wittgensteinians, and the neopragmatists are right in seeing metaphysical claims as requiring philosophical therapy to break their spell, we do not have three alternative perspectives here but one that in effect (a) summarizes a bunch of empirical observations and more or less concrete moral observations and (b) makes a morally freighted generalization about them, and two expressions of metaphysical fantasies that have crept into the language-games of *some* people. These metaphysical fantasies are, as Wittgenstein puts it in other contexts, wheels that turn no machinery, conceptions that do no work in these practices, and the people who use such phrases are only under the illusion that they have some understanding of what they are saying and that these metaphysical conceptions are functioning parts of our social practices with their embedded language-games. There are no metaphysical forms of life. (If it is replied they do rhetorical work this is in effect to concede the point.) And there are no metaphysical language-games, rule-governed social practices. The above cases are not like saying that we use physiological descriptions for certain purposes and action-intention descriptions for other purposes and that both can be perfectly in place for their own purposes but no one is just telling it the way things are. The three allegedly alternative characterizations under discussion consist in one actual characterization and two pseudo-characterizations and, of course, if this is so, we can, and should, say the one genuine one is more adequate. But that is not at all to say that it gestures at 'the one true description of the world'. There is no such thing (Nielsen 2005).

Some (including Wittgenstein) might deny that 'It's God's will' or 'It's the work of the Devil' are metaphysical utterances. And if 'God' and 'the Devil' are taken to denote Zeus-like empirical entities then these utterances are not metaphysical. They are implicit, very vague empirical hypotheses. They are just crude, plainly false empirical propositions plainly disconfirmed. *Such* religious beliefs are superstitions and Wittgenstein was keenly aware of that and rejected *such* religious beliefs and such a way of looking at religion with disdain. But it is very unlikely that now – or even for a long time – many reasonably educated and reflective Christians, Jews or Muslims so superstitiously conceive of God and the Devil. Indeed by now most of them do not. And where they do, Wittgenstein would have no sympathy at all with that. Where, alternatively, 'God' is construed as an infinite individual transcendent to the universe, we plainly do have a metaphysical claim – and a very esoteric one at that – and as such it is held to be nonsensical not just by positivists but by Wittgensteinians and neopragmatists such as Putnam, Rorty, and myself as well (Nielsen 1982, 1985, 1989a). If to that it is said that is not how to construe 'God' either, then it is difficult to know, unless we want to go back to the crude anthropomorphic construal or to a purely symbolic construal, how we are in some non-metaphysical way to construe 'God'. Just what is this non-Zeus-like, non-purely symbolic, non-metaphysical construal of 'God'? Do we really have any understanding of what we are talking about here?

If instead it is said, 'That's how things are' is itself a metaphysical statement this should be denied for it functions as a summarizing, somewhat moralizingly emotive, but all the same empirical, proposition standing in for (a) a lot more particular propositions such as people suffer, the wicked often flourish, starvation and malnutrition are pervasive, droughts and devastating earthquakes occur, people are struck down in their prime, alienation is pervasive, tyranny often goes unchecked, and the like and (b) the comment that this goes on at all times and in all places without much in the way of abatement. This – (b) in particular – *may* be an exaggeration, but that surely does not make it a metaphysical statement.

Suppose someone retorts that Jews and Christians do not have to treat 'That's God's will' or 'That's the Devil's work' in either the superstitious or the metaphysical way I attributed to them. Keep in mind, the response goes, that *practice* gives words their sense. Some mathematicians, when they speak of numbers, say they are abstract entities: real things but abstract things. And with this they become entangled in metaphysics. Indeed we have the shadow of Plato here. But they could, and most do, legitimately refuse to so theorize and just go on proving theorems, setting up axiomatic systems, or, as applied mathematicians, grinding out calculations for particular purposes and the like. Why cannot Jews, Christians and Muslims do a similar thing? Why could they not, and indeed why should they not, just stick with their practices in saying and thinking the things about God that their language-games allow them to say? They need no more theorize *about* God than mathematicians *need* theorize *about* numbers. Indeed it is not only that they *need* not theorize, Wittgenstein and Kierkegaard would insist, but that they *should* not theorize. That is destructive of faith. It is my *intellectualism* again – and here I am a token of a familiar type – that is leading me down the garden path, that is making me mistakenly think that practices which actually are not unreasonable – indeed are compelling for the people who engage in them – are unreasonable and irrational.

It should be responded in turn that there are at least two disanalogies between the language-games of mathematics and the language-games of religion. First we know, without any metamathematics, without any theory of numbers, at least if we are mathematicians, how to establish truth-claims, or at least assertability-claims, in mathematics. Mathematics is a theory-structured practice and mathematicians in doing mathematics cannot but use theory and in that way theorize. We need not theorize *about* mathematics, but we, not infrequently, theorize, often to good effect, *with* it. Second, we have in mathematics some ability to say what we are talking about. We often talk nonsense in talking *about* mathematics but not always. But actual mathematical talk is another matter. We have no such ability with our talk of God, the Devil, or the soul. It is not just the metatalk that is troubling.[8]

Suppose, it is in turn responded, that this only shows some of the differences between the language-games of mathematics and those of religion. We understand, if we are religious, that God is a *mystery* and – or so Wittgensteinians have it – that the very demand to be able to warrant our religious claims shows that we, in making that demand, do not understand them or understand what *faith* requires, including what it is to believe in God. Anything that we could warrant – establish the truth of – wouldn't be a genuine religious claim. To make such a rationalistic demand shows, Wittgenstein et al. would have it, that we do not understand religious language-games and that we are not operating from inside them. It would be like in logic to demand that an inductive argument be deductively valid. It would show that we understand neither what induction is nor what deduction is. We are just senselessly asking for induction to be deduction.

If this is what religious language-games are like, would it *not* be better *not* to engage in them? We do not know what counts for truth or falsity or in being reasonable or unreasonable here; indeed we do not even understand what we are saying. We are just in a fog. Nonsense engulfs us. Isn't talk of mystery just a high-fallutin' way of saying that? Once we see this clearly should we not desist – close up shop, so to say? Moreover, it is not just that we do not understand, we are forced, if we would play that language-game, to say things that we, if we reflect a bit, would not wish to say. Consider again Wittgenstein's remark in *Culture and Value* that we 'might speak of the world as malicious' or 'easily imagine the Devil created the world, or part of it' or that 'the whole scheme of things will be aimed at evil from the very start'. We not only *cannot* (*pace* Wittgenstein) easily imagine these things; we do not understand these utterances. We only, if we do not think, have the illusion of understanding them by extension from some familiar utterances we do understand. We understand what it is for a person to be malicious or an action or attitude to be malicious. We have truth-conditions or assertability-conditions for such claims. But for the *world* to be malicious? We can't intelligibly impute *intentions* to the world. That makes no sense at all. Speaking of the world being malicious is but a misleading way of making the perfectly secular utterance 'Many people are malicious and this maliciousness is pervasive in our lives.' Similarly while we understand 'Sven created a new recipe' or 'Jane created a more efficient electric car,' we do not understand 'The Devil created the world' or, for that matter, 'God created the world.' The former two sentences have truth-conditions or assertability-conditions. The latter two do not. Similarly language has gone on a holiday with 'The whole scheme of things will be aimed at evil from the very start.' Aside from not understanding what 'the very start' comes to here, more importantly, we are, with such a remark, again imputing intentions and aims to what it makes no sense to say has or can have intentions or aims. To say Shakespeare's Richard III aimed at evil or the Nazi regime or the Reagan regime aimed at evil makes sense, but the whole scheme of things, no more than the world, cannot be intelligibly said to *aim* at things either for good or for evil. A scheme of things or a world cannot have aims, form intentions, have desires, goals and the like. There is and can be no such teleology of nature. There is no such functional language-game. Language is idle here. In support of this, we have supplied what Wittgenstein has called grammatical remarks. But would not Wittgenstein, of all people, perfectly well realize that? That is the way he repeatedly reasons. And the grammatical remarks I have assembled above seem to be plainly so. It looks like Wittgenstein, or anyone who tries to so reason, is in a double bind.

Of course Wittgenstein is right, as he says in the sentence following the one quoted above, that 'things break, slide about, cause every imaginable mischief'. But that, minimally hyperbolic though it is, is a purely secular utterance. We have not even the hint of a *religious* language-game here. *If* that is what we '*really* are saying in saying that the whole scheme of things will be aimed at evil', we have turned it, by stipulative redefinition, into an utterly secular platitude without a whiff of religion or religious sensibility. Where we understand what we are saying we do not have a religious language-game at all; where we have one we do not – the superstitious anthropomorphic ones aside – understand what is said and thus cannot understand what it is for something to be, for example, God's will and thus we cannot do God's will or fail to do God's will.

Suppose someone says that that is a philosopher's hat trick. People do God's will. People, following God's will, make pilgrimages to Lourdes, go to confession, give up philosophy, lead a life of celibacy, go to the Congo or Haiti to alleviate suffering, etc., etc. But to this, it in turn can be responded, that this – this doing of God's will – is but to do things that some people take to be obligatory, the right thing to do, desirable to do, and the like and that some of them associate these moral commitments with their *avowals* that that is doing God's will without understanding what God is or what his will is or how one could ascertain what it is to do God's will. It is just a formula they recite with, if they are genuinely theistically religious, great conviction and sometimes with intensity of feeling. But that does not, and cannot, turn it into sense, into an intelligible utterance.

Your intellectualism continues to get in the way, some will respond or at least think. The aim in speaking of religion, as Kierkegaard and Wittgenstein do, is to expose the roots of the intellectual's compulsion in approaching religion 'always to reflect upon the task of living (a certain sort of life) rather than to attend to the task itself' (Conant 1993, 207). The thing to do is to go to church, to pray, to confess, to sing songs in praise of God, to alter your life by becoming more open and loving, to fight against your arrogance and pride, and above all help your fellow humans by engaging with them in their life struggles. Don't think, act! Thinking will never lead you to faith. To think that it can is a grand illusion of much of the philosophy of religion business. Philosophy will not lead us to God or help us in our religious endeavors or even our religious understanding.

There is, both Wittgenstein and Kierkegaard have it, no summing 'up the sense of a religion in philosophical or theological doctrines' (Winch 1994, 128). Kierkegaard stressed that religious belief stands at a very great distance from philosophical clarity. Such clarity is of no avail in coming to a religious life or, for that matter, in turning away from it and combating it. Wittgenstein, as we have seen, had scant use for religious doctrine, theology, or the philosophy of religion. He took it that one of the things that Christianity teaches us is that *even sound* doctrines are useless. The thing is to change your life or the direction of your life. Even achieving wisdom, if indeed we could do this, is of little value. Wisdom is cold and does not connect to your passions, does not grip your life, as religion does by taking hold of you and turning your life around (Wittgenstein (1980, 53). Wittgenstein, in a deeply anti-intellectualistic way, wrote, as we have already noted, that 'Wisdom is cold and to that extent stupid. (Faith, on the other hand, is a passion.) It might also be said: Wisdom merely *conceals* life from you. Wisdom is like grey ash, covering up the glowing embers' (Wittgenstein 1980, 56). Religious faith is a passion yielding a trust that grips your life and turns it around. Trying to be intellectual about religion – trying to rationalize religion – will never get you anywhere. People who are gripped by religious forms of life will not try to show how the religious life is reasonable, though they need not say it is unreasonable either. They will see all argument and attempts at reasoning here either on the part of the believer or the sceptic as utterly pointless.

V

Is this the end of the line? Should we, vis-à-vis religion, take some such anti-intellectualist stance and claim that philosophical thinking, or any kind of thinking, only stands in the way of coming to grips with religion whether by way of faith or by rejection of religious faith? Perhaps one way – a somewhat indirect way – of coming to grips with things here is to contrast Pascal, and the world he lived in, with that of Kierkegaard or Wittgenstein and the worlds they lived in. Pascal was as much of a fideist as Kierkegaard or Wittgenstein, though I now think it is better to say Wittgenstein was a passionate friend of fideism rather than a fideist. Pascal says very much what we have noted Wittgenstein and Kierkegaard saying above about religion and passion and about doing rather than thinking and about the role of faith. Yet for Pascal, in a way that is at a very great distance from both Kierkegaard and Wittgenstein, there 'was only one true religion, Christianity; only one true form of Christianity, Catholicism; only one true expression of Catholicism, Port Royal' (Winch 1994, 108). Kierkegaard was a Protestant, but, unlike Calvin and Luther who believed Protestant versions of what Pascal believed, Kierkegaard would never for a moment have believed anything like that. The confessional group that is Lutheranism could not have had such a standing for him. Indeed he thought little of the possibility of being a Christian in Danish Christendom. The times, we should note, they are a-changing. Kierkegaard's cultural life, and even more so Wittgenstein's, is very different than Pascal's. And our cultural conditions are not Wittgenstein's. Today someone with deep religious sensibilities and something like a university education could not, without self-deception and irrationality, respond as Pascal did, though the latter's religious sensibilities are as deep as they go and he certainly had a fine education and a keen intelligence. To respond in a manner similar to Pascal's would now be perceived as fanaticism, by intellectuals, and indeed be fanaticism, or at least blind dogmatism. Wittgenstein was a person passionate about religion and while he did not regard himself as a religious person, he had the deeply embedded 'ultimate' concerns and sensibilities of an intensely religious person. In that way he was a passionately religious person, if anyone ever was, but knowing what he does about religion, about the great diversity of religious responses, including in that diversity, deep religious responses and with them deep anti-religious *religious* responses, he could never attach his faith – his, if you will, 'infinite passion' – to any doctrine in the way that Pascal quite naturally did and as Luther and Calvin did. What was natural for Pascal's time and for Luther's is quite unthinkable for Kierkegaard's and Wittgenstein's (or for that matter for William James's). And for us the demystification of the world has gone even further. To repeat, 'the times they are a-changing.'

As we have seen, Wittgenstein wanted to eject all doctrine from the religious life or at least to regard it as of no importance. He, brought up a Catholic as he was, tended to use the vocabulary of Catholic Christianity; but it was clear enough that he attached little importance to the particular words that were used or, to be more specific and accurate, to the particular *doctrinal* formulae. Words used in prayer words used in hymns and in rituals were – in just the form they took – very important to him. But while remaining intense about religious commitment and ambivalent but intense about the Catholic faith, still, as he saw things, the doctrinal content of that faith was not, to understate it, very important. Indeed for faith to be genuinely faith, it must for the person *in* the faith (though not at every moment of his or her waking life) be a matter of intense passion. But, as Wittgenstein saw it, the content of that faith could, all the same, be very diffuse. Religious responses and religious conceptualizing vary greatly even within particular religious groups – say, Anglicanism, Presbyterianism, Reformed Judaism, Catholicism, Lutheranism. And, as things go on – as we stumble into our Brave New World – the diversity, and our sense of it, increases.

Wittgenstein was neither a believer nor a secularist, but there can be, and are, atheistical friends of religion and, what is something very different, even people who are antireligious *religious* persons. Santayana was the former; Lenin was the latter. We can be, as I think it is plain that Wittgenstein was, firm friends of fideism, believing that fideism is the only acceptable religious response, the only religious game in town, yet be quite unable and, perhaps even if able, unwilling to believe. Still, he was firmly convinced, if one is to be religious, one should be a fideist.[9] In this rather extended sense only was Wittgenstein a fideist. Here he differs from Kierkegaard and Pascal.

Atheists – or through and through secularizers if the word 'atheist' puts you off – come in various shapes and colours (Nielsen 1996, 427–50, 509–56). I am thinking of such different people as d'Holbach, Hume, Feuerbach, Marx, Gramsci, Santayana, Russell, Weber, Freud, Dewey and Rorty. Many atheists are passionately antagonistic to religion and could never be thought of as atheistical friends of religion. I am thinking classically of d'Holbach and Diderot and among contemporary philosophers of Paul Edwards and (until recently) Antony Flew. They see religion as a tissue of metaphysical errors and superstitions that yield no sound arguments for the existence of God at all and as being utterly incapable in any reasonable way of meeting the problem of evil or making sense of miracles or immortality. They see it as a groundless and pointless bunch of beliefs and practices that do more harm than good. Christianity, Judaism and Islam are irrational and immoral belief-systems and practices. Religion, they have it, just leads us down the garden path. For them it is little better than superstition and a superstition with largely evil results. Here the conflict with Wittgenstein or Wittgensteinians is (to understate it) in tone and over what belief in God comes to. Wittgensteinians could say to such an atheist 'Your conception of God and religion consists principally in a crude form of metaphysics or superstitions that we have been as concerned as you to reject. Indeed such religion is ridiculous and religiously offensive; it is a superstitious set of beliefs.' But Wittgensteinians will insist that religion isn't that. Religiously sensitive people would not so conceive of it, though they also stress that *some* people who are 'minimally religious' (what Wittgenstein and Kierkegaard would regard as not genuinely religious at all) and even some who vociferously claim to be religious are religious in this super-stitious and Neanderthal way. Some Wittgensteinians believe that 'religious Neanderthals' and the d'Holbachians complement each other; they take in, that is, each other's dirty linen.

Atheistical friends of religion will, however, agree with rationalistic atheists – the d'Holbach-Edwards sort described above – that sometimes religion integrally involves such crude metaphysics and they will believe, as well, that even in its genuinely religiously nuanced forms religion will contain cosmological elements that indeed are in error. Indeed they may think for *Tractarian* reasons that they are cognitively unintelligible. But with Wittgenstein they will agree that the cosmological side is not what is important about religion or what gives religion life. What gives it life is pretty much what Wittgenstein says it is, namely that religion helps us face and accept our tangled lives. They remain atheists because, setting cosmological conceptions aside as (to be pleonastic) bad metaphysics, as Wittgenstein does, what is left, as they reflectively sense these things, is inwardness and a certain kind of morality rooted in passion and the practices which are constitutive of religion. That, they agree, is all fine, but its substance, they point out, is *utterly secular*. Religious symbolism, however humanly important, is just that – *symbolism*. The substance is just that broadly moral substance and indeed it, given the incoherence of metaphysical concepts and most particularly supernaturalistic ones, can-not be anything but that. But unlike rationalistic atheists (the d'Holbach-Edwards sort) they think this particular moral substance – this sense of what our lives and our values should be – is terribly important. Wittgen-stein, and Kierkegaard as well, articulate for us, these atheistical friends of religion believe, a deep and compelling sense of what a really human life should be. So here we have what I have called atheistical friends of religion and *some* of them are even atheistic friends of fideism. George Santayana is a good example of such an atheist friend of religion.

What of what I have, not unparadoxically, called antireligious *religious* persons? Where do they stand in such a conversation? Like the atheistical friends of religion, they agree that Wittgenstein and Wittgensteinians with finely attuned religious sensitivity capture something that is deeply important in human life concerning which rationalistic atheists have a tin ear. This religious sensibility, they stress, is something that should not be lost. They see it in its strongest forms as a deep, humanly important response to life. Because of this stress, I have called them anti-religious *religious* persons. Perhaps, less provocatively, they should be called instead intense religiously sensitive people – people such as Friederich Nietzsche, Ludwig Feuerbach or George Eliot – but not literally religious

persons, for, though they are sensitively attuned to religion, they passionately combat and reject religion. In this way they are not like the atheist
friends of religion. (Contrast here Feuerbach and Santayana.) They
believe that such finely tuned religious sensibilities should not be lost,
while still believing that religious belief and practice should be firmly
rejected, only kept in mind for what these beliefs and practices have been
for some people – and not just for what they have done to people – but
still not to be lived, taken to be part of the repertoire of our affective and
cognitive existence. The doctrines, many of the particular religious moral
beliefs, religious stances, many of the attitudes toward life of religious
persons and the institutional structures of religions should, they believe,
drift, but not without continued remembrance, into obsolescence. In that
they importantly differ from atheistic friends of religion. They actively –
though, of course, without force – want to see Christianity, Judaism,
Islam, Hinduism and the like come to an end (quietly fade away) and a
genuinely secular age come into being. But they also differ from such
genial and bemused dismissers of religion as Bertrand Russell and W. V.
Quine who could hardly be bothered to think very much about it. (When
Russell, for example, did think a bit about it he stayed very much on the
surface.) Feuerbach and Nietzsche, by contrast, passionately reject it, and
not *just* because of its metaphysical nonsense, but for the human harm –
or what they take to be the human harm – religion does and not just, as
it were accidentally, but just in being what it is. Contemporary anti-
religious *religious* people (me, for example), if they were to study Wittgenstein, would recognize insights in Wittgenstein's understanding of
what morality demands of people, but they (we) also see it as one-sided,
and, if stressed, just as Wittgenstein stresses it, it does not yield the fullest
kind of human flourishing of which we human beings are capable. Such
a conception of the moral life feeds too much on a one-sided diet.

  Such matters need long pondering and careful dialectical examination
and I am not confident that there are the resources within Wittgenstein's
conception of what philosophy sensibly can be to come to grips with
such issues. (But *perhaps* we deceive ourselves in thinking there is any
intellectually oriented way of coming to grips with them?) Remember
that for him good philosophical work, work with a therapeutic intent, is
an activity and not an articulation of a theory of any kind or the taking
of any kind of moral or otherwise normative position or stance. He is
bent solely on elucidation, though elucidation for a particular purpose.
And this comes to giving a perspicuous representation through clear
description – leaving all explanation, normative *theorizing* and criticism
aside – of those stretches of language (which also, remember, are parts
of our forms of life) that we get confused about when we think about
them. Though we typically do not see that, it is so being entangled in our
language that generates the urge to do philosophy in the bad metaphysical

sense that Wittgenstein would therapize away. However, remember that for him it is a therapy which, as he sees it, will never end and will yield (and then only sometimes) only small temporary victories where we in some particular areas come, perhaps, only for a time, to command a clear or a clearer view (though always for a particular purpose) of the workings of our language and thus of the forms of our life. Though we should also recognize that Wittgenstein thought of his elucidations as having, in a very broad sense of 'ethical', an ethical point. But, be this as it may, this clear or clearer view is given by attentive description, a description which shows that everything is there before us, that nothing is hidden. There is, that is, nothing somehow revealing fleetingly in its hiddenness some essence or fundamental underlying structure there to be unearthed or something deep and unstateable that cannot be said, not even indirectly, but can only be shown to us as some unsayable deep something, some 'ineffable truth' (Malcolm 1986). There is nothing like this and there is no logical form of the world or of language or of thought. There are rather our practices there plainly to be seen, if only we will look, and, if we become perplexed about them, to be clearly described. What Wittgenstein calls for is description, though (*pace* Strawson), always for therapeutic purposes and not for theory-construction or for criticism. It is not even to be systematic description for its own sake. It is this that has been taken to be Wittgenstein's *quietism* or *neutralism*. But this – or so it at least seems – leaves us without the resources to come to grips with the issues mentioned in the previous paragraph.

There *may* be something more here that can be said, and of a *philosophical* sort, something that Wittgenstein's very way of construing philosophy *may* block. It will perhaps surface if we contrast Wittgenstein's way of construing philosophy with Rorty's or with a Deweyan pragmatism. Consider Rorty's remarks concerning the distinction he draws between Philosophy and philosophy (Rorty 1982, xiii–xlvii, and Nielsen 2005, 2–10). Wittgenstein's conception of philosophy, as therapeutic conceptual elucidation, should be located *as part of, but not the whole of*, what Rorty calls philosophy. Philosophy, by contrast, has been a central part of the tradition from Plato and Aristotle down to Edmund Husserl and Brand Blanshard.[10] This tradition of Philosophy has many variants. But they all claim to yield, and as part of a *discipline*, distinctive philosophical knowledge: some a priori knowledge that the Philosopher can grasp, utilizing some specialized philosophical technique, that cannot be gained from common-sense reflection and inquiry or from empirical inquiry. Philosophy is the attempt either in the grand metaphysical tradition or in the tradition of foundationalist epistemology or in the philosophy of logic or language to construct a systematic a priori theory which, as part of an *autonomous* discipline, would in one way or another found or ground the various forms of life and critique or at least clarify our ordinary and scientific beliefs, as well as our nonordinary religious, moral, and aesthetic beliefs and responses, showing what their real nature and import is. Wittgenstein and Wittgensteinians as well as neopragmatists such as Putnam, Rorty and myself, take Philosophy, in all of its various forms, to be houses of cards: as something, root and branch to be exposed as incoherent. It takes in some difficult cases the genius of Wittgenstein's probing to enable us to see how some bit of disguised nonsense is really plain nonsense and nothing more (Conant 1989). The very idea of having any such Philosophical knowledge or understanding makes no sense. We have only the illusion of understanding here and there is nothing with such Philosophy that we could build on to make sense of our lives or to understand our world more adequately. This is common ground between Wittgensteinians and neopragmatists including, of course, someone like Putnam, who seems to be a Wittgensteinian pragmatist (Putnam 1995, 27–56).[11]

However, Rorty argues, there is a contrasting activity he calls philosophy which, unlike Philosophy, he takes to be unproblematical. Wittgensteinian therapeutics is a part of this, but by no means the whole of it. I follow Rorty here in articulating such an activity, though I am less confident than he is that it is so entirely unproblematical (Williams 1986, 21–4). But surely, if not securely unproblematical, it is not nearly as problematical as Philosophy is. Rorty, following Wilfrid Sellars, construes philosophy to be the attempt to see how things, in the broadest sense of the term, hang together in the broadest sense of the term. Doing philosophy in this sense requires no specialized knowledge (no expertise in metaphysics, epistemology, logic, semantics, linguistics or anything of the sort) and it is not something that has a disciplinary matrix and it is as old as the hills: people at all times and places have engaged in it. No matter what happens to Philosophy, philosophy, like Old Man River, keeps right on rolling along, as an attempt, common to critical intellectuals – but not limited to them – to see how things hang together.[12] Giving up any claim to Philosophical knowledge or expertise, philosophers are general all-purpose critical intellectuals (among other things critics of society) including, as I put it in my *Naturalism without Foundations*, 'in their ranks all sorts of scientists (from both the natural and human sciences), historians, scholars in cultural studies and religious studies, former Philosophers (reformed into philosophers), novelists, poets, dramatists, literary critics, literary theorists, legal theorists, and the like' (Nielsen 1996, 540). Anyone can join in; it is not a prerogative of the 'experts', though no doubt, as an utterly contingent matter, some people, given what they have learned, have come in how they have lived their lives – including what they have been able to do with their leisure – to be a little better at forging a coherent conception of how things hang together and of understanding how they are to live their lives than others.

(They may, of course, be better at *understanding* it while still being hopelessly inept at living it, a point not lost on Kierkegaard.) But there is here, as elsewhere, no a priori knowledge gained from the Philosophical tradition, no 'esoteric knowledge' or any kind of any privileged knowledge and there are no overall experts in seeing how things hang together. Foundationalist epistemologists as cultural overseers are out of business. In that important way there has been a demise of Philosophy (Nielsen 1991, 1995).

I added the following in *Naturalism without Foundations*:

So construed philosophy is not an a priori purely conceptual investigation. It will be broadly empirical and historicist and rooted in a consideration of the problems of the epoch in which the philosopher philosophizes. In doing philosophy, such all-purpose critical intellectuals (philosophers), coming from all over the place, with a heterogeneous bunch of skills, notions, and sensibilities, will be starting with their traditions, their own preconceptions, and their considered convictions. Some of them will, as well, sometimes use, in a pragmatic manner, certain Philosophical notions or conceptual analyses, where philosophy, now as conceptual elucidation, functions purely as an elucidatory second-order discourse. But these things will be used with caution by the philosopher and only where they have a chance of working. And in being so used pragmatically, they will not be taken as contributing to or as presupposing a foundational theory or any kind of a priori theory or perhaps any theory at all. They will just be something which such philosophers (critical intellectuals) use in their attempts to see how things hang together and in looking with a critical eye for a conception of how things might better hang together. These philosophers – these critical intellectuals – will try to see how things hang together and they will, in doing so, and quite properly, ask critical questions concerning religion or any other practice, including philosophy itself. (That is why we have such a thing as metaphilosophy.) They will most particularly ask questions about how these beliefs fit together with our other beliefs, if indeed they do. Repairing the ship at sea, including sometimes throwing overboard some rotten planks, they will try for a time, but only for a time, and thoroughly fallibilistically, to see how things hang together. In doing so, the philosopher will not infrequently reject certain beliefs and conceptions – and indeed sometimes, though rarely, very fundamental ones – as not being conducive to our being able to forge a coherent picture of how things hang together and thus to a gaining of a better understanding of our lives and perhaps, as well, to a coming to understand a little more adequately how we might best live our lives both together and as individuals.

What I characterized in section III.5 of this chapter, with my use of wide reflective equilibrium, was just such an attempt to articulate how to do that and something of a conception of what this would come to. It was not an attempt to articulate a foundational theory or indeed any kind of theory. And it most certainly was not an attempt to articulate an autonomous Philosophical theory. But it was an attempt to do philosophy. It pragmatically used a few Philosophical notions coming principally from positivist and other analytical traditions, but, in my utilization, they were not systematically tied to those traditions or to any Philosophical view. Like any good carpenter, pragmatists use whatever tools and materials that come in handy for the problem at hand. There is, in such work, a Deweyan pragmatist philosophy and a roughly Wittgensteinian therapeutic metaphilosophy. The latter has the purely negative task of making the world safe from Philosophy. It is in this contextualist way in which we, without the 'aid' of some superdiscipline, can critically appraise our practices, including some-times showing that certain ones should be put out to pasture as in the past we put out to pasture our astrological and magical practices. (Nielsen 1996, 540–1)

I think Wittgenstein would resist much of this. He would be sceptical that with or without Philosophy we can get very far with seeing how things hang together. I think *au contraire* that this is only true if we think, as I guess Wittgenstein supposes, that we would only be satisfied if we got something that was 'completely clear' and 'completely certain' and this, of course, as he has powerfully contended, is impossible. We, as the *Philo-sophical Investigations* well argues, do not even have any criterion for, or conception of, what is to count as 'complete clarity'. He seems to think in going on this quest for being able to understand how things hang together, that we could not help but be driven into being Philosophers and thus be taken down the garden path. People with the Philosophical itch – and there will always be such people – will never stop being compelled to do Philosophy; the quest for complete clarity is difficult and perhaps impossible to exorcise. *Perhaps* this is one with a common religious impulse? Be that as it may, there will never be (*pace* Habermas), if Wittgen-stein is near to the mark, a post-Philosophical age. But we – that is 'we' as individuals – need not be such Don Quixotes. Sometimes the therapy has worked. Moreover, there have been all kinds of attempts at coherence that make no such extravagant claims. Dewey's is a prominent one. And philos-ophers and other intellectuals can sometimes profit from Wittgensteinians' therapeutic accounts and no longer be a prey to such conceptual obses-sions. Rorty is a very good example. Wittgensteinian therapy worked on him and, turning away from the obsessions of and about Philosophy, he seeks to articulate a more adequate conception of life and of society, using wide reflective equilibrium (Rorty 1991, 175–96). By looking care-fully and reflectively at our practices, seeing how they fit together, some-times seeking to forge a better fit, sensing the historicity of things and the contingency of our various fittings, but also seeing that some of them answer better to our needs (including, of course, our intellectual needs) than others, we will – particularly if we sense the impossibility of meeting some of the more esoteric of them – gradually lose the need, in our attempts to see how things fit together, to have some metaphysical backing or irredu-cibly metaphysical religious orientation – some grounding of our practices and language-games. Wittgensteinian therapy, on a metalevel can, and should, go hand in glove with a Deweyan-Rawlsian broadly historicist and contextualist forging of a wide and general reflective equilibrium.

We should also be more *holist* than Wittgenstein or most Wittgen-steinians are prepared to be. We should not take distinctive language-games to be autonomous, yielding their own wholly distinctive criteria of what it makes sense to say, what is justified, what is acceptable, and the like. We need repeatedly to attend to how our various language-games and practices relate, criss-cross and effect, or would effect, each other, if we saw with any clarity how they are related. Though no doubt, without any clarifying articulation, these different practices just do affect each other. But with a clearer understanding of how they relate and affect or could affect each other, we may gain a more adequate understanding of how things hang together and of the import of it. This may not happen, but it is not impossible that it could and it is worth struggling to attain. Here there should be no *quietism*. Such a struggle is both reasonable and worth the candle.

If we look at our religious practices, including those containing rather well firmed-up secular knowledge claims, we can come to see without any theory at all that certain religious notions make such a bad fit with other things that are very pervasive in our culture and important to us; in coming to understand that, we will come to see that there is very little, if any, sense in these religious notions. With respect to that it is surely right to tell us not to be so sure of ourselves and to look again to see if we are being blind to a fit that is there before our eyes which we simply do not see (Rhees 1997). (Perhaps we are ideologically blinkered here?) Wittgenstein has given us reason to believe, over the language-games he agonizes over, how often this is the case. But it is also possible that there is no fit – just clashing irreconcilable beliefs (sometimes just attempts at belief) and conceptions – or that a better fit can be made of the various things we know, reasonably believe, and care about, by jettisoning religious beliefs and practices; setting them aside so that they, though no doubt this takes time, will no longer play a part in our thought and behaviour and in our conception of how we should guide our lives. It may be the case that there is a severe strain and indeed even a clash between different elements in our forms of life and that the religious element will, if we really press things with integrity, be the odd man out. It may be that, in the attempt to overcome the tension by making our religious beliefs and conceptions fit with the rest of our beliefs and conceptions, we will have to resort to increasingly ad hoc assumptions or esoteric readings of our religious beliefs and conceptions. It seems to me that something like this is actually happening and indeed has been happening for some considerable time (Nielsen 1996, 79–155).

Holistic description here also can serve as criticism. Philosophy, little p *philosophy*, utilizing the method of wide reflective equilibrium, need not, and sometimes should not, leave everything as it is. A critical *philosophy* will utilize Wittgensteinian elucidation principally to break the picture that certain *Philosophical* conceptions seek to impose on us, but it will also engage in critical assessments – engaging with our lives as well as just with our cogitations – that pass without metaphysical extravagance or any other kind of extravagance beyond Wittgensteinian philosophical *quietism* and *neutralism*. This is done without trying to have some 'ultimate vocabulary' or some ultimate point of reference or to claim that there is one and only one true description capturing how the world just is anyway. Indeed such talk makes no more sense than William James's talk of an 'ultimate datum'.

Wittgenstein well shows us the incoherence of such conceptions. But we have seen how we can, and sometimes should, criticize practices, and not just stop with the reminder that this language-game is played. But our criticism will itself rest on other practices. There is no Archimedean point, *independent of all practices*, from which to criticize any of them. But from this – to make a good Peircean point – it does not follow that *any* practice is immune from or beyond criticism. We can't criticize them all *at once* or stand free of all of them and criticize them. But where there is a clash among the practices or the irritation of doubt is at work – real live Peircean doubt, not what Peirce well called Cartesian paper doubt – concerning any one, or several, of our practices, criticism is possible and in order. So we can see how a pragmatist need not, and should not, acquiesce in *quietism* (philosophical or any other kind). And we can see also how we can be pragmatists and consistently say that the Christian faith or any other faith or any set of beliefs and responses embedded in practices can rest on a mistake or (*pace* Putnam) be in deep and massive error (Putnam 1995). And this holds true not only for religious forms of life, but for *any* practice or form of life. We start with practices and it is important to see both that and in what ways many of them are crucial for our understanding and our lives and are irreplaceable. There is no place else for us to be than to start with practices and to remain with practices. Moreover, *taking them together*, we are stuck with them. There is no perspective outside of or beyond our practices as a whole. There is, that is, no leaping out of our skins, but for any one or several or for particular clusters of practices, where for *specific reasons* we come to have trouble with some specific practice or specific cluster of practices, it or they can either be reformed (sometimes deeply reformed) or sometimes even set aside. There is, to repeat, no practice that is immune from criticism. And the same is true, at least in principle, of clusters of particular practices. So we can repeatedly, relevantly and intelligently criticize our very practices and the beliefs and attitudes that are a part of them. This includes our faiths – that is, our trustings. It is just that (1) we cannot criticize *them all at once* or stand free of all of our practices and (2) that in criticizing a practice or a cluster of practices we must also be using practices. Thus we have Peircean *fallibilism* and Peircean critical commonsensism – something that was fully incorporated into the texture of Dewey's philosophical practice (Peirce 1935, 293–304, 354–67; Nielsen 1996, 295–328). With this, and without falling into Philosophy and the conceptual confusions Wittgenstein was concerned to dispel, we can do something critical concerning our forms of life. We can reasonably engage in an activity here for which Wittgenstein did not make space and indeed did not envisage.[13] With his feeling for a religious sense of life he would probably have thought it all *hubris*. But need it be?[14]

Notes

1 Wittgenstein rejected the idea of 'metaphilosophy' for he thought, and rightly so, so-called metaphilosophy was itself philosophy. What has come to be called 'metaphilosophy' is indeed itself philosophy. It is (among other things) philosophical thinking about what we are doing, can intelligibly be doing, should be doing, and the point(s) of our doing it when we philosophize (Couture and Nielsen, 1993).

2 Andrew Lugg has remarked (*pace* Conant) that it is hard to avoid the impression in reading the *Tractatus* that Wittgenstein is putting forward views. Indeed, Lugg continues, he says as much in the so-called framing remarks. That impression is indeed hard to resist and hence the pervasiveness of the traditional interpretation. But this would saddle Wittgenstein with either or both an atomistic metaphysics and a doctrine of ineffability. The former would not sit well with his own conception of what he is doing and the latter is obscurantist. To make maximal sense of Wittgenstein it seems as if we are driven to something like the Conant/Diamond reading.

3 Andrew Lugg, who knows a lot more about the *Tractatus* than I do, says he would argue that what Conant says here has no basis in Wittgenstein's text. Even if that is so, it has a basis in Wittgenstein's 'Lecture on Ethics' and has a considerable interest in its own right. Moreover, the 'Lecture on Ethics' remains in the *Tractarian* spirit.

4 It is not that Wittgenstein came to have a new view about logical and mathematical propositions. He never thought they described anything or were in anyway informative, but he came to have a new view about how they as nonrepresentational are to be understood. Again I am indebted to Andrew Lugg.

5 It might be argued that Malcolm's appeal to concepts as well as my own in the last few sentences is more Platonic than Wittgensteinian. But I do not reify or objectify the notion. I stick with *uses* of words, but I speak of concepts as a convenient way of noting I am, though I talk about the uses of words, not just talking about the uses of words in a *particular* language. Wittgenstein most of the time wrote in German and he has been translated into French and English (among other languages). What he calls, rather eccentrically, 'grammatical remarks' in the English translation carries over into the French and German texts. It is to make plain that 'carrying over' that I speak of concepts.

6 I do not mean to suggest that religion or Judaism or Christianity are language-games. That is neither Wittgenstein's view nor my own. However, Judaism and Christianity contain language-games embedded in their practices and are not understandable without reference to them.

7 It could be said that Wittgenstein should be understood as only denying that it is possible to give reasonable *philosophical* criticisms or defences of a form of life, but that he is not ruling out the possibility of giving any kind of reasonable criticism or defense of a form of life. But, given Wittgenstein's way of going about things, it is unclear what kind of criticism or defence of a form of life would be reasonable or that engaging in it would be a coherent activity. See more on this in Section V of this chapter.

8 One reader has remarked that the parallel with mathematics seems to beg the question. Many, he claims, of the same issues crop up in mathematics. And is it clear that all of the troubling issues can be shunted off to the metalevel? Why not say that metaphysics is intertwined in the practices of mathematics? Mathematics and religion run parallel here. I say in response that we can do mathematics, engage in the practices of mathematics, reason mathematically without ever raising the kinds of issues that Plato, Frege, Russell and Quine raise. We cannot, however, escape metaphysics when it comes to religious belief and practice. It is right there in our very first-order religious beliefs and discourse.

9 What I have in mind here in saying he was a 'friend of fideism' rather than a fideist is explained two paragraphs after the paragraph in which I signalled the occurrence of this note. I have in the past (Nielsen 1982, 43–64) thought of Wittgenstein as a fideist. My remarks in my present text indicate a correction. But Wittgensteinian Fideism is alive and well and paradigmatically exemplified in the work of D. Z. Phillips (Phillips 1970; Nielsen 1982, 65–139).

10 Rorty would say 'Rudolf Carnap and Hans Reichenbach' where I said 'Husserl and Blanshard'. Perhaps, as is frequently said, Carnap and Reichenbach were unwittingly entangled in metaphysics, that is, they did metaphysics in being anti-metaphysical. Their critique of metaphysics, the claim goes, rests on meta-physical premises. But that that is so is not so evident as it is usually assumed. After all, they did not think there was any a priori *philosophical* knowledge. And it is not evident that they in effect assumed any.

11 Putnam's attitude toward metaphysics is somewhat different than Rorty's

or my own. He agrees that metaphysical utterances are nonsensical, yet he thinks we need to acknowledge and keep firmly in mind the importance they have had in the history of human thought and that they continue to have in philosophical thought. I am less willing to genuflect before the tradition and would seek a more thorough transformation of philosophy (Nielsen 1991, 1995).

12 Remarking on the last few pages above, Lugg comments: 'This seems to suggest there is one correct view and one right vocabulary, contrary to what you said earlier.' *If* what I said in the past few pages, or anywhere else, commits me to that I would immediately retract it and go back to the drawing board. Neither my antirepresentationalism, perspectivism, or fallibilism fits with this. And, though I deploy the method of wide reflective equilibrium, I also argue that the very idea, *sans* particular context, of the widest or broadest equilibrium does not have a coherent sense. One reflective equilibrium can be wider or broader than another one at a given time and in a distinct context. At least in certain respects and in a determinate context one equilibrium might reasonably be thought to be the widest and broadest on offer, but we have no idea of what the widest possible reflective equilibrium would be. Wide reflective equilibrium is at home in assessing accounts of justice, morality, law and science. I also use it to apply to world-views. There it is *somewhat* problematical, but not, I believe, impossibly so. But it is certainly not unreasonable to be sceptical about it in that context. But even this application of wide reflective equilibrium does not commit me to the idea of the one true description of the world or to speaking of the way the world is in itself. What it does commit me to is to the possibility that we can gain a coherent account of how and why our practices just happen to hang together and to how it may be possible to forge an even more adequate way for them to hang together. But there is no reaching for the Absolute or for a conception of the way things just are anyway or of the one correct view or right vocabulary. Such notions are at best mythical.

13 Perhaps I am too harsh on Wittgenstein here. He did not engage in critical social inquiry into social and moral issues in anything like the way in which Dewey did and Rorty does. I do not think Wittgenstein would have thought that was a philosophical activity at all. But Lugg may be right in saying that Wittgenstein leaves plenty of room for critical discussion of our forms of life. Wittgenstein only rejects the idea that this can be done in some sort of an a priori philosophical way. But it would have been useful if he had done some of this non-philosophical criticism or have shown how he thought we should go about doing it.

14 I want to thank Stanley French and Andrew Lugg for their perceptive criticisms of an earlier version of this chapter. Their comments helped me very much. Sometimes, in the face of their criticisms, I have remained stubborn and did not budge. I hope that is not pigheadedness on my part.

Bibliography

Ambrose, Alice (1950), 'The Problem of Linguistic Inadequacy.' In *Philosophical Analysis: A Collection of Essays*, edited by Max Black. Ithaca, NY: Cornell University Press, pp. 15–37.

Braithwaite, Richard (1975), 'An Empiricist's View of the Nature of Religious

Belief.' In *The Logic of God*, edited by Malcolm L. Diamond and Thomas V. Litzenberg Jr. Indianapolis, IN: Bobbs-Merrill, pp. 127–47.

Copleston, Frederick (1956), *Contemporary Philosophy*. Burns and Oates.

Copleston, Frederick and A. J. Ayer (1957), 'Logical Positivism – A Debate.' In *A Modern Introduction to Philosophy*, 1st ed., edited by Paul Edwards. Glencoe, IL: The Free Press, pp. 586–618.

Copleston, Frederick and Bertrand Russell (1975), 'The Existence of God – A Debate.' In *A Modern Introduction to Philosophy*, 3rd ed., edited by Paul Edwards and Arthur Pap. New York: The Free Press, pp. 473–90.

Conant, James (1989), 'Must We Show What We Cannot Say?' In *The Senses of Stanley Cavell*, edited by Richard Fleming and Michael Payne. Bucknell, PA: Bucknell University Press, pp. 242–83.

—— (1990), 'Throwing Away the Top of the Ladder.' *Yale Review* 79, 328–64.

—— (1993), 'Kierkegaard, Wittgenstein and Nonsense.' In *Pursuits of Reason*, edited by T. Cohen et al. Lubbock: Texas Tech University Press, pp. 195–224.

Couture, Jocelyne and Nielsen, Kai (eds) (1993), *Mèta-philosophie/Reconstructing Philosophy*. Calgary: University of Calgary Press.

Diamond, Cora (1991), *The Realistic Spirit*. Cambridge, MA: MIT Press.

Hacker, P. M. S. (1999), 'Wittgenstein.' In *A Companion to the Philosophers*, edited by Robert L. Arrington. Oxford: Blackwell, pp. 538–50.

Hägerström, Axel (1964), *Philosophy and Religion*. Translated by Robert T. Sandin. London: Allen & Unwin.

Hare, R. M. (1973), 'The Simple Believer.' In *Religion and Morality*, edited by Gene Outkan and John R. Reeder Jr. New York: Anchor Press, pp. 393–427.

Hyman, John (1997), 'Wittgensteinianism.' In *A Companion to Philosophy of Religion*, edited by Phillip L. Quinn and Charles Taliaferro. Oxford: Blackwell Publishers, pp. 150–7.

James, William (1935), *Varieties of Religious Experience*. New York: The Modern Library.

Luckhardt, C. G. (ed) (1979), *Wittgenstein: Sources and Perspectives*. Ithaca, NY: Cornell University Press.

Malcolm, Norman (1960) 'Anselm's Ontological Arguments.' *Philosophical Review* 69, 378–90.

—— (1986), *Nothing Is Hidden: Wittgenstein's Criticism of His Early Thought*. Oxford: Blackwell.

—— (1994), *Wittgenstein: A Religious Point of View?* Ithaca, NY: Cornell University Press.

Maslow, Alexander (1961), *A Study in Wittgenstein's Tractatus*. Berkeley: University of California Press.

Nielsen, Kai (1973), *Scepticism*. London: Macmillan.

—— (1982), *An Introduction to the Philosophy of Religion*. London: Macmillan.

—— (1985), *Philosophy and Atheism*. Amherst, NY: Prometheus Books.

—— (1989a), *God, Scepticism, and Modernity*. University of Ottawa Press.

—— (1989b), 'The Faces of Immortality.' In *Death and Afterlife*, edited by Stephen T. Davis. London: Macmillan, pp. 1–30.

—— (1991), *After the Demise of the Tradition*. Boulder, CO: Westview Press.

—— (1995), *On Transforming Philosophy*. Boulder, CO. Westview Press.

—— (1996), *Naturalism without Foundations*. Amherst, NY: Prometheus Books.

—— (1999), 'Atheism without Anger or Tears.' In *Walking the Tightrope of Faith*, edited by Hendrik Hart et al. Amsterdam: Rodolpi, pp. 82–127.

—— (2001), *Naturalism and Religion*, Amherst, NY: Prometheus Books.

—— (2005), 'Pragmatism as Atheoreticism: Richard Rorty.' *Contemporary Pragmatism* 2, 1, 1–34.

Peirce, Charles (1935), *Collected Papers, Vols. V and VI*, edited by Charles Hartshorne and Paul Weiss. Cambridge, MA: Harvard University Press.

Phillips, D. Z. (1970), *Faith and Philosophical Inquiry*. London: Routledge and Kegan Paul.

Putnam, Hilary (1992), *Renewing Philosophy*. Cambridge, MA: Harvard University Press.

—— (1995), *Pragmatism*. Oxford: Blackwell.

—— (1997), 'God and the Philosophers,' *Midwest Studies in Philosophy* 21: 175–87.

Rhees, Rush (ed.) (1984), *Ludwig Wittgenstein, Personal Recollections*. Oxford: Oxford University Press.

Rhees, Rush (1997), *Rush Rhees on Religion and Philosophy*. Edited by D. Z. Phillips. Cambridge: Cambridge University Press.

Rorty, Richard (1982), *Consequences of Pragmatism*. Minneapolis: University of Minnesota Press.

—— (1991), *Objectivity, Relativism, and Truth*. Cambridge University Press.

Williams, Michael (1986), 'The Elimination of Metaphysics.' In *Fact, Science and Morality*, edited by Graham Macdonald and Crispin Wright, Oxford: Blackwell, pp. 9–25.

Winch, Peter (1994), 'Discussion of Malcolm's Essay.' In *Wittgenstein: A Religious Point of View?* Ithaca, NY: Cornell University Press, pp. 95–135.

Wittgenstein, Ludwig (1921), *Tractatus Logico-Philosophicus*. Translated by D. F. Pears and B. F. McGuinness. London: Routledge and Kegan Paul.

—— (1953), *Philosophical Investigations*. Translated by G. E. M. Anscombe. Oxford: Blackwell.

—— (1961), *Notebooks, 1914–1916*. Translated by G. E. M. Anscombe. Oxford: Blackwell.

—— (1966), *Lectures and Conversations on Aesthetics, Psychology and Religious Belief*. Edited by Cyril Barrett. Oxford: Blackwell.

—— (1967), *Zettel*, edited by G. E. M. Anscombe and G. H. von Wright. Translated by G. E. M. Anscombe. Oxford: Blackwell.

—— (1969), *On Certainty*. Translated by Denis Paul and G. E. M. Anscombe. Oxford: Blackwell.

—— (1978), *Remarks on the Foundations of Mathematics*, edited by G. E. M. Anscombe, et al. Cambridge, MA: MIT Press.

—— (1980), *Vermischte Bermerkungen*, edited by G. H. von Wright. Translated by Peter Winch under the title *Culture and Value*. Oxford: Blackwell.

—— (1993), 'A Lecture on Ethics.' In *Ludwig Wittgenstein, Philosophical Occasions, 1912–1951*, edited by James Klagge and Alfred Nordman Indianapolis: Hackett, pp. 36–45.

—— (1993), 'Remarks on Frazer's *Golden Bough*.' In *Ludwig Wittgenstein Philosophical Occasions, 1912–1951*, edited by James Klagge and Alfred Nordman. Indianapolis: Hackett, pp. 119–55.

14. Religion and Obstacles
of the Will

D. Z. PHILLIPS

I   Obstacles of the Will

I want to discuss Wittgenstein's distinction between obstacles of the intellect and obstacles of the will. It is important not to confuse the distinction with one between intellectual and psychological obstacles to accepting an argument. For Wittgenstein, it is a distinction of considerable importance *within philosophy*. This is because, as Rhees says,

> The difficulties of philosophy have in certain ways the character of moral difficulties. This is what Wittgenstein implies when he says that in philosophy one has to struggle constantly against a resistance within oneself, which is resistance of *will*. One is unwilling to let certain ways of thinking go. It was in such connexions also that Wittgenstein said that whoever does philosophy will have to *suffer*. (Rhees 1994, 577)

The resistance of the will is not due to the fact that the objections being put to one are too difficult, intellectually, to grasp. *That* is not the difficulty.

I discuss obstacles of the will because, rightly or wrongly, at this stage of the dialogue, I detect them in Nielsen's philosophical attitude to religion. As we shall see, I have misgivings about some of Nielsen's readings of Wittgenstein, but the main problems are not intellectual. Though appreciating central aspects of Wittgenstein's conception of philosophy, he resists applying it to the tensions between religious belief and unbelief. Wittgenstein said that, in his philosophizings, he is not trying to get people to believe what they do not believe, but to do what they will not do. But contemporary philosophy of religion is dominated by apologetic concerns, concerns with the truth or falsity of religious beliefs, or with the issue of whether anyone has an epistemic right to hold them. In the end, these are the concerns that dominate Nielsen's philosophical relation to religion.

Wittgenstein, by contrast, does not engage in philosophical disputes by countering theses with a counter-thesis of his own. He asks, rather, about the sense of things, and whether we are behind our words when we speak of it. If we grasp his conception of philosophy, we will see why it has no triumphant truths, no theses. Nielsen, on the other hand, longs for the triumph of atheism, and the demise of religion.

It is important to recognize how difficult it is for many philosophers of religion to grasp the character of Wittgenstein's methods. Richard Swinburne finds it a frustrating experience. Bewilderment and anger are frequent reactions, despite being accompanied by an acknowledgement that Wittgenstein is rightly named among the great philosophers. Swinburne tells us that the way he, and 'indeed most analytical philosophers approach some writer is to try to analyse what they have written in terms of a few philosophical claims and various supporting arguments; and then to attack or defend those claims by further arguments' (Swinburne 2001, 16). On the other hand, he says, 'To approach any Wittgensteinian in this way can be a frustrating experience. One is told that one's account of the philosophical claim is far too naïve, and that to produce head-on arguments for or against such claims is a naïve way to deal with them' (Swinburne 2001, 16). He concludes, 'One is finally left with the impression that one can only understand what the writer is saying if one endorses it' (Swinburne 2001, 16). Swinburne says more than he realizes in this remark, since if we are enquiring into the sense or meaning of things, shouldn't we agree with each other in this respect, if we are giving things the conceptual attention they deserve?

As William Wainwright says, in the 1950s there was a 'preoccupation with the question of religious discourse's meaningfulness'. But he also says, 'most of us lost interest in the debate' (Warnwright 2001, 21). For Wittgenstein, that is tantamount to losing interest in philosophy, in questions concerning logic and language, and language and reality. Contemporary philosophy of religion has paid a high price for this neglect. It has led to what I have called philosophy by italics; placing terms in italics to clinch an argument, when it is these very terms which cry out for conceptual elucidation. This is a case of philosophical impatience. The same impatience is shown in the uncritical acceptance of definitions whose coherence can be questioned. The definition of God as a person without a body is one of these. The definition of a human being as a person with a body is another.

Wittgenstein was extremely pessimistic about whether he would succeed in getting people to think of philosophical problems differently, so much so, that he said that he felt he was writing for another generation. Anyone influenced by him in the philosophy of religion will not find it difficult to share his reaction. But doesn't Nielsen appreciate this fact? He certainly recognizes that contemporary philosophers of religion discuss questions as though Wittgenstein had never written. Furthermore, he regards this fact as a philosophical disaster (see Nelsen 2001, 19). That being so, how can I find an obstacle of the will in his work with respect to Wittgenstein? It will take the whole of this chapter to give an adequate answer to that question, but, first, giving some examples of obstacles of the will may be of some help.

After 1931, Wittgenstein did not tell his pupils that they ought to renounce or refute metaphysics. 'But', Rhees says,

> he did want to bring them to see what metaphysics is, and in this way to free them from the special hold that it has on you when you feel that 'this is the only way it can be' ... I remember him telling, in 1938, of discussions he had been having with Ursell regarding Cantor's 'diagonal proof' of transfinite cardinals. Ursell agreed finally with Wittgenstein's criticisms, but he added: 'Still I must admit that such proofs have a very great charm for me.' When he was told of this, Wittgenstein said with a smile of real pleasure: 'Well that is fine, if anyone can say that. They have no charm whatever for me. But some-one like Ursell finds charm in them. O.K.' His point was that Ursell was not any longer trying to find some further significance in Cantor's proofs; he recognised that it was just that they had a certain charm for him. In this sense he was not calling on Ursell or anyone to 'renounce them utterly' – although he was calling on him to recognise that they were not what Cantor (and Ursell) had taken them to be. (Rhees 2001, 159)

A few months later, Wittgenstein, in conversation with Rhees, referred to Hilbert's remark in his essay 'On the Infinite': 'No one is going to drive us out of the paradise which Cantor has created for us.'

> Wittgenstein commented, 'I would never dream of trying to drive anyone out of paradise. I would try to do something quite different: to show you that it isn't paradise. And then you'll go of your own accord.' But the reference to 'paradise' does show that Wittgenstein was up against a powerful *mythology* here ... I said there would be value even in his negative criticisms of 'the Cantor business'. Wittgenstein replied, 'Certainly you can criticize the Cantor business. You can knock the Cantor business sky-high. But people will go on clinging to it nevertheless. They have other reasons for wanting to cling to it.' This is an illustration of the way in which philosophical discussion has to fight against tendencies of the *will*. It is not that Wittgenstein's criticisms would be too difficult (intellectually) for the mathematicians to follow. (Rhees 2001, 160)

Freud's attitude to dreams provides another illustration of an obstacle of the will. What would his response have been if someone convinced him that all dreams are not the product of unfulfilled sexual desires – not an intellectually difficult suggestion to grasp? Freud would have said, 'Well, in that case, what is the nature of all dreams?' He would not have given up the 'all' (see Wittgenstein 1966, 47–8). For him, there must be 'earliest' things which are the explanatory foundations of other things, including religious belief. With respect to religion, Wittgenstein shows that Freud was doing something very different from what he *thought he* was doing.

> Freud refers to various ancient myths in these connexions, and claims that his researches have now explained how it came about that anybody should think or propound a myth of that sort.
> Whereas in fact Freud has done something different. He has not given a scientific explanation of the ancient myth. What he has done is to propound a new myth. The attractiveness of the suggestion, for instance, that all anxiety is a repetition of the anxiety of the birth trauma, is just the attractiveness of a mythology. 'It is all the outcome of something that happened long ago.' Almost like referring to a totem. (Wittgenstein 1966, 50–1)

In accepting Freud's myth, we may find out things about ourselves, but not what Freud thought he was revealing. We do not discover the explanation of our dreams, but that we are prepared to link them, in certain ways, with other aspects of our lives. As Frank Cioffi has said, it is impossible to understand the hold Freud may have on our thinking without invoking what Wittgenstein called 'charm': 'We are caused to re-dream our life in surroundings such that its aspect changed – and it was the charm that made us do it' (Cioffi 1969, 209–10).

Someone accepting this critique of Freud[1] might still say, 'I admit that I still find great charm in the way I'm invited to look at my life.' But then he would not be claiming the status for it that Freud wants it to have. Wittgenstein suggests that it would be difficult for Freud or Freudians to give up their way of thinking. Doing so would involve suffering.

Despite his detailed discussions of Wittgenstein, Nielsen wants to advance, in the name of atheism, a claim that religious belief is inherently incoherent. He claims to have explained this by exposing its metaphysical, cosmological and anthropomorphic pretensions. What he has actually done, is to advocate one way of looking at the world, instead of another, while thinking 'that this is the only way it can be'.

Wittgensteinianism challenges this philosophical assumption, but Nielsen understands the challenge as a case of a rival apologetic – 'the strongest intellectual challenge to secularism and naturalism – to the very idea of the desirability of a postreligious culture' (Nielsen 2001, 14). The way in which Nielsen resists the philosophical character of the challenge, illustrates how he, too, is saying in effect, that nothing will drive him out of the paradise his philosophical atheism has created for him. He asserts that the Wittgensteinians, 'significant as they are . . . do not undermine or even render fragile, a through and through atheistic and secular orientation. And they do not shield religion from the wolves of disbelief (if that is what they are)' (Nielsen 2001, 14).

In what remains of our dialogue, I, like Wittgenstein and other Wittgensteinians before me, have to show Nielsen that I would not dream of driving him out of paradise. Like them, I have to show him that it is not paradise, and then he'll go of his own accord. This does not mean, necessarily, that he would cease to be atheist. The 'charm' of that view of the world might still command his allegiance. But he would no longer propound the philosophical claims he now makes on its behalf. In using the word 'paradise' in relation to Nielsen's view, I, too, recognize that I am confronting a powerful mythology. Giving it up, for one in the grip of it, entails suffering, since an obstacle of the will has to be overcome.

II Religion and Nielsen's Four Critical Categories

Readers of Nielsen's critique of religion soon became aware of the four critical categories within which that critique moves. His use of each category has to face Wittgensteinian criticisms of which Nielsen often seems to be aware. Faced by these, in the case of a given category, however, Nielsen has a tendency to rhetorically invoke an alternative category, conveniently forgetting, for that moment, that it, too, has to meet Wittgensteinian objections. For this reason, his apologetic strategy exhibits an unprofitable circularity. Clarity can only be achieved by stepping outside this apologetic circle. I shall give a brief indication of Nielsen's four critical categories before discussing three of them in the present section, and the fourth in the next.

According to Nielsen, religious beliefs have strands that are unmistakably metaphysical, cosmological or anthropomorphic. An attempt may be made to rescue religion from unanswerable objections to these strands, by emphasizing its essentially moral core. When this is done, however, the moral core revealed will be utterly secular. An attempt may be made to reintroduce religious elements into the moral core. The trouble is that such elements are logically dependent on the metaphysical, cosmological and anthropomorphic strands in religion that have already fallen foul of unanswerable objections, and so, the critical strategy has turned full circle. Postponing a discussion of Nielsen's relation to metaphysics until the next section, we shall now examine, in turn, the feasibility of Nielsen's other critical categories.

Let us begin with Nielsen's claim that the objects of religious belief are anthropomorphic. At times, Nielsen seems to appreciate Wittgensteinian grammatical cautions in this context. He writes, 'Some words refer or stand for something. They have a reference. But "Hans", "blue", "2", "the Empire State Building", "grace" and "God" do not all refer in the same way. We must, in particular, not assume that "God" refers like "Hans" or "the Empire State Building"' (Chapter 13, p. 245). If one learns from this, as Nielsen appears to, one will conclude that the reality of the divine must not be confused with the reality of human beings, or the reality of physical objects. If, however, one learns from Wittgenstein, one proceeds from this point to enquire into what it means to talk of a divine reality, and not assume that, given the above distinctions, it *cannot* mean anything. Nielsen's critical categories prevent him from taking this further step.

In Chapter 4, I argued that we should benefit from Rhees's analysis in which he showed that 'grace', 'love' and 'creator of heaven and earth', are related to 'God' as 'hands', 'feet' and 'face' are related to 'human being'. Nielsen insists that we cannot speak of these attributes of the divine without predicating them of a God whose prior existence we are assuming in the use of these terms. This, he claims, is the anthropomorphic strand in religious belief. But, in making this claim, Nielsen is reintroducing notions of a *kind* of reference that he has already admitted do not apply where 'grace' and 'God' are concerned.

Yet, even if Nielsen is made to be consistent concerning the grammar of *the object* of reference in religious belief, his critical strategy is not over. He argues that if the object of belief is not understood anthropomorphically, religion is reduced to a morality that is utterly secular in character. In this sense, the content of the belief remains anthropomorphic.

Nielsen's reaction to the alleged reduction of religion to morality is reminiscent of Feuerbach, and runs into comparable difficulties. The problem is that the logical space occupied by 'grace', where the whole of life is seen as a gift, could not be occupied by a human being. No human being can be seen as 'the giver of life' in this way, as the element in which one lives, and moves, and has one's being. 'God' is that element. At this point, Nielsen is likely to revert to his claim that 'God' must be conceived anthropomorphically, so negating Rhees's grammatical point about the relation in which 'grace' stands to God. This is one example of Nielsen turning within the closed circle of his critical categories. It may be a biographical fact that he does not understand a religious belief whose grammar is outside these constraints, but this is different from the philosophical claim that there is no such grammar to be elucidated.

Sometimes, Nielsen becomes a victim of a crude anthropomorphism he ascribes, uncritically, to certain religious traditions. He says that

'Zeus-like empirical entities' do not involve metaphysics. 'They are implicit, very vague empirical hypotheses. They are just crude, plainly false empirical proportions plainly disconfirmed. *Such* religious beliefs are superstitions and Wittgenstein was keenly aware of that and rejected *such* religious beliefs and such a way of looking at religion with disdain' (Chapter 13, p. 260). There is no doubt that Wittgenstein recognizes possibilities of superstition, conceptual confusion and harmful pictures in religion, but Nielsen's claims are, to say the least, premature. He does not even consider the possibility that, in belief in Zeus and the gods, we are given a language, or a system of reference, to use Wittgenstein's term, in which to understand human life. Winch finds such a language in Aeschylus' *Prometheus Bound*, where, he says, 'these stories are not merely told for the entertainment value (though that is of course, sometimes, a significant element), but are intended to convey important insights about the nature of human life, about "the human condition"' (Winch 2001).

Zeus is dismayed at Prometheus' gift of fire to human beings, since he realizes what the gift involves. The features of the gift which give life its tremendous potentialities, are the very features which can occasion its agonizing disappointments and diverse sufferings. In Aeschylus' story, there is no hint of theodicy. The gift of life is not *for* something. The story is devoid of the instrumentalism and consequentialism so central in any theodicy. In the relation between Zeus and Prometheus, Aeschylus is exploring relations between different aspects of the divine, and even tensions between them. On the one hand, since the givenness of life is not for anything, it can be seen under the aspect of love. On the other hand, the gift is that of human life, one that is, of necessity, imperfect. Aeschylus shows how love and suffering are both involved in the notion of the gods: love in the givenness of life, but compassion for what it involves. Suffering, Winch argues, belongs to Aesychylus' conception of the divine and the human. The divine suffers at the existence of imperfection – a compassion for human beings – while human beings suffer in the knowledge of a purity and perfection that can never be theirs. The essence of religious belief, here, is the task of accepting the gift of the gods, of living life in gratitude to the gods. Nielsen, of course, will argue, that such a response is logically parasitic on a prior belief in the existence of the gods. But, once again, he needs the Wittgensteinian reminder that it is only in terms of the response that one has any idea of what 'acknowledgement of the gods' amounts to. As Wittgenstein says, belief and practice go together here.

Acceptance of the gods' gift is no easy matter. Winch says,

> I wonder if this is part of the meaning of Io's semi-transfiguration into a beast, a cow, in her attempt to flee Zeus' love. She sees the suffering

that love involves and tries to escape it by rejecting its gifts. Only, of course, once the nature of the gifts have been comprehended, it is too late, for such comprehension comes only with these gifts. The eventual salvation which Prometheus prophesies for her is an acceptance of the gifts: Zeus' impregnation, 'without fear', an acceptance, that is to say, of the gifts along with their cost. Whereas, on the contrary, any historicist hope . . . that all may one day be made well (the cost eliminated), when the revolution comes perhaps, is just a continuation of the original refusal to accept the god's gifts, their cost being an inextricable part of the package; it takes one farther from the possibility of salvation and reconciliation with Zeus. (Winch 2001)

Would Nielsen still see only crude anthropomorphism here, a set of 'crude, plainly false empirical propositions plainly disconfirmed'? If so, it would be interesting to hear what form the empirical disconfirmation would take. Here we have a religious picture that says itself.

In the light of Winch's comments on Aeschylus, it is difficult, not only to interpret them anthropomorphically, but also to appeal to a second of Nielsen's critical categories, namely, the claim that *Prometheus Bound*, if read non-anthropomorphically, simply gives us an account of a thoroughly secular morality that can dispense with the gods. Is the story simply one of 'morality touched by emotion'?

There are signs in Chapter 13 that Nielsen is no longer content with this way of talking. He now says that when Wittgenstein speaks of ethics, 'it is always in a distinctively religious way.[2] But this would be badly misunderstood if it were taken, after the fashion of Richard Braithwaite and R. M. Hare, to be a reductive view of religion in which religion is viewed as morality touched with emotion associated with certain traditional narratives which may or may not be believed' (Chapter 13, p. 225). But, in that case, what becomes of Nielsen's claim that, if we dispense with religious terms, we can recognize, in what is said, an utterly secular morality? He seems to recognize, as I insisted in my early criticisms of Braithwaite, that there is an internal relation between the language of religion and the content of the religious morality.[3]

Nielsen, however, is not consistent on these issues. When Wittgenstein says, in his *Notebooks*, 'to pray is to think about the meaning of life' and that 'to believe in God means to see that life has a meaning' (Wittgenstein 1961, 73), he finds the remarks 'against most of the philosophical temper of Wittgenstein, utterly reductionistic' (Chapter 13, p. 248). Nielsen concludes, 'By verbal magic, all sensitive, reflective, caring people become religious believers.' There are, without doubt, problems concerning Wittgenstein's early remarks on ethics and religion,[4] but, even allowing for these, it cannot be said that Wittgenstein is trying to *reduce* prayer to *something else* called 'the meaning of life'. Rather, Wittgenstein is showing, what we have already seen in our other examples, namely, that in the language of prayer, we are offered a language in which to understand the whole of life (see Phillips 1965). To pray is one form of recognition that life is a gift of the gods or God. One may, in a prayer, ask to be worthy of the gift. At the end of his life, someone may feel that he has not used the gift as he ought, that he has failed to show sufficient gratitude for it in his dealings with others. Such a person may then seek the judgement of God or the gods, as the only hope: an eternal judgement, which cannot be reduced to anthropomorphic or moral terms. The distinction between temporal and eternal judgement has been insisted on by many philosophers, even before Socrates and Plato. The following is a remarkable example of seeking such a judgement from the Christian God:

> The great revelation of religion: that when it is clear that one's own life is a disgrace – better not to have lived than to have lived in this way – that then *death* can appear as something wonderful and holy ... (And I do not mean this in a negative sense: that here at last will be an end of my own adding to my degradation.) ... I know that with death I shall reach something not myself. That – saving possible nonsense in this – even my damnation will have something divine about it ... My tendency to write *meluis fuerit non vivere*[5] is an expression of ... *unwillingness to know* – which – if it masters me – will keep me from seeing death as the sole beauty and majesty; as the centre of 'Thy will be done'. To look on death if this means looking away from the world – is again a from of deception: a *failure* to see death as the word of God ... This is what especially falsifies my longing for death and makes it a form of idolatry (Is this the tendency which finds its most vulgar expression in 'That will be glory for me'?) (Rhees 1997, 235–7)[6]

Having commented on the anthropomorphic and moral categories in Nielsen's critique of religion, I want to comment on its third category, namely, the claim that there are untenable cosmological strands in religious belief. Nielsen ignores internal relations between belief and cosmology, between the so-called cognitive and the expressive in religious conceptions of the natural world. Consider the following comments by Stoney Indian Walking Buffalo:

> Indians living close to nature and nature's rules are not living in darkness. Did you know that trees talk? Well they do. They talk to each other, and they'll talk to you if you listen. Trouble is, white people don't listen. They never learned to listen to the Indians so I don't suppose they'll listen to other voices in nature. But I have learned

a lot from trees: sometimes about the weather, sometimes about animals, sometimes about the Great Spirit. (McLuhan 1980, 15)

Mario von der Ruhr has brought out why many philosophers would say that this anthropomorphic cosmology cannot be taken literally. Trees cannot be said to love, hate or say anything. They do not participate in a form of life in which such activities have sense. But if one extracts these elements, all one has left, it will be said, is symbolism. Nielsen says, 'Religious symbolism, however humanly important, is just that – *symbolism*' (Chapter 13, p. 267). As von der Ruhr points out, the problem with saying that the words should be understood symbolically, is that this suggests that there is only a contingent relation between 'what is said' and 'what it means'. The meaning could be expressed in some other way:

When the Wintu woman says that trees don't want to be hurt, she is not ascribing to them states of consciousness, but condemning the practice of felling trees. Her remark has the force of a reproach. Similarly, the expression 'spirit of the land' is just a poetic way of saying that the ecosystem should not be upset in that way, etc. And when Walking Buffalo insists that trees 'talk' to him about the weather, he is simply using the term to express, metaphorically, the idea that trees may be used in a primitive sort of weather forecast, etc. Hence, we can make perfectly good sense of what the North American Indians say, once we recognise that they are speaking metaphorically rather than literally, there is no need to accuse them of conceptual confusion. (von der Ruhr 1996, 29–30)

Unwittingly, Nielsen expresses what is wrong with this symbolic interpretation in words I could have chosen myself. He says that believers

do not have religious feelings which swing loose from religious concepts. Both their very understanding and deepest reactions are tied up (internally linked) with doctrines and creeds ... And their reactions and understanding here cannot be split apart (as if there were a 'cognitive' and a 'non-cognitive' side to them). *There is no religious understanding without the reactions and no reactions which are intelligibly religious without that understanding.* (Chapter 13, p. 256)

Nielsen, of course, is hoping to draw a distinction between religious practice and the problematic cosmological beliefs he thinks it presupposes. But if he had taken his own talk of an internal link seriously, he would see, once again, how belief and practice go together here. One would not hunt animals in the mountains, unless one believed that there were animals there. The practice is a consequence of the belief. But

Walking Buffalo's relation to nature is not a consequence of his beliefs, but an expression of them. Consider his reaction to the suggestion that he should plough the earth:

> You ask me to plow the ground. Shall I take a knife and tear my mother's breasts? Then when I die she will not take me to her bosom to rest. You ask me to dig for stone. Shall I dig under her skin for bones? Then when I die I cannot enter her body to be born again. You ask me to cut grass and make hay and sell it and be rich like white men. But how dare I cut off my mother's hair. (McLuhan 1980, 31)

I commented: ' "Not being taken into the bosom of the earth" is not a *consequence* of the spiritual relation with the earth, but an *expression* of it' (Phillips 2001b, 159).[7] Wittgenstein's notion of a 'world-picture' is relevant here. Walking Buffalo's spiritual relation to the earth, is not *enabled* by a world-picture. It is his world-picture. This is a major theme of Wittgenstein's *On Certainty*. Scientists do not conduct experiments, abide by their results, etc., as a result of their world-picture. Conducting experiments, etc., *is* their world-picture.

Nielsen writes, 'Wittgenstein is likely to have had a keen sense of what a religious form of life is. I have claimed . . . that there is no doctrineless religion and that religion inescapably involves making cosmological (metaphysical) claims . . . Wittgenstein firmly rejects this. Is he right to do so?' (Chapter 13, p. 250).

What Wittgenstein rejects is the misunderstanding of religious belief as something that logically entails the anthropomorphic and cosmological strands Nielsen attributes to it. He also rejects the view that without these strands, religious belief is reduced to a secular morality. Is Wittgenstein right to do so? I have argued that he is.

III   The Lure of a Philosophy of Life

Let us now turn to the fourth strand in Nielsen's critical categories, namely, his relation to metaphysical thought, and what he takes the implications of that relation to be for religious belief. These issues take us to the heart of the question of the nature of philosophical enquiry, and show why Nielsen turns from Wittgenstein's contemplative conception of philosophy, and gives in to the lure of a philosophy of life.

In what sense does philosophy investigate the nature of reality? I am assuming that Nielsen agrees that it is not like investigating the reality of a thing or a substance, since that would invite further questions about the reality of any thing or substance that is postulated as the measure of 'the real'. Plato recognized, in the theses of the Presocratics, this problem of measuring the measure. It follows that it makes no sense to say that reality exists, since nothing could explain the conditions of its existence. What could be 'other than' reality to constitute those conditions?[8]

Nothing occupies the space of 'reality' so conceived, since that notion is confused. Therefore, any attempt to place 'God' in that space will be equally confused. Since, for Nielsen, religion is unavoidably metaphysical, he thinks it 'should be said by Wittgenstein and Wittgensteinians to be incoherent. But this is not at all what they say' (Chapter 13, p. 247). Why not? Not because Wittgenstein turns from the big question concerning the nature of reality to a therapeutic conception of philosophy, as Nielsen is prone to think, but because he answers it in a different way. He still asks what it means to be in contact with reality, what it means to say something. His earliest form of that question is to ask, What is a proposition?, and he looks for one answer to that question. He thinks that if 'saying something' is not to be an arbitrary matter, it must always amount to the same thing, and that propositions should hang together in a system in a way akin to the parts of a calculus.

In his later work, the notion of 'practice' becomes more fundamental than that of a 'proposition', but in a reaction against the formality of the calculus conception of language, Wittgenstein sometimes goes to the other extreme in Part One of his *Investigations*, and says that language is a family of self-contained practices, logically complete in themselves. As we saw in Chapter 5, Rhees criticizes Wittgenstein for this excessive use of the analogy between language and games. In his reaction against the analogy between language and a calculus, Wittgenstein overlooked an important feature of it, namely, that of the interlocking intelligibility between different forms of discourse. If language were as compartmentalized as Wittgenstein sometimes suggests, then, as Rhees points out, nothing would be said. That is why Wittgenstein's claim that to imagine a language is to imagine a form of life is so important. What we say has its sense in the stream of life.[9] It may seem that this point is closely connected with Nielsen's appeal to a more holistic conception of language than the one he finds in Wittgenstein's thought, but that is not the case. I shall argue that his appeal, in fact, is a yearning for a metaphysical replacement for the systems of metaphysics he attacks.

We can appreciate the deficiencies in Nielsen's appeal to holism if we attempt to lay to rest, once and for all, his conviction that if one proceeds in philosophy in a Wittgensteinian way, 'this means that no philosophical or any other kind of reasonable criticism, or for that matter defence, is possible of forms of life'. Nielsen asks, 'Is this where we are? Is this the end of the line?' (Chapter 13, p. 246). But, as we have seen, everything depends on where Nielsen thinks we are. Many of his misgivings are seen to be groundless, once we distinguish between the grammatical and sociological meanings of 'practice' which we distinguished in Chapter 4, section V on 'Language and Wittgenstein's Philosophical Method'. None of the following criticisms are ruled out by Wittgensteinians:

1 There are the metaphysical confusions Nielsen notes, which may be present either in accounts people give of their religious beliefs or in the beliefs themselves.

2 There may be other confusions to be found in religion such as religious superstitions or a magical view of signs. The latter confusion may be found in rituals where a gesture, such as beckoning someone to return, may be thought to be effective *in itself*, without the surroundings in which the gesture is effective. It is an attempt to achieve an effect by baptism, where the effect is achieved 'all at once'.

3 Harmful religious pictures such as those that read predestination in a way that makes nonsense of morality; theodicies whose instrumentalism and consequentialism fail to take suffering or moral responsibility seriously; the confusion of eternity with the incoherent notion of endless duration; and so on.

4 There can be contradictions between religion and other forms of human activity, but these are dealt with as they arise. In other words, it makes no sense to ask, in the abstract whether, for example, science contradicts religion. It depends on what the religion or science amounts to. The confusion is in thinking that, somehow, there is a latent necessary contradiction waiting to be discovered. For example, Edmund Gosse tells of his fundamentalist father who was an eminent geologist. He believed that the Bible was correct in saying that the earth is 4000 years old. The dating of fossils which showed that the earth was much older was, therefore, a real problem for him. He tried to resolve it by saying that the Bible was correct, but that God created the fossils looking much older. Here we have a real contradiction, and Gosse's attempt to resolve it meant his end as a serious geologist (Gosse 1970). By contrast, the king Wittgenstein imagines Moore meeting in *On Certainty*, who imagines the world beginning with him, does not make an historical error. The biblical Gosse trades dates with geologists; he tries to play the same game with them. The king has no conception of, or interest in, history. If he is to acquire it, it will not be by a correction of previous mistakes, but by being initiated into an interest of a different kind.

5 There can be clashes, and criticisms, between ways of looking at the world which, as we have seen in the course of this dialogue, are not commensurable. Many philosophers see the anomaly between science and miracles in the claim made that the latter are violations of laws of nature – a confused notion in itself. The real anomaly is

between what a scientific interest in the natural world asks of us, and what the acknowledgement of a miracle asks of us. The latter asks that we do not pursue the explanatory questions which dominate our culture. So the tension between science and religion, in this respect, is not an accidental one (see Winch 1983, 1995; Rhees 1997; Phillips 1993, 2000).

6 Finally, there are criticisms which go *either way* between religious and secular responses to the tangled complexities of life. There are criticisms where the values of one reaction are criticized in terms of the values of another. It is in paying attention to these criticisms that we see the difficulties involved in Nielsen's holistic appeals.

Nielsen considers three responses to the complexities of life. Some people see them as an expression of God's will. Other people see them as the work of the Devil. Nielsen says,

> Some would say, as I would, 'That's how things are' without reference to God or the Devil ... I think (to abandon for a moment a Wittgensteinian commitment to description and to speak normatively) this austere approach reflects a more proper frame of mind ... I think myself 'That's how things are' is by far the more adequate way of viewing things. It is cleaner with less mystification and comes closer to – or so I think – telling it like it is. (Chapter 13, p. 258)

Nielsen could establish his conclusion by arguing that the appeals to God and the Devil involve the cosmological or anthropomorphic assumptions he has already claimed to be confused. But this is not what he does. He admits that those assumptions are not present in Wittgensteinian accounts of religion. Nevertheless, even if these confusions are absent, he still wants to say that his secular response is *closer to reality* than the others. His problem is that he thinks that a proper understanding of Wittgenstein would prevent him from saying what he wants to say.

Nielsen acknowledges that in their responses to life, 'People, including reflective people of integrity, often differ here' (Chapter 13, p. 258). We must say that no response is 'closer to reality' than any other response. At the root of this view is a misunderstanding of Wittgenstein that we discussed in Chapter 4. Nielsen attributes to Wittgenstein the view that language describes reality. As I have pointed out already, we offer descriptions, true or false, in various contexts, but the language in which we do so is not itself a description of anything. Because he thinks otherwise, Nielsen is led into saying that Wittgenstein and Wittgensteinians are 'set against the idea that there could be a one true description of the world' (Chapter 13, p. 245). But if I say that there is a chair in a room, or that a person is lying, when in fact there is a chair in the room, or a person is lying, I have given two true descriptions of the world.

As a result of his view that language is a description of reality, Nielsen is led into the further confusion of thinking of different forms of discourse as 'alternative descriptive and explanatory-practices utilized for different purposes'. He reiterates the view that 'none of these descriptions are "closer to reality" . . . than any other. We can only say that for different purposes one is more adequate than another'. (Chapter 13, p. 259) Nielsen gets into trouble by running different contexts together which should be kept apart. His talk of utilizing conceptual categories has some credence in physics, for example, where different categories or models may be used for different purposes. But, for the most part, we do not use or utilize language in this sense at all. I do not utilize language when I greet you, although my greeting has its sense in the language. Niether do we utilize language in expressing our value judgements. We are not using language for anything. If, like Nielsen, we think of our responses to the tangled complexities of life as descriptions, none of which is closer to reality than another, this encourages the very metaphysical view of a hidden reality that Nielsen thinks he is free of. His admiration for Rorty is no accident, since he, too, holds the view that all we are ever confronted by is 'alternative descriptions'.[10]

Even if these confusions are overcome, however, Nielsen is still faced with this essential problem: given the three responses to life's tangled web he considers, he wants to say that his is 'closer to how things are' than the others. He wants to know whether Wittgensteinian thought allows him to do so. What needs to be faced here is the issue of what is meant by the reality in values, and the character of criticism when different evaluative points of view criticize each other. To do so, we must turn from Nielsen's confused use of 'description', to Wittgenstein's use of that term in his philosophical method.

By 'description', Wittgenstein means the elucidation of the place concepts occupy in our practices. This will apply to the concept of criticism as much as to any other. Remember, that at this stage of the discussion, we are putting aside the admitted possibility of conceptual confusions, and asking, in their absence, what form criticism may take. My reply is that it takes the form of criticism *in terms of the values themselves*. In contexts such as these, we do not have reasons for our values; our values are our reasons.[11] In a critical clash, one person may or may not succeed in getting another to see something about a set of values he had not appreciated before. This may bring about a change in his own values, but it may increase his objections to the values he opposes. This is what a clash of values is like. This is what Wittgensteinian description should get one to appreciate. It is what Nielsen misleadingly calls 'quietism'. Why does he say this?

Nielsen exhibits an impatience with a contemplative conception of philosophy. He says that 'we need also to realize here that we are not just playing a little philosophical game. Matters of the heart, and deep and persistent matters of the heart, and not *just* matters of the head are at stake' (Nielsen 2001, 395). In this reaction, Nielsen is bereft of the philosophical 'wonder that there should be the problems that there are, and that they should have the solutions that they do' (Rhees 1994, 578) – a wonder one finds in Wittgenstein and Rhees. This is wonder at the fact that what will be a huge problem for some people, will not be a problem at all for others, and that what counts as a solution for some, would not count as a solution for others. But Nielsen wants to go beyond all this. He looks for a 'philosophy of life' which will show why his secular response to life should prevail over all others. Ironically, his 'philosophy for life' fails to do justice to the 'matters of the heart' Nielsen wants to emphasize, and to what might be meant by responding to them in a certain direction.

What is a philosophy of life? According to Nielsen, it is an intellectual attempt, in the broadest sense, to see 'how things hang together' (Chapter 13, p. 270). He thinks that there is 'an activity here for which Wittgenstein did not make space and indeed did not envisage' (Chapter 13, p. 275). On the contrary, if we allow the term 'philosophy of life', Wittgenstein was saying that here, we must all speak in the first person. Nielsen needs to heed the reminder, given to him by Andrew Lugg, that what Wittgenstein is opposing is the view that an answer to such personal quests can be found in 'an a priori philosophical way' (Chapter 13, p. 277, n. 13). It is for this reason, despite Nielsen saying that he does not care whether his quest is called 'philosophical' or not, that it is important to be clear about what we mean by 'philosophy'. Otherwise, we may, like Nielsen, want to have our cake and eat it; to have a quest which is called personal, but which has an outcome backed by philosophy. How does this come about in his case?

As we have seen, despite the fact that language does not have the unity of a calculus, Rhees thinks it important to emphasize its 'interlocking intelligibility'. Things bear on each other in innumerable ways. Discourse wouldn't be discourse were this not the case. But this 'interlocking intelligibility' is not a matter of a moral, political or religious consensus. It is marked by distances and differences, as well as by agreements and proximities. What would it mean to try to get 'behind' or 'beyond' them philosophically? To try to do so is reminiscent of Wittgenstein's early conviction that he ought to be able to show that a value has a value; to discover a set of properties that would show, of themselves, that a value is of value (see Phillips 2001a). Nielsen, too wants to show that his atheistic values are of value. He realizes that he cannot do so by an appeal to an Archimedean point outside all our practices, but he hopes they can be shown to be the product of the 'reflective equilibrium' we have already had reason to criticize. There are times when Nielsen recognizes that 'what is of value' cannot be equated with 'what prevails' in a cultural conversation. Critics, from Plato onwards, have pointed out that decadence may prevail, and often has. Furthermore, why should people forsake their values on realizing that they are not going to prevail? Rhees is worth quoting at length for the light he throws on the confused assumptions discussed in this last paragraph.

> If a man is determined to fight for liberty (for the furtherance of liberty in this society) – then fine. But if he says he is determined to fight for liberty for the reason that . . . then I lose interest. It is not as though 'there is something about a liberal society from which anyone can see that liberty is important.' No doubt there would be differences between a liberal society and an authoritarian one; different institutions (free and frequent elections, limitations on police powers: 'inviolability of the domicile,' etc.) and different methods of enforcing them. And I might describe these. I might emphasise that in an authoritarian society 'people are never allowed to' do this and that, and I might call this tyranny – although this is no longer pure description. The man devoted to order and strong government might answer that the does not find tyranny so very objectionable; things like insecurity, uncertainty, time-wasting disputes, want of any clear regularity in the life of the community, not knowing what one can expect – there are greater evils for the mass of the people than any tyranny would be. And so on. It is not that he and I understand something different by 'liberty'. We may agree on that. In other words, if I do care about liberty, then I shall want to defend the freedom of the press, the inviolability of the domicile, etc. We might even say that caring about liberty *means* inter alia, wanting to defend these institutions and practices. But then we should add that I do not have any *reason* for wanting to defend them. (Rhees 1970b, 54–5)

Once again: we don't have reasons for our values, our values are our reason. To seek a further reason for them via an appeal to a 'reflective equilibrium' seems like a lack of confidence in the values themselves. But doesn't remaining with the heterogeneity of values lead to relativism? Wittgenstein gives this suggestion short shrift: 'If you say there are various systems of ethics you are not saying that they are all equally right. That means nothing. Just as it would have no meaning to say that each was right from his own standpoint. That could only mean that each judges as he does' (Rhees 1970a, 101).

Nielsen's 'philosophy of life', arrived at via a 'reflective equilibrium', falls foul of a temptation which Wittgenstein thinks it is important to resist: 'In considering a different system of ethics there may be a strong temptation to think that what seems to us to express the justification of an action must be what really justifies it there, whereas the real reasons are the reasons that are given. These are the reasons for or against the action. "Reason" doesn't always mean the same thing; and in ethics we have to keep from assuming that reasons must really be of a different sort from what they are seen to be' (Rhees 1970a, 103).

When we contrast this Wittgensteinian caution with Nielsen's account of the facts of religion in the cultural conversation (is there only one?), the contrast could hardly be greater. Its fate can be seen under five aspects:

First, Nielsen says, 'If we look at our religious practices, including those containing rather well firmed-up secular knowledge claims, we can come to see without any theory at all that certain religious notions make such a bad fit with other things that are very pervasive in our culture and important to us; in coming to understand that, we will come to see that there is very little, if any, sense in these religious notions' (Chapter 13, p. 273).

Apart from the tautologous character of these remarks, Nielsen has not earned his confident use of 'us' and 'we'. What people will take to be 'fitting' or 'not fitting' varies. Even if something does not fit, that in itself would settle nothing for those once called 'upsetters of the world'. As with 'contradictions', each example would have to be met as it arises to see what 'not fitting' amounts to.

Second, but without very serious intent, Nielsen considers the possibility that he and other atheists simply do not understand religious beliefs: '(Perhaps we are ideologically blinkered here?) Wittgenstein has given us reason to believe, over the language-games he agonizes over, how often this is the case' (Chapter 13, p. 273). Interestingly, this possibility is not pursued. The reason why is found in the third aspect of religion's fate in the cultural conversation.

Third, even if there are important differences between religious and secular responses to life, the solution, according to Nielsen, is simple: get rid of the religious responses. He writes, 'But it is also possible that there is no fit – just clashing irreconcilable beliefs.' What then? – 'a better fit can be made of the various things we know, reasonably believe, and care about, by jettisoning religious beliefs and practices; setting them aside so that they, though no doubt this takes times, will no longer play a part in our thought and behaviour and in our conception of how we should guide our lives' (Chapter 13, p. 273). No sign of 'rational equilibrium' here. The gloves are off: if it gets in the way, get rid of it. Victims of cultural genocide would understand this policy all too well. The fact that this is the last thing Nielsen has in mind simply underlines the importance of his premature references to 'us' and 'ours'.

Fourth, the rationalistic appeal in the cultural conversation reasserts itself, but in a way which amounts to a blatant begging of the question. Nielsen says that 'the religious element will, if we really press things with integrity, be the odd man out' (Chapter 13, p. 274). I am sure that, on reflection, Nielsen would want to reconsider this exclusive atheistic appropriation of integrity, if only by recalling his earlier recognition of the fact that 'People, including reflective people of integrity, often differ here' (Chapter 13, p. 258).

Under the fifth and final aspect of religion's cultural fate, an offer of accommodation is made which might secure its survival. This is found 'by making our religious beliefs and conceptions fit with the rest of our beliefs and conceptions [by resorting] to increasingly ad hoc assumptions or esoteric readings of our religious beliefs and conceptions' (Chapter 13, p. 274). For Wittgenstein, this offer of accommodation would be a case of conceptual condescension.

When we read the five aspects of religion's cultural fate, as envisaged by Nielsen, we see how great was the need for his appropriation of Winch's warning about 'reflective equilibrium' which, clearly, went unheeded. Nielsen had expressed a worry about the fact that some disagreements are not benign, hence his faith in arriving at a reflective equilibrium. Winch said he did not share this faith, and pointed out that the agreement arrived at need not be benign either – 'It can suffer from intolerable smugness which ignores or distorts real differences.'[12] It is important to recognize that this may happen on the theistic, as well as the atheistic, side of the fence. In any event, we are far from Wittgenstein's contemplative conception of philosophy.

In a spirit that Nielsen admires, Charles Taylor has tried to show that we need a 'philosophy of life' very different from that envisaged by Nielsen. He argues that, faced with life's complexities, things hold together better, if we adopt a theistic conception of the self (Taylor 1989). It can be shown, philosophically, to be superior to any rival conception in our culture. Just as the atheistic Nielsen reaches atheistic conclusions, so the theist Taylor reaches theistic conclusions. This should, at least, give us pause for thought about the nature of the quest for a 'philosophy of life'.

In a critique of Taylor, Stephen Mulhall argues that Taylor has not established the philosophical superiority of a theistic conception of the self. What he has, in fact, been doing from the outset, is simply elucidating this one theistic concept (Mulhall 1996). Has Nielsen been engaged in a similar exercise for atheism? If so, Mulhall accuses them of 'stage strutting' while thinking that they were 'stage setting'. His advice is to be passionately open about this. Winch, in reply to Mulhall, says that, from the point of view of a contemplative conception of philosophy, Mulhall's advice would be disastrous (Winch 1996).

Winch points out that while a stage is sometimes used for monologues, or for plays with a didactic purpose, these are minority occasions. The main use of the stage is to represent segments of life, as faithfully as possible, which involve a number of different voices; voices which may end in tragic irreconcilability. One need only think of Shakespeare. But Winch points out that there is a comparable philosophical tradition which he finds in Plato's early dialogues, in Kierkegaard's pseudonymous works, and in Wittgenstein's struggles with the voices in his *Investigations*. It is 'a philosophical tradition which has concerned itself precisely with the problem of how to present moral or religious world-views in such a way that the passion behind them, which has to be evident if one is to recognize them for what they are, is clearly in view, along with a conception of the good that they embody, while at the same time equal justice is done to alternative and even hostile conceptions' (Winch 1996, 173). As Winch says, 'Achieving this is a task of enormous difficulty, both at the technical level and also because of the moral demands it makes on the writer who will him or herself have strong moral or religious commitments and will also be hostile to other possibilities' (Winch 1996, 173).

Wittgenstein said, 'My ideal is a certain coolness. A temple providing a setting for the passions without meddling with them' (Wittgenstein 1984, 2e). Wittgenstein is not ignoring the passions – the matters of the heart that concern Nielsen – he provides a setting for them. But he doesn't want to meddle with them. He wants them to be themselves. One way of meddling with them is to make them subject to a Nielsen-like 'philosophy of life'. The objections to such a 'philosophy' are not intellectually difficult to grasp, but its lure is very strong. To give that up, if we are in the grip of it, involves overcoming an obstacle of the will.

IV What Price 'Wittgensteinian Fideism' Now?

We seem to have come a long way from the accusations of Wittgensteinian Fideism I defended myself against in Chapter 2. There, Nielsen used it as a term of philosophical censure; the exposure of an attempt to shield religious belief from rational criticism. He expressed doubts over whether Wittgenstein would welcome any form of fideism. At other times, Nielsen says, he thought of Wittgenstein as a fideist. But in Chapter 6, Nielsen corrects these views (Chapter 13, p. 276, n. 9). He now recognizes that Wittgenstein was neither a believer nor a secularist (Chapter 13, p. 266), but he wants to call him a friend of fideism. What does this mean? According to Nielsen, it means 'that fideism is the only acceptable religious response' for Wittgenstein, although he was 'quite unable and, perhaps even if able, unwilling to believe. Still, he was firmly convinced, if one is to be religious, one should be a fideist' (Chapter 13, p. 266). Where is such fideism to be found? Nielsen replies, 'Wittgensteinian fideism is alive and well and paradigmatically exemplified in the work of D. Z. Phillips' (Chapter 13, p. 276, n. 9).

What is one to make of all this? Nielsen locates my fideism in my collection, *Faith and Philosophical Inquiry*, published in 1970. I do not know whether Nielsen sees me as a religious opponent to his atheism in an apologetic combat. For reasons which should be obvious by now, I would resist that view of my work; work that I see as firmly rooted in a Wittgensteinian tradition. I do not know either whether my work since 1970 would change Nielsen's view of what I am doing. Whatever of this, it may seem as though there has been a revolution already in Nielsen's view of it. From being the paradigm of a fideism that evaded philosophical scrutiny, my work is now a paradigm of 'the only acceptable religious response'!

But, as always with Nielsen, there is a sting in the tail. He describes himself as an atheistic friend of religion, and explains the relation in which he stands to Wittgensteinian thought. First, Wittgensteinians and such atheists can agree that the metaphysical, cosmological and anthropormorphical assumptions Nielsen has discussed need not be part of religious belief. Second, atheistic friends of religion, while insisting that religion may take confused forms, agree with Wittgenstein that what gives religion its life, is the way it helps us to accept our tangled lives. Religion is morality, rooted in passion.

Now comes the sting in the tail. When we understand that religion is a morality, rooted in passion, we understand, at the same time, that it is utterly secular. Nielsen wants to call himself, paradoxically, a religious atheist, because he claims to be sensitive to what is the core of religion, though it is a core that needs to be supplemented with additional moral insights. He sums up his relation to Wittgenstein as follows:

> Contemporary anti-religious *religious* people (me, for example), if they were to study Wittgenstein, would recognize insights in Wittgenstein's understanding of what morality demands of people, but they (we) also see it as one-sided, and, if stressed, just as Wittgenstein stresses it, it does not yield the fullest kind of human flourishing of which we human beings are capable. Such a conception of the moral life feeds too much on a one-sided diet. (Chapter 13, p. 268)

The outcome of Nielsen's long philosophical journey with Wittgensteinian Fideism seems to be this: Wittgenstein and I, albeit in different ways, recognize that fideism is the only adequate religious response, but fail to recognize, presumably, that a response we take to be religious, is, in fact, utterly secular. I do not know what has happened to the fideistic theses of Chapter 1, and which I discussed in Chapter 2. They seem lost without trace. Whatever of that, Nielsen's new thesis will take some maintaining. In the course of the present chapter, and in Chapter 7, I have discussed conceptions of divine grace and love which would simply make no sense in secular terms. Part of the difficulty of Nielsen's discussion is its comparative lack of examples. We still await his response to the countless religious examples found in Wittgenstein and Wittgensteinian thinkers. To complain, as Nielsen does, in these circumstances, of a one-sided diet of examples, is a complaint which is hard to take.

In my collection, *From Fantasy to Faith*, I related issues in the philosophy of religion to the literary work of 20 twentieth-century writers. Hopefully, I give full conceptual weight to rival secular and religious points of view. Among secularists, I discuss, for example, Frank Baum, Wallace Stevens, Ernest Hemingway, Philip Larkin and Albert Camus. Among those portraying religious insights, I discuss R. S. Thomas and Flannery O'Connor. But I also discuss writers who wrestle with tensions between different views of the world, such as Tennyson, Isaac Babel, Edith Wharton, Elie Wiesel, while not excluding, in this category, some of the others I have already mentioned. But I could not have done justice to these voices if I had tried to put them into one choir.

In working on the essays, I found, again and again, Christian and secular critics who would not let voices, other than those they admired, be themselves. Hemingway's old man in *The Old Man and the Sea*, and Nathanael West's *Miss Lonelyhearts*, were appropriated as Christ figures, while in the hands of a secular feminist, the complex self-sacrifice of the elder sister in Edith Wharton's *Bunner Sisters*, simply becomes a demonstration of the illusory nature of that virtue. I want to say that it was an obstacle of the will which made these critics do what they did, a conviction that 'things can be no other way'. I want to say that the same obstacle leads Nielsen to see only the secular in the religious.

Perhaps there is also a resistance in Nielsen which comes from the thought that to admit 'religious realities', philosophically, is to believe in them, and to confess them. Wittgenstein himself shows that that is not the case. At one time, Habermas thought that religion would disappear from the cultural conversations of humankind. Nielsen still entertains that hope. Habermas now thinks his view was not only premature, but that some religious meanings are *sui generis*. I am told that he came to this view with great reluctance (Cook 2001, 246). That is to his credit. It shows that he overcame an obstacle of the will. An appreciation of realities, in philosophy, is an appreciation of meaning. But, as Wittgenstein and Kiekegaard would say, mere clarity about religious meanings, is at an infinite distance from faith. I do not love God in being philosophically clear about 'God'.

Notes

1 For my critique of Freud's monistic vision, see Chapter 8 in my *Religion and the Hermeneutics of Contemplation*, Cambridge: Cambridge University Press 2001.

2 This is not true. Wittgenstein recognizes the heterogeneity of morals. For example, he notes how certain moral dilemmas will not arise for someone who has a certain Christian ethics. He also recognizes the importance, in moral matters, of recognizing that people's reasons really are their reasons, and not those which we would count as acceptable reasons. See Rhees (1970a).

3 For my criticism of Braithwaite see *Religion Without Explanation*, Oxford: Blackwell 1982, pp. 140–5. This early criticism is completely ignored by those who insist on comparing my work with Braithwaite's.

4 For my discussion of the development in Wittgenstein's views on ethics and religion see my 'Ethics, Faith and "What Can Be Said"', in *Wittgenstein: A Critical Reader*, ed. by Hans-Johann Glock, Oxford: Blackwell 2001.

5 'It would have been better not to live.' (Ed.)

6 Rhees's judgements are made in the *first person*. We who knew him, could never concur with his view of himself, which, of course, is not the same *at all* as saying that what he says is false.

7 See Chapter 7 for a fuller discussion of these issues.

8 I discuss this metaphysical conception of reality in *Philosophy's Cool Place*, Ithaca: Cornell University Press 1999, but what I say is deeply indebted to Rhees's *Wittgenstein and the Possibility of Discourse* ed. by D. Z. Phillips, Cambridge: Cambridge University Press 1998, and to his two-volumed work *In Dialogue with the Greeks: Vol. I: The Presocratics and Reality* and *Plato and Dialectic*, Aldershot: Ashgate 2004.

9 A major theme in Rhees's *Wittgenstein and the Possibility of Discourse*.

10 For my criticisms of Rorty see Chapter 4: 'Rorty's Lost Conversations' in Phillips 1998.

11 See my 'Allegiance and Change in Morality' in Phillips 1982b.

12 See 'Voices in Discussion' in *Philosophy and the Grammar of Religious Belief* ed. by Timothy Tessin and Mario von der Ruhr. Basingstoke and New York: Macmillan and St Martin's Press 1995, p. 392. Winch's views are represented by Voice J.

Bibliography

Cioffi, Frank (1969), 'Wittgenstein's Freud' in *Studies in the Philosophy of Wittgenstein*, ed. Peter Winch. London: Routledge.

Cook, Maeve (2001), 'Critical Theory and Religion' in *Philosophy of Religion in the 21st Century*, eds D. Z. Phillips and Timothy Tessin. Basingstoke: Palgrave.

Gosse, Edmund (1970), *Father and Son*. Harmondsworth: Penguin Books.

McLuhan, T. C. (1980), *Touch the Earth: A Self-Portrait of Indian Existence*. London: Abacus.

Mulhall, Stephen (1996), '*Sources of the Self's* Sense of Itself: A Theistic Reading of Modernity' in *Can Religion Be Explained Away?* ed. D. Z. Phillips. Basingstoke and New York: Macmillan and St Martin's Press.

Nielsen, Kai (2001), *Naturalism and Religion*. New York: Prometheus Books.

Phillips, D. Z. (1965), *The Concept of Prayer*. London: Routledge, 1965. (Oxford: Blackwell, 1981).

—— (1982a), *Religion Without Explanation*. Oxford: Blackwell.

—— (1982b), *Through a Darkening Glass*. Oxford: Blackwell.

—— (1991), *From Fantasy to Faith*. Basingstoke: Macmillan.

—— (1993), 'Waiting for the Vanishing Shed' in *Wittgenstein and Religion*, Basingstoke and New York: Macmillan and St Martin's Press.

—— (1998), *Philosophy's Cool Place*. Ithaca: Cornell University Press.

—— (2000), 'Miracles and Open-Door Epistemology' in *Recovering Religious Concepts*. Basingstoke: Macmillan.

—— (2001a), 'Ethics, Faith, and What Can Be Said' in *Wittgenstein, A Critical Reader*, ed. Hans-Johann Glock. Oxford: Blackwell.

—— (2001b), *Religion and the Hermeneutics of Contemplation*. Cambridge: Cambridge University Press.

Rhees, Rush (1970a), 'Some Developments in Wittgenstein's View of Ethics' in *Discussions of Wittgenstein*. London: Routledge.

—— (1970b), *Without Answers*, ed. D. Z. Phillips. London: Routledge.

—— (1994), 'The Fundamental Problems of Philosophy', ed. Timothy Tessin. *Philosophical Investigations* 17: 4, October 1994.

—— (1997), 'Miracles' in *On Religion and Philosophy*, ed. D. Z. Phillips. Cambridge: Cambridge University Press.

—— (1998), *Wittgenstein and the Possibility of Discourse*, ed. D. Z. Phillips. Cambridge: Cambridge University Press (second edition, Oxford: Blackwell, 2005).

—— (2001), 'On Wittgenstein', ed. D. Z. Phillips, *Philosophical Investigations* 24: 2.

—— (2004). *In Dialogue with the Greeks* Vol. I: *The Presocratics and Reality*. Vol. II: *Plato and Dialectics*. Edited with an introduction by D. Z. Phillips. Aldershot: Ashgate.

Ruhr, Mario von der (1996), 'Is Animism Alive and Well?' in *Can Religion be Explained Away?* ed. D. Z. Phillips. New York: St Martins Press.

Swinburne, Richard (2001), 'Philosophical Theism' in *Philosophy of Religion in the* 21st Century, eds D. Z. Phillips and Timothy Tessin. Basingstoke: Palgrave.

Taylor, Charles (1989), *Sources of the Self*. Cambridge: Cambridge University Press.

Tessin, Timothy and Mario von der Ruhr (eds) (1995), *Philosophy and the Grammar of Religious Belief*. Basingstoke and New York: Macmillan and St Martin's Press.

Wainwright, William (2001), 'Philosophy and Theology at the End of the Century' in *Philosophy of Religion in the* 21st Century, eds D. Z. Phillips and Timothy Tessin. Basingstoke: Palgrave.

Winch, Peter (1983), 'Ceasing to Exist' in *Trying to Make Sense*. Oxford: Blackwell, 1983.

—— (1995), 'Asking Too Many Questions' in *Philosophy and The Grammar of*

Religious Belief, eds Timothy Tessin and Mario von der Ruhr. New York: St Martin's Press, 1995.

—— (1996), 'Doing Justice or giving the Devil His Due' in *Can Religion Be Explained Away?* ed. D. Z. Phillips. Basingstoke and New York: Macmillan and St Martin's Press, 1996.

—— (2001), 'What can Philosophy say to Religion?', ed. D. Z. Phillips. *Faith and Philosophy* 18.

Wittgenstein, Ludwig. (1961), *Notebooks: 1914–1916*. Oxford: Blackwell.

—— (1966), *Lectures on Aesthetics, Psychology, and Religious Belief*, ed. Cyril Barrett. Oxford: Blackwell.

—— (1969), *On Certainty*. Oxford: Blackwell.

—— (1984), *Culture and Value*. Oxford: Blackwell.

15. Avoiding Nonsense, Keeping Cool: Nielsen, Phillips and Philosophy in the First Person

STEPHEN MULHALL

Interesting though its twists and turns may be to historians of ideas and biographers, I don't intend to pay very close attention in these remarks to the genealogy of the debate between Nielsen and Phillips. Neither will I be much concerned with establishing in any detail what the appropriate criteria might be for applying the label of 'Wittgensteinian Fideism'. My primary concern is rather with the question of what Wittgenstein's familiar view of philosophical method does and does not entail for those interested in applying it in the specific context of the philosophy of religion. In pursuit of this goal, I will advance a number of more or less critical comments on the papers by Nielsen and Phillips.

I Nielsen: 'Wittgenstein and Wittgensteinians on Religion'

Austere Nonsense

I was glad to see that Nielsen is inclined to find much of philosophical value in James Conant's and Cora Diamond's reading of the *Tractatus*; but I doubt whether that reading can really be used as Nielsen seems to want to use it – namely, as showing that the *Tractatus* does not in fact endorse the idea that religious mysticism intuits or indicates a domain of ineffable truth, but rather aims to disabuse us of that very misconception by enacting its inevitable self-dissolution into simple nonsensicality. My worry is not that the *Tractatus* in fact does retain the idea of ineffable ethical and religious truths; it is rather that attempts to give expression to ethical and religious values in the *Tractatus* do not appear (or at least, not simply) to dissolve into thin air or emptiness.

This worry is certainly shared by many of those who support this austere reading of the *Tractatus*, which suggests that they agree with Nielsen's interpretation of their work. For example, Diamond (2000) argues that while 'ethical' nonsense is on all fours with any other kind of nonsense from the point of view of logic, it has a very distinctive character from the point of view of psychology. For even when we have been shown its nonsensicality, we do not lose our inclination, or compulsion, to employ it – something that cannot, on her view be said of our attraction to more straightforwardly metaphysical nonsense.

More specifically, I am inclined to believe that the relevant sections of the *Tractatus* seem to employ a figurative register (invoking such images as the waxing and waning of the world, wonder at the fact rather than the form of its existence, the happy as opposed to the unhappy man) that is not simply jettisoned when the futility of attempts to model ethical discourse on fact-stating discourse are rejected as nonsensical. Its retention amounts to the impress in language of a practical attitude to the vicissitudes of one's experience – one that does not embody an answer or solution to life's problems, but the transcendence of any sense of life as a (set of) problems in need of a solution. This hardly amounts to a complete denial of significance to the domain of ethics; and it may even be regarded as a precursor to Wittgenstein's later sense of ethics as grounded in practice. I will return to this last point a little later.

Winch and Malcolm

Nielsen is wrong to think (see Chapter 13, p. 238) that Winch's critique of Malcolm is intended as the beginnings of a probing critique of Wittgenstein; it is rather a critique of Malcolm's reading of Wittgenstein in Wittgenstein's name. So Winch shouldn't be recruited to Nielsen's critique of Wittgenstein and Wittgensteinianism on these grounds at least.

Metaphysics, Doctrine and Nonsense

In my view, Nielsen misrepresents Wittgenstein's portrayal of religion in a number of important ways.

1 Wittgenstein does say that doctrine in the absence of practice is not enough for true faith; but that is not equivalent, as Nielsen appears to think, to his claiming that doctrine has no significance in religious life.
2 Similarly, Wittgenstein does say that it is a mistake to offer philosophical justifications of religious belief; but, contrary to Nielsen's assertion on p. 243, this does not amount to claiming that no justifications (or criticisms) of such beliefs can intelligibly be offered.
3 More generally, to say – as Wittgenstein and Wittgensteinians certainly do – that religious belief has and needs no rational foundations does not entail that it can neither be defended nor criticized

from without. Wittgenstein's objection is to the 'foundations' model, not to the idea that specific religious beliefs or religion as a form of life might be the object of reasonable objections and/or defences. One might instance Wittgenstein's own critique of the scapegoat ritual, or of St Paul's letters. And of course a Nietzschean critique of Christianity is hardly an attack on its rational foundations.

4 It sometimes seems that Nielsen thinks that all doctrinal elements in religion are metaphysical (cf. p. 247: 'religions ... are inescapably in part metaphysical religiosities ... There are no doctrineless or creedless religions'); but he gives no justification for this contentious assumption. The Creed tells us, among other things, that Jesus was crucified, died and was buried; are these metaphysical claims?

5 In the same vein, it sometimes seems that Nielsen thinks that all religious concepts are metaphysical (cf. p. 259, where he treats 'That is God's will' as a metaphysical utterance); but no reason is given for this tendentious assumption either. Why *must* all talk of God's will involve the assumption that God is a metaphysical entity?

6 Nielsen often talks of doctrine (which he equates with metaphysics) as a component or element of religious life, but his argumentative strategy commits him to the incoherent assumption that doctrine is both detachable from and integral to the whole. He needs the latter assumption, because he wants to argue against the possibility (erroneously attributed to Wittgenstein) of jettisoning doctrine and keeping practice by emphasizing that religious attitudes and practices are given the sense they have by the doctrines to which they are linked (p. 247). But he also needs the former assumption, because he wants to deny Phillips's view that we can only properly comprehend the substance of doctrine by seeing how it fits into and finds expression in the believer's life (p. 249ff., and *passim*, where Nielsen assumes that we can see the metaphysical import of doctrine without any need to consider its links with practice). It seems to me that Nielsen simply can't have it both ways here.

7 Nielsen never explains in any detail (at least in this chapter) what he means by 'metaphysical' – he simply treats it as a synonym for 'nonsensical'. The impression is sometimes given that it means 'just like a claim about the natural world except that it concerns the supernatural world' (cf. the discussion of Zeus on p. 260). Certainly, some religious claims made by some religious believers might be so understood; but Wittgenstein and Phillips would both then identify them as philosophically confused, and hence metaphysical, as quickly as Nielsen. And why assume a priori that all religious claims must be so understood? Particularly when, as Phillips points out, Nielsen accepts Wittgenstein's view that not all putatively referring

expressions refer in the same way, or even should be treated as referring expressions at all (see p. 285)

8 Nielsen has a remarkably impoverished conception of the kinds of non-factual or non-descriptive uses of language that there might be. The picture seems to be: Religious utterance that is non-metaphysical can only be a symbolic expression of moral substance, and hence wholly secular. It would be interesting to know how Nielsen would analyse moral utterances themselves: they're presumably not factual, and not (necessarily) metaphysical; so how exactly do they function? And the same set of questions arises for aesthetic and political uses of words. It would be equally interesting to know what 'symbolic' means; does it include the whole range of figurative modes of utterance (metaphor, simile, secondary sense, etc.)? If so, which subset do religious utterances fall into?

II Phillips: 'Religion and Obstacles of the Will'

A Lack of Cool

Much of Phillips's discussion is devoted to establishing critical concerns about Nielsen's views with which I am in much sympathy. But he really doesn't help his case by allowing an unseemly and self-defeating degree of irritation to keep on showing through. The most egregious example of this is the association of certain aspects of Nielsen's attempts to argue for his atheistic philosophy of life against religion with the practice of cultural genocide (Chapter 14, p. 297). This hardly amounts to 'doing justice to alternative and even hostile conceptions' – a principle he claims (p. 299) to be central to his own philosophical practice of hermeneutical contemplation.

The Very Idea of Coolness

In my view, there might be rather more substantial difficulties in the way of keeping to the path of methodological coolness than mere human frailty.

1 Why is it so important to distinguish any kind of speaking in the first person from any kind of philosophical discourse? Phillips isn't prepared to allow that certain kinds of first-person speech (stage-strutting, as he reminds me that I once called it elsewhere) can have any kind of claim on the name of philosophy – despite the centrality of such speech in the philosophical traditions of the West since Plato (as Nielsen rightly points out). The rigorous and passionate intellectual advocacy of one perspective on a range of problems or

on human life as a whole need not present itself as 'backed by philosophy' (p. 295), if that means it is presented as having an authority going beyond its own cogency, rigour and capacity to compel conviction – for example, as depending solely upon uncovering conceptual or logical commitments that any rational being as such is bound to acknowledge on pain of intellectual confusion. Charles Taylor's work (in *Sources of the Self* and elsewhere) doesn't really, and certainly does not need to, cloak itself in such misleading terms; this was one of the points of my paper on his work, to which Phillips refers and which Winch criticized. But why shouldn't such work, if carefully distinguished from other kinds of philosophical work such as grammatical investigations, be regarded as one way of continuing one kind of perfectly respectable philosophical tradition?

2 Shakespeare is presented to us as the theatrical equivalent of the methodological coolness Phillips and Winch desire in philosophy (p. 299). We are told that he uses the stage not to speak to us in monologue, but to 'represent segments of life, as faithfully as possible, which involve a number of different voices ... which may end in tragic irreconcilability' (p. 299). But can we really argue that Shakespeare's plays do not also present us with a distinctive vision of the world? To choose an example of some relevance to this particular context of debate, many critics say that religion is pretty much entirely absent from Shakespeare's theatrical universe – Santayana claimed to find everything in it but religion. Others say that the reason for this is that religion is Shakespeare's pervasive, hence invisible, business – Stanley Cavell says that Shakespeare puts or finds his theatre in competition with religion, perhaps as its successor. This is hardly – at least, not necessarily – a way of trying to do justice to a variety of views about religion. And anyway, how could any playwright not find that her distinctive view of the world informs and pervades her theatrical universe?

3 Whatever the merits of the above analogy, it seems plain that the fact that a thinker is committed to a certain kind of neutrality with respect to a range of substantial and competing moral visions is no guarantee that this commitment is not itself the embodiment or expression of a moral vision. Rawlsian political philosophy is a good example: his veil of ignorance denies us any reference to our specific conceptions of the good; but this neutrality is in the service of a distinctively liberal commitment to freedom and equality. We might then want to ask: what value-commitments lie behind the idea that we philosophers should provide a setting for the passions without meddling with them, that we should show one another differences, that we should remind one another what is ordinarily done with words? Perhaps this is where the *Tractarian* vision of

ethics finds its late expression. The happy man is one who over-
comes any dissatisfaction with the specific ways in which the world
is arranged, who is capable of accommodating himself not only to
whatever the world throws at him but also to the sheer existence of
the world – whose happiness consists in a calm, wondering acceptance of what is, as what it is (and not another thing) and as being
(rather than not-being).

4 More specifically, what conception of human beings is encoded into
Wittgenstein's therapeutic conception of philosophy? He presents
us to ourselves as systematically self-exiled from the ordinary, as
becoming aware of the everyday only through its loss, as the peculiar
animal whose burden of language condemns us repeatedly to lose
control of our words, to finding the words in our mouths to be
empty of meaning just when we are most convinced of their deep
significance. His methods are designed to reveal to us the depth and
constitutive force of this desire of ours to transcend the conditions
of meaningful speech, the linguistic dimension of our finitude, and
to overcome the specific expressions of this desire in the name of a
certain kind of acknowledgement of our conditionedness, call it the
human condition. Can such a portrait of humanity, and such a
therapeutic commitment, really be thought of as spiritually neutral?
To my ear, it rather forms part of a complex lineage in modern
philosophy whose members find it central to philosophy's present
task to settle accounts with Christianity. Like Nietzsche and Heid-
egger, Wittgenstein finds that Christianity's conception of humanity
as at once originally sinful and yet always already open to redemption embodies a vision of the world that must be recovered and
re-presented, recounted otherwise, rather than simply rejected. Is it
his unwavering preoccupation with this inflection of the perennial
human desire to be God that explains why Wittgenstein famously
declared that 'I cannot help seeing every problem from a religious
point of view'?

Bibliography

Diamond, Cora (2000), 'Ethics and Imagination in the *Tractatus*', in *The New
    Wittgenstein*, eds Alice Crary and Rupert Read. London: Routledge.
Taylor, Charles (1989), *Sources of the Self*. Cambridge: Cambridge University
    Press.

16. On Obstacles of the Will

KAI NIELSEN

I

D. Z. Phillips and I are, to put it mildly, at loggerheads. We both think of each other, at least on the issues before us, as a philosophical disaster. We think of each other not only as more than typically confused, but as blinded, caught in obstacles and obstinacies of the will, engaging in apologetics and so on and so on. I see Phillips as at least in effect a preacher mounting the pulpit to preserve religion from any fundamental criticism, while thinking of himself as a neutral contemplator of the actual and the possible operating in a cool place; and he sees me as a fervent – perhaps an evangelical – atheist riding the hearse proclaiming that God is dead and a good thing too. Be that as it may, let us see what can be done.

II

I start by saying something in this section about what Phillips calls my 'four critical categories' and the devious 'apologetic strategy' to which, he has it, I put them. When he characterizes my views, and I *suspect* those of others as well, he gives them a 'creative interpretation'. And I don't mean that as a compliment. He gives a careless and inaccurate reading of me, sometimes even badly misquoting me or, as has already been noted, he creates a figure of straw to use for his own dialectical and apologetic purposes.

His talk about the four critical categories he attributes to me is a good illustration of his 'creativity'. The four categories are the metaphysical, the cosmological, the anthropomorphic and the moral. For starters, revealing Phillips's careless way of going about things, for me 'the cosmo-logical' as I use it is not a distinct category from the metaphysical, but is included in the metaphysical. Indeed I do not appeal to it as a category at all. There is plainly in physics scientific cosmology: a rather speculative side of physics. It may unfortunately have its metaphysical residues but still it is fundamentally a part of physics and when I talk about cosmology I am not concerned with that scientific enterprise. It is unclear what Phillips means by 'cosmology', but I suppose we can safely take it to be some kind of 'metaphysical world-picture' (metaphysics II, as I shall call it) and contrast this metaphysics with a theory of being (metaphysics I). But whether we are talking about metaphysics I or metaphysics II, we still get, on Wittgenstein's understanding, nonsense. But, *for the sake of the discussion*, let Phillips have his four categories. After all they were not of my choosing and they are not mine. I didn't conceive of things in that way, but let's see what sneaky apologetic work Phillips thinks they do. He says Nielsen's 'use of each category has to face Wittgensteinian criticisms of which Nielsen often seems to be aware. Faced by these, in the case of a given category', Nielsen conveniently forgets for the moment that it, too, has Wittgensteinian objections (Chapter 14, p. 284). But I do nothing of the kind. To think what he says here reveals a thorough misunderstanding of what I am doing. Where I speak vis-à-vis of religion (more accurately of theistic religions) of the anthropomorphic, the metaphysical and the moral (a religiously freighted moral), I am giving a diachronic picture, not a synchronic one. In early forms of Judaism and Christianity, the conception of God and the attributes that go with such a conception are standardly crudely anthropomorphic. As these religions developed – or at least changed – as a result of philosophical and theological criticism and greater scientific sophistication in the culture in question, they became less and less anthropomorphic and more and more metaphysical until, with Maimonides, Scotus and Aquinas, and later with Calvin, the conception of God became almost completely metaphysical. As we move into the nineteenth and twentieth centuries and metaphysics becomes increasingly under attack, we get with Friedrich Schleiermacher and Rudolph Otto a conception of God that is even more elusive than the robustly metaphysical conceptions of Aquinas et al. and, as the disenchantment of the world continued to deepen, conceptions of God became even more de-metaphysicalized until we finally get, with Richard Braithwaite and R. M. Hare, a conception of God that is utterly naturalistic. (Remember Hare's remark that 'the transcendent God is bound always to be an idle element in our religious life' [Hare 1973].) Many have thought of the Braithwaite–Hare account as in effect, though certainly not in intention, a *reductio* of what Christianity is. This seems to me right. Religion cannot be understood in those terms and still be seriously *and* clearheadedly entertained as religion (Nielsen 1989a, 172–89). Theologians such as Rudolph Bultmann and Martin Buber have had views that are substantively similar but their accounts veil the naturalism of their views so that they often pass theological and religious muster while Braithwaite's and Hare's do not because their stark naturalistic substance is so evident while Bultmann's and Buber's is not. The obscurity of their writing hides that.

The point of giving this picture, oversimplified in certain ways but sufficient for my purposes here, is that in different historic times within Judaism and Christianity different conceptions of God have held front and centre stage. For an anthropomorphic conception of God empirical objections are crucial. The existence of such a God is testable and has been disconfirmed. That is to say we have very good reasons to say that it is false that such a God exists. However, for a metaphysical God empirical testability is *at best* problematic and claims of incoherence are in order. And, if I am right, such a conception of God is actually incoherent. (But note I am not saying *pace* Phillips, as if I were an essentialist, '*inherently* incoherent'.) For the Braithwaite–Hare characterization where God is reduced to a moral category – if you will, a religious-moral category – consider the objections concerning principally its adequacy for the *expectations* of religious people and secondarily concerning its moral adequacy (Nielsen 1962; Nielsen 1989a, 172–89).

I give this condensed version of something I have on several occasions elaborated on with care (Nielsen 1971, 93–134; Nielsen 1973; Nielsen 1982; Nielsen 1985; Nielsen 1989a). When looking at versions of Christianity that are thoroughly anthropomorphic, a particular sort of criticism is principally in order, namely evidential. When we move to a metaphysical conception of God – the God of Aquinas and of Calvin – where there is no question of a God to be observed or encountered, either directly or indirectly, another type of criticism is in order since we have a radically different conception of God (Hepburn 1958). And again where we have a conception of God that rejects theism altogether, where talk of the transcendent God is taken as just speaking of the meaning of life, another type of criticism is in order (Nielsen 1989a, 172–89). Here the term 'God' does duty for speaking of 'the meaning of life' such that to speak of one is to speak of the other. 'God', on such a conception, does not stand for a transcendent supernatural being but 'God' means the same as 'the meaning of life' or at least is extensionally equivalent to it. That is to say that to speak of God, as Wittgenstein himself said, just comes to speaking of the meaning of life. When this is the conception of God then, to repeat, another type of criticism is in order. There is no shifting back and forth, engaging in what Phillips calls my 'apologetic strategy' – my little dialectical dance – employing *for the same conception of God* one 'critical category' at one time, conveniently forgetting the other criticisms of it while doing so, and then, when difficulties are brought to bear, rhetorically invoking an alternative category, now conveniently 'forgetting, for that moment, that it, too, has to meet Wittgensteinian objections' (Chapter 14, p. 284). There is no circularity at all here, let alone what Phillips rather vaguely calls an 'unprofitable circularity'.

When I criticize a conception of God that identifies God with a belief in the meaning of life or with a categorical prescriptivity (as Wittgenstein appears to do in his 'Lecture on Ethics'), I do not criticize that conception for having a conception of a necessary being transcendent to the world or for having a conception of a desert God – Yahweh – where no one has ever seen this anthropomorphic deity, but who nevertheless is supposedly seeable though never in fact seen. There is no slippery slithering from one 'dialectical category' to another to avoid what otherwise would be crushing criticisms. There is on my part no such dialectical twisting and turning at all. Phillips forgets that my account here is *diachronic* not synchronic. I have been keeping in mind how conceptions of God have developed or at least changed. What we have instead is a figment of Phillips's imagination, which he then turns into 'Nielsen's view' without good reason.

I do have, taking these various conceptions of God diachronically and not synchronically, a sense of the historical progression of these concepts or at least historical change if 'progression' is question begging. We start in the Old Testament with a God that is typically rather crudely anthropomorphic and we end up – junking even a sophisticated theism as we go along – with a post-metaphysical conception of God where in speaking of God we are speaking of the meaning of life or accepting that there are moral imperatives that are categorical or that religious belief is no more than the expression of a moral vision. I then point out – sociologically, if you will – that when such post-metaphysical conceptions of God are *clearly presented*, as they usually are not, most Christians will feel cheated, for what they get with Braithwaite and Hare is plainly in substance atheistic. They feel, and rightly, the life-string of their religion has been cut (Nielsen 1962; Hägerström 1964). This starkness that we find in Braithwaite and Hare is disguised from the plain believer in the writings of Phillips and Buber, for example, by a lot of scarcely intelligible religiose moral-talk linked with associated narratives similarly religious or religiose but again, *if taken literally*, is often scarcely intelligible, for example Phillips's use of the narratives of certain native peoples (Chapter 14, pp. 288–90). They are fine as metaphors or narratives carrying insights that we would do well to remember. But Phillips tries as well to treat them as something *more than* metaphors or stories and thereby ends up in incoherence. He wants to avoid the utterly secular, but to do so he ends up in incoherence.

I have argued that post-metaphysical conceptions of God reduce to a moral core. Religious belief for such conceptions is itself just the expression of a moral vision. This is disguised from us because they are usually wrapped up in religiose verbiage. I have called this morality touched with emotion. Phillips responds rightly, pointing to Wittgenstein's treatment of morality, that the morality of which he speaks is a *religious* morality. But the trouble with such a morality is that it is dependent on either anthropomorphic or (more likely for us) metaphysical elements. We do not get our morality straight. I did not say, as Phillips says I say, that religious ethics – the addition to the secular moral core – is *logically* dependent on metaphysical or anthropomorphic conceptions of God, but I did say they are dependent. The religious person who says God's will *must* be done has as a background belief the belief that God is all powerful, all knowing and perfectly good. So he or she concludes, reasonably, given that background belief, that God's will must be done. For someone who construes 'God' as Wittgenstein and Phillips do, it is, to put it minimally, not so inescapable. Indeed it is not clear on such a Wittgensteinian reading of 'God' that we can even understand what doing 'God's will' means. If, following Wittgenstein, and if I have argued rightly, we see that metaphysical claims are nonsensical, and yet that key religious claims that are doctrinal claims are themselves inescapably metaphysical, then, unless we want to embrace nonsense, we must reject them.

Phillips responds, and he believes rightly, that what Wittgenstein rejects is the misunderstanding of religious belief as something that *logically* entails anthropomorphic and cosmological strands. They obviously cannot be that for then, on Phillips's own conception, they would be either false or incoherent. This being so, such religious beliefs, to the extent they are acceptable, must, it seems to me, be reduced to secular moral beliefs. The *religious* side of religious morality, if this is so, is just emotive rhetoric (Chapter 14, p. 287). But I claim no logical entailments here but only a link which is *inescapable*. There are plenty of things that are inescapable that are not a matter of entailments, for example, without water for a long period you will die, a baby left untended for a considerable time will die, a person utterly without recognition or companionship will not flourish and without something like a reasonably equal or at least equitable distribution of power there will be no genuine democracy. Similarly, though more controversially, without some *believed* metaphysical backup, Christian belief will wither. It will have lost its life-string (Nielsen 1962). Hare's post-metaphysical conception of God clearly does that when, as we have seen, the 'Transcendent God' is thought 'always to be an idle element in our religious life' (Hare 1973). I leave it an open question here whether, without a metaphysical backup – a doctrinal link – we can maintain coherently, without obfuscation, *religious* morality: a *religious* moral vision. There is (assuming for the nonce intelligibility) no *contradiction* in either affirming or denying that. There could be, let us assume, as far as *logical* possibilities go, a morality that is not *substantively* secular. Similarly I leave it an open question whether without some recognition and companionship human beings could live a flourishing life or that without some reasonable equitable dispersal of power we could have a flourishing democracy. These appear at least to be logical possibilities. I guess their denials are not logical contradictions, but some of these things, perhaps all of them, are inescapable all the same. *Mere logical possibilities* are usually not very significant and a Wittgensteinian, of all people, should recognize that. Possibly (logically possibly) there is some reasonable conception of religious morality distinguishable from secular morality that is not a metaphysical religiosity nor does it rely on anthropomorphic conceptions of God. I leave this as possibly a *logical* possibility. But I want to see it filled in with something that is not just religiose moralizing.

When I speak of 'religiose moralizing' here I mean the saying of something in a high literary tone – something that a post-modernist might go in for – that is so unclear and so vague and metaphorical, without even a hint of how to cash the metaphors in, that we are at a loss as to what is being said and at a loss of any way, or at least any reasonably apparent way, of how to put more literally what is being said without invoking at least seemingly mysterious metaphysical elements, while at the same time disavowing metaphysics. This, I believe, is what Phillips, again and again, dishes up for us. Suppose it is said in a poem, 'She heard a fly buzz as she died' and in reacting to it we feel it, though rather obscurely, to be a powerful emotionally contentful sentence. But we also have a philosophical itch to say rather more clearly what it means and we get this response from Phillips: 'It is a grammatical confusion to think that this language is referential or descriptive. It is an expression of value. If we ask what it says, the answer is that *it says itself*' (Phillips 1976, 147 italics mine). But '*It says itself*' is a deviant utterance and the trouble about this deviance is that it is quite unclear what, if anything, it means. I guess it is best taken to be a warning to us not to expect for every sentence a paraphrase that will capture its meaning, and also to be sceptical about whether this remark about paraphrasing is so and how we could determine whether it is. Phillips just leaves us with the obscurity 'It says itself' and with the impression – a kind of giving us to understand we know not what – that something profound is being adverted to or hinted at. Phillips should be less like Gabriel Marcel and more like G. E. Moore including an adapting of Moore's adroit practice of paraphrasing and paraphrasing again to try to capture more adequately what is being said. Moore does not leave us with dark, obscure but profound *sounding* sayings – what I have called religiose moralizings.

Phillips might say in response that I am in effect ignoring Wittgenstein's stress on the importance of pictures. *Perhaps* I am, but saying this does not help much. Stony Indian Walking Buffalo and *some* physicists no doubt have a world-picture, but we need to ask what is a world-picture? Clearly it is not literally a picture. If it is a metaphysical view it is, according to Wittgenstein, and I think rightly, nonsense. If it is instead a symbolic or metaphorical expression of something then we need to know, at least when we are doing philosophy, what it is symbolic of or meta-phorical of. If this is not just difficult to say – which it often is – but cannot be said, we are back in the stew, and, if it is metaphysical, we are also back in the stew, and if it is naturalistic we are also, for religious persons, back in the stew. I do not assert, though I suspect, that a world-picture cannot be anything else. But I await Phillip's or anyone else's alternative characterization of it in clear non-evasive terms.

III

In speaking of contemporary novelists, both Christian and secular, whose writings he examined, Phillips remarks that he 'found again and again, Christian and secular critics who would not let voices, other than those they admired, be themselves' (Chapter 14, p. 301). Then he comments, 'I want to say that it was an obstacle of the will which made these critics do what they did, a conviction that "things can be no other way". I want to say that the same obstacle leads Nielsen to see only the secular in the religious' (Chapter 14, p. 301). Of course that is not what I say. But still that does not touch Phillips's basic point, for what I do say is that the only plausible thing that can be seen, standing where we now stand, in the religious is the secular. The disenchantment and demystification of the world has gone that far. Religious views or orientations not reduced (typically unconsciously) to the secular, I claim, either make false claims or are incoherent. Which they are depends on what kind of religious views they are. But that view of mine still runs afoul of Phillips's point about obstacles of the will. But, perhaps not accurately understanding myself, I do not think that the obstacles of the will business is true of me or of anyone who has sincerely and successfully abandoned what John Dewey called the quest for certainty and has, as well, gone resolutely post-metaphysical. It is not true, that is, of anyone who has integrated the rather different lessons of John Dewey and Ludwig Wittgenstein into a genuinely fallibilist view. They are not going to think or are even going to be unconsciously caught up in the view that things *must* be a certain way or *must* go in a certain way or that they *must* take it, concerning their pet views, that things can be no other way. They no longer have such religious or metaphysical instincts. Such persons will think rather that some ways of viewing things are more plausible or reasonable than others, but all the same it will be the case that, and repeatedly and rightly, matters that we humans take to be of vital interest will be contested and some of the contestants, though of course not all, will be reasonable persons reasonably informed and tolerant. In arguing as I have, I think, hardly surprisingly, that for people standing where we stand, secularism all the way down is a more plausible, more reasonable and a more

morally attractive way of living and thinking than any religious alternative (see Chapter 13 and see Nielsen 2001a, 56–76). But I did not say or
think that for anyone sufficiently rational there can be no other way. I
cannot see that there is another way, but then, of course, I may be
mistaken – indeed perhaps blind about some things. *Perhaps* suffering
from what Phillips calls aspect blindness. None of us are embodiments
of reason marching through history. Reasonable persons will always be
open to the possibility, even the likelihood, that they in some way or
another are in error, that they may even be blind to certain possibilities.
That should be a platitude. If we have any intellectual humility we should
acknowledge that. I would go even further and say, if we are reasonable,
we will recognize what Rawls calls 'the burdens of judgment' and recognize that unfortunately these burdens often are not acknowledged and
not treated as things which are commonsensically evident, though reasonable bits of common sense. Such phenomena point to at least two rather
different things: (1) that fanaticism and *hubris* run deep and (2) that
metaphysical orientations, including unwitting metaphysical orientations, are hard habits to kick. With such phenomena plainly in our
cultural space, we not infrequently get some not easily untangled, and
perhaps untanglable, mixture of obstacles of the intellect and obstacles
of the will. And this blocks enquiry and impedes reflective endorsement.
Perhaps it will always be this way with us, but then again perhaps not.
Or perhaps with more education, more wealth and more security it will
grow weaker. With luck – religious people will speak of God's grace –
we may become able to see things more reasonably than we do now,
have a little more humility and have passions and commitments that are
of more enduring value than those that are now in our possession. We
should hold on to our brains, be reflective about our sentiments, realize
there is no paradise and chase ourselves out of any imagined paradise
that we have deceived ourselves into thinking we have gained or may
gain. With things like this thoroughly ingrained in us, we might, just
might, get something a little bit like a pilgrim's progress.

IV

We live in a world that is increasingly disenchanted. Sometimes it gets
re-enchanted in some places for a while, but where a stability in reasonable wealth obtains and a high level of education obtains the disenchantment prevails. We become aware that there is a surfeit of religions around
(particularly if we go anthropological) with conflicting or at least (if that
notion makes sense) incommensurable claimed revelations and that in
Western cultures at least there are conflicting understandings of morality
and different responses to it are around, including amoralist responses

(Nielsen 1982 and Nielsen 2001b). We are aware, if we have a good philosophical understanding, including a good understanding of the history of philosophical discussions of religion, that we have no sound arguments for or evidences of the existence of God. Or to put things more cautiously, that any claims to a proof of or evidences of God are very, very problematic.[1] We will also be aware that we live in a moral and political wilderness. In such a situation some reflective persons, at some stage in their lives, will ask themselves, 'Should I believe in God?' This is not like an idle metaphysical or epistemological question 'Is time real?' or 'Can we ever know anything?'. With 'belief in God' there are real doubts, not just what Peirce called paper doubts. So not a few people will set out, and not in a *merely* contemplative spirit, on a *quest for God*. They want to ascertain, if they can, whether God exists or even if there is any good reason to believe in God or to be religious. They will soon realize, if they persistently pursue such matters, that there are all kinds of conflicting things that are said here and that among them the sceptical things are very strong. (They will also see, if they are perceptive, that this is quite independent of a *general* philosophical scepticism.) They cannot but ask themselves, if they are serious, whether they should be atheists or agnostics or some kind of sceptic concerning religion and its claims. (This need have here nothing to do with epistemological scepticism.) But that notwithstanding, religion may be very important to them and they may very much want to believe in God yet they may worry about the cogency or the reasonableness of their belief. They may worry about its legitimacy. Here Wittgensteinian Fideism, if on the mark, can help them not just apologetically but rationally as well. If Wittgensteinian Fideism is a justified way of looking at things, it makes no sense to ask if belief in God is reasonable or justified or, for that matter, unreasonable or unjustified. These are, Wittgensteinian Fideists will maintain, pseudo-questions rooted in a misunderstanding of our forms of life, our uses of language and of what philosophy or thought of any kind can achieve.

A person, if Wittgensteinian Fideism is on the mark, is not being unreasonable in believing in God though he should understand that reason does not require it, but it does not, and cannot, undermine it either if the conception of God we have is a proper one. And it will be a proper one, though neither reasonable nor unreasonable, if it is the one that is in accord with what Wittgensteinians and some others call the religious language rooted in our forms of life. This will exclude superstitious, metaphysical and reductive conceptions of God, but if we can obtain a perspicuous representation of our religious discourse we will have a conception of God which cannot be in error and there will and can be no sound grounds for doubting the reality of God, for thinking belief in God rests on a myth, is an illusion or is just a projection of our emotions or anything of the kind. If we have a proper understanding of the use of 'God', Wittgensteinian Fideism has it, belief in any of those sceptical things must be rooted in a failure to understand the workings of our language in its living contexts. If we have a proper understanding of 'God' belief cannot rest on a mistake.

We should recognize the extent in nearly all domains of life, indeed perhaps in all domains of life, of our *groundless believing*. But we should recognize as well that that does not usually make things untoward for us or land us in irrationality (Malcolm 1977). A person's religious belief can be acceptable and indeed crucial for her, yet still, as Norman Malcolm puts it, groundless but perfectly acceptable all the same. This is, when the form of life in question is religious, some from of fideism and Wittgensteinian accounts, or at least the accounts I have called Wittgensteinian, provide what appears to be a reasonable rationale for believers, both simple and sophisticated, to continue with their Christianity, Judaism, Islam, Buddhism, Hinduism and the like in good conscience and without crucifying their intellects or indeed believing anything untoward.

Such an account is surely of deep religious interest in a disenchanted world. It looks as if we could be, if we so chose, religious without engaging in re-enchantment. This being so, it is of considerable significance to human beings, situated as we are, to come to have a clear understanding of Wittgensteinian Fideism and to have a clear understanding of it as something we can perhaps reflectively and knowledgeably endorse.

V

Having posed things in this manner, I now want to conclude this chapter by doing four things. I aim to: (1) briefly articulate what I take to be the core conception of Wittgensteinian Fideism; (2) bring out how, without it effecting how Wittgensteinian Fideism is to be construed, I, in my *Naturalism and Religion* and in discussions with Béla Szabados, created unnecessary perplexities about who is or isn't a Wittgensteinian fideist or a friend of Wittgensteinian Fideism and the like. I explain here how all this is unnecessary and why it should never have been raised; (3) set out my more fundamental criticisms of Wittgensteinian Fideism; and (4) turn to an examination of Phillips's crucial criticisms of me in Section III of Chapter 14.

First, my brief characterization of Wittgensteinian Fideism. It is the view that to imagine a language is to imagine a form of life and that the only thing a *philosopher* can legitimately do is perspicuously display the workings – including the interrelations – of these forms of life and that there is no privileged perch for philosophy or science or history or anything else to assess these forms or life or to enable us to gain religious knowledge, for example, knowledge of whether there is a God, of what he requires of us or of whether we shall have everlasting life. Indeed there is no assessing forms of life, any forms of life, period. They are *our given*: just there like our lives. *Within* a form of life or a mode of discourse there is justification and lack of justification, evidence and proof, mistaken and groundless opinion but one cannot apply these terms to the forms of life or modes of social life themselves. Science is one such mode, morality is another and religion still another. Each has criteria of intelligibility peculiar to itself. *Within* science, morality or religion, actions or beliefs can be reasonable or unreasonable, rational or irrational, justified or unjustified, and beliefs can be worthy of acceptance or not worthy of acceptance and some can be proved and some cannot. But we cannot sensibly speak of modes of social life or forms of life themselves as reasonable or unreasonable, rational or irrational, justified or unjustified. They rather supply the core of our criteria for what is rational and what is not, what is reasonable and what is not. There are no context-independent and form-of-life-independent practice-transcendent criteria of rationality or reasonability by which our modes of social life can be assessed or criticized for they supply our very standards of assessment or criticism and criteria of intelligibility. These standards being peculiar to each mode of social life itself, we cannot relevantly criticize one mode of social life in terms of another. Science cannot legitimately be criticized by criteria distinctive of morality or morality by that of science or religion by either nor can religious criteria be used to assess the reasonability or unintelligibility or legitimacy of morality or science.

However, in stressing the above we should not go on to say that the modes of social thought are Balkanized from each other. They have connections both causal and internal. But this does not undermine their distinctiveness. It is what Wittgenstein would say is a grammatical remark to say that God could not pointlessly torture people. Any being who did that would not be God or at least the Judaeo-Christian-Islamic God. But that notwithstanding, given the distinctiveness of criteria of intelligibility and reasonability peculiar to each mode of social life, what is reasonable and what is not is determined by the mode of social life itself. This being so, it is incoherent on this account to say that religion is irrational or belief in God a myth or an illusion. So, if this account is sound, religion, or indeed any mode of social life, is perfectly protected. There can, as Phillips avers, be criticisms from *within* a mode of social life itself; we can, for example, show that one conception of God is more adequate than another, but we cannot show that the very concept of God is incoherent or unintelligible or that all religious beliefs are in error or that religion rests on an illusion or that belief in God is unreasonable or anything of the like. So if Wittgensteinian Fideism is a telling it like it is (if indeed there is such a telling) we have, as Kenny well puts it, 'a stonewall defense against any demand for a justification of belief in God' (Kenny 1975, 145). The faithful have been protected from the wolves of disbelief and fideism rides triumphant.

However, before I set out something of my critique of Wittgensteinian Fideism, I want to correct an error I slipped into in responding to critics and in having new thoughts about Wittgensteinian Fideism myself. I have come to see, or at least to think I see, that it is a mistake to go around asking who are the Wittgensteinian fideists. What is crucial is to give, as I hope I have just done, a clear characterization of Wittgensteinian Fideism and show that it yields some plausible grounds for being called Wittgensteinian even *if* no Wittgensteinian on record ever held *exactly* that position, took *exactly* that stance. I think it is recognizably Wittgensteinian and as far as particular philosophers go, if the shoe fits, let them wear it. I think it fits for Malcolm and Phillips – though Phillips is not clear enough so that I can be sure – and it fits for at least the early Winch. I am less sure for his later work. But who (if anyone) should wear the shoe doesn't matter a lot. What matters is the position itself and its claims and implications. What matters is whether (on some reasonable reading) it is recognizably Wittgensteinian and whether it has force and is not an arbitrary view.

Probably most Wittgensteinian fideists will be religious, as Malcolm was and Phillips is, but I believe Winch was not. Probably *most* Wittgensteinian fideists will be at least religiously inclined or at least attuned. But what their religious orientation is (or lack thereof) doesn't matter for what I want to say about Wittgensteinian Fideism. What I now realize, as I didn't earlier, is that that does not matter in the slightest. It, to repeat, is the view and its implications that count. A thoroughgoing atheist could be a Wittgensteinian fideist though *probably* a rather resigned, pessimistic and conservative one and not likely to be one to use it, as I believe Phillips and Malcolm do, for apologetic purposes. What would not fit well with Wittgensteinian Fideism are those radical change-the-world atheists such as Holbach, Feuerbach, Nietzsche, Marx, Lenin and (to go to the small fry) myself, Paul Edwards, John Mackie and Walter Kaufmann. But it is possible that even a radical change-the-world atheist, if she did not have metaphysical baggage and rationalistic beliefs – as is perfectly possible – could be a Wittgensteinian. The point is, contrary to what I thought when I wrote *Naturalism and Religion*, that those issues – who is and who is not a Wittgensteinian fideist – are not very philosophically important. That belongs to the gossip columns around philosophy. What is important is the position itself and its cogency and implications. I see Wittgensteinian Fideism as a powerful challenge to a secularism all the way down, for it would deprive secularists of the full strength of their argument that we should – we people standing where we stand now – be secularists all the way down if we want to be non-evasive. That non-rationalist but not irrationalist enlightenment stance would be undermined.

If Wittgensteinian Fideism is the very confused thing that Phillips takes it to be, we could, and should, just forget about it. Put it in the dustbin of history. But if I am near to the mark it is (1) a challenging philosophical position; and (2) a normative challenge concerning how, religiously and morally, we should be and act in the world and how we should conceptualize that.[2] Challenging as it is and, while still feeling its attraction, I also thought, and still think, that there is something very mistaken about Wittgensteinian Fideism and that one does not have to be a rationalist or an heir of the logical positivist tradition, including, as Hilary Putnam sees, Quine and Michael Friedman, to think that is so. In most of my writings concerning religion, from 'Wittgensteinian Fideism' (1967) to my *God, Scepticism, and Modernity* (1989a) to my *Naturalism and Religion* (2001a), I have sought to critique while also sympathetically explicating Wittgensteinian Fideism.[3] I want here briefly to state the criticism I have most persistently deployed and then to add two new ones.

1. The argument I most frequently use and the one Kenny notes and fairly states (Kenny 2002) claims that religions inescapably involve metaphysical beliefs but metaphysical beliefs on Wittgenstein's view are incoherent yet religions are also believed by Wittgenstein and Wittgensteinians to be forms of life and forms of life, they believe, cannot be incoherent. So they end up in a contradiction saying that religion is inescapably both incoherent and coherent.

The standard Wittgensteinian response is to reject the belief that key religious claims are inescapably metaphysical. Historically they were so intertwined, but they need not be, and should not be but should be viewed instead as a matter of a passionate orientation of one's life. I in turn respond, as we have seen, that indeed for genuinely religious persons religion is a matter of a passionate orientation of one's life. But that is only a *necessary* condition for being genuinely religious and for there being religion. Through and through atheists can, and not infrequently do, have a passionate orientation of their lives. Sometimes, that is, such an orientation takes a non-religious or sometimes even an anti-religious form. However, given a Wittgensteinian way of construing things, if it is a passionate orientation of your life then it is a religious response. But that is conversion by stipulative definition. Even Paul Tillich, who was not clear about very much, went around talking of religion as ultimate commitment, but when he was doing theology and not preaching a sermon or giving a popular talk, he insisted that for this ultimate commitment to be a genuinely religious commitment it must be an ultimate commitment to the unconditional ground of being and meaning – the

Ultimate Unconditional, whatever that means. Similarly the person claiming that the 'essence of religion' is a matter of a passionate orientation
of her life needs to distinguish herself from the atheist or the secularist
with a passionate orientation of her life. Both have a passionate orientation of their lives. What distinguishes them is the *object* of that orientation. For religious persons who are Jews, Christians or Muslims, the
object of that orientation is God and the unconditional love on the
believer's part of God. But with that we have metaphysical beliefs. Indeed
with the spelling out of these beliefs additional metaphysical beliefs come
tumbling back again and we are back, as Wittgenstein sees things, to
trying to hold beliefs which are incoherent – so incoherent that they are
unintelligible. We cannot, to escape these difficulties, even move from
being a Wittgensteinian fideist to being a Kierkegaardian one, for we
cannot – logically cannot – have faith in something we do not understand
at all for then we cannot understand what it is we are to have faith in
(Nielsen 1963 and Nielsen 1965).[4]

So Wittgensteinian Fideism is caught in a contradiction. The only
escapes I can see involve (1) rejecting Wittgenstein's belief that metaphysics is nonsense; or (2) claiming that religious belief need not involve
having metaphysical beliefs. But if either such turn is taken we will have
to face the above objections plus, and perhaps even more fundamentally,
the conviction of theists that their religion involves a deeply embedded
belief that without a belief in the transcendent God, and thus the having
of a metaphysical belief, the life blood of their faith will be drained, the
very hopes and beliefs that fuel the passionate orientation of their lives
will be undermined. What gave their faith its strength will be eviscerated.
(I am, of course, here talking of the theistic strands of religious discourses.
Such considerations do not touch a Theravada Buddhist.)

2. A second criticism of Wittgensteinian Fideism is that it neglects the
distinction, to adopt Rudolph Carnap's terminology, between questions
internal to the framework and questions *external* to the framework
(Carnap 1956, 205–21 and E. W. Hall 1964, 106–32).[5] Wittgensteinian
fideists neglect the distinction between justification *within* a system and
justification *of* a system: the latter comes to pragmatic vindication (Feigl
1950). Carnap, who first drew this distinction, pointed out here, unlike
the well-regulated arguments that we can make *within* a system, that in
giving a proof or vindication *of* a system we involve ourselves with a
host of pragmatic considerations: the vitality of the system, the extent
that it answers to our needs and interests, facilitates our flourishing, more
readily gains our reflective endorsement than some other system, fits in
best with other beliefs we have, makes fewer contestable or problematic
assumptions and the like. (See here, as well, Hall 1964 and Feigl 1950).
Things are not as neatly charted here as they often are over questions
internal to the framework or (if you will) to a form of life.[6] But questions

external to the framework are crucial questions for us. And we have resources to respond to them, though lacking the probative force of proofs *within* a system or form of life or of straightforward evidential claims made within a system or form of life, still they have force for us though perhaps never conclusive force. But that should not bother those acculturated into a fallibilistic ethos (Peirce 1998, 44–56). We are never just left with this is what we do around here, this is the language-game we play, this is our form of life, these are our framework beliefs, take them or leave them if you can or perhaps if you wish. We are never in the position – indeed we can never be in the position – where we have reached the *last word* and we *must* just say 'my spade is turned', though we may say that where we *feel* that we have reached bedrock, for example, with 'So what was so wrong with the Holocaust?' Things can pinch so that we can say that we do not want to argue about that, for example, argue about the evil of the Holocaust. We just feel that that would be obscene. But, if pressed, we could. There is never, except sometimes practically speaking, for a reasonable philosophically sophisticated contemporary, 'the last word' and there never was for anybody. It was just that some were under the illusion there was.

Hilary Putnam wonders whether Wittgenstein was a pragmatist, but over the issues gestured at above Wittgenstein and Wittgensteinians are distant from pragmatists – at least pragmatists of the Peircean-Deweyian-Meadian sort (Putnam 1995 and, for a key contrast, Cavell 1998). Normally we do just accept – perhaps better acquiesce – in our forms of life. We are just enculturated into them. Without them we could not reason or think at all or make sense of our lives. But that notwithstanding, we can, though typically with great difficulty, come to question them, change them in certain respects or even in the extreme case to reject at least some of them, though surely not all of them *at once*. Religion, it seems to me, is one of the best candidates here for this, given its bad fit with some of the rest of our beliefs. However, we have to have some practices, though they need not be the same ones, standing fast in any circumstance where questions of vindication arise. Without some practices for the nonce standing fast, we would never be able to question, criticize, reform or reasonably reject, perhaps even reject at all, any other practices. If we try to reject them *all at once* – somehow, without any practices, 'standing beyond' or 'transcending' all our practices – we get incoherence. Pragmatists and Wittgensteinians are agreed on this, but pragmatists, unlike Wittgensteinians, will not take forms of life as being beyond criticism or even beyond reasonable outright rejection.[7]

Most Wittgensteinians will not like Carnap's talk about questions internal to the framework and questions external to the framework or E. W. Hall's talk of proof in a system and proof of a system; and, rightly wary of scientism as they are, they will usually not like talk of systems.

That way of viewing things, they believe, is too regimented, too rational-istic and too scientistic. They prefer, and not without reason, to talk of forms of life, modes of social thought, practices and of language-games. But the same, or at least very similar, considerations as Carnap and Hall bring to bear in talking about proof *in* or justification *in* and distinctly of proof *of* or justification *of* a system can be utilized concerning practices embedded in forms of life or of forms of life themselves. Never transcend-ing practices *überhaupt*, we can, and sometimes do, rebuilding the ship at sea, come to question certain practices and this can lead to question-ing other practices until eventually a whole mode of life, a whole form of life, is so chipped away that it is abandoned and not arbitrarily or groundlessly so. We come to have new practices rather than the old ones. A form of life is abandoned, that is, for good pragmatic reasons. We need not take a form of life as something sacrosanct, permanently given and rationally unquestionable. *Synchronically* something must be given – be there like our lives – but *diachronically* nothing must remain fast though some things very likely will. Everything can at least in principle be questioned, but not everything at once. And those beliefs (or at least some of them) that Wittgenstein calls groundless beliefs may be such that questioning them in most circumstances at least is perfectly pointless or, for some, questioning them is even insane, for example, 'Do you have a head?' (But note asserting 'You don't have a head' would be equally insane.) But at least the pointless ones can be questioned and sometimes with a good point showing that questions here were not really pointless. This seems at least to undermine Wittgensteinian Fideism. Neither religion nor anything else need be permanently shielded and all of this without the invocation of metaphysics or ideology.

There is a third criticism of Wittgensteinian Fideism, a criticism of Davidsonian and Rortian inspiration, but paradoxically it will – or so it seems – involve setting aside the Carnapian-Hallian-rooted criticism just made, resting on a distinction between questions internal to the framework and questions external to the framework. This criticism made by Davidson and Rorty rests on challenging the making or just uncriti-cally assuming an essentially Kantian *distinction between scheme and a ubiquitous content*. It is a Kantian distinction but it is also a distinction, though of Kantian inspiration, that is widely assumed by modern and contemporary philosophers who do not regard themselves as Kantians. It is, to repeat and expand, the distinction between scheme and a ubiquitous content: a sense manifold or a blooming buzzing confusion that is just ubiquitously given. Put otherwise, it is a distinction between, on the one hand, a scheme or set of categories or a set of conceptual distinctions that the mind or language just imposes and, on the other hand, an undifferentiated given. We have the analogy of the cookie cutter (the scheme) imprinting itself on a plate of uniform dough: the pervasive undifferentiated sensuous given. The scheme/content these philosophers have it, must always obtain; without their interaction there would, it is claimed, be no understanding. Concepts without precepts are empty; precepts without concepts are blind. This is the distinction challenged by Davidson (1974, 5–20) and Rorty (1982, 3–18).

Standard sceptical epistemological questions arise from the deployment of this Kantian distinction. There seems to be no reason to believe, if we operate *within* its confines – if we just take the scheme/content distinction as ubiquitous – that we can have any knowledge or understanding of the external world at all. But Davidson and Rorty are not interested in that sceptical worry or more likely pseudo-worry for they think the very distinction between scheme and ubiquitous content is unintelligible (Davidson 1974, 5–20; Rorty 1982, 3–18). We have no way of distinguishing mind and its contents. We are language-using animals with our practices firmly embedded in the world – where else could they be embedded? – which is not identifiable apart from these practices. And we do not have questions external to the framework and questions internal to the framework that are in any fundamental sense different kinds of questions, for we have no inner/outer distinction. There is no intelligible question about how mind or language hooks on to the world. Both are part of the world. Where else could they be? What we always have is part of the world interacting with other parts of the world. There are these big-brained language-using animals – macroscopic objects (though rather distinctive ones) clearly a part of the world with their practices, which are bits of their behaviour, their characteristic ways of acting, but norm-governed all the same. However, there is no access to the norms apart from the behaviour – no discernable acting and doing – that is not rule-governed behaviour. There is no need to reify the norms as existing apart from the behaviour. Indeed we have no understanding of what this would be. And there is no acting and doing that is not norm governed. The scheme/content distinction presupposes the mind/body distinction or language/world distinction but those distinctions, if Davidson and Rorty are at all on the mark, cannot get off the ground.

How is this a criticism of Wittgensteinian Fideism? I should have thought Wittgenstein, having a practice conception of philosophy himself, would welcome what Davidson and Rorty argue here. We can't speak here for Wittgenstein, but Wittgensteinians do not welcome this Davidson–Rorty move for the Davidson–Rorty criticism is of the very pervasive scheme-like idea that there are forms of life that are just given and must just be accepted and that, with these forms of life holding fast, and with, as Malcolm puts it, these framework beliefs in place, we can go on to justify certain things, establish certain things as reasonable or unreasonable, true or false, but no question can intelligibly be raised of the truth or falsity, reasonability or unreasonability of these alleged framework beliefs or the forms of life themselves. There is no conceptual space, on Wittgenstein's way of looking at things, for that, for these forms of life are just given like our lives. They are, that is, just there like our lives. But these 'framework beliefs' embedded in forms of life are treated by Wittgenstein and Wittgensteinians like schemes that can at another time and in another context come into question. And here they begin moving out of Wittgensteinian Fideism. There are no forms of life – conceptual or grammatical schemes or frameworks – that are forever and that in *any context* are just given and must just be accepted. There is nothing that so stands in such a strong and ubiquitous way. And with this Wittgensteinian Fideism collapses. And with that religious believers are no longer protected – insured against all climes and times – from the wolves of disbelief.

VI

I come now to Phillips's criticisms of me in Section III of Chapter 14. There Phillips turns to a central issue between us, namely whether, as he puts it quoting me, 'if one proceeds in philosophy in a Wittgensteinian way [that] "this means that no philosophical or any other kind of reasonable criticism, or for that matter defence, is possible of forms of life"' (Chapter 14, p. 246). Phillips wants very much 'to lay to rest, once and for all, his [my] conviction' that this is Wittgenstein's view or the view of Wittgensteinians such as himself, Winch or Malcolm. Here he again creates a straw Nielsen. As I have repeatedly made clear, I claim that the Wittgensteinians' claim was that no criticism of a form of life is possible that would allow us to say that a form of life itself (assuming that it was a genuine form of life) was irrational or unreasonable such that it would even make sense, let alone to say that it would be justified, or that would allow us to say that a form of life was incoherent, rested on a myth or an illusion, was unreasonable or irrational and that for any of these reasons that a form of life was to be rejected. The Wittgensteinian claim is that no such *fundamental* criticisms of a form of life can even be intelligibly made, let alone rationally or reasonably made. I cited plenty of chapter and verse for that. Phillips seems at least to accept this and, Phillips apart, indeed it is a fundamental belief for Wittgenstein and Wittgensteinians.

When Phillips says forms of life can be criticized he means nothing at such a fundamental level such that we could be justified, or even coherently assert, that a form of life was unreasonable or irrational and to be set aside. When he speaks of forms of life being criticizable he does not mean criticism at such a deep level. We can, he rightly says, discover some metaphysical or conceptual confusions in *some* of the ways that

some philosophers talk about a form of life, or in some of the superstitious beliefs that some religious believers attach to their conception of
forms of life or in how they appeal to certain theological interpretations
(e.g. confused conceptions of predestination) that make, if accepted, nonsense out of morality or to contradictions between *some* scientific beliefs
and *some* believers' conceptions of some rather superstitious religious
beliefs about, for example, the age of the earth. Moreover, there can be
conflicts concerning values (conflicts concerning what is taken to be
really humanly important) between people accepting a certain religious
tradition and some secularists. Sometimes for some of these issues, there
can, and should be, some philosophical (i.e. conceptual) untangling of
these conflicts or tensions. But – and this is the crucial point here – at no
point does Phillips or any other Wittgensteinian make a conceptual space
that would allow any criticism to push so far as to claim legitimately
that we have evidence, grounds or sufficient reasons for saying that the
form of life that religion is or is part of (take your choice) is such that it
is unreasonable and is to be set aside. And that, after all, is what is at
issue between people I have called Wittgensteinian fideists and myself.
Phillips just dances around this. That is, he evades the issue. If we have,
given a form of life, a perspicuous representation such that we clearly
see what it is, so that nothing is lacking here by way of clarification or
elucidation, there is nothing of a critical kind we can say of these forms
of life. If we have a clear command of our language-games making up
our practices, which taken together constitute our forms of life, there can
be, if Wittgensteinians are right, nothing left to assume or to criticize for
we are given with this our very *norms* of assessment. There is, as we
have seen, no Archimedean point outside our practices with which to
assess our practices so that we could justify a form of life or show it to
be unreasonable or irrational. Phillips, I fear, has not laid to rest what is
for him 'the ghost of Wittgensteinian Fideism'.

 This, I take it, is the central consideration that Phillips wishes to deploy
in laying to rest what he takes to be that bit of bad philosophy that is
Wittgensteinian Fideism. But he also has a number of subsidiary claims,
some linked with something of an argument. Again they seem to me to
rest on various confusions or on misconstruals of my views. I shall
consider them briefly. In rejecting metaphysics, criticizing religion and
assessing Wittgensteinian Fideism, Nielsen, Phillips has it, shows 'a yearning for a metaphysical replacement for the systems of metaphysics he
attacks' (Chapter 14, p. 291). Well, as I have already made clear, I am
not on the quest for certainty; fallibilism for me is the name of the game.
I appeal to or yearn for no *synthetic a priori truths*. I seek no foundations,
nor do I yearn for them, to underpin our practices (Nielsen 1995). I don't
even understand what that would come to. In what sense, then, if at all,
do I yearn for a metaphysical replacement for the systems of metaphysics

I attack? This is something Phillips must say is unconscious with me, but what evidence does he have for that claim?

For Phillips I think the key to it is in my talk of a philosophy of life, a notion, and understandably, of which Phillips is very suspicious. A philosophy of life could, and sometimes has, turned into the worst sort of moralizing – a smelly little ideology. He opposes to that what he calls a *contemplative* conception of philosophy that sticks to striving for perspicuous representation and eschews normative argument or an articulating of a way of life and avoids efforts, as a bit of philosophy, to change the world no matter how reflectively and carefully argued. Philosophy conceived as contemplation will have no truck or trade with anything normative, with anything that would guide conduct or seek to orient our lives. Perhaps, because he seems at least to be rather apolitical and individualistic, he sees a philosophy of life as exclusively a *personal* quest, while for me a philosophy of life is centrally social. It is, or at least should be, an attempt by us to try, not only to decide how we should live our lives as individuals, but also to set out how we should live our lives together and to try to ascertain what our social order should be like and to find, or more likely to forge, a view of things – principally of social things – that is a little more reasonable and closer to something we would reflectively endorse than the rather inchoate one we habitually carry around with us under our hats (to gesture here at a remark by William James). A philosophy of life, as I see it and have articulated it, would be an attempt by us, in the broadest possible sense, to see how things hang together in the broadest sense of the term (Nielsen 1996 and Nielsen 2001a). But in advocating such an attempt, I am clearly not talking about self-help books and the assorted *schmaltz* we typically find in the philosophy section of airport bookstores.

It is also important to make clear in trying to come to grips with the problems of life that we cannot reasonably do this in an a priori way. We observe and reflect, draw inferences, set out hypotheses or conjectures and then test them, in whatever ways are appropriate, and in doing these things try to see how things hang together and look at what we have done and then endorse what we take to be the best fit, squaring with our considered judgements, that we can for a time forge (Scanlon 2003). Whatever for a time we forge here will have repeatedly to be revised. Permanence is a false assurance of a pre-post-metaphysical age: a time before the fly got out of the fly bottle.

In doing this we have a crucial place where we use the method of wide reflective equilibrium. Winch, and Phillips following him, show their utter failure to understand wide reflective equilibrium when they point out that agreements need not be benign. Reflective equilibrium does not just seek consensus or agreement but agreement that rests on a set of consistent beliefs, well supported by evidence (where this is relevant), considered judgements and always beliefs which are reasonable in the sense that they aim to be such that no reasonable person could reject them.[8] If that does not obtain or could be made to obtain by people reflectively deliberating and acting together and then reflectively and with integrity endorsing the conclusions that emerged from their impartial and mutually respectful deliberation, we do not have something that is a considered judgement in wide reflective equilibrium.

This conception is light years away from Winch's haughty and ignorant judgement – ignorant about what reflective equilibrium is – that agreement arrived at in reflective equilibrium 'can suffer from intolerable smugness which ignores or distorts real differences'.[9] This is precisely what it does not do or cannot allow, for if it did it would not be reflective equilibrium. Moreover (*pace* Phillips), such a deployment of reflective equilibrium, far from being distant from Wittgenstein's alleged 'contemplative conception of philosophy', fits nicely with it.

Philosophy, recall, is not the name of a natural kind and it does not have an essence. (Surely Phillips should not just grudgingly acknowledge but applaud that. What kind of Wittgensteinian would he be if he did not?) Philosophy as in Wittgensteinian therapeutic analysis – if you will, anti-philosophy philosophy (Nielsen 1994) – tries to make evident the nonsense that is disguised nonsense in metaphysical views and in the traditional problems of philosophy that most professors of philosophy try to sucker students of Philosophy 101 into taking seriously. Philosophy conceived in this therapeutic manner is sometimes one useful thing that philosophy can do as is, as well, when carefully constrained, philosophy as contemplation. But so is philosophy as normative critique and articulation.[10] These are different activities but not incompatible unless made so by *arbitrary* stipulation claiming just *one* of these activities to be 'real philosophy' or 'true philosophy' (Nielsen 1993, 4).[11] Phillips just arbitrarily selects his horse and rides it, thinking of it exclusively as 'proper philosophy'. (This itself is hardly done in a contemplative spirit. The tides of ideology are running high here.)

I take philosophy as contemplation *as but one conception* of philosophy among others. Philosophy of life is another and, often takes as a back-up for philosophy of life, philosophy as normative articulation and critique is still another. I take this activity very seriously (again *pace* Phillips). But this, to be worth anything, must be a disciplined critique and articulation utilizing careful elucidatory work of philosophers, work becoming increasingly marginalized, and, for the most part, lacking in cultural significance, with little critical clout and only sometimes relevant to philosophy as normative articulation and critique. However, I take Wittgensteinian therapeutic analysis as a crucial propaedeutic to a disciplined and clear-headed engaging in philosophy as normative articulation and critique. It cuts down the warbling, the hot air and its irrelevance to the problems of life: something that neither philosophy as contemplation Phillips's style nor traditional description, explanation and demanding elucidation of what can be soundly argued and reasonably reflectively endorsed does much to cut down. Otherwise a philosophy of life turns into mush, engaging in warbling and sweet singing. It is ideology without awareness, that is, preaching without awareness (and even with a denial) that it is preaching. This deserves the scorn that both Wittgenstein and Carnap heaped on it.

Wittgensteinian philosophy as therapeutic analysis is, to repeat, a crucial propaedeutic. It sweeps away the debris so that philosophy in a good Deweyan spirit as normative articulation and critique without metaphysical encumbrances and distractions can get on with its business. If we ever get to a situation where a post-metaphysical philosophy is a secure paradigm, where the revolution in philosophy has securely triumphed and we have a genuinely Kuhnian paradigm shift and no counter-revolution is in sight, we can let the Wittgensteinian propaedeutic wither on the vine. We will no longer need it.

My *Naturalism Without Foundations* and my *Naturalism and Religion* do not limit themselves to setting out, explicating and defending some fundamental conceptions. They also engage in a normative examination and critique of our condition and of our prospects, standing where we are now in the world. I try to say something in a disciplined, informed and hopefully perspicuous and reflective way concerning what is to be done. Such a normative philosophy is concerned with our coming to grips with our lives without evasion or self-deception. Such efforts are, philosophically speaking, as old as the hills and some (indeed most) have been done in very problematic ways. They have been tied to metaphysical, theological and foundationalist accounts where they often have given *lebensphilosophical* accounts a bad name. They have been obfuscating and sometimes ideological.[12] But while this is often so there is no necessity that this be so. Philosophies of life justly have a bad name – evoking a sneer or dismay by many who are serious – because sloppy thinkers and schmaltzing Matildas are so common among philosophers so engaged. Perhaps because Phillips can imagine no alternatives in philosophy between philosophy being an activity dominated by schmaltzing Matildas and being an activity dominated by philosophers attempting to offer in a clear normatively neutral manner, at least in intent, descriptions of 'the logic of our discourses and their relations one to another' that he cannot bring into focus, in philosophy at least, an activity that is neither schmaltzing nor *parti pris* proclaiming, on the one hand, nor *just* normatively neutral conceptual description and perspicuous representation on the other. Delete the scientism and hang-ups with verificationism and Phillips's account of philosophy is very like that of the logical positivists. He erects for himself an exclusive and exhaustive divide and then is blind to other possibilities. Many of us, repulsed by the phenomena of schmaltzing Matildas hinting at depth when they only offer obscure empty verbiage, depressed by scientistic types with their narrowness and blindness to things that matter most to many human beings and often to themselves when they do not have their blinkers on, and disgusted by metaphysicians who just jazz things up to no avail, turn away from philosophy altogether and abandon the attempt at having anything like a reflective reasonable overview of our lives. Like John Dewey, I think there is something more for philosophy to do and I try to make a stab at that, or the beginnings of that, in *Naturalism Without Foundations* and *Naturalism and Religion*. Phillips thinks that is love's labour lost, but that is because he is so blind to the very possibility of a disciplined, empirically responsible, critical normative articulation and critique of our forms of life – of our asking and answering (fallibilistically, of course) what sorts of life among the actualities and possibilities thrown up by our actual living and striving are most worthy of our endorsement. He thinks in a kind of individualistic Protestant fashion that is something we can only finally decide for ourselves, speaking in the first person. It *may* well be that such deciding for ourselves may even be a conceptual necessity. Conceptual necessity or not, this is so whether there is a lot of deliberating together or the influence of what has been deliberated where being felt through by others bears heavily on the decisions and choices we make. But we never choose in a social and historical vacuum. So in trying to sort out how we should live collectively and individually and what should be done in our world and in seeking to ascertain whether, and if so how, to think and feel through what this would in general terms come to, we (1) need to deliberate together for this could never just be an individual project; and (2) must seek something in the sense previously specified that no reasonable person could reject where this is understood in a Scanlonian-Rawlsian fashion. We have here an informed, reflective intersubjectivity that is the strongest sense of objectivity that we can in such contexts attain or even need (Davidson 2001). The resulting philosophy of life will be based on such a seeing of how things hang together in the widest manner and in the most general sense of 'hang together'. It will also be rooted in what we, in the light of informed and impartial reflection, most care about and could reflectively endorse. Such things will be central ingredients in any reasonable world-view that we could come to have.

Phillips would presumably say that in articulating such a world-view, as I do in *Naturalism without Foundations* and *Naturalism and Religion*, I have given voice to what he calls my 'yearning for a metaphysical replacement for the systems of metaphysics he [Nielsen] attacks' (Chapter 14, p. 291). What I have just articulated is indeed holistic, but that is neither necessary nor sufficient to make it metaphysical. A 'metaphysical world-view' is *not* pleonastic. Seeing how things hang together makes no claim to even the possibility of completeness. In articulating and defending a normative (though not only normative) contextualist, non-scientistic naturalistic world-view, what I set out is fallibilistic, does not deploy transcendental arguments or appeal to *synthetic* a priori propositions, foundational principles, esoteric non-naturalistic characterizable conceptions, truths which are not warrantedly assertable and the like. There is nothing in my conception that the philosophical tradition would recognize as metaphysical (Nielsen 1995). Surely, in a way Wittgenstein would disapprove of, I try holistically to ascertain how things hang together. But how does that make this effort metaphysical? It may make it unrealistically utopian perhaps; perhaps it is only a heuristic to be approximated; perhaps it is something that distracts us from what is really important. But then we need to say something about what is important and as well show how such philosophical concerns distract us from concern with it (Nielsen 1995).

Isn't it just a central part of what it is to be reasonable to want, if we can, to see things steadily where we can, see how the various things that are important to us fit together, if they do, into a coherent whole? Maybe they don't; maybe, using the method of wide reflective equilibrium, we will not be able to forge such a coherent conception of how things hang together. But that would be a human loss and if we are reflective and reasonable we will acknowledge that is so. But remembering that conceptions of coherence admit of degrees and that there are approximations of seeing things steadily and seeing them whole, we have no good reason for thinking such a thing is not approximatable and desirable – something that reasonable people would like to see obtain and make at least some small effort towards the realization of (Nielsen 1995).

Neither Phillips nor Winch have given us good reason to think such an approximation is not possible or desirable or that inquiry into it and an attempt to articulate and assess such a normative order is beyond anything that philosophy can reasonably aspire to. They have not given us any reason to believe that the use of the method of wide reflective equilibrium messes up such a normative endeavour or pushes it in complacent conservative directions, diverting our attention away from what may be tragic irreconcilabilities with the complacent belief that there will be an answer for everything if only we search hard and long enough. But that is not a consequence of reflective equilibrium or of my naturalistic world-view. It *may* be a consequence of scientism but that is a quite different matter. And it is not a matter of having the rationalistic belief that there *must* be a reason for everything.

VII

There is a further connected matter that I believe is of considerable importance where Phillips alerts us to a conception of philosophy articulated by Winch that is different from anything I have previously considered here or in my earlier chapters. Though it does not, as far as I can see, touch the conceptions I have characterized as Wittgensteinian Fideism, it alerts us to different conceptions that are also Wittgensteinian in content and inspiration and which give us an alternative Wittgensteinian way of doing philosophy than the one that I have articulated. It is important to recognize that it does not replace the therapeutic one I have articulated and that it is compatible with Wittgensteinian Fideism but certainly does not require it.

Phillips sets out this Winchian conception as follows:

> Winch points out that while a stage is sometimes used for monologues, or for plays with a didactic purpose, these are minority occasions. The main use of the stage is to represent segments of life, as faithfully as possible, which involve a number of different voices; voices which may end in tragic irreconcilability. One need only think of Shakespeare. But Winch points out that there is a comparable philosophical tradition which he finds in Plato's early dialogues, in Kierkegaard's pseudonymous works, and in Wittgenstein's struggles with the voices in his *Investigations*. It is 'a philosophical tradition which has concerned itself precisely with the problem of how to present moral or religious world-views in such a way that the passion behind them, which has to be evident if one is to recognize them for what they are, is clearly in view, along with a conception of the good that they embody, while at the same time equal justice is done to alternative and even hostile conceptions'. As Winch says, 'Achieving this is a task of enormous difficulty, both at the technical level and also because of the moral demands it makes on the writer who will him or herself have strong moral or religious commitments and will also be hostile to other possibilities'. (Chapter 14, pp. 298–9, quoting Winch)

This is an attractive way of thinking about and doing philosophy, which is little in evidence in Wittgensteinian Fideism or in my critique of it or in my critique of Phillips or Phillips's critique of me or in his remarks about philosophy and about secularism. None of these things proceed in this spirit, nor does philosophy as therapeutic analysis, nor does (at least directly) philosophy as a normative guide and/or as normative critique. We are in debt to Winch for putting the matter so clearly and forcibly and it is something that should be integrated without evasion in our practice as philosophers.

Now consider Phillips, building on this, in his final paragraph of Section III. There Phillips remarks:

> Wittgenstein said, 'My ideal is a certain coolness. A temple providing a setting for the passions without meddling with them.' Wittgenstein is not ignoring the passions – the matters of the heart that concern Nielsen – he provides a setting for them. But he doesn't want to meddle with them. He wants them to be themselves. One way of meddling with them is to make them subject to a Nielsen-like 'philosophy of life'. The objections to such a 'philosophy' are not intellectually difficult to grasp, but its lure is very strong. To give that up, if we are in the grip of it, involves overcoming an obstacle of the will. (Chapter 14, p. 299, quoting Wittgenstein's *Culture and Value*, p. 2e)

But this is almost certainly mistaken, revealing an overly narrow conception, but still a penetrating conception, of philosophy. It is penetrating in that it attempts to keep, without meddling, in full view the passion behind religious or moral world-views. This is something, as I remarked in discussing Winch, that is seldom done when we do philosophy either in characterizing moral and religious world-views (philosophies of life, as it were) or in trying to appraise them philosophically. But philosophers, such as William James and Simone Weil perceptively saw that these matters were crucial for understanding what is going on in religion, religious morality or secular morality and in orienting one's life religiously, non-religiously or anti-religiously. We need, as Winch stressed, to have these matters and their relations with each other on full, clear and sympathetic display. We can hardly reasonably critique with integrity and force until we have these matters clearly before us. Critique and normative construction or articulation clearly must, if they are to yield anything of acceptable substance, have that before us. Moreover, strong moral passion often, *perhaps* even usually, should not be something with which we should meddle. But also, clearly, meddling should not be proscribed. Sometimes meddling is mandatory. Some primitive societies have brutal initiation rites, which sometimes cause great pain and lasting harm to certain people in the society – female circumcision is a vivid example – but strong moral passions are linked with these rites. It is not obvious, to put it mildly, that we should *not* meddle with some of these passions unless it is the case that eveything considered we would by doing so cause more pain and more harm all around. Then, it would seem, we should not intervene. But even here such consequentialism may not be the decisive thing. However, the crucial point is that it certainly appears to be the case that there are situations where the passions should be meddled with. Moreover, there are other cases alive and well in our societies of which similar things should be said. The Catholic Church even faced with the horrendous harm caused by AIDS still disapproves of the use of contraceptives and for some Catholics (though not all) their passions are tied up with that belief. Is it so clear we should not meddle with the passions here? It seems, to put it mildly, that we should. Or consider that in the time of Ferdinand and Isabella, with the aid of the Inquisition and the Spanish Church hierarchy, Spain ethnically cleansed Muslims and Jews, murdering them in great numbers or (for those lucky enough not to be murdered) driving them from Spain, and as well the Church–State allegiance destroyed a great library of Arabic documents central not only to Arabic culture but to Western culture as well. Powerful passions deeply rooted in religion and the state were invoked and were involved there. Should there have been no meddling with the passions? To even ask the question is to answer it. Similar things should be said about the Turks' often vicious slaughter of Christian Armenians who were seen as the infidel corrupting the land or now for Hindus murdering Muslims and Muslims murdering Christians and Jews murdering Palestinians. It seems at least to be plainly evil *not* in such situations to meddle with the passions if we can. If Wittgenstein and Winch, as Phillips says, want without meddling with them to let them be themselves, they plainly have in this respect an unthought out and impoverished moral view. (Or can they legitimately say this is all distant from philosophy? But still the impoverished moral view causing severely damaged lives hangs on. Does philosophy have nothing to say about this?) Wittgenstein, it might be said, should have stuck to the things he was really good at, like showing that there can be no private languages or a genuine problem of other minds or of the external world or of epistemological scepticism.

The reminders I have assembled using his own and G. E. Moore's technique of translating into the concrete and of using *reductio* arguments, undermines Wittgenstein's claim that we, at least in doing philosophy, 'should provide a setting for the passions without meddling with them.' The obvious and correct thing to say about that is sometimes yes and sometimes no. Sometimes yes, we should meddle with the passions and sometimes no, we shouldn't, and sometimes we do not know what to say and do.

Let me give one more case where meddling is in order that is not like the gruesome cases I have used above. Suppose a talented and intelligent and reflective young woman wanting to go to university very much has been raised in a very religiously orthodox family. It could be Jewish, Christian or Islamic. Suppose further she has a brother who is untalented, not very energetic and not very interested in going to university. But she still feels, given the orthodox ambience of her life, that she should, following the family's wishes, step aside so that her brother can go. (I am assuming they do not have the resources to send them both.) She recognizes both his lack of talent and lack of interest beyond securing for himself a better job with minimum effort. But she feels so strongly the pull of her religion that says that even in such situations males should take precedence over females. Holding fast to this belief, she sacrifices herself for her brother with the full support and urging of her family. Is there no reasonable case for meddling with the passions here? In talking about morality and in thinking seriously about morality we should criticize such a way of looking at things and argue that such a moral point of view is irrational and deeply destructive of human flourishing. Is there any case at all for claiming that in saying this we are just being ethnocentric and giving voice to a liberal morality? *Maybe*, everything considered, passions shouldn't be meddled with even here, but there is at least, to understate it, a strong *prima facie* case for such meddling.

Counter-examples to Wittgenstein's and Phillips's claim concerning philosophy – a claim Phillips makes much of – come trippingly on the tongue. It hardly withstands translating into the concrete. It makes one think that they have not thought deeply and carefully about the moral life. It is particularly difficult (some might say outrageous) to think *that* of Wittgenstein, who was both so intensely concerned with the moral life and so incredibly perceptive concerning plainly philosophical matters, for example, the problems he confronts in the *Philosophical Investigations*. With Phillips the explanation is a little more obvious; he is plainly blinkered by his arbitrary constraining philosophy to contemplation and not allowing any role for normatively critical *philosophy*. That kept him from seeing what is plainly before his eyes. Should we here speak of the distorting effect of obstacles to the will? Genuine philosophy, he has it, must just be contemplative and nothing else! But this is just arbitrarily asserting a 'must' here and unwittingly engaging in a *persuasive* definition.

VIII

I have responded to what I take to be the most crucial criticisms that Phillips has to make of me in Section III of Chapter 14. I now turn briefly to some other objections he makes, which I take (perhaps mistakenly) to be less crucial. In handling them briefly I may create the *appearance* of being dogmatic but that is dictated solely by the necessity of saving space.

1. Phillips maintains that many of my claims will be seen as groundless once we distinguish between the grammatical and the sociological uses of 'practice'. That is a very un-Wittgensteinian point. But that aside, there are no such separate uses of 'practice'. A practice, as rule-governed,

has both normative and factual components and, like the descriptive and evaluative components of 'rude' or 'fearsome' they cannot be unscrambled into distinct uses.

2. Phillips claims that there are ways of looking at the world that are not commensurable (Chapter 14, p. 292). I, following Donald Davidson and the later Richard Rorty, deny that beliefs are incommensurable. The most fundamental form of alleged forms of incommensurability is to claim that there are terms expressive of concepts that are not in any way translatable into terms of another language such that there are concepts (uses of terms) of a speaker of language A that cannot be translated or in any way paraphrased in language B. There are concepts of language A that can in no way be understood by someone using language B or any other language and who does not understand language A. But if this were so we could not know that it was so. All we could know is that no one had yet succeeded in translating into language B the terms expressive of some concept or concepts of A into language B. To the users of language B they just sound like noises. But we have no genuine cases of where this is so. There are as a matter of fact no untranslatable languages or concepts of some language that, directly or indirectly, are not translatable. That *perhaps* there could be does not establish that there is. Given the track record of successful translation there is no good reason to believe that there are some concepts which are untranslatable and thus incommensurable.

Some theories do not claim incommensurability with respect to untranslatability but incommensurability with respect to *justification*. It is claimed that some theories are incommensurable with respect to justification because they so deeply differ about fundamental forms of reasoning. But we could differ in this way without our beliefs being incommensurable. I might be an ordinary language philosopher and adopt fundamentally different forms of reasoning than that of a Carnapian formalist without it being true that our beliefs are, or even could be, incommensurable with respect to justification. It would not follow that we disagreed and disagreed about justification such that we could know, or have good reason to believe, that we had reached bedrock such that we could know that there was nothing further that we could say to each other that might lead to agreement. We could only know *that* if we could know that our beliefs would be non-comparable and we could only know *that* if we could know that they were untranslatable, either directly or indirectly, into each other and, as we have seen, we cannot know that. All we can know is that if p adopts form of reasoning y it makes it very difficult for s, who does not adopt form of reasoning y but form of reasoning w, to understand p or to be understood by p. But that does not show that it is impossible and that is what is required for incommensurability.

Finally, someone might claim that two views are incommensurable
with respect to appraisal in the sense that sometimes we cannot intelligibly claim that theory or account N is superior to theory or account M.
But the only way this evaluative incommensurability could be established
is by showing that N and M are in evaluative incommensurability. And
this would be to show that they are incommensurable justificatorily or
by way of being untranslatable into each other. But we have seen that
there is no good reason to believe in justificatory incommensurability or
in incommensurable meanings or uses. We could never discover that the
latter was so and this being so the latter rests on a dogmatic claim. And
it is always possible that a justification could be found just as it is always
possible that commensurable evaluative criteria could be found. The
fundamental form of incommensurability claims is that of meaning or
use incommensurability: *untranslatability*. (When he does so in the next
chapter, Phillips gives a characterization which is both vacuous and
eccentric.) But all known languages are translatable and if M was
untranslatable into N or to any other language we would never be able
to discern it. Phillips does not clearly say what he means by 'commensurability' or 'incommensurability'. But on any of the familiar claims to 'being
incommensurable' there is no good reason to believe that commensurability (*pace* Phillips) rests on a mistake. We have no good reason to
believe there are any incommensurable concepts or beliefs.

3. Phillips claims that while we 'offer descriptions, true or false, in
various contexts, . . . the language in which we do so is not itself a
description of anything. Because he thinks otherwise, Nielsen is led into
saying that Wittgenstein and Wittgensteinians are "set against the idea
that there could be a one true description of the world". But if I say there
is a chair in a room or that a person is lying when in fact there is a chair
in the room or the person is lying, I have given two true descriptions of
the world' (Chapter 14, pp. 293–4). In spite of sounding here like a good
Moorean common-sense philosopher, Phillips is confused. He thinks
because I somehow mistakenly think that language 'is not itself a description of anything', it is a mistake to say that there is a one true description
of the world. But it does not follow from that fact (if it is a fact) that
there is *one true* description of the world. Imagine an Inuit who had
never seen or heard of a chair but who knows English. Where the ordinary speaker of English would truly say 'There is a chair in the room',
the Inuit could as truly say 'There is some firewood in the room'; or an
English-speaking Amazonian who had never learned the word 'chair' or
had such a concept could as truly say 'There is some wood for making
paddles in the room'. All three statements can be true and none *is the
one true description of the world*. Which one will be appropriate to say
will depend on the interests, the enculturation of the speakers and the
situation they are in. Similar things obtain for saying a person is lying.

We do have, depending on who we are, how we are situated and what our purposes are, alternative descriptions, all of which may be true but none of which is the one true description of reality (even in that situation) and that does not at all mean that 'truth is relative'. (Phillips should have studied carefully Hilary Putnam and Richard Rorty.)

4. Phillips maintains I have a confused conception of criticism. I do not see, he has it, where criticism is not a matter of criticizing conceptual confusion but where instead we criticize someone who is not confused, or at least may not be confused, for the stance she takes towards life. There Phillips remarks we are criticizing someone in terms *of the very values themselves that they take or hold toward life.* (Could this *for him* be a matter of philosophy?) These are contexts where we get a clash of values – sometimes a tragic clash of values. Phillips tells us what 'needs to be faced here is the issue of what is meant by the reality in values and the character of criticism when different evaluative points of view criticize each other' (Chapter 14, p. 294). We need properly to understand the place concepts occupy in our practices. Criticism there takes the form 'of criticism *in terms of the values themselves.* In contexts such as these, *we do not have reasons for our values, our values are our reasons*' (Chapter 14, p. 294, latter italics mine). Well, sometimes they are and sometimes they are not. Suppose I am asked, as I was asked during the conference, whether religion is, everything considered, a bad thing. Some will say we are in no position to determine or even reasonably conjecture anything like that and people who say that may be either believers or non-believers. But some believers and some non-believers will bite that bullet. Some believers will say, though religion sometimes does harm, it is, everything considered, a good thing that people are religious. Some atheists, say Nietzsche or Marx, will deny this. Some atheists will point to the harm that religion does, the diminishment of human flourishing it engenders and the credulity it gives rise to and with this the lack of clarity about oneself and the world one lives in. In such situations one gives reasons for holding the values one does. Perhaps inadequate reasons but reasons all the same. At other times our reasons are our values. Sometimes, for example, we seem at least to run out of reasons. I say, for example, that we must treat people – all people – with respect and add that the life of everyone is to count and to count equally. A tough-minded Nietzschean anti-egalitarian faces me and says that that is just an egalitarian prejudice of mine. We can offer reasons for and against my egalitarian claims but it might not – probably will not – get us anywhere with the Nietzschean. I *may* finally get to the point with the Nietzschean where I just give expression to my values and assert that people must be treated with respect and I further assert that the life of everyone matters and matters equally. Here I appeal to my values. *Here* they are my reasons. I can't in that situation back off them. But there is no rule here. Sometimes in very

fundamental contexts 'we do not have reasons for our values; our values are our reasons' *and* sometimes not and sometimes, indeed frequently, our reasons and our values are so intermingled that we have no way, except arbitrarily, of asserting one thing or the other (Nielsen 1985, 13–41). Phillips, as we have seen, too often lives on a one-sided diet. There is no *one way* to so describe a clash of values and he too easily assumes there will be ultimate clashes of value where nothing more can be said.

5. Phillips returns to his misunderstanding of wide reflective equilibrium but now from a different angle. I claim, Phillips thinks mistakenly, that when certain religious notions make such a bad fit with many other things that are very pervasive in our culture, among believers and non-believers alike, that it is important to us, in coming to understand that and taking into account its import, to come to recognize that there is very little, if any, sense in these religious notions.

There is nothing tautological (though Phillips without argument says there is) about my claim. But without pursuing that unsupported claim of his, Phillips contends 'Nielsen has not earned his confident use of "us" and "we". What people will take to be "fitting" or "not fitting" varies' (Chapter 14, p. 297). Well of course it does, but we native speakers of some natural language can and do often agree about what fits and doesn't fit and we can, and sometimes do, make mistakes about this, but we will agree that if Hans is in the room and sitting in a chair and speaking, he has a bodily identity and occupies space in the room at a particular time and place. To say he has a spiritual identity and has no body does not fit with these other things we competent speakers of a natural language (in this case English) can recognize or can readily be brought to recognize. It is *not* the case that what, between beliefs in situations such as this, is fitting or not fitting varies or is in some instances perhaps not settleable. We can often recognize in a particular context what fits and does not fit and there often is no dispute about that.

Then Phillips goes on to say, 'Even if something does not fit, that in itself would settle nothing for those once called "upsetters of the world".' But the 'upsetters of the world', to settle anything, would have to provide us with value judgements or considered judgements that had such an overwhelming appeal and an *initial credibility* that they outweighed the other considered judgements taken together. Otherwise the reasonable thing to do would be to reform through modification, or even reject, the belief that keeps us from having a consistent set. Consistency and coherence, having a bunch of beliefs that fit together, is something that reasonable creatures prize. If the belief that does not fit with the rest has initial credibility and is a value judgement that is much prized and seems on reflection crucial to us, then *perhaps* some other adjustment should be made in the belief set but nothing like this has been shown to be the case where religious belief is concerned. If this is felt to be cultural genocide people must sincerely ask what are we to do when, after considerable reflection, we still find one belief conflicting with the mass of other beliefs. We have carefully searched for a fit, but have not been able to find one. We are faced with the choice between just living with what appears at least to be an inconsistency (as the Azande did) with its resulting incoherence or modifying or perhaps even rejecting the conflicting religious belief. I am saying that the reasonable thing here for persons aware of the choice is to modify the religious belief, if that belief does not fit with the rest, until we have a coherent set or, if that cannot be done, to reject the conflicting religious belief. That is not callously and thoughtlessly to throw out the religious belief. We should try very hard to see if it can be made to fit. Moreover, if the religious belief is strong enough some other adjustment will perhaps have to be made for the one who has a *deep need* to religiously believe. Still there is at least a prima facie deficit in reasonability here.

I do not claim an exclusive atheistic appropriation of integrity. My point was to show that integrity is at risk if we do not push the deliberation (*pace* Winch) as far as it can go. If we continue to accept a belief conflicting with the mass of other beliefs we also accept and that is furthermore plainly shown to be in conflict with the other consistently held beliefs we firmly accept our integrity is under threat when we clearly see that. That is not atheistic *hubris*, but just what it is to be reasonable. *If* that be rationalism, so be it.

IX

I have sought in this chapter and in the ones preceding it as well to articulate (hopefully perspicuously) what I have called Wittgensteinian Fideism against various charges brought against it, principally by D. Z. Phillips. I have said what it is, shown how it is Wittgensteinian, and shown how it provides a considerable challenge to a naturalistic thinking about religion and how this challenge is to be met and how and why Wittgensteinian Fideism is not the poor, confused thing that Phillips scorns.

Notes

1 The history of attempts to in some way prove God's existence and the move away from such attempts in later religious thought is particularly evident. A new attempt at proving the existence of God is likely to provoke a yawn in most of us.

2 I actually would not make such a sharp separation between (1) and (2) as the above remark suggests. I am too much of a pragmatist and anti-essentialist for that. I let it stand in this context in deference to tradition but I do so with some misgivings.

3 Three essays that nicely show the progression of my thought are reprinted in Mostafa Faghfoury, ed., *Analytical Philosophy of Religion in Canada* (University of Ottawa Press, 1982, 71–124). See also Benoît Graceu's comment on them in his 'On Dining with the Meta-theological Skeptic' (Faghfoury 1982, 125–37).

4 It might be thought that I am deploying a royal 'we' here. But surely there is a considerable, though by no means universal, consensus among philosophers and theologians that what I have said in the last two sentences above is so. To most people that might very well be mistaken, but that is not to the point. The truth of the above two sentences (if they are true) as *a sociological fact* is sufficient to justify my use of 'we' and 'our'. *Perhaps* the remarks above should be softened to the remark that it is widely believed among most present day philosophers and theologians that these claims are true. That would be sufficient for my purpose. I am not trying to establish truth by a claim about what most of us *say*. But remember my claim cuts across believers and non-believers alike who are philosophers or theologians.

5 Hall does not use Carnap's terminology but very similar distinctions are being made that are crucial for what I say above.

6 Most Wittgensteinians will not like the juxtaposition of 'system' and 'framework' with 'forms of life'. The former two are at least too scientistic sounding for them. But whatever we want to say here, the distinction between questions *external to* and *interior to* or justification *within* and justification *of* applies in both cases. We could be speaking of 'forms of life' or of 'modes of social living' rather than 'system' or 'framework' and still make much the same distinction.

7 The objection that Phillips keeps putting to me is also not to the point here, as it was not on the other occasions previously discussed in one or another of the chapters in this volume. If all we mean by criticizing a form of life is that we are offering some more perspicuous articulation of it, or scrubbing away some accretion to it resulting from bad philosophy, then criticism can be made. But, as I have repeatedly pointed out, what Wittgensteinians repeatedly *reject* is fundamental criticism that would justify rejection of a form of life. They stick with proof *in* and justification *in* and arbitrarily rule out questions of proof *of* or justification *of* as bad incoherent metaphysical questions that no one would pose if one had a good understanding of what one was doing. This I have challenged.

8 As for an unanalysed, unexplicated 'reasonable' popping up at the end, like a logical primitive, we should say of it that we have an old-as-Socrates sense of the concept 'reasonable' working that has been pervasive in the history of at least Western Culture and that does not leave us completely at sea. See McCarthy (1994), Nielsen (1998) and Mandle (1999). A reasonable person will be impartial, fair, aware of what Rawls calls the *burdens of judgement* and act within the constraints of those burdens. She will pay attention to evidence where that is relevant, follow the force, or try to follow the force, of the better deliberation or, where relevant, and the force of the better argument. That we work in a circle of terms which are interdefinable does not mean we have a vicious circle. The size and nature of the circle is relevant here. See here Rawls (1999, 86–7 and 177).

9 Quoted by Phillips, Chapter 14, p. 298, from a remark correctly attributed to Winch, p. 392, voice J in Timothy Tessin and Mario von der Ruhr, eds., *Philosophy and the Grammar of Religious Belief* (New York: St Martin's Press, 1995).

10 Anthony Kenny in effect gives a constrained reading of this Phillipsian conception of philosophy which he attributes to Wittgenstein and shows that it is in Wittgenstein and indicates ways in which it is not incompatible with Wittgenstein's more negative therapeutic conception of philosophy. See Kenny (1982, 4–10).

11 I am not suggesting by any means that these exhaust the conceptions of philosophy. Let many flowers bloom, even though some of them – perhaps many of them – may turn out to be weeds.

12 There have been foundationalist accounts that have not been obscurantist. Sometimes 'foundationalism' is taken in such a *wide* way that any clear, rationally argued account will count as foundational thereby turning Blanshard, Quine, Rawls and Davidson into foundationalists by stipulative re-definition. Other times this error has been avoided while claiming that if we appeal to considered judgements as Rawls, Daniels, Scanlon and I do, we have appealed to basic beliefs which are foundational. But a considered judgement is not like a sense-datum or a qualia supposedly is. Something that is a considered judgement has in itself a nest of relations. To be *considered* it could not stand by itself as an expression of a kind of protocol sentence. I am thankful to Jocelyne Couture for discussion on this matter.

Bibliography

Carnap, Rudolf (1956), *Meaning and Necessity*. Chicago, IL: University of Chicago Press.

Cavell, Stanley (1998), 'What's the Use of Calling Emerson a Pragmatist?' in Morris Dickstein, ed., *The Revival of Pragmatism: New Essays on Social Thought, Law, and Culture*. Durham, NE: Duke University Press, pp. 72–83.

Davidson, Donald (1974), 'On the Very Idea of a Conceptual Scheme.' *Proceedings and Addresses of the American Philosophical Association*, Vol. 47, pp. 5–20.

—— (2001), *Subjective, Intersubjective, Objective*. New York: Oxford University Press.

Faghfoury, Mostafa (ed.) (1982): *Analytical Philosophy of Religion in Canada*. Ottawa: University of Ottawa Press.

Feigl, Herbert (1950), '*De Principus Non Disputandum* . . . ? On the Meaning and Limits of Justification' in Max Black, ed., *Philosophical Analyses: A Collection of Essays*. Ithaca, NY: Cornell University Press, pp. 119–56.

Hägerström, Axel (1964), *Philosophy and Religion*. Translated by Robert T. Sandin. London: George Allen & Unwin.

Hall, E. W. (1964), *Categorial Analysis*. Chapel Hill, NC: University of North Carolina Press.

Hare, R. M. (1973), 'The Simple Believer' in *Religion and Morality*, edited by Gene Outlean and John H. Reeder Jr. New York: Anchor Press, pp. 393–427.

Hepburn, Ronald (1958), *Christianity and Paradox*. London: C. A. Watts.

Kenny, Anthony (1975), 'In Defense of God.' *The Times Literary Supplement* February 7, p. 145.

—— (1982), 'Wittgenstein on the Nature of Philosophy' in Brian McGuinness, ed., *Wittgenstein and His Times*. Chicago, IL: University of Chicago Press, pp. 1–26.

—— (2002), 'A Genial Solitude.' *The Time Literary Supplement* January 18, p. 281.

Malcolm. Norman (1977), 'The Groundlessness of Belief' in Stuart C. Brown, ed., *Reason and Religion*. Ithaca, NY: Cornell University Press, pp. 186–90.

Mandle, Jon (1999), 'The Reasonable in Justice as Fairness.' *The Canadian Journal of Philosophy* Vol. 29, no. 1.

McCarthy, Thomas (1994), 'Kantian Constructivism and Reconciliation: Rush and Habermas in Dialogue,' *Ethics* vol. 105, no. 1 (October), pp. 50–68.

Nielsen, Kai (1962), 'On Speaking of God.' *Theoria* Vol. 28, pp. 110–37.

—— (1963), 'Can Faith Validate God-Talk?' *Theology Today* Vol. 20, pp. 173–84.

—— (1965), 'Religious Perplexity and Faith.' *Crane Review* Vol. 8, no. 1, pp. 1–17.

—— (1967), 'Wittgensteinian Fideism.' *Philosophy* Vol. XLII, no. 161, pp. 191–209.

—— (1971), *Contemporary Critiques of Religion*, London: Macmillan.

—— (1973), *Scepticism*. New York: St Martin's Press.

—— (1982), *An Introduction to the Philosophy of Religion*. London: Macmillan Press.

—— (1985), *Equality and Liberty: A Defense of Radical Egalitarianism*. Totowa, NJ: Rowman and Allenheld.

—— (1989a), *God, Scepticism, and Modernity*. Ottawa: University of Ottawa Press.

—— (1989b), *Why Be Moral?* Buffalo, NY: Prometheus Press.

—— (1993), 'Is "True Philosophy" Like "True Art?"?' *Philosophic Exchange*, pp. 107–23.

—— (1994), 'Anti-Philosophy: Some Programmatic Remarks.' *Diálogos* Vol. 64, pp. 149–58.

—— (1995), *On Transforming Philosophy: A Metaphilosophical Inquiry*. Boulder, CO: Westview Press.

—— (1996), *Naturalism Without Foundations*. Amherst, NY: Prometheus Press.

—— (1998), 'Liberal Reasonability as a Critical Tool? Reflections After Rawls.' *Dialogue*, pp. 739–59.

—— (2001a), *Naturalism and Religion*. Amherst, NY: Prometheus Press.

—— (2001b), 'Moral Point of View' in L. Becker and C. Becker, eds., *Encyclopedia of Ethics* Volume II, second edition, pp. 1141–45).

Peirce, C. S. (1998), *The Essential Peirce, Volume 2 (1891–1915)*. Edited by the Peirce Edition Project. Bloomington, IN: University of Indiana Press.

Phillips, D. Z. (1976) *Religion Without Explanation*. Oxford: Blackwell.

Putnam, Hilary (1995), *Pragmatism*. Oxford: Blackwell.

Rawls, John (1999), *The Law of Peoples*. Cambridge, MA: Harvard University Press.

Rorty, Richard (1982), *Consequences of Pragmatism*. Minneapolis: University of Minnesota Press.

Scanlon, Thomas (2003), 'Rawls on Justification' in Samuel Freeman, ed., *The Cambridge Companion to Rawls*. Cambridge: Cambridge University Press, 139–67.

Sellars, Wilfrid (1963), *Science, Perception and Reality*. London: Routledge & Kegan Paul.

Tessin, Timony and Von Der Ruhr, Mario (eds) (1995), *Philosophy and the Grammar of Religious Belief*. New York: St Martin's Press.

Wittgenstein, Ludwig (1953), *Philosophical Investigations*. Translated by G. E. M. Anscombe. Oxford; Basil Blackwell.

—— (1984): *Culture and Value*. Oxford: Basil Blackwell.

17. Wittgenstein: Contemplation and Cultural Criticism

D. Z. PHILLIPS

I   Philosophical Deadlock?

Kai Nielsen thinks that our discussions have ended in philosophical deadlock. He begins Chapter 16 as follows:

> D. Z. Phillips and I are, to put it mildly, at loggerheads. We both think of each other, at least on the issues before us, as a philosophical disaster ... I see Phillips as at least in effect as a preacher mounting the pulpit to preserve religion from any fundamental criticism, while thinking of himself as a neutral contemplator of the actual and the possible operating in a cool place; and he sees me as a fervent – perhaps an evangelical – atheist riding the hearse proclaiming that God is dead and a good thing too. (p. 311)

For Nielsen, my calling 'Wittgensteinian Fideism' an unscholarly term, simply shows that I have not understood what he means by it. If I did, I would regard it, as he does, as the most powerful contemporary challenge to natuaralism and secularism. His reaction notwithstanding, I do not share Nielsen's pessimistic view of our discussions. There have been changes in the course of them. Nielsen now thinks that it is a mistake to worry too much over who can and cannot be called a Wittgensteinian fideist. More importantly, from my point of view, as we shall see in the present chapter, is his admission that perhaps no one has ever held the view quite as he described it (see section III, pp. 317–18). For my part, I have come to appreciate, more than I did at the outset of our discussions, why Nielsen finds Wittgensteinian Fideism to be such a powerful challenge to his position. More importantly, I should have conceded, as I shall do later in this chapter, that some of the ways in which Wittgenstein and Wittgensteinians have talked, at some stages of their discussion, would give grounds for ascribing something like Wittgensteinian Fideism to them.

Such changes, however, are minor compared with what I think can be achieved. What is more, the progress to be made depends on nothing more than paying attention to the logical issues that have arisen in our discussions so far. The issues to be discussed would involve the relation of religion to metaphysics, belief and atheism, cultural criticism, and the nature of enquiry. Progress between Nielsen and myself on all these fronts would be progress indeed, and I admit that one huge difficulty, which will be with us to the end, stands in the way. Examples play an enormous role in Wittgenstein's philosophy, but when I provide religious examples, drawing on the power of literature, Nielsen says that they do no philosophical work. There is no denying the enormity of this difficulty, and I shall return to it. Nevertheless, before we reach that point, I believe that progress can be made on a range of relevant philosophical issues. I am unlikely to make any progress at all, however, unless I can convince Nielsen that I do understand the powerful challenge he finds in Wittgensteinian Fideism. I hope to do so, at this early stage, by putting in my own words his philosophical frustration with me, in this respect.

For Phillips, 'Wittgensteinian Fideism' is a term of abuse. Why can't he appreciate the respect I have for a powerful point of view I find in Malcolm, Winch and himself? Why does he think I have returned to this topic again and again, over the years, if I did not find it challenging? I do not return to consider Swinburne's appeals to probability, or the dogmatism I find in Reformed epistemology. These philosophers write as though Wittgenstein had never existed. No doubt their views dominate contemporary philosophy of religion, but this simply puts the philosophical clock back as far as I am concerned. Wittgenstein's work is quite a different matter. It has had a deep influence on Malcolm, Winch and Phillips. Well, it has had a deep influence on me too. I think that Wittgenstein's view that all forms of discourse do not have a common form, and that they are not answerable to a transcendent reason, independent of them, are deep philosophical insights. But I also think that these insights have been developed in problematic ways. Language is said to be made up of distinct modes of discourse. Science is one such mode, religion is another. Within each mode of discourse, there are criteria by which beliefs and claims are assessed, and criteria by which mistakes are identified and corrected. These modes of discourse are not isolated from each other, but although they bear on each other in innumerable ways, they retain their conceptual distinctiveness. As a result, it is argued, while justifications can be found within modes of discourse, it makes no sense to ask for a justification of a mode of discourse as such. Armed with such a view, religious believers, in our disenchanted world, can adhere to their beliefs, immune to fundamental criticism. Why, given all this, can't Phillips see what a powerful challenge Wittgensteinianism is to my naturalism and atheism? It is the most powerful challenge to secularism in our culture. Yet Phillips treats it as such a poor thing! How ironic it is that Phillips can so misrepresent a tradition he is part of, while I, though outside that tradition, can appreciate its power and find it eminently worthy of critical, philosophical engagement.

Despite his respect for Wittgensteinian Fideism, Nielsen thinks it is ethically and politically imperative to expose its confusions. For Nielsen, as Béla Szabados says in his introduction to this volume,

> Wittgenstein's philosophical outlook is ethically and politically irre-sponsible, since its attitude of quietism leads us to a pernicious disen-gagement from the world and robs us of the critical tools to assess our culture and change it for the better. To put it bluntly, a philosophy that leaves everything where it is hinders the struggle for social justice, peace and human flourishing. It is an obstacle to human solidarity. (p. 4)

Why, then, despite all this, do I continue to think, along with Rush Rhees, that the effect of the phenomenon of Wittgensteinian Fideism has been to deflect us from the *logical* issues that are at the forefront of Wittgenstein's work? My bold claim, in this concluding chapter, is that, if we pay attention to these logical issues, we shall actually *advance* our understanding of the possibility of cultural criticism, which Nielsen, rightly, wants to protect. Nielsen thinks that Wittgenstein's views threaten this possibility, but it is worth paying attention to Szabados's reaction to this claim: 'It may strike some as ironic that one of the deepest critics of our culture, concerned with its reanimation, is charged with complacency and quietism' (p. 4).

The irony Szabados refers to consists in the fact that one of the con-cepts in our culture that Wittgenstein reanimates is *the concept of criti-cism*. Criticism is rescued from what philosophy tries to make of it. By reflecting on contexts where *real* criticisms have their life, these criticisms, including the most radical, are allowed to be themselves. So far from advocating quietism, Wittgensteinian contemplation allows real battles to be themselves.

Apologists need to pay attention to the logic of criticism. Nielsen's primary interest in Wittgensteinian Fideism is apologetic. He sees it as a *challenge* to his naturalism and atheism. It is difficult for him to accept that my interests are not of the same kind. He sees us as locked in an apologetic battle. If I claim to be reflecting on the logic of criticism in a cool place, Nielsen accuses me of self-deception.

If my aims were apologetic, my hope, in discussing with Nielsen, would be his *conversion*. I have no such aim, whereas he wants to lead people from the darkness of religion to the light of atheism. Neither am I engaged in the negative apologetics of Reformed epistemology, committed to showing that, to date, no intellectual attack on the rationality of religion has been successful. Wittgensteinian reflection allows belief and atheism to be themselves. It rescues *both* from the intellectualist fantasies that so often surround them. That is why, even if Nielsen's interests are apologetic, he has good reason to heed the logic of criticism. At least, Nielsen and I can agree that we want disagreements to be real disagreements, free from philosophical shadowplay.

II   'No Last Word' – An Intellectualist Fantasy

It is an intellectualist fantasy to think that the integrity of criticism demands a culture in which *any* question can be asked. It is confused to argue that, while it may be *practically* unprofitable to ask a further question, *it always makes sense to do so*. Nielsen accuses Wittgensteinian Fideism, via the notions of a 'form of life', or 'world-view', of closing down that possibility of asking the further question. The logically prior question, however, is whether the possibility of always asking a further question, thought of as the cornerstone of intellectual criticism, is even a coherent idea. An attempt to make this possibility coherent is found in Nielsen's apologia for what he calls 'a fallibilistic ethos'.

> We are never just left with this is what we do around here, this is the language-game we play, this is our form of life, these are our framework beliefs, take them or leave them if you can or perhaps if you wish. We are never in the position – indeed we can never be in the position – where we have reached the *last word* and we *must* just say 'my spade is turned', though we may say that where we *feel* that we have reached bedrock, for example, with, 'So what was so wrong with the Holocaust?' Things can pinch us so that we can say that we do not want to argue about that, for example, argue about the evil of the Holocaust. We just feel that that would be obscene. But, if pressed, we could. There is never, except sometimes practically speaking, for a reasonable philosophically sophisticated contemporary, 'the last word' and there never was for anybody. It was just that some were under the illusion there was. (Chapter 16, p. 325)

I want to counter these claims, initially, by considering some of Wittgenstein's arguments in *On Certainty* with respect to scientific explanation and our day-to-day dealings with empirical matters. I shall do so via the notion of 'world-picture', which Nielsen regards as a Wittgensteinian aberration and an obstacle to appreciating his fallibilistic ethos. He says that he awaits an explanation of it in non-evasive terms (see p. 317).

It will be useful to begin with Rush Rhees's comparison of Wittgenstein's conception of philosophy with that of G. E. Moore's 'In Defense of Common Sense' (2001). Moore wants to defend certain propositions against the assaults of the sceptics. In this respect, Moore could be said to want an error-free philosophy. When the sceptic says that we cannot know whether a picture of the world is the true one, Moore wants a philosophy that will enable him to reply, 'Yes, we can.' On this view, a philosopher is someone who *establishes* that a picture of the world is the right one. To use Nielsen's language, it is a philosophy that provides a 'last word'. What of Wittgenstein? Rhees writes,

> Wittgenstein's use of 'world-picture' is different from that. Wittgenstein wouldn't say it is the task of philosophy to *establish* a world-picture, to show that it was the *right* one, or that it could be *known*. He wouldn't call it *the* right one, since it may undergo changes. There are also the differences between peoples. So Wittgenstein isn't saying anything about *the* structure of the world. (Rhees, 2003, 89)

So far, these remarks should be quite congenial to Nielsen's insistence that we are never in a position to have a 'last word'. This conclusion seems to be reinforced when Wittgenstein compares a scientific culture with one devoid of science, and concludes that neither can be said to have *the* right picture of the world. In reaching this conclusion, Rhees insists, 'Wittgenstein is not presenting a form of relativism: each man has the right to regard his world picture as *the* right one. That is not Wittgenstein's use of world-picture' (Rhees 2003, 89).

At this point, Nielsen begins to feel uneasy, since he regards any appeal to cultural incommensurabilities as an appeal to 'last words' that prevent further questions from being asked, for example, about magical or religious practices. Nielsen claims that I have never made clear what I mean by 'incommensurability'. He wonders whether I mean that certain aspects of a culture *cannot* be understood by another culture, or translated into its language. I hold no such thesis. I am saying that when we understand the multiplicity of concepts in our own and other cultures, we see that they are not all of the same kind. They are *conceptually incommensurable*. If they were commensurable, they could all be talked and argued about in the same way. Nielsen's difficulty puzzles Mulhall (see Chapter 15) as it puzzles me, since, as Mulhall says, Nielsen would surely not deny important conceptual differences between moral, political and aesthetic concepts (see p. 308). In his very first chapter, Nielsen says, 'if we try to construe moral statements as if they were empirical statements, and moral reasoning as if it were scientific reasoning, we would make nonsense out of morality. We have learned to treat these concepts and modes of reasoning as being *sui generis*' (p. 23). Here,

Nielsen is pointing out conceptual incommensurables. He has no objection to doing so. His objection is to saying that religious concepts are ever examples of it. This is because he thinks that religious beliefs are either false or incoherent.

There are times when Nielsen is attracted to my appeal to conceptual incommensurabilities. He thinks 'There is something here which is important and has . . . a "ring of truth" about it' (see Chapter 5, p. 79 and Chapter 7, p. 138). The ring does not last long since, unlike his caution with regard to so treating morality, Nielsen does treat magical and religious practices, often, as though they were inadequate or false instances of scientific reasoning. Nielsen would say of the Azande belief in witchcraft, as Rhees says others have done,

> these people do not know a lot that we know. And let them be ever so sure of their belief – they are wrong and we know it.
>
> If we compare our system of knowledge with theirs then theirs is inevitably the poorer one by far. (Wittgenstein 1969, para. 286)

For Rhees, this reaction not only ignores conceptual incommensurabilities, but also succumbs to what Nielsen says he wants to avoid doing, namely, giving one view of the world the 'last word'. Rhees shows why we should resist doing so. He imagines someone asking whether we can really imagine inhabitants of a non-scientific culture getting better results than we do by our scientific methods. Rhees replies,

> I do not think they would get the results as well by other methods. I.e. they would not develop our engineering and our medicine and our industry. They would not know the answers to the problems in physics and problems in chemistry and problems in biology and other methods. They would not *have* these problems.
>
> There is a tendency to ask: 'Aren't our methods the best fitted for finding out what there really is: for finding out what the world is like?' whereas: they are best fitted for finding out what scientists do find out. (Rhees, 2003, 74–5)

An *absolute* conception of reality, *the* right picture of the world, would be one beyond the scientific and the oracle-seeking cultures, by which they could be assessed. It would be the 'last word' about the world. For a thinker like Max Horkheimer, that absolute conception is unattainable due to the limitations of our finitude.[1] For Wittgenstein, the conception makes no sense. So far, Nielsen would agree with Wittgenstein, rather than with Horkheimer. Where Wittgenstein would not agree with Nielsen, is in the latter's claim that we are *never* in any position where we have a last word, where our spade is turned. It all depends what one means. If all Nielsen means by his fallibilism is that there is no *necessity* for a culture to have scientific or magical practices, all well and good. As we have seen, Rhees says that Wittgenstein would not speak of *the* world-view partly because of differences between peoples. 'Fallibilism' is still an odd word to use in this context, since there is nothing 'fallible', in the normal sense of that term, in having the interests they pursue. But let that pass. The important point is that it does not follow from this conclusion that it *always* makes sense to ask a further question about anything in relation to these practices, or to ask it of every general feature of the practice itself.

Take a simple example. Does it always make sense to ask for a further justification of whether I am confronted by a chair? When I see a chair in a room, isn't that the last word on the matter? Nielsen is reluctant to admit this, because someone devoid of the concept of the chair may only see wood in the room (Chapter 16, p. 340). But this changes the context. There is no 'last word' about what is in the room *must* mean; we didn't have to have the concept of a chair. But what if we *are* talking about the concept 'chair'. Won't there be 'last words' in connection with it, in the sense that further questions would be unintelligible? In fact, in order to grasp any concept, we must see that certain questions simply do not arise. It is the same with the mathematical series 2, 4, 8, 10 . . . There comes a point where one cannot ask, 'And how do you know you are going on in the same way?' In fact, one can say that unless there were a 'last word', there could not be a 'first word' either. In grasping *any* concept, we also learn what not to say with respect to it. To go on to say such things would not be the mark of intellectual rigour, but an intellectualist fantasy. These points are not affected by the fact that circumstances may change. At other times, it is difficult to know what 'change' would mean. If I were thrown into doubt over my name (what I go by), my friends, my familiar surroundings, I'd think I was going insane!

There are not only 'last words', in the sense specified, about particular things within a practice, but also about general features of a practice. A culture need not have science, but, given scientific practices, does it make sense to seek a general justification of its inductive procedures?

Wittgenstein in *On Certainty*, shows that a scientific world-picture is not a hypothesis about the world, but the element, the mode of thought, *in* which we think about the world. With respect to it, certain questions *do* not arise. Notice, Wittgenstein does not say that they *cannot* arise, but that they *do* not. He is not invoking a transcendental logic, or necessary conditions of sense, but pointing to certain features *in* our scientific thinking.

A child may ask a scientist, 'Why are you arguing like that?' The answer would be an initiation into inductive reasoning, not a justification of it. When experiments go awry, the same methods are appealed to in locating the mistake. Rhees writes,

> Suppose you say that a certain theory is now not probable. Or suppose you want to dispute the claims that have been made for it. You may examine reports of the experiments and say that they do not support the theory: these occurrences could be explained more simply otherwise; this effect was due to something in the apparatus, etc. – Here your criticisms themselves presuppose an accepted technique. You are relying on induction when you say it is '*due to*' something in the apparatus, and so on.
>
> So that if anyone were to ask, 'But why does this make it possible that . . .', we should wait for him to state the particular objection. And the objection would operate *within* the developed technique of setting up and testing theories. (Rhees 2003, 76–7)

Rhees asks us to contrast this familiar context of justifying scientific conclusions, with a request to justify the reliance on tests at all. He imagines this request coming from a tribe

> Who has never heard of experiments or of putting forward theories to be tested, [but] were told what scientists had done. If they were to ask 'But why does that make it probable that . . .' you wouldn't know what to answer, and you wouldn't know what they were asking. (Rhees 2003, 77)

Showing that certain questions simply do not arise with respect to science's inductive procedures, is not to restrict their critical effectiveness. Ruling out the unintelligible is not a restriction of criticism, but a condition of it. In exposing the intellectualist fantasy of open-endedness, with no 'last word' in any situation, Wittgenstein reanimates criticism by refusing to cut it loose from the very surroundings in which it has its life.

III   The Collapse of Wittgensteinian Fideism

What is Nielsen's likely reaction to the conclusions reached in the previous section? I think he would say that the discussions, especially those relating to the inductive procedures of science, confirm his attribution of Wittgensteinian Fideism to Wittgenstein and his followers. The discussions seem to depend on a distinction between criticisms which can be made *within* a framework, and the framework itself which is immune to criticism. What is this if not pure Wittgensteinian Fideism? Further, Nielsen is likely to see the argument as an apologetic preparation for application to religion, since, if criticisms can be made within frameworks, but never of frameworks themselves, it will follow that religious frameworks, like all others, will be immune to criticism. And *that*, as Nielsen tells us over and over again, in every chapter, is the essence of Wittgensteinian Fideism. It is at this point that Nielsen hopes to deliver a fatal blow to the whole conception:

> These 'framework beliefs' embedded in forms of life are treated by Wittgenstein and Wittgensteinians like schemes that can at another time and in another context come into question . . . There are no forms of life – conceptual or grammatical schemes or frameworks – that are forever and that in *any context* are just given and must just be accepted. There is nothing that so stands in such a strong and ubiquitous way. And with this Wittgensteinian Fideism collapses. (Chapter 16, p. 328)

What if I could show that, in the considered view of Wittgenstein and most of the Wittgensteinians Nielsen criticizes, Nielsen's version of Wittgensteinian Fideism cannot be sustained? What if I can show that they actually *work through Nielsen's distinction between frameworks and their contents and end up by rejecting it*? Then, Nielsen, surely, would have to concede that he was mistaken in attributing Wittgensteinian Fideism to Wittgenstein and those followers. Wittgensteinian Fideism would indeed collapse, but not because it could not withstand the weight of Nielsen's criticisms, but because, as Wittgenstein's considered view, it never existed in the first place! This is why I called it an unscholarly term. The texts do not support it. This is not as harsh a criticism as Nielsen takes it to be, because *in the course of arriving at* their considered view, Wittgenstein and the Wittgensteinians *work through a position* that does resemble Nielsen's notion. So although, *in the end*, the term is unscholarly, the twists and turns in the philosophical discussion can easily tempt, not only Nielsen, but other Wittgensteinians, to see, in Wittgenstein, a distinction between criticisms within a framework and uncriticizable frameworks. To see the distinction there is not a simple mistake, but a powerful temptation. Nevertheless, to succumb to it, is to create something called 'Wittgensteinian Fideism', which neither Wittgenstein, nor most of the Wittgensteinians Nielsen criticizes hold. In the remainder of this section of the chapter, I hope to establish these conclusions.

Chapter 16 is, without doubt, Nielsen's most powerful attack on Wittgensteinian Fideism. It is meant to show why Wittgenstein, Rhees, Winch and myself cannot rid ourselves of its yoke. Nielsen's attack is two-pronged, depending on whether or not we allow the distinction between frameworks, schemes or systems, and what goes on within them.

What if, along with Carnap, we allow the distinction, and insist that frameworks cannot be criticized because they cannot be said to be true or false? Nielsen's reply is that it is evident that this claim cannot be sustained, because we can ask whether the framework itself 'answers to our needs and interests, facilitates our flourishing, more readily gains our reflective endorsement than some other system, fits in best with other beliefs' (p. 324).

What if, on the other hand, we agree with Davidson, that the whole distinction between frameworks and schemes, and what goes on within them, is a bogus one? Nielsen thinks that the distinction *is* bogus. Once we accept the Kantian distinction between 'an unformed sensory given', and the conceptual schemes we impose on it, we open the door to scepticism, since how could we ever know that these schemes reflect reality? What Davidson and Rorty have shown, according to Nielsen, is that we should not accept the Kantian distinction in the first place.

We are language-using animals, with our practices firmly embedded in the world – where else could they be embedded? – which is not identifiable apart from these practices. And we do not have questions external to the framework and questions internal to the framework that are in any fundamental sense different kinds of questions, for we have no inner/outer distinction. . . . There is no need to reify the norms as existing apart from the behaviour. Indeed we have no understanding of what this would be. (p. 327)

Nielsen says that with their emphasis on *practice*, Wittgenstein and Wittgensteinians should welcome Davidson's and Rorty's conclusions. What prevents them from doing so, according to Nielsen, is that they accept a Kantian distinction between forms of life and what goes on within them – the cornerstone of the Wittgensteinian Fideism Nielsen has been urging them to acknowledge in their work.

[With] . . . these framework beliefs in place, we can go on to justify certain things, establish certain things as reasonable or unreasonable, true or false, but no question can intelligibly be raised of the truth or falsity, reasonability or unreasonability of these alleged framework beliefs or the forms of life themselves . . . They are, that is, just there like our lives. (pp. 327–8)

When we put together our acceptance of the arguments of Davidson and Rorty, and our criticisms of Carnap, the net effect, Nielsen argues, is that we realize that there are no forms of life, frameworks, schemes, or world-views. With that realization, we are told, Wittgensteinian Fideism collapses.

As I have said, Nielsen misconstrues the reasons for the collapse of Wittgensteinian Fideism. It collapses because it is not the considered view of Wittgenstein, Rhees, Winch or myself. It is time to establish this textually. First, I want to show how Wittgenstein himself wrestled with these issues himself in *On Certainty*. The tensions, at certain stages in his thinking, can be illustrated by two well-known passages.

Think of chemical investigations. Lavoisier carries out experiments with substances in his laboratory and concludes that this and that happens when he burns them. He doesn't say that something different might happen at another time. He has got hold of a definite world-picture: not one that he invented, of course; rather he learned it as a child. I say world-picture and not hypothesis, because it is the foundation of his research which he takes for granted and as such is also unarticulated. (Wittgenstein 1969, para. 167)

All testing, all confirmation and disconfirmation of a hypothesis takes place already within a system. And this system is not a more or less arbitrary and doubtful point of departure for all our arguments; no, it belongs to the essence of what we call an argument. The system is not so much the point of departure, as the element in which arguments have their life. (Wittgenstein 1969, para. 105)

There is clearly a tension in these passages between calling a world-picture a foundation, a system, or a point of departure, on the one hand, and the denial of all that in saying that it is 'the element in which arguments have their life', and that 'it belongs to the essence of what we call an argument'. The latter option, which eventually becomes Wittgenstein's considered position, makes no mention of frameworks or of foundations. It refers to the *character* of our thinking and activities. This gets rid of Wittgenstein's problematic reference to a foundation, which he claims, at the same time, is unarticulated. The central notion becomes, as Nielsen rightly surmises, *practice*.

The emphasis on 'practice' is as central to Rhees and Winch as it is to Wittgenstein, but each is tempted by an alternative that, rightly, Nielsen would say that they should reject. In the passages I have quoted, Rhees, like Wittgenstein, is tempted to speak of a scientific world-picture as *presupposed* by our scientific activities. His considered position, however, is to deny that a world-picture is the presupposition of our thinking. Rather, it is a way of referring to features that go deep *in* our thinking. Thus, in the case of science, Rhees insists that the world-picture is not something that *enables* the scientist to construct theories, test hypotheses or conduct experiments. Rather, constructing theories, testing hypotheses, conducting experiments *is* his world-picture.

In the case of Peter Winch, matters are even clearer, as he couples Wittgenstein's working through the difficulties Nielsen mentions, with the way he works through them in his own thinking. Further, he shows that the importance of the claim that, in certain circumstances, certain questions *simply do not arise*, in no way depends on holding, as Nielsen thinks it does, a distinction between framework and other kinds of belief.

In *On Certainty*, Wittgenstein is interested in the kind of *sureness* that exemplifies itself in our language-games. As Winch points out, Wittgenstein uses different analogies to capture this 'sureness', and some are better than others. In fact, some are bad. It is these which encourage us to ascribe a belief in frameworks to Wittgenstein. For example, at one stage, Wittgenstein suggests that we can distinguish between propositions that cannot be doubted, and propositions that can be doubted. He calls the former hinge, or framework propositions. Clearly, here, we have a distinct similarity to the cornerstone of the Wittgensteinian Fideism Nielsen wants to ascribe to Wittgenstein. The problem, for Nielsen, is that Winch clearly objects to the very notion Nielsen says that Winch holds. What Winch says of 'hinges' can easily be applied to 'frameworks'.

A hinge exists in a fixed position independently and in a sense prior to the motion of the door which hangs on it; the hinge is a causal condition of the door's movement. And though the 'hinge theorists' have by and large, I think wanted to see this as an example of Wittgenstein's anti-foundationalism, it seems to me a bad example for the purpose and obscures the radical nature of Wittgenstein's position. It suggests that Wittgenstein had not *abandoned* the search for a 'foundation', but is simply pointing to a foundation of a kind different from the usual. For a hinge *is* a kind of foundation. (Winch 1998, 198)

Winch finds an earlier analogy in *On Certainty* far more satisfactory:

I do not explicitly learn the propositions that stand fast for me. I can discover them subsequently like the axis around which a body rotates. The axis is not fixed in the sense that anything holds it fast, but the movement around it determines its immobility. (Wittgenstein 1969, para. 152)

Winch contrasts the two analogies as follows:

Hinges after all *are* held fast by something besides the movement around them. 'Axis' on the other hand is a purely geometrical concept; not merely the 'immobility' of an axis is 'determined by the movement around it', *it itself* is so determined. It is a reference point for the description of the movement. It has no existence or meaning apart from the movement. We can of course make a mark to indicate where the axis is located. But the mark itself is not the axis. (Winch 1998, 198)

As we have seen, Wittgenstein, at one stage does talk of 'propositions which stand fast for me'. They have been called hinge or framework propositions, and a large literature has grown around these terms.[2] How do we stand in relation to these propositions? If we say that we *know* them to be true, there seems to be no answer to the question of *how* we know this. As a result, for much of *On Certainty*, Wittgenstein seems to be searching for a substitute for 'know' to explain our relation to such propositions. Do we 'believe', 'trust', 'presuppose' or 'take for granted' that they are true? Wittgenstein gradually comes to see that he's looking in entirely the wrong direction to resolve his difficulties. What is basic, is not a special set of propositions, called 'framework propositions', but our *practice* – the very conclusion Nielsen wants us to reach. Recall Nielsen's conclusion, 'There is no need to reify the norms as existing apart from the behaviour. Indeed we have no understanding of what this could be' (p. 327).

In the course of our practice, certain questions simply *do not arise*. To say that they *cannot* arise suggests a conception of logic, independent of our practices, which determines what *can* and *cannot* be said. Wittgenstein's radical position calls into question the sharp distinction between the logical and the factual. It is not, as Nielsen thinks, that the questions make sense, but for pragmatic purposes are not asked, but that *in* practice, certain questions and responses simply do not arise, and we wouldn't call them, say, 'doubting' if they did. When Wittgenstein has a choice, in these contexts, between 'could not doubt' and 'do not doubt', he invariably chooses the latter. What if someone asks, 'What stops us from doubting?' Winch replies:

But it isn't that anything stops us: rather that whatever anyone did, we *could not* call it 'doubting all these facts.' Behavior, however superficially similar to behavior that expresses doubt, counts as expressive of doubt only in the right circumstances. In particular, we look for contrasts: certain things are doubted against the background of our *not* doubting other things. And these contrasts are not haphazard. (Winch 1998, 200)

Wittgenstein allows for a fluid change of circumstances in which what was not questioned is questioned, but the circumstances are never haphazard, never completely open-ended in the way Nielsen suggests.

Nielsen's 'unrestricted fallibilism', which looks radical on the surface, lacks the very circumstances that radical doubt needs to be itself. Wittgenstein and Winch reanimate the possibility of radical doubt, by emphasizing that it occurs in situations where a great deal will not be doubted. They will not be contexts, as Nielsen thinks, where no spade is ever turned. Nielsen's unrestricted fallibilism is no more real fallibilism, than Descartes' methodological doubt is real doubt. Real open-mindedness has to be brought back from an intellectualist fantasy of itself.

Winch says that his own thinking was held up by the tensions at different stages of Wittgenstein's thought which we have noted, until he realized that, in Wittgenstein's *considered* position, 'world-picture' and 'practice' go together. The world-pictures cannot be the *foundation* of the procedures, their 'point of departure', 'since it is the procedures which make them the pictures they are' (Winch 1998, 195). Given these procedures, certain claims, responses and questions are simply ruled out. This can be illustrated by the much misunderstood moon travel example in *On Certainty*.

Wittgenstein said that it made no sense to say that one had been to the moon. When human beings achieved that, some critics said that this showed the absurd consequences of Wittgenstein's restrictions on questions that can be asked. In fact, the achievement shows no such thing. Wittgenstein had cited the technical and other difficulties in his day, which stood in the way of anyone going to the moon. No one could have claimed to have done so. But when moon travel became possible, this did not cast doubt on scientific and technological methods, since it is by such methods that the prior difficulties were overcome. Wittgenstein wanted to distinguish, however, between claims that do not arise, because of our competence at a given time, and 'claims' that one has difficulty in recognizing as claims at all. He imagines a tribe who justify their claim to have been to the moon as follows:

'We don't know *how* one gets to the moon, but those who get there know at once that they are there; and even you can't explain everything.' We should feel ourselves intellectually very distant from someone who said this. (Wittgenstein 1969, para. 108)

If one challenges a claim to have been on the moon by asking a person how he got there, and he responds, 'What's that got to do with it?', one is completely nonplussed. Something relevant has been asked, but rejected. Wittgenstein doesn't call the rejection 'wrong'. It is too distant to be 'wrong'. The rejection makes one wonder what 'relevance' could mean for the person making the claim. Wittgenstein goes on to discuss a number of strange happenings asking, in each case, how we could 'go on' if they occurred. In some, as I have already indicated (see Section II), it would be hard to envisage what 'going on' would be. One would think one was going insane. I wouldn't stand in need of correction, but in need of treatment.

How would Nielsen react to the conclusions of this section? It seems to me that he could point out, as he does, that doubts *are* expressed, not simply about the intelligibility of some aspect of religious belief, but about the intelligibility of religious beliefs as such. Therefore, arguments in *On Certainty* that concern other matters cannot be used to make religious belief immune from doubt and criticism. Such doubts and criticisms can assail the primary language of faith. I agree entirely on this point, and nothing said in this section is meant to beg that question. The point of this section is to show that the source of Nielsen's concerns is not to be found in his conception of Wittgensteinian Fideism.

I cannot see, in the light of the textual discussions I have provided, how Nielsen can continue to ascribe Wittgensteinian Fideism either to Wittgenstein, or to most of the Wittgensteinians he criticizes.[3] I have shown how Wittgenstein, and some Wittgensteinians, wrestled en route to their considered conclusions, with the distinction between framework and other kinds of belief (the cornerstone of Wittgensteinian Fideism), but moved beyond it to their emphasis on *practice*.

The result is that disputes with Nielsen about the *character* of religious belief will continue. In *that* context, I am pessimistic about the prospects for progress. Where progress *can* be made is in seeing that those disputes and difficulties do not depend on, and have little to do with, so-called Wittgensteinian Fideism. As far as its usefulness is concerned for the future understanding of Wittgensteinianism, or disputes between belief and atheism, 'Wittgensteinian Fideism' can be laid quietly to rest. It has indeed collapsed. For Nielsen, it collapses because it cannot be held as an intelligible philosophical position. For Wittgenstein, Rhees, Winch and myself, it collapses because it is not their considered position. It has taken a long time for some to find that out, hence the necessity for this section of the chapter.

IV   Criticism in a Form of Life

What happens to Nielsen's attacks on Wittgensteinian fideists when he discovers that there aren't any? He could regroup, and argue, as he already does, that in moral and religious matters, one's spade is never turned. Here, open-minded fallibilism is essential. The alternative, for Nielsen, is a Wittgensteinian quietism that, as Szabados says, he thinks of as 'a pernicious disengagement from the world [which] robs us of the critical tools to assess our culture and change it for the better' (p. 4).

When Nielsen says that our moral spades are never turned, is he saying that this is something that *cannot* happen, or something that ought not to happen? I suspect it must be the former, since he holds that our reflective questions are endless as we move in the direction of human solidarity. What is more, the 'coming together' of human beings must be a *rational* 'coming together'. It is neither unity of the herd, nor the tyranny of the majority. Nielsen has to believe in the commensurability of values, since they have to be answerable to the *same* reflective rationality. Such reflection is supposed to show us which values will lead to human flourishing.

One fundamental difficulty for Nielsen, is that 'human flourishing' cannot mediate between different values, since it is those values which inform, not only different, but also moral conceptions of human flourishing.[4] Nielsen admits as much in his last chapter, but doesn't seem to realize the logical implications of doing so. For example, he accuses Winch of a haughty dismissal of the notion of 'reflective equilibrium', but what Winch has done, with others, in Wittgensteinian ethics, is to achieve *the reanimation of moral differences both between and within cultures*. Such reanimation avoids the confusion of calling adherents to different values irrational or deluded. Think of the condescending misunderstandings of primitive magical rituals. Wittgenstein's account of them helps to reanimate their significance for us, after which, he says 'Laugh if you can' (Wittgenstein 1993, 123) – that is, do you still want to accuse them of making simple mistakes because of their undeveloped intelligence? When I spoke of 'cultural genocide', it was not with the slightest intention, as Mulhall thinks, of suggesting that Nielsen would indulge in it, but with a view to pointing to dangers in his argument that he is unaware of. After all, his view of Azande magic is that *we* know that it is obviously wrong (see Chapter 1, p. 27). but one does not have to go so far afield to see the dangers of a kind of rationalist social policy. Unlike myself, as a Welshman, Mulhall does not find himself being asked why he bothers to speak his language. Nor does he have to tolerate the reasoning (offered as often, as anywhere, by some of one's own people) that states that the usefulness of doing so is obviously in doubt given the existence of such a powerful linguistic neighbour.

The search for a 'reflective equilibrium' is simply another candidate in the history of ethics, for the attempt to determine which values are of value. If it is simply an emphatic expression of a moral view – always try to seek compromise where there is conflict – all well and good. Some will argue with that view, others will not. But it is offered as more than that. The compromise is supposed to be *rationally* desirable. If you are for compromise, that's fine. The 'because'. . .' is philosophically superfluous. Nielsen does not respond to Rhees's example of the dispute between a liberal and a defender of central state control (Rhees 1969, 84–5). The liberal simply *is* someone who has liberal values. His opponent need not misunderstand him, but still support other values. It is not as though we cannot 'go on' (whatever that means) with such conflicts in our midst. As Rhees says, that's how we *do* go on.

In his last chapter, Nielsen provides a controversial example of his own. He is reacting to the claim that some people can reach bedrock, in certain moral cases. Although they may *feel* this is so, Nielsen argues, we are never in this position. This is so, in his view, with respect to the question, 'So what was so wrong with the Holocaust?'

> Things can pinch so that we can say that we do not want to argue about that, for example, argue about the evil of the Holocaust. We just feel that that would be obscene. But, if pressed, we could. (p. 325)

Who is the 'we' being referred to? It must mean 'anyone', since anyone refusing to do so is held to be irrational. On this argument, Primo Levi, who argued that to think such justification is necessary *is* simply obscene, must be held to be irrational. Levi argues of the dangers involved in treating the evils of the Holocaust in terms of the 'free' language of everyday life. To do so, is to fail to give sufficient recognition to the systematic attempt in the Holocaust to destroy a sense of 'the human'. The point is not to advocate Levi's moral reaction, or to accept his distinction between 'free' and 'unfree' language (Levi 1969, 112–13), but to insist on the possibility of such a reaction as 'complete', and not as one which is logically incomplete without a wider justification. Nielsen's insistence leads from the 'thick' concepts of actual moral values, to the 'thin' concepts of theoretical philosophy. What Wittgensteinian ethics does is to reanimate Levi's response and the reality of moral conflict. If, on the other hand, one heard someone ask what is wrong about systematically stubbing out one's cigarette on one's child's cheek, the task facing one would not be to find a justification of why the cruelty is wrong, but to instil that very judgement in the person by elucidation, not by fruitless justification. As G. K. Chesterton said, somewhere, the madman is not the person who has lost his reason, but the person who only has his reason. That is why I insisted that our values *are* our reasons.

Some have asked how, if certain moral values are incommensurable, there can be moral change. Instead of asking how this *can* happen, we should concentrate on how it *does* happen. One may come to recognize, and be attracted by, some features of new values one had not noticed previously. Certain values may become so dominant in the culture, that the very possibility of certain other values is eroded. But it may be the case that different values exist in an unresolved tension in one's life. The art of the writer Isaac Babel grew out of such a tension between Jewish piety and the morality of the Red Cossacks (Babel 1961).

In different situations such as these, it is important, philosophically, to do conceptual justice by them, and to rescue them from intellectualized fantasies of moral values, moral arguments and moral change.

V   Contemplation and Meddling

In the concluding section of the previous section, I am citing the fruits of a contemplative conception of philosophy. I have contrasted it with Nielsen's desire to arrive at a philosophy of life (see Chapter 14, section III). The contemplative conception of philosophy is captured in Wittgenstein's remark, 'My ideal is a certain coolness. A temple providing a setting for the passions without meddling with them' (Wittgenstein 1977, 2e). Mulhall asks,

> what value-commitments lie behind the idea that we philosophers should provide a setting for the passions without meddling with them (Chapter 15, p. 309) [because] it seems plain that the fact that a thinker is committed to a certain kind of neutrality . . . is no guarantee that this commitment is not itself the embodiment . . . of a moral vision. (Chapter 15, p. 309)

Mulhall is thinking of John Rawls's political philosophy. Wittgenstein's moral vision is very different. His is the ethic involved in disinterested enquiry, and a desire to do conceptual justice to the world in all its variety when faced with philosophical theories that distort it. It wants to show us the city with no advocacy of a main road. As I have said before, I know of no better expression of this contemplative conception of philosophy than the following remarks by my teacher, Rush Rhees:

> Wonder is characteristic of philosophy anyway, as it is of the thinking of less corrupted peoples. Wonder at death – not trying to escape from death: wonder at (almost reverence towards) madness; wonder that there should be the problems that there are, and that they should have the solutions that they do. (Pythagoras treating the 'discovery' that any triangle inscribed in a semi-circle is right-angled, as divine revelation, as a word to be reverenced.) Wonder at any natural scene that is beautiful. Wonder at the beauty of human actions and characters when it appears in them. And in the same way, wonder at what is terrible and what is evil. (We cannot say 'wonder at what is mediocre' . . .) Wonder at – treating as important – what is terrible just *because* it is terrible; as primitive peoples may celebrate it in rites: the burning of human figures, perhaps of children, in effigy; treating what is terrible as a sacrament. If someone can think of these practices only as 'morbid' or as 'perversions' – or if he can think of them only as methods to *ward off* the terrible things they celebrate – this means he cannot

imagine how people might wonder at terrible events because of what they are (as opposed to: wondering what neglect should have allowed them to happen, how they might be avoided, etc.). (Rhees 1994, 578)

Similarly I do not know any better expression of the *demands* of a contemplative conception of philosophy than the following by another of my teachers, in which it is compared with the obligations involved in depictions of characters and events on a stage.

> to stand on the stage and speak in one's own voice is not the only, or even the most characteristic use of the stage. One also stages dramas in which a *diversity* of characters speaking in different voices are portrayed ... One need only think of Shakespeare, for instance. The aim may be to portray as faithfully as possible a segment of life, without shying away from the possibility of there being unsolvable conflicts (not merely divergencies) which can only have a tragic outcome. (Winch 1996)

I am not, as Nielsen thinks, denying that other activities go on in the name of philosophy. Mulhall does not make that mistake, but he wonders what I make of philosophy that speaks in the first person, since, as Nielsen points out, such philosophy has been part of the philosophical tradition of the West since Plato. Mulhall argues,

> The rigorous and passionate intellectual advocacy of one perspective on a range of problems or on human life as a whole need not present itself as 'backed by philosophy' ... Rawlsian political philosophy is a good example: his veil of ignorance denies us any reference to our specific conceptions of the good; but this neutrality is in the service of a distinctly liberal commitment to freedom and equality. (Chapter 15, pp. 308–9)

The first thing to be said is that *if* someone openly puts philosophy in the service of some political ideal, all well and good. In that case, I would *contrast* it with the character, aspirations and ethic of contemplative philosophy. No doubt all the great political philosophers have expressed substantive political views, but the great ones have also raised questions about *the very possibility* of society and political authority (Winch 2002).

The second thing to be said, is that what I am protesting against is philosophers who *are* speaking in the first person, but who *think* they are invoking values, moral or political, to which philosophy gives a rational justification. It would be relevant (but not here) to look critically at the alleged relation between the 'veil of ignorance', its alleged lack of presuppositions, and Rawls's eventual liberal conclusions. After all,

Mulhall's criticism of Charles Taylor is precisely that, while thinking he was arriving at a theistic conception of the self, as the one which can be shown, disinterestedly, to serve the needs of modernity best, he was, in fact, using philosophy to advocate it from the outset. I criticize Nielsen's philosophy of life in a similar way. That is why, as I have said, I was surprised to find Nancy Bauer thinking that I, too, was saying that philosophy can determine how we should react to the vicissitudes of life.

Nielsen says that he is impressed by Winch's analogy between contemplative philosophy and the obligations involved in presenting different, conflicting voices on the stage.

> This is an attractive way of thinking about and doing philosophy . . . We are in debt to Winch for putting the matter so clearly and forcibly and it is something that should be integrated without evasion in our practice as philosophers. (Chapter 16, pp. 335–6).

Two points need to be made in relation to Nielsen's response. First, it is not a matter of integrating anything into different philosophical practices. Winch is talking about *a conception of philosophical practice*, one that excludes what Wittgenstein disapproves of, namely, 'meddling'. Second, Nielsen misunderstands what Wittgenstein means by 'meddling'. He says that there are times when we *should* meddle. He himself would meddle with the Catholic view on contraception, with Catholic crimes of ethnic cleansing, with inner-religious killings, and with unequal opportunities for women in education. In relation to these issues, he writes,

> If Wittgenstein and Winch, as Phillips says, want without meddling with them to let them be themselves, they plainly have in this respect an unthought out and improverished moral view. (Or can they legitimately say this is all distant from philosophy?) (p. 337).

Wittgenstein and Winch are clearly using 'meddling' as a pejorative term. It is meant to refer to philosophically misleading accounts of the emotions, including moral emotions. The examples Nielsen gives are simply expressions of his moral opinions. They are not examples of meddling at all. 'Meddling' would be the attempt to get behind the values expressed in Nielsen's judgements, in an attempt to ground them in a conception of rationality provided by philosophy. This would be an example of 'the chatter in ethics' which Wittgenstein said he wanted to get rid of. Nielsen's conception of a philosophy of life would fall into this category. Nielsen recognizes this, to some extent, when he says that Wittgenstein would not have approved of his conception of 'how things hang together' in the broadest possible sense (p. 334).

Nielsen thinks that our exchanges show little sign of philosophical contemplation. Given his apologetic concerns, and his imputation of such concerns to me, that is not surprising. For me, the demands of contemplative philosophy are at the heart of our dispute. Speaking of the difficulties faced in contemplative philosophy, Winch writes that it

> concerned itself precisely with the problem how to present moral or religious world-views in such a way that the passion behind them, which has to be evident if one is to recognize them for what they are, is clearly in view, along with the conception of the good which they embody, while at the same time equal justice is done to alternative and even hostile conceptions. Achieving this is a task of enormous difficulty, both at the technical level and also because of the moral demands it makes on the writer, who will, of course him or herself have strong moral or religious commitments and will also be hostile to certain other possibilities. (Winch 1996, 173)

Nielsen denies the truth or coherence of religious beliefs. I have not denied the possibility of Nielsen's atheism. This affects the character of our exchanges, something that will become more evident in the remainder of the chapter.

VI 'Fundamental Criticism': Nielsen's Challenge

Nielsen thinks that I dance around a challenge that he puts to me again and again. When we look at what it amounts to, however, it turns out either to have been met many times, or to be senseless, and, hence, impossible to take up.

The challenge often takes the form of asking me whether I allow that, after giving a perspicuous representation of a religious belief, it can turn out to be incoherent. In Wittgenstein's terms, a 'perspicuous representation' is a *clear* presentation of the conceptual status in our language of whatever segment of it is being discussed. In Chapter 14, I said that after perspicuous representations have been given, religious beliefs may turn out to be metaphysical confusions, superstitions, examples of a magical view of signs, creators of harm, and contradictions of science and history. I am saying that at *any* time religion is a mixed bag. I am rejecting Nielsen's diachronic account of religion as too simplistic. Sometimes, Nielsen says that I only allow criticisms that are recognized within religion. That, too, is not so. Many religious believers do not recognize the confusions I point out. Further, in the case of religious beliefs that are not confused, there can still be external criticisms of them, for example, the kind of criticism made by Nietzsche and others.

So what exactly does Nielsen's criticism amount to? What does he mean by *fundamental* criticism? He would say that the give-away is in my reference to religion as a 'mixed bag'. I will not allow that *every* religious belief could be confused. If that is meant to refer to a factual possibility, of course I will allow it. A time could come when all surviving forms of religion are superstitious. But Nielsen wants me to say *now* that all religious beliefs are either false or incoherent. Since I do not think this is so, I obviously cannot meet *that* challenge, since it asks me to say that what makes sense is senseless!

Nielsen will say that I am still missing the point of his challenge. He may say that he is not addressing any of the circumstances I mention, but something he believes to be a *logical* impossibility for me. As we have seen, he thinks I hold the thesis that whereas there can be confusions within religion, religion as such, can never be said to be confused. In short, we are back to Wittgensteinian Fideism, to the claim that Wittgenstein and Wittgensteinians hold that whereas beliefs within frameworks can be confused, this can never be said of the frameworks themselves. As we saw in section III of the present chapter, this distinction between 'scheme' and 'content' is not only the cornerstone of Nielsen's criticism, but also of his very conception of 'Wittgensteinian Fideism'. But the title of section III is 'The Collapse of Wittgensteinian Fideism'. I showed, with detailed textual references to Wittgenstein, Rhees and Winch, how they consciously worked through the confusions Nielsen ascribes to them, to an emphasis, not on 'framework beliefs', but on *practice*. So Nielsen's challenge was taken up in that section. Like the label he created, it collapses.

VII   Where 'Seeing' Need Not Mean 'Believing'

As we saw in section V, Nielsen is impressed by Winch's analogy between contemplative philosophy and the representation of different voices on the stage. Where the voices are religious, however, Nielsen finds them either false or incoherent. Putting Wittgensteinian Fideism aside, why should this be so? Three reasons emerge from his arguments.

First is the objection that, according to Nielsen, he uses most often against religious belief. He believes that religious belief *must* involve metaphysics. In saying that metaphysics is incoherent, but that religious forms of life must be accepted, Wittgensteinians 'end up in a contradiction saying that religion is inescapably both incoherent and coherent' (p. 323).

Nielsen gives no argument for saying that religious beliefs *must* involve metaphysics. For Nielsen, the term 'metaphysics' is a synonym for 'nonsensical'.

The impression is sometimes given that it means 'just like a claim about the natural world' except that it concerns the supernatural world (cf. the discussions of Zeus on p. 260). Certainly, some religious claims made by some religious believers might be so understood; but Wittgenstein and Phillips would both then identify them as philosophically confused, and hence metaphysical, as quickly as Nielsen. (Chapter 15, p. 307)

To associate metaphysics with Wittgensteinianism is extremely odd, since, in opposing metaphysics, Nielsen says that we are on the same side of the fence. The fact of the matter is that the *substantive* accounts he gives of the religious beliefs he opposes belong to that form of philosophy of religion he thinks that he and I have moved beyond. So despite all his talk of Wittgensteinian Fideism, his *actual* engagements, as far as his substantive accounts of religious beliefs are concerned, are still with traditional philosophy of religion. His rejections are simply the flip side of the coin within the same intellectual game.

Nielsen's second reason for opposing religious beliefs is a consequence of the first. Failing to get beyond the accounts of religious belief offered in traditional philosophy of religion, the only alternative he sees to them is limited by that fact. If religious beliefs are not metaphysical beliefs (and he admits that, for Wittgensteinians they are not), the only alternative is to see such belief as 'a passionate orientation of one's life' (p. 323). Thus, according to Nielsen, God is ignored as the *object* of the orientation.

When writers, such as Kierkegaard, say that, in religion, proof is from the emotions, they have wanted to contrast it with speculative theories. So far from ignoring the concept of God, they are endeavouring to indicate the context in which it has its sense. Every object of belief is not an object. Keeping in mind the discussions of *On Certainty* in section III, we can see that the religious practice being appealed to is not a doubtful point of departure, with the existence of God as its presupposition, but the element in which believers live, move and have their being. It is in that context that substantive accounts of belief in God are to be sought.

Nielsen's third objection to religious belief is also linked to the other two. He thinks that if we say that religious belief is 'a passionate orientation', things are made too easy, since any such orientation would thereby be religious. He thinks it is 'conversion by stipulative definition' (p. 323). In referring to such an orientation, one is only advocating the general direction in which to look if we want to understand religion. It is the first necessary step away from theory. But not all such orientations are religious. Nielsen is right: further elucidation is called for.

At this point, at the end of our long road, we come to the real problem in my dispute with Nielsen. When I provide the elucidations he rightly demands, providing example after example in my work, Nielsen fails to see any sense in them, though plenty of non-believers do. We are back to the sensitive issue of meaning blindness (see Chapter 9, section III).

It may be helpful to go back to the discussion of Nancy Bauer's example, in which the religious words with which her father comforted her as a child were not available to her when her own child needed comforting. Somehow or other, the sense of her father's words had gone astray. Am I trying to get Nielsen to appropriate religious sense as her father did? No. It would be a contemplative advance if I could get Nielsen to say, as Bauer does, not that the religious words are senseless, but that their sense, if any, is not available to him. But this would not satisfy Nielsen, since he claims to have understood the primary language of faith; he has *seen through* it to the falsehood or incoherence that it is. I, on the other hand, think that Nielsen misses what is there to be seen. The contemplative task becomes harder at this stage. It is the struggle to do conceptual justice to perspectives and points of view *other than one's own*. As an aid to that struggle, I presented my literary examples. Sometimes, Nielsen seems to regard them as impure intrusions into philosophy. As I have said, however, it may be that the language Nielsen wants philosophy to remain with, is not, as he thinks, *clean*, but, rather, *narrow*. Mulhall comments on the narrowness of his critique. In relation to my use of Sophocles, Horace and R. S. Thomas, Nielsen simply stops thinking too soon. I think that there is an obstacle of the will involved in this, and that there is an indication of it as early as Chapter 1. Nielsen writes,

> I agree with such Wittgensteinians that to understand religious discourse one must have a participant's understanding of it. However, this certainly does not entail that one is actually a participant, that one *accepts* or *believes* in the religion in question. But I do *not* agree that the first-order discourse of religion is in order as it is. (p. 23)

But suppose that at least *some* examples of first-order discourse of religion are in order. Suppose further that Nielsen could be brought to see the sense they have. Does that mean that he would be a believer? Obviously not, since some of the Wittgensteinians Nielsen argues against, who appreciate this religious sense, are not believers, and Wittgenstein himself did not regard himself as one. They are philosophers who have seen something through contemplation of religious belief. This is at a distance from actual religious belief in one's own life. As Winch has pointed out, Wittgenstein never spoke of them in the same way, or suggested that philosophy can turn one's life around in the way religion can (Winch 1994, 128–9).

Philosophical contemplation seeks to do justice to belief and atheism, to the confusions and the sense that can be found in each. An atheism that holds that *all* religious beliefs are either false or incoherent will be unable to do that. But, then, it has always been recognized that one's own beliefs can get in the way of the kind of attention called for by a contemplative conception of philosophy.

Notes

1 See Max Horkheimer, 'Erinnerung an Paul Tillich' in *Gesammelte Schriften* Bd. 7, Frankfurt 1985, quoted by Matthias Lux-Bachmann in 'Critical Theory and Religion' in *Philosophy of Religion in the 21st Century* ed. D. Z. Phillips and Timothy Tessin, Basingstoke: Palgrave 2001, p. 204.

2 See, for example, Norman Malcolm, 'Wittgenstein's "Scepticism" in *On Certainty*', *Inquiry* Vol. 31; Deborah Jane Orr, 'Did Wittgenstein have a theory of Hinge Propositions?' *Philosophical Investigations* Vol. 12 No. 2 April 1989; Jon Dorbolo, 'What Turns on Hinges?' *Philosophical Investigations* Vol. 11 No. 2 April 1988; John Cook, 'The Metaphysics of Wittgenstein's *On Certainty*' *Philosophical Investigations* Vol. 8 No. 2 April 1985.

3 I say most of the Wittgensteinians because I do think that Norman Malcolm, in *some* of his pronouncements, laid himself open to Nielsen's attacks.

4 For my arguments on this issue see my, 'Does It Pay To Be Good?' and 'On Morality Having A Point' (with H. O. Mounce), in my *Interventions in Ethics*, Basingstoke: Macmillan and New York: SUNY Press, 1992.

Bibliography

Babel, Isaac (1961), *Collected Stories*. London: Penguin.

Cook, John (1985), 'The Metaphysics of Wittgenstein's *On Certainty.*' *Philosophical Investigations* 8: 2.

Dorbolo, Jon (1988), 'What Turns On Hinges?' *Philosophical Investigations* 11: 2.

Levi, Primo (1969), *Survival in Auschwitz: The Nazi Assault on Humanity*. New York: Collier Books.

Lux-Bachmann, Matthias (2001), 'Critical Theory and Religion' in *Philosophy of Religion in the 21st Century*, eds D. Z. Phillips and Timothy Tessin. Basingstoke: Palgrave.

Malcolm, Norman (1988), 'Wittgenstein's "Skepticism" in *On Certainty.*' *Inquiry* 31.

Moore, G. E. (2001), 'A Defense of Common Sense' in *Philosophy of Religion in the 21st Century*, eds D. Z. Phillips and Timothy Tessin. Basingstoke: Palgrave.

Orr, Deborah Jane (1989) 'Did Wittgenstein have a theory of Hinge Propositions?' *Philosophical Investigations* 12: 2.

Phillips, D. Z. (1992), *Interventions in Ethics*. New York: SUNY Press.

Rhees, Rush (1969), *Without Answers*, ed. D. Z. Phillips. London: Routledge.

—— (1994), 'The Fundamental Problems of Philosophy', ed. Timothy Tessin. *Philosophical Investigations* 17: 4.

—— (2003), *Wittgenstein's 'On Certainty'*, ed. with an Afterword by D. Z. Phillips. Oxford: Blackwell.

Winch, Peter (1994), 'Response to Malcolm's Essay' in *Wittgenstein: A Religious Point of View*, ed. Norman Malcolm. Ithaca, NY: Cornell University Press.

—— (1996), 'Doing Justice or Giving the Devil his Due', in *Can Religion Be Explained Away?* ed. D. Z. Phillips. Basingstoke: Macmillan.

—— (1998), 'Judgement: Propositions and Practices.' *Philosophical Investigations* 21: 3, July 1998.

—— (2002), 'How is Political Authority Possible?' *Philosophical Investigations* 25: 1.

Wittgenstein, Ludwig (1969), *On Certainty*. Oxford: Blackwell.

—— (1977), *Culture and Value*. Oxford: Blackwell.

—— (1993), *Philosophical Occasions*, eds James Klagge and Alfred Nordmann. Indianapolis: Hackett Publishing Co.

Index

morality
  religious *see under* religion;
  religious beliefs
secular 200, 287, 290, 316, 336
motives 243
Mounce, H. O. 94n, 148, 151,
  152, 153, 156, 157, 160n, 169,
  170, 173, 181n, 372n
Mulhall, Stephen 298
  305–10 (ch. 15), cited 352, 363,
  365, 366, 369–70
Murphy, Arthur 162n
mysticism 153–4, 157, 158

Nagel, Thomas 153, 211
natural theology 7, 17n, 75, 144,
  163n, 245–6, 254
Niebuhr, Reinhold 163n
Nielsen, Kai *passim*
  obstacles of the will (ch. 16)
    311–47, cited 348, 351, 352,
    354, 356–7, 360, 364, 367,
    369, 370
  understanding: limits on
  (ch. 8) 143–64, cited 165, 167,
    170, 171, 173, 174, 175, 176,
    181, 206, 213n, 215–16, 217
  (ch. 10) 184–202, cited 210,
    218–19
  Wittgenstein and
    Wittgensteinians on religion
  (ch. 13) 225–79, cited 285,
    286, 287, 289, 290, 291,
    293–4, 295, 297–8, 299–300,
    306–8
  Wittgensteinian Fideism
  (ch. 1) 21–38, cited 3, 66, 73–4,
    76, 80, 81, 82, 83–5, 87, 88,
    90, 134, 135, 137, 138, 168,
    209, 371
  (ch. 3) 53–64, cited 65, 133,
    137, 166
  (ch. 6) 97–131, cited 133, 134,
    165, 299

Nietzsche, Friedrich 88–90,
  114–16, 133, 269, 310, 322,
  341, 368
nonsense, 228–9, 232–4, 305–6,
  307–8; *see also* incoherence
  under God; religious beliefs

obstacles
  of the intellect 280, 318
  of the will 280–3, 301, 317–18,
    338, 371
O'Connor, Flannery 301
Orwell, George 152, 170
Otto, Rudolph 312

Paley, William 61, 88
Pareto, Vilfredo 27, 31
Pascal, Blaise 14, 15, 61, 88, 249,
  250, 265, 266
passions: meddling with 299, 309,
  336–8, 367
Passmore, J. A. 48, 52n
Paul, St 14
Peirce, C. S. 130n, 198, 252, 274,
  275, 319, 325
Penelhum, Terence 10, 75, 129n
Pfleiderer, Otto 163n
Phillips, D. Z. *passim*
  contemplation and cultural
    criticism (ch. 17) 348–72
  obstacles of the will (ch. 14)
    280–304, cited 308–9, 312,
    314, 317, 320, 328, 329, 333,
    335, 336, 339, 340, 341, 342,
    345n
  understanding: limits on (ch. 9)
    165–83, cited 169, 187, 189,
    190, 191, 193, 194, 196,
    197–8, 199, 206, 210, 211,
    370; (ch. 12) 215–22
  Wittgensteinian Fideism
  (ch. 2) 39–52, cited 53–4, 55,
    57–9, 65, 66, 109, 110, 133,
    136, 165, 166, 299, 300